GARDENING WITH GOD

GARDENING
WITH GOD

Light in Darkness

JANE MOSSENDEW

BURNS & OATES
A Continuum imprint
LONDON • NEW YORK

First published in Great Britain in 2002 by
Burns & Oates
A Continuum imprint
The Tower Building
11 York Road
London SE1 7NX
www.continuumbooks.com

British Library Cataloguing-in-Publication Data
A catalogue record for this book is available from the British Library

ISBN 0 8264 6102 6

Line drawings by Penelope Harter

Typeset by Bookens Ltd, Royston, Herts
Printed and bound in Great Britain by
MPG Books Ltd, Bodmin, Cornwall

Dedicated to Our Lady of the Annunciation, in memory of Margaret and Bill Mossendew

CONTENTS

Part Two: SOLEMNITIES AND SAINTS' DAYS

ACKNOWLEDGEMENTS

Copyright material is quoted by permission of the following: Dame Felicitas Corrigan, OSB, *Benedictine Tapestry*, quotations and extensive reference: the author; 2 Sam. 7 from *The Jerusalem Bible*, published and copyright 1966, 1967, and 1968: Darton, Longman and Todd; Margaret Baker, *Folklore and Customs of Rural England*: David and Charles; *The Rule of St Benedict*, trans. A. C. Meisel and M. L. del Mastro: Doubleday, Random House, Inc.; Pierre Teilhard de Chardin, *The Heart of Matter*: English translation of *Le Coeur de la matière*: Editions du Seuil; Wallace Stevens, 'Sunday Morning', in *Collected Poems* ...: Faber and Faber and Alfred J. Knopf; Psalm 85: The Grail and Gregorian Institute; notes on prophecy and the *Bibliae pauperum*: John Greenhalgh; Elizabeth Jennings, 'In a Garden', in *New Collected Poems* ...: (Carcanet Press): David Higham Associates; Jan Struther, 'Daisies are our silver', in *Enlarged Songs of Praise 1931*: Oxford University Press; Richard Mabey, *Flora Britannica* (Chatto and Windus), quotations and extensive reference: Random House Group Ltd; Sutton and Sons, *The Culture of Flowers and Vegetables*: Suttons Consumer Products Ltd; 'Pain and the paschal Mystery' in *Priests and People*, March 1994, quotation and extensive reference: The Tablet Publishing Co. Ltd. Every effort has been made to contact copyright holders and any inadvertent omissions will be made good in future editions.

I should like to express gratitude to the following, without whose temporal and/or spiritual support and encouragement this book could not have been written: the former community of Augustinian Canonesses, Abbotskerswell, Devon; Emily, Emma, Nadia, and Ben Asprey; Elsie M. Byard; Brigitte and Serge Bonneau; Dame Felicitas Corrigan, OSB; Jacqueline and Camille Chatellier; Christine Cleveland; Malcolm Cottle; Catherine Dubarry Martin; the Cistercian Community at Echourgnac, Dordogne; Dame Philippa Edwards, OSB; Kathleen and Robert Fulthorpe; Dame Anne Field, OSB; Bridget Garrett; Florence Gledhill; Steve Gledhill; Carmen Hughes; Sr Agnes Hurley, DC; Peter Jones, choirmaster; Julie Layton; Aileen McGinlay; Sr Catherine Mulligan, foundress of the Daughters of Our Lady Mother of the Church; Sr Mary

St Peter, of the Sacred Heart of St Aubin and the former community at Barnes; Diane Pierce-Harvey; Kevin Reid; Michael David Renason; Canon Michael Richards; Dame Teresa Rodrigues, OSB; Astrid Rowsell; Revd Bill Scott; David Speake; David Spriggs; Ken Stanion; Mgr George A. Tancred; the fomer community of St Scholastica's Abbey, Teignmouth, Devon; Douglas Walker; Adrienne Witczack; Margaret Woods.

Thanks also to Br John Hart, CFX, for current statistics of his Congregation; Henry Hely-Hutchinson for his remark about Lennox Berkeley's 'I sing of a maiden'; Revd Nick Mercer for the loan of a Breviary when my own was in France; Fr Chris O'Brien, OSM, prior of Fulham, for advice on the Servite entry; Canon Lord Pilkington for the history of Canon Robin Lamburn and the Kindwitwi Leprosy Trust; and to William Whitehead for the words and music of 'Jesus Christ the apple tree'.

My profound gratitude and appreciation also go to the Irish writer and historian Martin Dillon for early encouragement and for telling me to 'Stop talking and start writing'; Edna and John Greenhalgh, who 'took over', with John supplying patient technical and theological help, when Martin went to New York; Elizabeth Russell for her wise counsel; David Denning for gifts of seeds and Paeonies and for 'keeping my hair on'; Sue and John Gregson for their loyal friendship and creative understanding; to Thomas O'Neill, my faithful and gifted student, for I.T. assistance at crisis points; and to Franck Petit, whose fax machine proved indispensable on many occasions.

Every person in the foregoing list is very special. But there are four others whose contribution has been crucial throughout and who have understood and shared my vision. My undying gratitude goes to Penelope Harter for the plant drawings that grace this book and, I believe, are a grace within it; to Revd Stephen Young, whose spiritual guidance underpins it; to Colin, my husband, whose patience and love have proved rock-solid in the face of severe testing. Lastly, in Paul Burns I have been privileged to have an editor of experience and seemingly bottomless forbearance and tact, from whom I have learned a tremendous amount and, as if all that were not enough, who shares my love of gardening with God.

Warning

Always seek the advice of a professional medical herbalist or homeopathic doctor before taking plant remedies.

'Thy word is a lamp to my feet and a light to my path' (Ps. 119:105)

'The light shines in the darkness, and the darkness has not overcome it'
(Jn 1:5)

'And God said, "Behold, I have given you every plant yielding seed which
is on the face of the earth, and every tree with seed in its fruit"'
(Gen. 1:29)

'Bless the Lord, all things that grow on the earth,
Sing praise to him and highly exalt him for ever'
(Additions to Dan. 3:54)

INTRODUCTION

For as long as I can remember, prayer and gardening have been mutually supportive, and it was a joy when, in the early 1990s, after a garden-less decade in central London, I was at last able to move to the countryside of southwest France. During those London years, the idea had come to me of eventually making a garden for God. Now it would be possible to begin. Four years later, I had reached the point where gardening had become not merely an aid to prayer, but increasingly synonymous with it; more and more I was gardening *with* God as well as *for* God; and the effect was spilling over into the rest of my spiritual and practical life. Then, in 1998 came the terrible blow of forced exile from the garden, the original design of which was by no means executed. Back amid the noise, rush, and polluted air of London, I struggled spiritually across a dark and barren plain, and I found at first that the only way to accept my lot was not to think of the garden at all. Isaiah 38:12 came frequently to mind in those early days: 'My dwelling is plucked up and removed from me like a shepherd's tent; like a weaver I have rolled up my life; he cuts me off from the loom; from day to night thou dost bring me to an end.'

In retrospect, the only obvious blessing on the day I left home was that I did not know how long it would be before my return. Other blessings lay hidden in my spiritual luggage, which would not come to light for some time. The realization soon dawned, however, that moping, fretting, and chafing did me no good at all. Somehow strength was given, and I knuckled down to city life and became deeply involved again in the parish. At no point was I cut off from it: faith did not waver, and the effort to pray was ceaseless. In the Sacrament of Reconciliation, I found me a wonderful guide. Every time, he would say something that had an immediately healing effect, and every time he gave specific advice for the next step on the path. At daily Mass and Office, phrases of Scripture would pierce my exile's shell and flood me with a joyous certainty in God's promise. 'I will return you to the land from which I have exiled you.' I knew in those moments that the return was not a merely physical journey and arrival, taking place on some unknown day in the future, its nature was spiritual and I was already on the road.

The long barren plain of seeming 'exile' from God was behind me now, and I began to draw on my memory bank of plants to lead me into meditation, in the process re-addressing the writing abandoned since the return to London. At last I saw the exile as a God-given opportunity to learn acceptance and detachment. The physical homecoming would happen only if and when God willed. Had I not been forced back to London, I would never have learned that lesson. And moreover, because gardening is so demanding, had I remained at home there would not have been time to write a book. Exile had been essential for my spiritual development as an active witness, in the mostly unbelieving workplace, and among my fellow Christians, who in their turn gave unstintingly to me. I had felt God testing, stretching, pulling me into shape, and I had listened to his message for all of us, collectively as the body of Christ, the Church, and as individual members within it: 'Remember not the former things, nor consider the things of old. Behold, I am doing a new thing; now it springs forth, do you not perceive it? I will make a way in the wilderness and rivers in the desert' (Is. 43:18–19).

At my eventual homecoming in May 2001, I knew at least part of a personal answer to the psalmist's question, 'Why then hast thou broken down its walls so that all who pass along the way pluck its fruit? The boar from the forest ravages it and all that move in the field feed on it. They have burned it with fire, they have cut it down' (Ps. 80:12–13, 16). And on the morning of first seeing the garden again, the words of another psalm, whose ecclesial, apostolic, and eschatalogical significance I had long appreciated, now also took on a deep personal symbolism. 'He that goes forth weeping, bearing the seed for sowing, shall come home with shouts of joy, bringing his sheaves with him' (Ps. 126:5–6). A first cursory inspection made it clear that the work begun that day must continue for at least five years, before the garden would be restored to its former state. It took a week of cutting through brambles, nettles, and tall grass to reach the enclosed herb garden at the end of my plot. The arch that had supported climbing roses had collapsed, but the roses themselves had made their own natural arch across the entrance. 'Paul's Scarlet' was ablaze with colour, and, just inside, a few shy blooms of 'Peace' waited to greet me. This was the moment for which I had longed, this the place where I had yearned to be. In pre-exile days it had been my favourite place for saying the Office; here I had taken first steps in mental prayer, and had begun to write about gardening and the spiritual life. And it was to be here that, during those first joyous weeks of homecoming, the idea would come for a new spiritual map for the restored garden (see First Monday of Ordinary Time to Shrove Tuesday). But on my first morning back in the blessed little enclosure of my heart, there was only one thing to do. After a struggle I managed to pull my old prayer bench from under the choking vicious brambles. Sitting down to pray, I noted approvingly that the trees surrounding the herb garden had grown to about seven feet and now created the total privacy that had been my aim in planting them. Then as I prayed it seemed that they were protecting the air in the place so that it was filled with the intensity of my prayer, which rose steadily in wordless worship and love of God, from that roofless sanctuary. It is difficult to describe the experience; I can only offer phrases: 'out of myself', 'annihilated and yet exultantly alive', 'suspended in time'. Later that year, one early August afternoon, when reflecting on the phenomenon of birdsong, I was arrested by the last two lines of Sassoon's poem 'Everyone Sang'. And I suddenly saw the similarity between the wordless birdsong of his poem and my wordless May-time prayer in the herb garden. Just as Sassoon's birds' song is ceaseless, so must mine become. By praying in the garden, or through the act of gardening, or, in London, by letting the thought of my plants lead me to prayer, the garden will itself increasingly become an offering of living and loving witness to God. Yet again, words that have other all-embracing interpretations now assumed personal significance: 'You shall no more be called Forsaken, and your land shall no more be termed Desolate; but you shall be called my delight in her, and your land Married; and as the bridegroom rejoices over the bride, so shall your God rejoice over you' (Is. 62:4–5b).

There is a complementarity between the natural cycle of seasons and the Church's year, the one making a backdrop for the other. November always reminds me of Shelley's 'dirges in the wind', and it is somehow appropriate that we remember our dead in that month when church and natural years have run their course. The Christian year ends but also begins when the natural one seems dead; the garden may look increasingly sparse and dun-coloured, but the foundations of next year's rebirth lie dormant under the rough digging completed before the first frosts. In faith we begin the long wait through the dark days before Christmas, the herald voice of Advent calling us to consider both the First and Second Comings, and its steady flame of hope guiding us through the gloom towards the great mystery of the incarnation – birth in midwinter. The gardener must wait through Lent until early spring for life in the garden to reburgeon. At Easter the two cycles meet in seed-time, resurrection and redemption.

Then, Christ ascends as the garden greens and blossoms; the promised Comforter is bestowed, and Mary's month is with us again. The garden begins to yield its produce and flowers for the great summer feasts – Corpus Christi, the Sacred Heart, SS Peter and Paul, the Transfiguration, the Assumption. At harvest time we can assess the year's achievement in the garden and in the soul, before closing it in thanks and praise to Christ the King; winter looms again, but so does Advent.

Every garden in the world is potentially a place of prayer. Whether we are gardening or appreciating the results of our own or someone else's labour, we are reflecting the active and contemplative lives. A gardener must be a 'Martha' busy about many things, but Mary's 'better part' is always there for the choosing. Indeed it is possible to balance the two, as the Benedictines have been demonstrating for centuries. And Kipling reminds us: 'O Adam was a gardener, and God who made him sees / That half a proper gardener's work is done upon his knees.' A great deal of the other half, in my experience, is spent doubled over in a frequently painful attitude of submission. Both praying and gardening demand discipline, stamina, and consistency. In either activity, an hour's daily attention will yield a more abundant harvest than if one goes at it in an excess of enthusiasm for several days and then neglects it for weeks. The attempt to gain a semblance of control over weeds, in the garden or in the soul, is a lifelong business. As believers, we turn to prayer in all experiences – happy, sad, or harsh – and through all rites of passage – joyful, solemn, or anguished. As praying gardeners, we find the garden a celebratory place in the good times, and a therapeutic, even cathartic one in the bad. I know this to be true from my own experience, even in the very pit of grief in a new bereavement.

Gardening is supportive of prayer because it stimulates awareness of God's presence, praise of his eternal creativity, and awe of his power. When we are among plants, tending and nurturing them with close concern, it is difficult not to be continually and pleasurably astonished by their intricacy and delicacy, their simplicity and complexity, their variety and beauty of form, scent and colour. How is it possible to adore and glorify the design and not the Designer? How is it possible to withhold gratitude not only for the design but also for the senses with which we appreciate it? Herbs and herbal trees are particular favourites of mine because so much religious lore and symbolism attaches to them. Also, apart from their aromatic qualities, they suggest so many other reasons for gratitude to their Creator. Many that have culinary, medicinal, decorative, and cosmetic uses are also good companion protectors of other plants; there are herbs whose every part is edible – root, stem, leaf, flower, and seed – and almost every commonly known herb has uses beyond those generally employed nowadays. A herb garden sharpens the senses in a special way – so many different perfumes from the clean astringency of southernwood to the delicate sweetness of woodruff; and the scents of lemon balm and lemon grass differ subtly from one another. Nothing demonstrates so clearly as a herb garden that green is not one colour; it is as many colours as there are plants growing there.

Long years of city dwelling may so deaden the sense of hearing that gardens can seem very silent places. But at dawn and dusk in spring and summer the birds make them jubilantly noisy. The more time one spends in the garden, the more one's ear becomes attuned to the glorious variety of bird-call and song, and to the different noises made by insects and small mammals among the plants. The great black beetle begins to sound as if he's wearing hiking boots, and out of the corner of my ear I can hear a lizard darting into its home under the stones of Our Lady's grotto. One summer morning I discovered that an army of squashy, shiny red grubs, the size of five pence pieces, had invaded my potato patch, and I could only watch in astonished panic as they swarmed over the plants. But what amazed and horrified me even more was that I could actually hear them munching their way through the leaves.

It is a great privilege, from spring to autumn, to say the Morning Office in the sunlit dawn garden. It is so easy in such surroundings to be in accord with the Psalmist's outpouring of joy and praise: 'The pastures of the wilderness drip, the hills gird themselves with joy, the meadows clothe themselves with flocks, the valleys deck themselves with grain, they shout and sing together for joy' (Ps. 65:12–13). During our first year in the country we had the front of the house painted, and in my absence the decorator tore down some newly-built martins' nests from under the eaves. They have never nested there again and I am certain that each year a warning is handed on to the next generation. However, in the second year, I was delighted to watch them darting expertly through an open fanlight and building nests in the beams of my garden workshop. They have come annually ever since, and I am happy to recompense them for earlier and fatal inhospitality. My frequent presence has no effect on their daily round, and when poor weather keeps me in the workshop for Morning Prayer, they assist with their own calls and song, thus lending special significance to the verse, 'Even the sparrow finds a home, and the swallow a nest for herself, where she may lay her young, at thy altars, O Lord of hosts, my King and my God' (Ps. 84:3).

But all is not harmony, progress and jubilation. In gardening *and* prayer we learn not to look for short cuts or quick results. But at times we become daunted by the sheer hard work involved and find difficulty in beginning, let alone completing it. We are in Bunyan's 'Slough of Despond' and lack the strength to climb out. There are times of drought, disappointment, doubt, anxiety, and disease. We and the garden are parched and barren; the seed refuses to germinate. After an hour's prayer or gardening we seem to have achieved nothing, heard nothing, felt nothing. There is no consolation. All is dark, cold, and unproductive. Prayer and labour have become burdensome and fruitless duties. And at yet other times, some pest (like the nasty potato grub), kills plants, decimates a crop, and gnaws at the soul. 'If only I work hard enough,' we say to ourselves, 'things are bound to improve.' Of course we should work hard and have good intentions, but our wretched human insistence on being in control dictates that we cannot be at peace until *we* have rooted out the problem and set things right through our own efforts alone. We forget that without God we can do nothing and that only his grace, mercy, and power can lighten the darkness, send the rain, heal the disease, solve the problem, and enable us and our plants to develop. When the clouds break at the end of a difficult time in prayer or garden, they do so at his behest, not ours, and we realize anew that progress is not something *we* make. It is done *to* us and *for* us, not by us. William Cowper's lines come to mind:

> Ye fearful saints, fresh courage take,
> The clouds ye so much dread
> Are big with mercy, and shall break
> In blessings on your head.

As the darkness disperses we feel ourselves plucked out of the slough and drawn onwards and upwards to the next stage of growth, just as on a sudden we find one morning that the precious green of slow germinating parsley has at last spiked its way towards the light.

And what of the tedious, heavy work that breaks the back but leaves the mind relatively clear? Such tasks as clearing ground with a mattock, or digging over a patch, have rhythms that lend themselves to the use of a mantra, and admirably fit the Rosary. Sometimes I sing a hymn, but whether 'making a joyful noise unto the Lord', or meditating silently, whether praying freely or to a formula, I find that the concentration takes the mind from physical discomfort and ensures that the work is completed with increased thoroughness, and at a steady pace which does not exceed wisdom. And yet in spite of this, the ground seems to be covered more quickly than if the time had been spent thinking about next week's shopping list, or what I would do if we won the lottery.

The power of individual plants as an aid to prayer lies in symbolism, allegory, the association of ideas, and to their mention in the Bible. (Quite often it is the more humble and insignificant ones that yield the most fruit for meditation.) Many plants call to mind Old Testament incidents and verses from the Psalms. I cannot look at bulrushes or irises without thinking of Moses (Ex. 1–3), nor at hyssop without remembering the King James' version of Psalm 51: 'Purge me with hyssop and I shall be clean.' Plants and gardens feature prominently in the life and teaching of Christ – the vine, fig, mustard, sycamore, and 'lilies of the field', to name but a few. And if on Maundy Thursday you are unable to visit an Altar of Repose, where better to be than in a garden, which will become Gethsemane whilst you watch with him one hour.

In his masterpiece, *Introduction to the Devout Life*, St Francis de Sales entitles his twelfth article, in the second part, 'Spiritual Retreat'. He recommends that people should each day select a place in the Gospels, near Our Lord, and retire there mentally during the execution of their daily work. Souls who do this, says Francis, will be blessed in saying to Christ, 'You are my place of strength and my stronghold to give me safety, my roof against the rain, my shade against the heat' (Ps. 31). So for instance, if you have been led by St John's wort to meditate on the Gospel accounts of John the Baptist, you may come away with the occasion of the Lord's baptism by the Jordan as your place of spiritual retreat. The plant and the saint have led directly to Bible reading and meditation; indirectly they will keep you closer to God as you go about your daily tasks than may otherwise be the case.

The lore of plants is a treasury of verifiable history, as well as of legend and custom, much of it with a Christian significance or symbolism. Many plants have a traditional meaning, or are associated in the folk-consciousness, by their names, colour, or scent, with certain rites of passage, or with the feasts and seasons of the liturgical year. A knowledge of this lore opens up the power of plants to evoke specific attributes of Our Lord, Our

Lady, and the saints, and of events in their lives. In the same way plants can bring to mind the gifts of the Spirit, virtues to be sought, and vices to be eschewed; people to remember in prayer, either living or dead, individuals or groups, and nations; and events in the past to remember with thanksgiving or repentance. They can also evoke concepts such as justice, peace, liberation, and reconciliation. This last is important, as a snare of the gardener's calling is to become blinkered and insular and to forget that there is much in the garden of the world that is extremely unlovely. 'Father, may your spirit lead us forward out of solitude, may he lead us to open the eyes of the blind, to proclaim the Word of light, to reap together the harvest of life' (Intercession from the Divine Office Psalter, Saturday Week 4).

Many seasonal customs and beliefs connected with plants have their origins in pre-Christian cultures. The age-old ritual of 'crying the neck' (or mare), as the final sheaf of corn on the farm is harvested, would probably have been familiar to the reapers of Ancient Egypt. In *Folk Lore and Customs of Rural England* (1974) Margaret Baker quotes a north Devon farmer who said in 1828, 'I shall always patronise it [the custom] myself, because I take it in the light of a thanksgiving.' It is well known that the Church pragmatically transmuted the two great pagan festivals of winter and spring solstices into Christmas and Easter. Our Devonian countryman was in fact mentally transmuting a pagan practice into something that had Christian significance for him. The important thing is the symbolic meaning that any ritual act has for *you*. And it is in this spirit that I make no excuse for the inclusion in this book of customs and legends that without Christian transmutation would remain as mere superstition and fairy tale. Symbolism, metaphor, and allegory are mainsprings of poetic imagination. Indeed, according to Robert Lynd, editor of *An Anthology of Modern Verse* (1921), for William Blake 'imagination was almost another word for the Holy Ghost'.

Certainly I believe that the spiritual map for the restoration of my devastated garden, devised during the first months of homecoming, was the result of God-given imagination. The long rectangular plot is to be divided into six sections, rather than the present four:

1. The Advent, Christmastide and Pre-Lent enclosure;
2. A pleached Way of the Cross;
3. The 'Sanctuary' garden (the original herb garden);
4. The summer garden of Ordinary Time;
5. Autumn and winter beds of Ordinary Time;
6. Nourishment and healing plot.

Eventually, to walk round the whole will be to follow the cycle of the Church's year, both physically and spiritually. Detailed planning for the first enclosure is complete. The first task will be to install a long-desired water feature to signify the Baptism of the Lord, and our own. During this and future seasons I will put in as many of the plants mentioned in this book that are not already there, and for which time, money, and space can be found. *Rosa mundi* is a must to commemorate the Immaculate Conception; and a statue of a woman with a pitcher, bought some years ago, will go by the pond, recalling the Samaritan woman at the well. In that position, she will symbolize the Church waiting to be born before Christ's incarnation, and all women before they are converted.

This is a book of approaches to meditation, stimulated by plants and trees. They may lead readers in different directions from the ones I take, and a plant may not call forth the same response from year to year. In any case, to follow an approach slavishly is to run the risk of missing 'the many splendoured thing' of Francis Thompson's poem 'In No Strange Land'. Above all it is important to pray always to the Holy Spirit, who often has very different ideas. Originally written as a private spiritual manual for gardeners, the book may also help in the planning of retreats and house liturgies. Exile in London taught me that I could practise my plant method with a windowsill herb garden, with flower displays in church, by really *looking* at the displays in florists' shops, and simply by being more concentratedly observant when walking through urban parks, streets and squares; and as the seasons turned I was able to summon all my own plants from memory. But however or wherever *Gardening with God* is used, the literature and music listed in Appendix 2 are suggested for the lengthening and deepening of meditation and prayer.

The *Office of Readings* referred to throughout is always an excellent foundation for daily prayer and meditation.* The *Divine Office* in English is published by the Hierarchies of Australia, England and Wales, and Ireland in three volumes: 1. Advent, Christmastide, and Weeks 1–9 of the Year; 2. Lent and Eastertide to Pentecost; 3. The Weeks of Ordinary Time to the Feast of Christ the King. The volumes are expensive, but the investment for most of us will be a once-in-a-lifetime purchase and is worthwhile. The benefits to lay people of praying the Office are manifold.

---

* Unless otherwise stated, any reference to the writings of an early Father, or saint, or to the documents of Vatican II indicates that an extract from the named work forms the second office reading of the day on which it is cited.

It deepens our understanding of daily Mass and brings a myriad of blessings, insights, and knowledge; it is the prayer of the Universal Church, and to participate in it shows solidarity with her and increases our sense of membership of the Body of Christ; and it offers us the chance of adding, by supererogation, to the store of merit at the Church's disposal.

And so, for all gardeners, and for everyone who reveres the earth and its creator, I pray the healing peace and increased closeness to God that I find in my own garden. Be assured that that garden is neither large nor grand, and even before my long absence was never immaculately free of weeds. Nevertheless I remain undaunted by the lavish photographed perfection so beloved of gardening books and magazines, or by the 'quick-fix' stage management of some television programmes. As Elizabeth Jennings says in her poem 'In a Garden', 'Everything was too neat and someone cares / In the wrong way.' As all our prayer is characterized by faith, hope, and love, and a request for an increase in them, so the gardener has faith and hope that spring will be God-given each year, and that God's life-force will again engender the seed. I believe that the vision we have of our gardens and the love we lavish on them are reflections, however dim, of the Divine. Many writers before me have seen gardening as an expression of nostalgia for Eden, and as an attempt to regain the paradise lost at the Fall. Perhaps Teilhard de Chardin would call it our response to the 'Essence of all that is tangible', and enjoin us thus: 'You who have grasped that the world – the beloved of God, has ... a soul to be redeemed, lay your whole being wide open to my inspiration, and receive the spirit of the earth which is to be saved' (from *The Heart of Matter*). Were he alive today, he would be appalled, like us, at the mighty forces of godless greed and manipulation that threaten to destroy the Creation God loves. As individual Christian gardeners we know that our own tiny efforts must always fall short of perfection, this side of the grave. But we also know that because Christ has ransomed us, our gardening is blessèd. We know it from those rare moments of privilege when we hear the 'sound of the Lord God walking in the garden in the cool of the day' (Gen. 3:8).

J.M.
London, Feast of the Annunciation, 25 March 2002

INTRODUCTORY NOTE

Using this book as a gardener's companion to the liturgy

In the main, the Church's Year is structured according to weeks. This means that given days within those weeks do not occur on the same date each year. So certain Solemnities and the Saints' Days (now ranked as Feast, Memorial, or Optional Memorial) cannot be fitted in date sequence into this Part One. Part Two, which contains them, should therefore be read concurrently with Part One, rather as we use the Missal and the Breviary, turning on specific dates from the main seasonal liturgy to celebrate a Solemnity or to commemorate saints as their importance dictates.

Part One

ADVENT TO
SHROVE TUESDAY

INTRODUCTORY
LITURGICAL NOTE

The earliest date for the First Sunday of Advent is 27 November; the latest, 3 December. In 2000, for example, Advent began on the latter date, thus causing the Fourth Sunday of Advent to turn into Christmas Eve around midday! In years of longer Advent there can be up to a week between the Fourth Sunday and Christmas Day. In order to furnish plants for that extra week I have written the book as if the Third Saturday occurs on 17 December and the Fourth Sunday on 18 December. Whatever the length of Advent, the liturgy becomes specific to date from 17 December onward.

ADVENT

FIRST SUNDAY IN ADVENT

SILVER BIRCH *Betula pendula*

Cultivation Notes

This lovely deciduous tree is easily recognized from the satin silver of its bark. It improves soil rather than acidifying it, flowers from April to May, and produces catkin fruits in July and August. The leaves, similar to beech though smaller, turn yellow in autumn. *B. pendula* var. *laciniata* has a svelte elegance; *B. pendula* var. *tristis* is tall with gracefully drooping branches; and *B. pendula* var. *youngii* has a flattened dome-like crown with 'weeping' branches. These varieties can grow to between 25 and 30 feet and spread between 15 and 30 feet. Most of us, therefore, unless our gardens already have an established birch, must seek out its beauty in natural woodland or in botanical gardens.

History and Lore

The silver birch was important in the establishment of northern European forests after the last Ice Age. Ironically, its formidable regenerative powers have made it unpopular with present-day foresters, who sometimes control it by slashing, spraying, and ring-barking. And until its branches were banned as instruments of corporal punishment many generations of criminals and, sadly, children, had reason to hate and dread it. The tree itself has constantly pleaded a redemption of this shame, not only by its beauty, but by being useful in so many more constructive ways. Its oil is used in perfume and in dental products; its wood for paper, cotton reels, and toys, and in fish-smoking; its bark in tanning to add fragrance, as in Spanish leather. The sap is fermented to make beer, wine, spirits, and vinegar. One tree can produce almost 150 pints over a week in early spring. In past times twigs were bound together to make kitchen whisks and besoms. In parts of Sussex there is still a tradition of home-brewed birch wine, whilst in Siberia it is used to treat arthritis. The birch is the emblem of Russia and, with its connotations of new life born from the cold, perhaps never more appropriately so than now.

In the British counties of Shropshire and Staffordshire, our forefathers kept the Whitsuntide custom of decorating their parish churches with birch boughs. In the Bilston accounts for 1691 we read, 'Dressing ye chapel with birch, 6d'; in 1697, 'For birch to dress ye chapel at Whitsuntide, 6d'; and again in 1702, 'For dressing ye chapel, and to Ann Knowles for birch and a rose, 10d.' Countrywide, the tradition of using birch trunks to make maypoles is even more ancient. The fourteenth-century Welsh poet Gruffyd ap Dafydd expressed his Celtic spirituality in a poignant elegy.

> Long are you exiled from the wooded slope, birch-tree, with your green hair in a wretched state; you who were the majestic sceptre of the wood where you were reared, a green veil, and now turned traitress to your grove. You were made it seems, for huckstering, as you stand there like a market woman; and in the cheerful babble at the fair all will point their fingers at your suffering, in your one grey shirt and your old fur, amid the petty merchandise. No more will the bracken hide your urgent seedlings, where your sister stays; no more will there be mysteries and secrets shared, and shade, under your dear eaves; you will not conceal the April primroses, with their gaze directed upwards; you will not think now to inquire, fair poet tree, after the birds of the glen.
>
> (In *A Celtic Miscellany*, Kenneth Hurlstone Jackson (ed.), 1971.)

In his early poem 'The Dirge', Tennyson is believed to have been the first to describe the birch as silver:

> Now is done thy long day's work
> Fold thy palms across thy breast,
> Fold thy arms, turn to thy rest
> Let them rave.
>
> Shadows of the silver birk*
> Sweep the green that folds thy grave
> Let them rave.
>
> (*Juvenilia*, 1830)

* Birk: northern and Scots form of birch.

Towards Meditation
'And in earth's darkest place / Let there be light' (John Marriott, 1780–1825).

The skeletal yet still graceful birch tree of early December encompasses so many Advent themes. The few papery yellow fragments clinging futilely to the branches remind me that we are embarking on a penitential season: 'We all fade like a leaf, and our iniquities, like the wind, take us away' (Is. 64:6b); 'Your country lies desolate' (Is. 1:7). This is true in nature. How true is it of my soul? How seemingly beyond the light is our collective conscience? Apparently it is no longer safe to walk alone in the woods where, fifty years ago, I was taught the lore of trees by my father. Those glades, I recently learned, have since witnessed rape and other violent attack instead of the innocent wholesome pleasure of a little girl and her parents on their Sunday morning walks. Isaiah prays for mercy and help and so must we.

By the first Sunday in Advent the birches have gone to their winter sleep, but we must stay awake and watching, for we 'do not know when the master of the house will come' (Mk 13:33ff.). The trees will not awake until spring, but throughout the year bear a full harvest in their beauty and many practical uses. This is the season in which we pray that at Christ's Second Coming we may go to meet him bearing a harvest of good works. Then, with the birch trees, we will lift up our heads and see. But now we live and pray through the period that my grandmother, conscious, I'm sure, of deeper significance, always called 'the dark days before Christmas'. The birch, desolate and naked in the gloom, offers, in its gently lustrous bark, a pale hint of the glorious light of the Incarnation. Later, in spring, we may stand among its slender trunks, enjoying the dappling sun through a filigree of translucent green. Then we will note another symbolism. In every season, but perhaps most consolingly in Advent, the silver birch is indeed a tree of light.

Bible Readings
Isaiah 63:16–17; 64:1–8: Prayer for mercy and help
Isaiah 1:1–18: Your country lies desolate
1 Corinthians 1:3–9: Wait for the revealing of our Lord Jesus Christ
Mark 13:33–7: Watch therefore, for you do not know when the master of the house will come

5

Intercessions
For all who work in birch product industries; for the people of Russia; that we may not become so bound up in material things that we 'go to sleep', and are deaf and blind to Christ; for mercy and forgiveness for the way in which we have destroyed our natural environment and that even now better stewardship may prevail; for courage, strength, and alertness as we work towards our own harvest and the harvest of the world.

Place of Spiritual Retreat
With the disciples as they hear Christ's exhortation to stay awake, as in Mark 13

MONDAY WEEK ONE IN ADVENT

A Dried Arrangement for a Penitential Season

Flowers
heather; purple loosestrife; purple cone flower; everlasting flower; gladdon (see Saturday Week Two); lavender (see Sunday within the Octave of Christmas)

Foliage
eucalyptus (see Third Sunday); sweet bay (see Wednesday Week Two)

HEATHER *Calluna vulgaris*

Cultivation Notes
Botanists draw a distinction between the large family of ericas and *Calluna vulgaris*, or ling, which is the true heather of the moors, but British crossword compilers tend to regard heather and erica as synonymous. In the interests of achieving a range of colour, height, and flowering time, so shall I. Of late-summer flowering *Calluna*, the following are suggested:

Purple loosestrife

6

'Darkness' (deep rose-purple, 12–18 inches); 'Silver queen' (mauve flowers on silvery leaves, 10–16 inches); 'Alba plena' (pure white, 12–18 inches). For a dwarf white subject try *Erica vagans* 'Lyonesse'; and for deep purple, *Erica cinerea* 'P. S. Patrick'. *Erica darleyensis* is bushy and grows to about two feet, and its soft heather-purple flowers can bloom from November to April. All prefer sandy, acidic soil and dislike lime. Harvest for drying at the peak of flower maturity, but not when over-ripe. They dry well, and colour retention is good. Leaves tend to drop when dry so use a fixative, or glycerine method (see Appendix 3).

History and Lore

Calluna, sometimes known as ling, is the common heather that covers moors and woodland banks with pale purple in late summer. It is native to North America, Asia Minor, and northern Europe and is the only British example of its genus. There is, however, great variety in its shape, height, and habit. *Calluna* comes from the Greek *kalluna*, meaning to adorn or beautify. One thinks of the 'purple-headed mountain' of Mrs Alexander's hymn 'All things Bright and Beautiful'. Perhaps the name was given because it was made into brooms and did the beautifying by sweeping and cleansing. Heather is named from the places where it grows, a heath being defined as an open, untilled extensive tract of wasteland or wilderness. Caedmon uses the word, but according to the *Épinal Glossary*, it first appears as early as 700. In *King Lear* and *Macbeth* Shakespeare used the heath as the place for the outcast and outlaw, who would there descend into madness and perversion of truth; Emily Brontë's naming of Heathcliff in *Wuthering Heights* can hardly have been accidental; whilst in Thomas Hardy's *The Return of the Native*, Egdon Heath is just as much a character as the human figures whose story is played out on and around it. The word heather itself first appears in the eighteenth century. Ling comes from *lig*, Anglo-Saxon for fire.

In nature, heather provides valuable food for caterpillars of the emperor moth, which feed on its leaves in high summer. Bees love the nectar and produce a deep amber honey from it. At the end of the seventeenth century there were ten million acres of heath and moorland in Britain. This is now reduced to about two million, where it is conserved for sheep and grouse, and where heather is sometimes burned to encourage fresh shoots for their feeding. The plant has proved tremendously versatile in our traditions, being used as fuel, fodder, human and animal bedding, thatching material, and as a substitute for wattle in building. It has been used to make brooms and rope, and the roots have been carved into knife handles. The flowers produce an orange dye and can be used to make tisanes and beer. Not surprisingly, it was Scottish settlers who took it to North America. In more recent times Doctor Bach selected it as one of the original 38 flowers for his remedies, and it is used in modern homeopathy to treat arthritis, rheumatism, and insomnia. Briar-root pipes are made from *Erica arborea*, briar possibly being a corruption of the French *bruyère*, which has much the same cover-all meaning in layman's language as our word heather.

PURPLE LOOSESTRIFE *Lythrum*

Cultivation Notes
Two perennial varieties are recommended, *Lythrum salicaria* and *Lythrum virgatum* 'Dropmore purple'. From midsummer to early autumn both produce rosy purple flowers all the way up the tapering stems, which grow to as much as three feet. The natural habitat of loosestrife is on the margin of river banks, so you need to make sure the soil is moist and alkaline. It will self-seed readily in these conditions. Otherwise, propagate by division in autumn or spring. Harvest when in flower and dry immediately.

History and Lore
Lythrum is from the Greek *lythron*, meaning blood, possibly because of the colour of the flowers. *Loosestrife* comes from Lusimakhos (Lysimachus), who is said to have discovered the plant. *Lusimakhos* means 'loosing' (i.e., ending) strife. It is native to Europe, Asia, and North Africa. Pliny the Elder (23–79 AD) says it has a soothing effect on oxen and that it deters flies and gnats, thus relieving the animals from irritation. If you ride, try some in your pony's bridle. It has highly astringent properties and was once used for tanning leather and for dyeing. It has a long history of use in European folk medicine and was widely used during the cholera outbreaks of the nineteenth century.

PURPLE CONE FLOWER *Echinacea purpurea*

Cultivation Notes
An easily and therefore widely grown perennial, *Echinacea purpurea* is hardy and flourishes in rich well-drained soil. The strikingly tall and erect flowers are honey-scented, appear in colourful display from midsummer to

autumn, and are excellent for cutting and drying. Divide when still dormant in early spring or sow seed outdoors in April. Root cuttings can be taken in late winter.

History and Lore

Echinacea comes from the Greek *echinos* meaning hedgehog, probably because of the prickly scales of the flower's central cone. The plant grows wild on the prairies of southern North America and has long been used by native North American Plains tribes as a panacea and purifier. They particularly believe in its power to treat wounds and to ease coughs, colds, inflammations, and cramps. Roots would be sucked all day to ward off an incipient cold. It is listed in the United States National Formulary (1916–50). European homeopathy uses it in the form of tinctures, compresses, ointments, and flower essences. Domestically, you can lift roots in autumn to make a wash for acne or infected injuries.

EVERLASTING FLOWER *Xeranthemum annum*

Cultivation Notes

As its name suggests, the *Xeranthemum annum* is indeed an annual. Its daisy-like petals are naturally stiff and papery and therefore are easily dried. Many colours are available but I have chosen lilac, purple, and white for this Advent display (and pink for the third Sunday, *Gaudete* Sunday). Flowering is from late summer to early autumn. The grey-green foliage offers a contrast with other greenery. *Xeranthemum* will grow to a height of two feet, even in poor soil. It is important to harvest when flowers are at their best because they tend to discolour with age. If you pick bunches in various stages of development, including buds, take care to display in a dry atmosphere or the buds will absorb moisture and go limp.

History and Lore

Xeranthemum is a member of a group of plants called 'perpetuelles' by florists and flower arrangers. The group knows no boundaries, since people constantly experiment with new subjects. Like me, you may have memories of faded, brittle, and dusty arrangements, usually in the houses of older relatives. They need not be like this if care is taken at harvesting in summer. Autumn is too late. Choose subjects whose colour retention is good, as I have tried to do here, and consider the atmosphere in the place of display. Another advantage to the city dweller is that a garden is not necessary. Some nurseries specialize in plants for drying, and other outlets supply them ready dried (see Appendix 3).

Towards Meditation

'Restore us, O Lord God of hosts! Let thy face shine, that we may be saved!' (Ps. 80:19).

If there was not time yesterday, I will now begin my Advent arrangement, starting with a basis of dwarf heathers, violet ribbon, and a single white candle, adding the other flowers and foliage as the weekends of the season unfold, and on each Sunday, another candle. We only use our dining room on high days and holidays, so it is normally a cool dry room and therefore ideal for this display, which I usually put in the empty fireplace. As far as space is concerned, church florists have the best scope, but a small wreath, posy, or wall spray can still be made using the subjects described above.

The flowers give a range of colour from pale lilac to deep purple, and remind us daily that we are in a penitential season as well as one of hope. Later on, the ashen petals of Gladdon will symbolize the gleam of the Incarnation approaching in the darkness, and the white blooms, the purity of Christ and his mother. In former times, rose-coloured vestments were worn to express the joy of *Gaudete* Sunday, and this can still be reflected by pink heather and *Xeranthemum* on that day. Eucalyptus leaves provide hints of white and mauve, and their pale green is suggestive of young growth. Bay gives a strong, dark, glossy green, representing the eternal certainty of God's promise.

It is not just the colour and texture of the chosen plants that make them helpful to us in our journey through Advent to Christmas. Their history, lore, and present use can lead us to ponder several Advent themes. Ling, with its connotations of fire, suggests images of winter firelight, which, though it may be comforting, must not lull us into 'sleep'. We must stay alert and ready to meet Christ when he comes. Heather, loosestrife, and purple cone flower all evoke a beautifying, scouring, and purifying process. This may lead us to consider the Sacrament of Reconciliation as a necessary seasonal stocktaking, and make us more receptive to the insight of Charles Borromeo (1538–84). In today's second Office reading, he says in a Pastoral Letter that if we clear away impediments, Christ, who came once in the flesh for all of us, is ready to come again to each soul at any time. John Clare's poem 'The Winter's Spring' (1847) reminds me of this.

The plants of my arrangement also lead me to reflect on the reconciliation between races, and the fact that Christ came to heal differences, and to take the whole world into his saving love. He is the reconciliation between God and humankind. The heath is the wilderness, both of the individual soul and the world at large without God, but he still crowns it each year with royal purple. And Christ was born of a royal house. 'Everlasting' flowers cannot fail to remind me of the valley of dry bones, of his life-giving Holy Spirit, or of the fact that God will draw all nations together into the eternal peace of his kingdom. Despite everything that we make foul and cruel in his world, the Saviour is still prepared to come among us. He is at hand and we fear no more. For another year I am grateful to him for the reminders of Advent, and that I still have time to prepare.

Bible Readings
Isaiah 1:21–7: Lament for the Holy City; judgement and salvation
Isaiah 2:1–5: Let us walk in the light of the Lord
Ezekiel 37: The valley of dry bones
Ephesians 2:12–22: You who were far off are now brought near
Matthew 8:5–11: Many will come from east and west
Luke 12:35–8: Blessed are those servants whom the master finds awake when he comes

Intercessions
For victims of war, particularly children; for peace; for those who have power over our natural environment, and that our children will not be deprived of contact with it; for grace to clear away the barriers which keep Christ from our lives and prevent our reconciliation with God.

Place of Spiritual Retreat
At the scene of the healing of the centurion's servant, as in Matthew 8

TUESDAY WEEK ONE IN ADVENT

OAK *Quercus robur*; pendunculate oak; common English oak; Sussex weed

Cultivation Notes
Few of us have the pleasure of an oak in our gardens, but should you wish to plant one, lack of space would be the only drawback, as the oak

tolerates both acid and alkaline soils. A grown oak wood is a miniature nature reserve in its own right and even a single tree should eventually encourage wildlife to your garden. The crooked, open structure of its branches will let through a good deal of light, so that, while affording protection to birds and small mammals, it will allow plants and grasses to flourish beneath its spread. For woodland effect you can plant bluebell, early purple orchis, and primrose. Over 250 insect species can live in the oak tree, and this of course attracts birds – if you are lucky, woodpecker, nuthatch, and tree creeper. Acorns provide food for jays and squirrels. I have seen both in oaks near my outer-city workplace.

History and Lore
The word 'oak' is derived from the Anglo-Saxon *ac*. Acorn is literally corn of oak, the fruit being used as human food before the cultivation of corn, and later in pig fodder. It is native to the British Isles and most of Europe. The term 'pendunculate' refers to the stalks (penduncles) on which the acorns grow. In the Old Testament the oak figures as a favourite place to sit in shade (1 Kgs 13:14); to bury the dead (Gen. 35:8); and as an individual landmark (1 Sam. 10:3). However, it seems to have attracted idol worship, which is forbidden and criticized in Deuteronomy 16:21 and Hosea 4:13. The Celtic Druids held oak groves in great veneration. In *Hyperion*, Book I, Keats evokes an ancient mystic character for the trees:

> As when, upon a tranced summer-night
> Those green-robed senators of mighty woods,
> Tall oaks, branch-charmed by the earnest stars,
> Dream and dream all night without a stir.

In Britain, Christianity seems to have absorbed respect for the oak, and carvings of every part of the tree are to be found in cathedrals and older parish churches throughout the land, where it often symbolizes faith and endurance – on fonts, pews, choir stalls, and roof bosses. Ancient boundary oaks became stopping points during 'the beating of the bounds', a ceremony designed as an annual reminder of the parish boundaries and itself a transmutation of earlier fertility rites. It took place in Rogationtide just before Ascension Day. When the procession halted at the oak, crops would be blessed and passages from the Gospels read. George Herbert found spiritual value in the custom: 'A blessing of God for the fruits of the field; justice in the preservation of the bounds;

charitie in living, walking and neighbourly accompanying one another'
(*A Priest to the Temple*, 1652).

In Wishford Magna, Wiltshire, the villagers annually reaffirm their
ancient cutting rights in nearby Grovely Forest. At dawn on 29 May, oak
branches are cut there and taken back to the village to adorn the houses
amidst the blaring of horns and banging of metal dustbin lids. One large
branch is hoisted on to the church tower. Known as 'the marriage bough',
it is supposed to bring fertility to couples married in the church during the
following year. After this ceremony, four women go to Salisbury
Cathedral with sprigs of oak to present to the Dean. They are
accompanied by the villagers carrying banners bearing the motto 'Unity
is strength'. All enter the cathedral raising the shout essential to their
claim, 'Grovely, Grovely, and all Grovely!' They used to dance the whole
six miles until the practice was banned by the Victorian church.

The famous proverb, 'Great oaks from little acorns grow', is thought to
date from the fourteenth century, and many writers have used the oak as a
figure for longevity and slow growth. In 1658 Thomas Browne wrote,
'Generations pass while some trees stand, and old families last not three
oaks.' And in the nineteenth century G. H. Lewes, the partner of George
Eliot, put into his *Spanish Drama* the remark, 'Many a genius has been slow
of growth. Oaks that flourish for a thousand years do not spring up in
beauty like a reed.'

The present woodland canopy in the British Isles covers only about 15
per cent of the land. Nevertheless, we do have a legacy of ancient oaks that
exceeds that of any other Western European country. Many are over 250
years old, some much older. The Major Oak in Sherwood Forest, where
Robin Hood is supposed to have hidden, is said to have been a mature tree
during the reign of King John (1199–1216). The tree was cloned in 1992
to ensure that copies will be growing when it dies. Another Sherwood oak
believed to be 1000 years old was blown down in 1966. It was known as
Robin Hood's Larder, the tradition being that he used its hollow trunk to
store the deer he had killed. A remnant of this tree was sent to the Mayor
of Toronto by the Duke of Portland.

Between 1803 and 1814, when England was at war with France, the
Honour Oak at Whitchurch in Devon marked the limit for French
prisoners on parole from Princetown jail. Later, during the cholera
epidemic of 1832, money was customarily left by the tree in exchange for
food and, perhaps, even supplies of purple loosestrife. The Romans
awarded an oak chaplet to anyone who had saved the life of another. The

Victorians too held it to denote bravery and, if mixed with holly, hospitality. Acorn-shaped ends on their window blind pulls perhaps support this idea. The converse tradition of 'sporting (showing) one's oak' in our ancient universities meant closing the outer door of one's rooms to deter visitors. But this was only because most of those doors were made of oak. I prefer to think that a positively welcoming symbolism has a biblical origin in Abraham's meeting with the angels under the oak trees.

In nineteenth-century English lore the oak was a weather indicator: 'When the oak is out before the ash then there'll only be a splash; / When the ash before the oak, then there'll be a soak.' It was also a place unsafe for shelter during a storm: 'Beware of an oak, it draws the stroke.'

Oak wood is exceptionally strong and resistant to rot. Horace imagined that it must have been the first shipbuilding material: 'Oak was round his breast, / Who first launched his boat on the rough sea' (*Odes*, Book 1). This water-resistance has led to a variety of practical uses in furniture making, cooperage, and fencing. Oak is still widely employed in the parquet-flooring industry and in fishing-boat manufacture. Throughout Europe the major symbolism of oak comes from its durability and might, perhaps nowhere more so than in England. The decay of Britain's 'wooden walls' is 'nothing which seems more fatally to threaten a weakening, if not a dissolution of the strength of this famous and flourishing nation.' Ever since John Evelyn wrote these words to the Royal Society in 1662, these virtues of the oak have become synonymous with those of the nation, even with those of the very land that nation inhabits. The idea is enshrined in David Garrick's famous sea shanty, 'Heart of Oak are our ships, / heart of oak are our men; / we always are ready, / steady, boys, steady; / we'll fight and we'll conquer / again and again!' And even the Scottish poet Thomas Campbell acknowledged this English strength of character: 'Ye mariners of England that guard our native seas, / Whose flag has braved, a thousand years; / The battle and the breeze' (1801).

The pride of the English in their identification with the oak's fine qualities may be overweening. However, the facts are that they chopped down over 3,000 trees from which to select for the building of one three-deck warship; and the 'jolly tars' were often pressed into service and endured appalling conditions at sea. Whatever one thinks of the national policies under which they slaved, one still marvels at their strength. On a more humorous note, and to underline the affection in which Britons hold the oak, when some old oaks were felled in Great Windsor Park in 1955, one anonymous commentator, (according to Richard Mabey in *Flora Britannica*), remarked that it was like chopping down the Queen Mother!

Towards Meditation

'The voice of the Lord causes the oaks to whirl' (Ps. 29:9)

'The Lord of hosts has a day against all the oaks of Bashan' (Is. 2:13).

In King Lear's 'Blow winds' speech (Act 3, scene 2) Shakespeare describes lightning flashes as the heralds of 'oak-cleaving thunderbolts', and in so doing impresses us with the might of something even more powerful than the oak. Both the Psalmist and Isaiah use the same conceit, but in their case the 'thunderbolt' is the voice or Spirit of God, speaking of God's power over the mightiest on earth. As such, God's day against the oaks of Bashan inspires fear and trembling. But that day is a prelude to the salvific one in the New Testament, when Christ is born, the 'righteous branch' from Jesse's stock. And God's Spirit when it comes brings joy, peace, and comfort, not terror. In Luke 10 we read of Jesus being filled with the joy of the Spirit. That voice which brought down the mighty and rent the oak tree is now one that gives strength, if only we will ask and listen. The concluding prayer at today's Lauds and Vespers is for strength.

In winter the oak in its bareness lets in the short daylight hours. In spring and summer its structure still admits light so that a host of creatures may live in it. In all seasons it reminds me of the Light of the Word under which we flourish, by which we are guided and saved, and towards which we are specifically led in this Advent season. In one of his Orations St Gregory Nazianzen discusses the wonderful exchange wrought by the Incarnation. His description of Christ is full of images of immovable unchangeability. John the Baptist is the lamp that precedes the one who is the brightest possible light of all.

There is in the Holy Land, about two miles north west of Hebron, a tree known as Abraham's Oak, most probably named in commemoration of Genesis 18, in which Abraham, sheltering from the heat by the oaks of Mamre, looks up and sees three men standing in front of him. He seems to know their true identity straightaway and spares nothing in his efforts to make them welcome. His wife Sarah is sceptical of the news they bring that she will bear a child in her extreme old age. The story makes me think of 'saints' who have welcomed strangers and only afterwards come to realize their heavenly provenance, but perhaps most of all at this time of

15

year it echoes the great Advent message: stay awake for you do not know when the Master will come.

A copy of the Gaelic Rune of Hospitality hangs just inside our dining room in the country. If I'm there today a sprig of oak will be placed behind its frame; if not, the words of the Rune are etched in my mind so that I am reminded to leave my door open for the coming of the One who will keep me firm to the end.

> I saw a stranger yestreen
> I put food in the eating place,
> Drink in the drinking place,
> Music in the listening place;
> And in the sacred name of the Triune
> He blessed myself and my house,
> My cattle and my dear ones.
> And the lark said in her song;
> Often, often, often,
> Goes the Christ in the stranger's guise.
>
> (Anon.)

Bible Readings
Genesis 18:1–15: Abraham's hospitality
Psalm 29: The voice of the Lord
Isaiah 2:6–22: The Lord's day against all the oaks of Bashan
Isaiah 11:1–10: The Spirit of the Lord shall rest upon him
Ezekiel 34:15–16: I will strengthen the weak
1 Corinthians 1:7–9b: He will sustain you to the end
Luke 10:21–4: He rejoiced in the Holy Spirit

Intercessions
For workers in nature reserves and wild life sanctuaries; for ministers in our cathedrals; for shipbuilders; for mariners and submariners; for the families of victims of man-made disasters, such as those who died in the submarine Kursk; for those whose homes are lost or damaged in storm and flood; for members of emergency and air-sea rescue services; thanksgiving for their bravery; for all who gave their lives on 11 September 2001.

Thanksgiving for the happinesss of newly married couples.

For respect for God's presence and will; for open ears and eyes to hear and see it; for strength to carry it out and to take more care of our spiritual welfare. For light, joy, and peace in the world and in our own souls; for a greater spirit of generosity and hospitality; for greater awareness of the needs of those close to us.

Place of Spiritual Retreat
With the disciples when Jesus is filled with joy in the Holy Spirit, as in Luke 10

Note: Three days after I wrote this entry, the Boscabel Oak in Shropshire, offshoot of the famous hiding place of Charles II, was badly damaged in the worst storms to hit Britain since 1987.

WEDNESDAY WEEK ONE IN ADVENT

BOX *Buxus sempervirens*; common box

Cultivation Notes
If left to itself box can attain a height of up to ten feet, but in gardens the dwarf variety, *B. sempervirens* var. *suffructicosa*, is popular for low hedging. The purchase of sufficient plants to start a hedge tends to be expensive, so buy two or three and take three-inch cuttings in August or September. Keep them in a cold frame and maintain a balance between drying out and over-watering. Pot on at the start of the second year, then plant out in October. For a dense hedge, set six inches apart. Box likes a well-drained, neutral to alkaline soil, but it is greedy for moisture and nutrients, so water and compost/mulch nearby plants. The hedge should be clipped twice a year when established. Go for a single ornamental bush if you haven't time for the maintenance of a formal hedge. Box is very slow growing.

History and Lore
Sempervirens simply means evergreen, and indeed box is a source of glossy greenery for flower arrangers at a time of year when this is scarce. It is native to Europe and North America and has been used in topiary since classical times. Pliny the Elder (AD 23–79) describes 'a terrace adorned with representatives of divers animals in box'. It was much beloved of Tudor knot gardeners, and magnificent present-day examples can be found at Moseley Old Hall (Wolverhampton), at Hatfield House (Hertfordshire), and in the gardens of several National Trust properties.

It remains popular as an edging plant in herbaries but still grows naturally in many places, notably on Box Hill in Surrey.

Writers have disagreed as to the smell of box. One unacknowledged quote claims that it takes us 'out of time into the abysses of the unbeginning past'. Oliver Wendell Holmes (1809–84) also found it suggestive of eternity and of 'the incalculable remote time of childhood'. He had first smelled the box when he was not much taller than the hedge itself. Richard Mabey in *Flora Britannica* (1998) is scathing about the smell of box, likening it to tom cat. To say the least, it is pungent when cut, perhaps a reason for having just one and allowing it its way. However, I am happy to let John Evelyn, writing about Box Hill in 1706, have the last word: 'The Ladies and Gentlemen divert themselves among the Box-trees; without taking any such offence at the smell which has banish'd it of late from our Groves and Gardens; when after all, it is infinitely to be preferr'd, to any sweeter, less-lasting Shrub whatever.'

Box wood is yellow, very hard and even-grained; and because of this it gave its name to boxes. It has been used to make combs, spoons, rulers, rolling pins, chessmen, printing blocks, and mathematical, nautical, and musical instruments. It is still used for woodcuts, and is believed by some to encourage hair growth. Florists use young stems in their wreaths, perhaps an unconscious connection with the old tradition of carrying it with rosemary to funerals, to throw on the coffin.

Box is supposed to be as effective as quinine in the treatment of malaria but has fallen out of use because of its high toxicity. Probably it is best kept in gardens for its ornamental use and for its symbolism of stoicism. Isaac Walton claimed that angling is a good training in patient waiting; so too is the growing of box.

Towards Meditation

The King James Bible mentions the box twice only, and more modern translations tend to give 'pine' in those texts, as in Isaiah 41:19, where God promises to help the poor, needy, and thirsty by putting pools, rivers, and springs in the wilderness and by planting trees there. God's major purpose is that all may recognize him as sovereign creator. I have never been to the hills of Galilee, but I am told that box still grows there. According to Matthew, this is where Jesus healed many before feeding the four thousand. Perhaps the hungry crowds gathered about him among box bushes, patient without food for three days until he worked the miracle with the loaves and fishes. This, itself a symbol of the heavenly banquet, is prefigured in Isaiah, but even in his account of the Feast of Fat Things, there is an element of waiting, not just for nourishment, but for the Lord himself and the salvation he brings.

In a sermon on Advent, St Bernard of Clairvaux (1090–1153) speaks of the first coming of Christ in the flesh, and of the last, when all shall see the salvation of God and 'look on the one they have pierced'. But, in an echo of Gregory, he refers also to a coming in the spirit and in power. He says that this advent of Christ, to each one who earnestly seeks him, is like a path leading from his first coming as man to his last coming in majesty, glory, and judgement. For the next three weeks or so we are waiting again to celebrate that first advent; we do not know when the last advent will be, but the liturgy constantly enjoins us during this season to be spriritually on the watch. We may open ourselves to Bernard's intermediary advent at any time, and we have God's promise that if we do this the Spirit will console us through Word and Eucharistic presence. All three waitings demand a robust, rigorous steadfastness. But this still allows the urgent prayer, 'Come Lord, do not delay.' In his motet *Rorate Coeli* the composer Guerrero, a pupil of Palestrina, sets those words, '*Veni Domine et noli tardare*' to a falling cadence, but in the alto part with rising notes on the last two syllables. It perfectly expresses a yearning, profoundly earnest entreaty that is at the same time confident. Renaissance polyphony is like a tapestry. None of the lines rests much; one nano-thread of error and the fabric falls apart. To sing it is a hard and satisfying discipline. Fervour must not allow a descent into mawkishness, but in singing this phrase of Guerrero's I always had a struggle to prevent emotion from affecting evenness of voice.

Anyone familiar with Shakespeare's *Twelfth Night* will immediately associate the box tree with Malvolio's pride. There is a connection here with patience, my main theme today, for the moment we dare congratulate ourselves on our patience we risk a subtle pride, far more insidious than that of Shakespeare's puritan. Joseph Addison perfectly expressed the fine line between true patience and self-righteous endurance: 'Tis pride, rank pride, and haughtiness of soul; / I think the Romans called it stoicism' (*Cato*, Act 1, scene 4; 1713).

Knot gardens have a particular spiritual symbolism, and whilst admiring their geometric discipline, this gardener prefers an informal look on her own patch. One box tree allowed to grow naturally, and from which a sprig may at last be taken for an Advent flower arrangement, will more potently instruct her in the nature of patience and pride than any number of its sculpted relations could possibly do. 'You also be patient. Establish your hearts, for the coming of the Lord is at hand' (Jas 5:8).

Bible Readings
Isaiah 25:6–10: The Feast of Fat Things
Daniel 9:19: O Lord delay not
Isaiah 40:31 They who wait for the Lord
Psalm 40:1 I waited patiently for the Lord
James 1:4: Steadfastness
James 5:7–11: You have heard of the steadfastness of Job
Isaiah 2:11: The pride of men shall be humbled
Isaiah 26:9: My soul yearns for thee in the night, my spirit within me earnestly seeks thee
Matthew 15:29–39: He went up on the mountain and sat down there

Intercessions
For recognition of the value of the gifts of others; for the starving; for sufferers from tropical diseases; for church musicians and florists; for a greater awareness of God as Creator; for healing; for greater under-standing of the three Advents; for a better preparation for our encounters with Christ in the Eucharist.

Place of Spiritual Retreat
At the healing and feeding of the multitude in the Galilean hills, as in Matthew 15

THURSDAY WEEK ONE IN ADVENT

JUNIPER *Juniperus communis*; common juniper

Cultivation Notes
The juniper belongs to a special group within the cypress family. Its 'berries' are in fact cones, and normally one tree does not bear both male and female flowers. Many plants for sale are propagated from male-bearing trees, so if you want to grow for the 'berries', be careful how you buy. The flowers appear in late spring, the males being yellow and the females green and inconspicuous. Juniper does well on chalk and limestone and is found growing naturally on hills and heath-like downs

in Britain. Many forms are available for the garden, from a flat creeping type about two feet high to a single stemmed tree up to 35 feet. For the rock garden, the dwarf *Juniper c. compressa* reaches no higher than a foot and is one of the slowest growing. There is also the elegant *Juniper c. fastigia* (the Latin meaning 'of highest rank/dignity'). All varieties can be raised from cuttings of firm young growth in early autumn and put in sandy soil in a propagating frame. The 'berries' can take up to three years to ripen; they are green to blue in the first year and dark blue with a white waxy coating in the second. Pick when purplish-black and light brown inside, shaking them onto a light-coloured ground sheet. The spicy pine aroma and sweet resinous flavour are stronger in the southern-growing varieties.

History and Lore
Juniper was one of the earliest trees to establish after the last Ice Age. Today its area of growth constitutes the greatest spread of all the world's conifers, and it is native to Europe, North Africa, North Asia, and North America.

The Gaelic name is *aiteann*, a word linked with *teine*, meaning fire, because of the former use of its twigs for kindling; apparently it is still used as fuel in parts of Corsica and Spain. The heartwood is durable, tough, and reddish brown. It smells of pencils, and many are made from an American species. The larger varieties are used in high quality woodwork and the thinner branches and twigs in basket-work and in curing foodstuffs. The 'berries' contain 1 per cent Juniper oil, which is mentioned in the British *Pharmacopoeia* and used in the treatment of rheumatism and arthritis. It is thought to reduce the build-up of uric acid in the joints. An aphid causes needle galls or 'whooping berries', so called because of their former use as a remedy for whooping cough. A modern homeopathic medicine is available for indigestion. However it may cause an allergic reaction and should not be taken by anyone with a kidney complaint, or in pregnancy. In my girlhood, even good Catholics knew the old wives' tale about hot baths and gin. Perhaps the most common historical use for juniper has been as a flavouring in the manufacture of that drink. The word 'gin' comes from the Dutch *genever*, which in turn is derived from Latin *juniperus*.

For innocent and safe culinary use, store 'berries' in a spice jar and use whole or gently crushed. They go well with hearty meat dishes such as beef stew or in stuffings and marinades for game and pork and are a traditional ingredient in English salt beef and Welsh and York hams. In Germany a juniper conserve is eaten with cold meats. The flavour blends well with bay, garlic, marjoram, thyme, and fennel.

Towards Meditation

'Sweet berries ripen in the wilderness' (Wallace Stevens, 'Sunday Morning', 1923).

I am reminded of the passage in Isaiah 17 where God speaks of the punishment he will wreak on Damascus. The general picture is one of a land devastated by crop failure. Two or three berries may be found, but only on the topmost branches. In the previous chapter a similar fate has been prophesied for Moab, but here there is an injunction to shelter the outcast and dispossessed. God will bring down mighty cities, but in their place is prophesied the glorious new city the poor shall inherit. Today's Gospel tells us that unless we listen to God's Word and act upon it we will be building on sand and will not enter the kingdom of heaven. The juniper is a suitable plant for today because of these references, but also because of the story of Elijah in 1 Kings 19.

In Victorian times the juniper signified protection and asylum, probably because the 'Authorised Version' identifies it as the prophet's resting place on his flight from Jezebel. Modern versions render 'broom', but for me, reared on the same translation as my forebears, he will always be under a juniper. I see a traumatized Elijah after the immense faith demanded during his successful contest with the prophets of Baal and the amazing strength of will and body involved in his killing all 450 of them. In his flight from Jezebel's vengeance he sits under the tree and wishes to die; the angel wakes him with a touch, from what must have been the sleep of utter collapse. He does not come round properly the first time; the angel touches him again – there is such concern and gentleness in this. When he is fully conscious at last, the angel provides hot food and drink. (Interestingly, we know from Job and the Psalmist that the tree of 1 Kings was used in cooking fires, and modern reports from the Holy Land say that charcoal from its roots throws out the strongest heat for that purpose.) After the sustenance Elijah goes 'in the strength of it for forty days and nights' to Horeb. Later, on the Mount, God is heard, not in the wind or earthquake, and not in the fire. It is after these cataclysms, through a 'still small voice', that Elijah receives instructions for the future of the kingdom and the appointment of Elisha as his successor. God has tested him most terribly, but then at last there is this quiet tenderness as if to say, 'You have prevailed. The horror is over – for now.'

Elijah's tree was probably a broom, of the low-growing straggly variety. Apparently these are the characteristics of the plant that grows in the Holy Land today under the name of white broom or juniper. We are told that Elijah sat down under the tree. I do not find it too fanciful to imagine that it was the first thing he came across that afforded any protection at all. I think he may have crawled under it in exhaustion and despair. His were bloody times, but even for a man of his fierceness in mission, the killing of 450 must have been horrific.

The mystery of why God tests some of us more than others is for pondering another day. For now, I am humbled by Elijah's faith and strength. But I know that in a very, very minor way it is the same for me, after scorching under the slightest lick of the Refiner's fire. Sometimes he vouchsafes a sudden insight; at others he speaks in the silence through small things, like the juniper tree itself, a message of instruction or consolation no human language can translate or explain, and yet the receiving soul understands and benefits immeasurably.

The story raises many aspects of why, how, and when God speaks to us, but the main point today is that we should be alert to hear him. As a child I always thought of the Advent voice as startling and loud. So many hymns seemed to present it in this way, and certainly their authors meant to ensure we did not sleep and tasted the joy of anticipation. Every Advent morning of my girlhood, my father would bellow lustily in the bathroom, 'Hail to the Lord's Anointed', 'Hills of the North Rejoice'. Certainly nobody slept in our house once he was at his ablutions. He claimed to be practising for school assembly, but I know he just relished the words and tunes. However, as beloved as the memory of his voice remains, in middle age I find a gentler, more reflective approach developing with each successive Advent. We can be awake without roistering about the place. As children we were mainly concerned with Christmas; now we think more about the Second Coming. Ephraim (*c.* 306–73), in his Commentary on the *Diatessaron*, chapter 18, tells us that the very reason why the time of this is hidden is to keep us watchful. He refers to the signs Jesus gave of its imminence and remarks, 'In varied ways they have happened and are still happening.' From a twenty-first-century standpoint we cannot but agree with him. And yet Ephraim tells us we must not lose heart: 'I slept, but my heart was awake. / Listen! my beloved is knocking. / "Open to me, my sister, my love"' (Song 5:2).

23

Bible Readings
Isaiah 16 and 17: Zion the refuge of sinners; punishment on Israel
Haggai 2:6–9: In this place I will give you prosperity
Isaiah 26:1–6: He lays it low, low to the ground
1 Kings 19:4ff.: Elijah under the juniper tree.
Acts 28:28: The Gentiles will listen
Matthew 7:21–7: Build your house upon the rock

Intercessions
For all who work in the timber and food-curing industries; for arthritis, rheumatism, and whooping-cough sufferers; for relief for victims of drought, famine, flood, and volcanic eruption; for the persecuted, tortured, and dispossessed; for the traumatized and clinically depressed; for patience during growth, in faith, and in the garden; for greater commitment in mission; for a greater respect for others and for God's creation; for quiet in which to listen; for fortitude that we may not lose heart.

Place of Spiritual Retreat
With the crowds being taught by Jesus, as in Matthew 7

FRIDAY WEEK ONE IN ADVENT

FENNEL *Foeniculum vulgare*

Cultivation Notes
Fennel can be perennial or biennial. It likes sun and moisture but thrives on most soils. It can be confused with the annual dill and should not be grown near it; they may cross-pollinate, with a resulting impairment of flavour. Avoid planting near beans or tomatoes, as it is said to have an adverse effect on their health. If allowed to flower, fennel will self-seed readily, to the extent that it can become a nuisance. Certainly you should not need to worry about new plants. Simply dig up a likely specimen and transplant before the tap root forms (which it will if there is more than three inches top growth). Today might afford time to make war on the unwanted stragglers. The flowers appear from June to October. They are insignificant, yellow, and borne in clusters on umbels. After flowering, cut back, and the plant will produce a second crop of leaves before dying back

for the winter and reappearing the following spring. The plant tends to deteriorate after a couple of years, but as already noted can be replaced at no expense. Fennel is feathery and handsome, often growing to a height of six feet. A very attractive bronze variety is also available. Harvest seeds before they fall by cutting flower heads. Hang upturned in a paper bag for drying.

History and Lore

Fennel is a native of southern Europe and has been grown as a vegetable and herb since classical times. Believed to have been brought to Britain by the Romans, it was one of the nine sacred herbs of the 'old religion' and is mentioned in Anglo-Saxon herbals. It became popular with the medieval poor as flavouring for food; the seeds depressed appetite and were much used in Lent. More recently in England and America ladies carried it to church in Sabbath-day posies with caraway, dill, and southernwood. It revived them during long sermons and kept fidgety children quiet during the same. (Children have traditionally made 'pens' from the hollow stalks.) In America, I am told, the seeds were called 'meetin' seeds'.

Attractive to bees, fennel is also the food of the rare Swallowtail butterfly and is often found growing wild on wasteland in Britain. In some parts of Australia it is under control as a weed. The oil is claimed to reduce inflammation and to be an effective remedy for hiccups and conjunctivitis. Fennel is not given to pregnant women. On the other hand fennel tea, apart from being a digestive, is said to encourage milk in nursing mothers. The oil is also used in commercial production of toothpaste, soaps, air fresheners, gripe water, and insecticides.

All parts of fennel are aromatic, and its aniseed flavour is very powerful. My husband and I love strong Mediterranean cooking, but I use only two or three seeds in a recipe. Fennel gives their characteristic flavour to *Finocchiona*, the Italian salami, and to the French liqueur *Fenouillette*. Use chopped leaves in salads and in sauces for fish dishes. In some families it is traditional with pork and other rich meats. The bronze variety, though more ornamental, has a rather insipid flavour – so stay with green fennel for kitchen use. Both green and bronze provide graceful tall subjects for autumn arrangements, and they can both be dried. They are particularly effective when frosted for Christmas decorations. (*F. dulce*, sweet or Florence fennel, is the white bulbous beast used as a vegetable and is difficult to grow in Britain.)

Fennel is of ancient repute in strengthening eyesight. It is illustrated in the early fifteenth-century manuscript the *Tacuinum Sanitatis*, where it is described as cool and dry and good for eyesight. The nineteenth-century American poet Henry Wadsworth Longfellow complimented it thus: 'Above the lower plants it towers, / The fennel with its golden flowers, / And in an earlier age than ours / Was gifted with the wondrous powers / Lost vision to restore.'

Towards Meditation

'According to your faith, be it done unto you' (Mt. 9:29).

Lesley Gordon, in *Green Magic* (1977), reports that Peter Parley referred to fennel as 'theological smelling salts'. In former times, the men occasionally borrowed sprigs from the posies of their womenfolk, to prevent them from sleeping in church, or as Parley put it, to 'exorcise the fiend that threatened to their spiritual welfare', surely a literal interpretation of Ephraim, who tells us in his sermons that when the soul succumbs to sleep, 'the enemy takes control of it and works through it what it does not want to do'.

Fennel reminds me that being awake and alert means looking as well as listening and also of the truism enshrined in the common saying, 'None so blind as those who will not see.' Isaiah's prophecy can be taken metaphorically, that the souls of those who seek Him will at last see God. 'In that day, out of their gloom of darkness, the eyes of the blind shall see.' And we have faith that sight will be given in heaven to those who have been physically blind on earth. I know of no lines in literature that evoke the desolation of blindness so painfully as those of Milton in *Samson Agonistes*, made more truthful by the poet's own affliction: 'O dark, dark, dark, amid the blaze of noon, / Irrecoverable dark, total eclipse / Without all hope of day!' The blind themselves often say that lack of one sense sharpens the others and heightens their perception. Perhaps this is what Keats meant in his poem 'To Homer': 'There is a budding morrow in midnight / There is a triple sight in blindness keen.' (Homer is traditionally thought to have been 'the blind man living in rugged Chios'.)

For all of us, blind and sighted alike, it is God's will that we should see the face of his Son. But we must rouse ourselves to seek him. In his *Prosologion*, chapter 1, St Anselm (1033–1109) speaks of the human attempt to contemplate God as an inching towards 'inaccessible light'. He prays to be taught how to seek and for God's pity on his efforts and strivings. The Psalmist also pleads with God not to hide his face and asks to 'behold the beauty of the Lord and to inquire in his Temple'. And he too encourages us to 'wait for the Lord and to be strong and steadfast in prayer'. We keep climbing. In an echo of St John of the Cross in his *Ascent of Mount Carmel*, Tennyson describes the journey thus: 'I falter where I firmly trod, / And falling with my weight of cares / Upon the great world's altar-stairs / That slope thro' darkness up to God' (*In Memoriam*, Canto 55).

The story in Matthew of the healing of two blind men holds lessons for us, one of which is surely tied up with the efforts we make in prayer, with how much and how often we pray for our faith to be increased. And it raises the question of whether we listen to and obey him when he does heal us, when he does speak to us, when we are allowed a glimpse of him. No doubt the two healed blind men could not help their disobedience. And I have to ask myself: How often have I used that excuse? And yet whatever we do, whatever our physical or spiritual blindness, reconciliation is always open to us. And we may 'taste and see' in the Sacrament, where like Luke and Cleopas on the road to Emmaus we will recognize him in the breaking of bread.

Bible Readings
Isaiah 29:17–24: Out of their gloom and darkness the eyes of the blind shall see
Jeremiah 30:18: I will restore the fortunes of the tents of Jacob
Psalm 27: The Lord is my light and my salvation
Matthew 9:27–31: According to your faith be it done to you

Intercessions
For the starving; for those suffering from eating disorders; for nursing mothers and their babies; for those who work in industries where fennel is used; for the physically blind; for eye specialists and opticians.

For the spiritually blind and desolate; for progress in the prayer of 'inquiry'; for an increase in faith; for strength and steadfastness in prayer; for grace to resist the impulse to disobedience; for strength to carry our cares without faltering.

Thanksgiving for poets, whose words sharpen our insight and perceptions.

Place of Spiritual Retreat
At the healing of the two blind men, as in Matthew 9

SATURDAY WEEK ONE IN ADVENT

WINTER BARLEY *Hordeum hexastichum/polystichum*

Cultivation Notes
Barley has a shorter growing season than wheat and can flourish on poorer soils. There are two main types: *H. distichum*, known as 'two row' because it has two rows of seeds in each ear, and 'six row', *H. hexastichum*, which usually has six. Normally sown as winter barley, it is the first to come into ear in late spring. You need a big garden to grow barley and sufficient space to assign it a separate plot. Sown in autumn, it should grow to three feet by the end of winter.

History and Lore
The Greek word for barley, *krithe*, means piercing or pointed, and the Hebrew, *seorah*, means long-haired, describing the bristles or 'awns' on the ears. It is known to have grown in the Middle East some 12,000 years ago. Pliny mentions it as the oldest of human foods. Remains have been found in Egypt that date from 2,000 BC, and also under the alluvial basins of Swiss lakes. It is one of the hardiest of crops, even growing in Lapland, Siberia, Alaska, and Tibet, where it is the staple food. In the United States it was first grown in Massachusetts in 1602. In Britain, more acreage was recently under barley than any other arable crop, traditional areas being East Anglia, northern England, and Scotland.

From the many biblical references to barley we learn that it was a staple food in the Holy Land, particularly of the poor (Deut. 8:8; Ruth 2:17; Ezek. 4:9; Jn 6:9). In Leviticus 27:16 it is valued at 50 shekels of silver a homer (i.e. a dry measure of some 80 gallons), and 2 Kings 7:1 records that its price was half that of wheat. It provided fodder for horses, cattle, and dromedaries (1 Kgs 4:27); Solomon must have got through a tremendous amount for this purpose! Then there is the strange story in Judges 7 where, before Gideon's battle against the Midianites, a man has a dream about a barley cake falling upon an enemy tent and laying it flat. His friend interprets the cake as the sword of Gideon, which will prevail. Gideon accepts the reading, goes out, and is victorious. I am told that 'barley cake' as a derogatory term for Jew was in use in the Holy Land at least up to the 1970s. One wonders how old the expression really is. Is it symbolic of the belief that God's chosen poor will have the victory? Archaeological finds of drinking vessels suggest that the Philistines brewed barley, but I know of no evidence that the people of God drank alcoholic liquor made from it.

In our day it is still grown for livestock feed and used extensively in the brewing and distilling industries. For this purpose the 'two row' variety is apparently favoured. For beer, seeds are germinated and kiln-dried to produce 'wort' (barley broth at fermentation stage) or the 'barley bree' of Robert Burns' poem, 'Willie brew'd a peck o' maut' (1790). Burns was also responsible for the popular personification of 'dutch courage': 'Inspiring, bold John Barleycorn / What dangers thou canst make us scorn!' ('Tam o' Shanter', 1791).

The Barley Mow (stook) is prevalent in English folklore, and I remember with great affection several rollicking evenings in the inns of south Devon during the 1970s, singing folk songs that hail its produce. Not surprisingly, 'Barley Mow' is a popular name for public houses.

Barley is first recorded in medicinal use about 1500. Non-alcoholic barley water is rich in vitamins B and E and has long been used to stimulate the appetite and improve the digestion of convalescents. There are homeopathic treatments for asthma and bronchitis based on hordenine, which is similar to ephedrine, but nursing mothers should avoid it as it suppresses lactation. In the home, the six-rowed barley is more attractive in flower arrangements; cut when fresh green or later when golden.

Barley-sugar sweets, taken to allay travel sickness and popping ears when flying, were originally made from barley; I remember being given one in 1956 on a hair-raising flight by Dakota from Blackbushe to Basel. But the barley product I hold in deepest affection is the malt extract that was occasionally spooned out of a great jar on nursery school mornings in the 1940s. It was a treat to me then, and I would not learn for another twenty five years that it had been part of Magnus Pyke's wartime nutritional plan to safeguard the health of the nation's children.

Towards Meditation
'He that goes forth weeping, bearing the seed for sowing, shall come home with shouts of joy, bringing his sheaves with him' (Ps. 126:6).

Today, my own family roots in Cambridgeshire will probably make me think first of arable farmers and imagine them casting eyes over the fields to see whether the barley has germinated. For them, nowadays particularly, the thrill of seeing the first green tips may be reduced to weary relief. Barring disaster, they will harvest another crop. I have often seen barley stooked in the old way, like golden macaroons in shadows cast by the setting sun. It has always evoked Ruth, who came with Naomi at barley harvest. It was barley she gleaned and barley she was given by Boaz. Her story resonates with all those who have had to start again in an alien place and who feel that deep love and loyalty towards the person who helped them in those circumstances. Perhaps Ruth was not far from the mind of Wordsworth when he wrote of the song of the 'Solitary Reaper': 'The music in my heart I bore / Long after it was heard no more'. Both Keats ('Ode to a Nightingale') and Hood ('Ruth') were moved by the image of the exiled Ruth in the harvest fields. May Doney's less-considered poem 'Ruth' does not use the image *en passant*, but after opening with a line of Hood's goes on to present her as archetypal woman:

"She stands breast high amid the corn" –
The harvest of her love and tears
And every pain her soul has borne
Through the fulfilling years.

She stoops amid the golden wealth
That drops around her patient feet,
Gathering her suffering and her health –
Her spirit's ripened wheat.

She gleans, unwearied, evermore
The great ears of her joy and grief,
And binds the wonders of her store
Into a little sheaf.

Bruising the grain of all she is,
She kneads a little loaf of bread,
Mingling her life's strange mysteries –
Loins, bosom, heart and head.

And then upon herself she feeds
The life she loves, the lives she bears,

Breaking her passion for their needs,
Her pity for their cares.

So, through her days' allotted span,
She yields and binds and spends her truth;
The woman God has given to man –
The everlasting Ruth.
(Robert Lynd (ed.), *An Anthology of Modern Verse*, 1933.)

There is something tremendously reassuring about a field of stooks, something deeply satisfying and God-connected. Why is this? In the case of barley, it is history and nature that particularly impress. Wherever remains have been found, they have been of cultivated specimens. Like all cereals, barley is an annual, does not survive permanently on its own, and must be sown each year. It can be reared only on ground tilled by sweat of human brow and body – and yet it will grow almost anywhere if that effort is made. The Victorians had a notion that there had been some unrecorded miracle in the mists of time, when God had given barley to humans to farm for their food. He 'prepared them corn when he had so provided for it'. This miracle they thought of as a prefiguration of the one worked by Our Lord with the barley loaves in John 6. And here the mind turns to the differences between the Old and New Covenants and to how, even in the time of the Old, Isaiah prophesied the compassion and mercy of the New. We must labour, even for 'the bread of adversity', and we remember that barley is the bread of the poor. But God will help us; he will give rain for the seed; he will heal and bind up (see Is. 30:19–26). (I am tempted to add, 'As long as we do not continue to pollute and destroy the earth.') We shall see our 'Teacher' if we obey the urgent Advent demand for our effort: 'Seek the Lord while he may be found' (Is. 55:6).

Christ, 'the Teacher', comes to forge the New Covenant and fulfil prophecy. In John 6 he heals and then feeds them with the barley loaves taken from a poor boy. In Matthew 9 again he heals many. And we are told of his compassion for the crowds because they were harassed and dejected, 'like sheep without a shepherd'. He sees that their hunger and poverty is spiritual as well as physical and sends out the Twelve on their mission to the countless numbers not present at the miracle of the loaves and fishes. 'The harvest is plentiful, but the labourers are few' – perhaps never more so than in our own day. This must be our call to action. For our sustenance he has left us the spiritual food of Holy Communion, and

31

barley, being low in gluten, is really only of use in the baking of unleavened bread:

> The corn that makes the holy bread
> By which the soul of man is fed,
> The holy bread, the food unpriced
> Thy everlasting mercy, Christ.
> (John Masefield, 'Everlasting Mercy', 1911.)

The Word is like a seed of barley in our souls and we wait for it to germinate and swell. In his 'Treatise on the Advantage of Patience', St Cyprian (200–58) says we hope for what we do not see and that our waiting must be patient if we are to fulfil 'what we have begun to be'. We should not give up half way and lose the advantage of previous growth. We must 'do good to those of the household for in due season we shall reap'. Love for others is part of the mission, and we must nurture it so that its hold is tenacious like that of healthy barley in the soil. God is Lord of the harvest, his Son both the Lamb and Good Shepherd, and his Holy Spirit the supreme sower and germinator. Under the guidance of the Holy Trinity all of us must strive, in our small way, to be harvest and reaper, sheep and shepherd, seed and sower, germ and germinator. And so the barley draws together our Advent themes so far, in the need for alert, patient, and active waiting, 'for yet a little while, and the coming one shall come and shall not tarry' (Heb. 10:37).

Bible Readings
Isaiah 30:19–21: He will surely be gracious to you at the sound of your cry
Psalm 147: He heals the broken hearted and binds up their wounds
Isaiah 55:6: Seek the Lord while he may be found
James 5:7–8: Be patient like the farmer with his crops
Matthew 9:35ff.: When he saw the crowds he had compassion for them
John 6:8ff.: There is a lad here who has five barley loaves

Intercessions
Thanksgiving for our food and for the Eucharist.

For all who work the land; for those in the brewing and distilling industries and the licensed trade; for travellers and exiles; for sufferers from asthma and bronchitis, and for alcoholics; for improved nutrition of children throughout the world; for peace in the Middle East.

For the quality of our family life; for greater love for others and gratitude to our friends; for strength and courage to answer Christ's call to action; for an increase of labourers in the harvest; for a share in God's creative power in our work; for rest to renew our strength; for grace to wait in faith, love, and patience for his coming.

Place of Spiritual Retreat
At the sending out of the Twelve, as in Matthew 9

SECOND SUNDAY IN ADVENT

WINTERSWEET *Chimonanthus praecox*

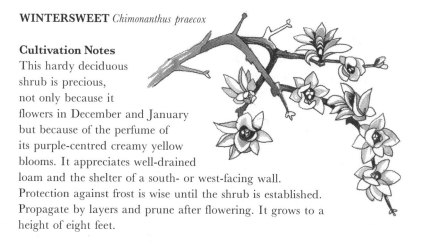

Cultivation Notes
This hardy deciduous
shrub is precious,
not only because it
flowers in December and January
but because of the perfume of
its purple-centred creamy yellow
blooms. It appreciates well-drained
loam and the shelter of a south- or west-facing wall.
Protection against frost is wise until the shrub is established.
Propagate by layers and prune after flowering. It grows to a
height of eight feet.

History and Lore
Wintersweet is named *praecox* because it blossoms before the leaves appear. It is a native of China and is widely available for sale in Britain. It is attractive in winter flower arrangements and useful, since it can precede forsythia by up to two months.

Towards Meditation
'We are waiting for a new heaven and a new earth in which righteousness dwells' (2 Pet. 3:8–14).

I have chosen wintersweet today because the symbolism of its fragrant flowering in the desert of winter calls to mind one of the major themes of today's liturgy, which is 'the voice crying in the wilderness'. And I think of John the Baptist when I am near the plant, not of classical heroes; 'Only the actions of the just / Smell sweet and blossom in their dust' (James Shirley, 'Ajax and Ulysses', 1659).

Mark opens his Gospel with a quotation from Isaiah and immediately identifies John the Baptist as the voice prophesied therein, who would appear in the wilderness preaching repentance and baptism for the forgiveness of sins and confessing himself as herald. 'After me comes one who is mightier than I. I have baptised you with water; but he will baptise you with the Holy Spirit.' In his 'Commentary on Isaiah' Eusebius of Caesarea (fourth century) gives us the interpretation that John appeared outside Jerusalem and baptized by the Jordan because God was about to come into the hitherto barren and impenetrable wastes of the nations who had no knowledge of him.

The wilderness is a symbol for 'all flesh'. That is why God ordered a path to be cleared beforehand and we can now take this as an instruction to open our souls to his coming. But before this could be possible, the good news had to be spread. Immediately after his prophecy about John, Isaiah becomes urgent on the subject of mission and who, in the first instance, should carry it out: 'Get you up to a high mountain, O Sion, herald of good tidings' (Is. 40:9). This suggests, again according to Eusebius, that the apostles are chosen to represent the people. They are to obey the call and preach first to the cities of Judah and then to the world, because 'the Glory of the Lord shall be revealed and all flesh shall see it together' (Is. 40:5). But the Second Coming is also evoked here, and my mind turns to the salutary lesson on the nature and meaning of time in 2 Peter: 'With the Lord one day is as a thousand years and a thousand years as one day. The Lord is not slow about his promise as some count slowness.' Patience becomes possible if we understand this: 'For still the vision awaits its time; / it hastens to the end – it will not lie / If it seems slow, wait for it; / it will surely come, it will not delay' (Hab. 2:3).

Bible Readings
Isaiah 40:1–5; 9–11: Comfort ye, my people
2 Peter 3:8–14: We are waiting for the new heavens and new earth
Mark 1:1–14: Make his paths straight

Intercessions

Thanksgiving for the life and work of John the Baptist and the Apostles, and for the writings of the early Fathers.

For those whose special ministry is preaching the Word; that those of us not called to preach may witness to Christ through our actions; that this Advent we may make a special effort to open our souls to Christ; that in the Eucharist today we may look forward with hope and patience to his Second Coming as much as to our celebration of his First; that our active lives may not prevent our attention to prayer.

Thanksgiving for the precious blooms and evergreen of winter.

Place of Spiritual Retreat

On the banks of the Jordan at the Baptism of Christ as in Mark 1

MONDAY WEEK TWO IN ADVENT

TEASEL *Dipsacus fullonum/silvestris*; brushes and combs

Cultivation Notes

Teasel is biennial. If possible collect seeds in the wild in autumn and sow straightaway. They will produce large rosettes of leaves in the first year and tall flower stems in the second. The spiny heads and rosy mauve flowers apppear in July and August. The plants should reach a height of up to six feet.

History and Lore

Teasel is native to Britain except in parts of the north and is often found on clay soils. The Anglo-Saxon word *taesl* means 'to pluck' and *dipsacus* is Latin for 'teasel'; *fullonum* refers to the fuller's craft of cleaning and raising nap on finished cloth. The plant is depicted on the inn sign of the Clothiers Arms in Stroud in Gloucestershire and grows wild in the traditional cloth-producing regions. Replaced for the most part in the nineteenth century by steel brushes, it has proved invaluable for cloth that needs a very fine and even nap, such as in the hat trade and the manufacture of baize for snooker tables. Its superiority is due to the small hooked spikes, which are gentler than steel. *D. silvestris*, the wild teasel, was probably used for wool-carding in the days of cottage industry, but it would not have been strong enough for nap-raising.

Richard Jefferies, in *Wild Life in a Southern County* (1879), shows how the plant's leaves and green membranes form cups that catch the rain around the stalks. The biggest, he says, can hold 'as much as three wine glasses'. Whatever the size of the cups, they catch and drown many small insects, and this led to the idea that teasel might be carnivorous. In English folklore 'teasel water' was thought to have rejuvenating properties, and in the eighteenth century it was believed to help remove freckles. Teasel has been known to grow near church porches, probably from seeds dropped as the parent plants were taken in for winter flower arrangements.

In 1998, a teasel sprang up in my garden, apparently from nowhere, since no parent exists on my neighbour's regimented patch. There must be some wild teasel not far away. Despite the fact that I'd always found the plant rather unattractive, I let my single specimen be. This tolerance was to be rewarded and I reflected later on the strangeness of having lived to fifty-five before nature put in my way the surprise and pleasure of the teasel in flower. But I made two mistakes. First, I did not pick it until the seed head was brown and dry, thus losing the versatility of mauve and green which, if gathered in August, it would have given to Advent flower arrangements. The second error was not to sow any seed from the 'gift'. That summer was a period of domestic crisis and spiritual aridity. I had neither time nor inclination to organize space for new plants. And so when I could have benefited from its lesson, I failed to let the uninvited guest remind me

> what fulling and faith were to mean.
> New woven cloth is not fit to wear
> Till it be cleaned underfoot or in the fuller's frame
> Washed well with water and with teasels carded,
> Tucked and stretched and under the tailor's hand.
> (William Langland, *Piers Plowman*, Passus 15: 449–53.)

Three summers have passed since my failure. Exile from home has prevented me from going in search of my teasel's ancestral patch. This year.

Towards Meditation
'If it were not for hope the heart would break' (mid-thirteenth century proverb).

It now seems appropriate that the stray teasel arrived in my garden at a time of spiritual anguish. The plant had always symbolized desolation and dryness, even cruelty, and would be one of the few stalks left after the destruction described in Isaiah 24, from which no one shall escape. 'The Lord will lay waste the earth and make it desolate.' Isaiah's prophecy presents an all too familiar picture. 'The earth is polluted under its inhabitants for they have transgressed the laws and violated the everlasting covenant.' This is terrifying, for I feel the Second Covenant is being spoken of here as well as the First. For two verses Isaiah sees a glimmer of light and then returns to his desperate theme of devastation and punishment.

Where is hope in all this? I muse on the chance that my teasel may have dropped a seed as I carried it out of the garden and am led to consider the leafy rosette that would then have been produced in 1999, followed by flower in 2000. These thoughts remind me of Isaiah's assurance that after the destruction, 'the Lord of hosts will manifest his glory.' I think too of the Psalmist acclaiming the One who is 'the hope of all the ends of the earth', and of Job, who with fainting heart cries out, 'I know that my Redeemer lives, and at last he will stand upon the earth. Then from my flesh I shall see God' (Job 19:25).

The uses of a plant often lead to a next step in meditation, and it is so with teasel. The thought of fine smooth-napped cloth immediately brings an image of the soldiers casting lots for the seamless robe of the crucified Saviour, source of all hope. Richard Jefferies, in his *Wild Life in a Southern County* (1879), shows how, with its 'green circle at the bottom of the dome, and two circles of gems above', the poor teasel is ennobled in its own small way by offering a symbol of the Redeemer's crown.

In his *Ascent of Mount Carmel*, Book 2, chapter 22, St John of the Cross (1542–91) tells us that in Christ we will find more than we can possibly know how to ask. He says it is as if God spoke to the patriarchs and prophets only to promise Christ, and that their very questions and requests are a means of leading them to hope for him. As the revelation of God's astounding love, mercy, and forgiveness approaches, we rejoice in the priceless gift of hope in him. The fine cloth traditionally associated with teasel reminds us, as we await both the First and Second Advents, that we should put on a garment of the worthiest fabric of all, namely 'the armour of light', 'the whole armour of God'.

'The woman said to him, "I know that the Messiah is coming." Jesus said to her, "I who speak to you am He"' (Jn 4:25–6).

Bible Readings
Isaiah 24:1–18: Judgement on the nations
Isaiah 10:20–1: The returning remnant
Isaiah 3:22: His time is close at hand
Psalm 26: Prove me O Lord and try me
Job 19:25–6: The hand of God has touched me
Romans 13:11: It is full time for you to wake from sleep
Ephesians 6:11–20: Awake O sleeper
John 11:17–44: I am the resurrection and the life

Intercessions
For those who entertain with their skill in snooker; for those in the cloth industry; for an end to prejudice and for respect for others; for those suffering from domestic crises or spiritual aridity; for those who have charge of the natural environment; for forgiveness for the times when we have been indifferent to the magnitude of God's gifts; for forgiveness of others as we are forgiven; that our minds may be turned back to the Lord and that he may send his light and truth; that we may prepare in humility to celebrate the birth of our Redeemer.

Place of Spiritual Retreat
At the raising of Lazarus as in John 11

TUESDAY WEEK TWO IN ADVENT

IVY *Hedera helix*

Cultivation Notes
Before planting ivy, it is wise to consider whether you will have the time to keep it under control by twice-yearly trimming. The stem can attain a diameter of 8–10 inches and it will climb up to 100 feet over trees and buildings. The greenish yellow flowers appear from early autumn to November; the berries are green in midwinter and ripen to a purplish-black the following June. Ivy dislikes being waterlogged but is tolerant of shade. Propagate by rooted layers and by softwood cuttings in late summer. It does not need to climb and makes a good ground cover. Alternatively, there is *H. helix* 'Erecta', a non-climbing bush that reaches about 4 feet. *H. helix* 'Goldheart' with its bright yellow-centred leaves is an

attractive specimen for indoor arrangements. Variegated types are less hardy and need more light. Opinion is divided as to the wisdom of growing ivy against houses. Some say it keeps cottages warm and dry, others that it has the reverse effect because the foliage holds the wet after heavy rain. Best therefore to avoid it unless you have cavity walls.

History and Lore

Hedera is the old Latin name for ivy, and *helix* is Greek and Latin for a twining plant. The name 'ivy' comes from Anglo-Saxon *ifig* meaning 'bitter', probably because of the toxicity of the berries. *H. helix* is our only British evergreen liana and is also native to a large part of the rest of Europe, Asia Minor, and Iran, though absent from most of Russia. As a dense carpet on the woodland floor, ivy forms a protective habitat for wildlife. It climbs by means of 'grips' on the underside of its stems. The flowers do not smell pleasant, but bees use them to stock up their larders at the end of the season.

In classical times ivy was sacred to Bacchus and was thought to prevent drunkenness, probably because of its ability to smother grapevines. To the Greeks it was symbolic of fidelity and featured in their marriage ceremonies. This use was later banned by the early Christian church, but ivy is later frequently depicted in the borders of illuminated 'Books of Hours', and there are carvings of it on supporting columns in Westminster Abbey. The medievals regarded ivy as a feminine plant, while the holly with its striking red berries was thought of as male. By Shakespeare's time the connection between ivy and alcoholic liquor was evident in the 'Bushes' used as advertisements outside taverns, hence Rosalind's comment at the end of *As You Like It* that 'good wine needs no bush'. By the eighteenth century ivy had become suggestive of melancholy as it grew over deserted ruins and in graveyards: 'From / yonder ivy-mantled tow'r / The moping owl does to the moon complain' (Thomas Gray, 'Elegy written in a Country Churchyard', 1751).

The Victorians loved it, but they knew it had to be trained to prevent it from becoming a pest. Nowadays in many parts of Britain it is cursed as a tree killer, and it can certainly do more damage than a true parasite. However, it takes about thirty years for ivy to cover a tree or building, and it is then that its weight becomes dangerous. Clearly, the answer is a rigorous and concerted programme of control. It has long been part of Christmas evergreen decoration, and in the Fens, when holly berries were scarce, ivy berries were collected and painted. In Chudleigh, near where I lived in Devon, there was a tradition of searching the woods for 'coloured ivy' with its pretty leaves. The heartwood is a lustrous ivory cream and is most attractive in driftwood arrangements. Ivy leaves can be used in poultices for boils and abscesses, but all parts of the plant are poisonous and should be left well alone by all but qualified medical practitioners.

Towards Meditation
'Thou hast been a stronghold to the poor, a stronghold to the needy in his distress' (Is. 25:4).

The ivy flower has five sepals, five petals, five stamens and a five-celled ovary. In nature the figure five always reminds me of the Rosary mysteries and of the wounds of Christ. The Church at large maintains an ambivalent attitude to the plant. It is for instance not welcome in church with the other evergreens at Christmas, but it is quite acceptable in the home, where it has probably been used since pre-Christian times. However, in spite of its connections with paganism, ivy in Church symbolism still represents faithfulness because of its clinging habit and everlasting life because it is an evergreen. It is these two qualities that will today lead me to think of God's promises and faithfulness to his people. Isaiah's prophecy is a most tender and wonderful consolation for them. The ivy will remind me of this because in Devon I heard many stories about its use in feeding sick or poisoned livestock and claims that is it the only other thing they will eat if there is a breakdown in the supply of normal fodder. It is sometimes used to tempt ewes to eat again after a difficult lambing.

'He will feed his flock like a shepherd, he will gather the lambs in his arms, he will carry them in his bosom, and gently lead those that are with young' (Is. 40:13). In fulfilment of this Christ teaches, through the parable of the lost sheep, that 'it is not the will of my Father that one of these little ones should perish.' Ezekiel consolidates Isaiah's comforting words, but there is a warning: 'Behold I judge between sheep and sheep, rams and he-goats.' There will be no life everlasting for the 'remnant' before the righteous judgement. In Matthew 25 Jesus again endorses the words of the prophets and shows us plainly how we should live our lives as we wait for the separation of 'sheep from goats' at his Second Coming. Christ fuses the two greatest commandments into one, so that to love God means to love others and to love others means to love God. How often have I thought, when listening to the destiny of the sheep, 'Well of course I know what must come now.' But Our Lord goes on to make us face up to the fate of the goats, hammering it home, negative by inexorable negative, like a series of nails in the coffin lid of selfishness. Love in the heart and love in action must be the same thing.

The documents of the Second Vatican Council characterize the Church as an imperfect pilgrim. How could it be otherwise since we are part of it? But as we move forward with the help of grace, we call to Christ on behalf of this world and its pain, fear, and greed. We turn to him because in his loving faithfulness to his promises, he has made our restoration possible with his life, death, resurrection, and the sending of the Holy Spirit. Only he enables us to live our lives to the full and transfigure them with hope in the future glory of the new heaven and new earth.

So when I come to consider the part ivy is to play in this year's Christmas decorations, it will lead me to a wry acknowledgement of my own need for control, and to further reflection on the teaching of Christ, which clearly shows that the path to everlasting life lies in our efforts, however feeble, to imitate his own loving faithfulness to us. Ivy, despite its ill repute, will stir anew my conviction: 'He will keep you firm to the end without reproach on the day of our Lord Jesus Christ' (1 Cor. 1:7b–9).

Bible Readings

Isaiah 40:1–11: God's consolation
Psalm 96:11–13: The trees of the wood sing for joy
Isaiah 4:2–6: Salvation of the remnant
Isaiah 25:4: You have been a stronghold
Ezekiel 34:4–17: I will feed them in justice
Philippians 3:20–1: We await a Saviour
Titus 2:12–13: Godly lives in this world
Matthew 18:12–14: The one who went astray
Matthew 25:21–46: Parable of the talents; fate of the sheep and goats

Intercessions

For livestock farmers, particularly those nursing sick animals or who have lost animals to disease; for the imminent lambing season; for sufferers from boils, abscesses, and ulcers; for botanists; for students and actors of Shakespeare; for innkeepers; for married people; for an avoidance of over-indulgence and extravagance during the coming festivities; for those whose weakness or illness lead them to alcohol abuse; for control and order in our working lives; for those in pain or fear or who are victims of the greed of others; for increased faithfulness to God and thanksgiving for his faithfulness, protection, and mercy.

Place of Spiritual Retreat
With the disciples being taught by Jesus, as in Matthew 25

WEDNESDAY WEEK TWO IN ADVENT

BAY *Laurus nobilis*; sweet bay; bay laurel

Cultivation Notes
Bay is native to the Mediterranean region and therefore likes warmth. In favourable conditions it can reach up to 30 feet. Once established, it is safely hardy in southern England, and I remember a healthy specimen in a garden of my northern girlhood. It is wise, though, to give protection during the first winter after planting out. Greenish-yellow flowers appear from April to June and fruit sometimes in September and October. It is possible to propagate by heel cuttings in late summer, but the purchase of a young tree is the more reliable option.

History and Lore
Laurus, the Latin for bay, also means 'triumph', and it is difficult to know which connotation came first. *Baca* is Latin for berry, and the Old French (still current) is *baie*. Since classical times, bay has been known as a symbol of success and victory. The Ancient Greeks thought Apollo himself regarded it as such. Daphne had changed herself into a bay tree to escape his amorous attention. The Romans believed it brought victory as well as being an appropriate reward for it. Asclepius, the Greek hero and god of healing (Roman: Aesculapius), is often depicted wearing the leaves, and the Romans chewed them to keep away disease. The present-day Baccalaureat originated in the old French practice of awarding laurel berries to young doctors of physic. In order to keep them totally devoted to their calling, these early *bacheliers* were not allowed to marry. English has kept the word 'bachelor' both for single men and first degree graduates, but modern French uses it only in its academic sense. There is a hint of old custom in the modern French word *célibataire* to describe a single person, which in these days of sexual freedom strikes a note of

incongruous *pudeur*! The heraldic device of the Count of Dunois was a bay tree, with the motto 'I defend the earth that bears me.' In English tradition, bay leaves under the pillow were supposed to induce prophetic dreams, and they were hung about the doorways of dwellings to keep away thunder and lightning. It was sometimes sprinkled along the paths of funeral processions, and in *Richard II* Shakespeare records an earlier superstition: ''Tis thought the king is dead; we will not stay, / The bay trees in our country are all withered' (Act 2, scene 4). It is still the tradition that bay trees did wither and flourish again after the death of Richard.

For centuries bay was thought to be a powerful antiseptic, but nowadays the oil is used only for rheumatism, sprains, and bruises. A very little in a hot bath is particularly soothing for an aching, weary gardener. Some claim it as an aid to concentration and suggest burning a few drops of oil whilst studying. A connection with those early *bacheliers* here?

I shall never forget being told as a child to crush the glossy, leathery leaves for a surprise. My pleasure in that first experience of their wonderful spicy aroma has not been dulled by many intervening years of culinary use. Bay leaves seem to have a special affinity with tomatoes, soft cheese, and pastas, and I sometimes use the smaller ones to decorate sorbets. Collect the leaves in summer and dry whole. I use sprays in arrangements in a cool airy atmosphere and then store the leaves for the kitchen when dry. Apparently they lose flavour after a year. In most households it is unlikely they will have the chance.

Towards Meditation
'Let the favour of the Lord our God be upon us, and establish thou the work of our hands upon us, yea the work of our hands establish thou it' (Ps. 90:17).

There is a bay tree on either side of the rose archway that forms the entrance to the 'sanctuary' of our herb garden. I say sanctuary because it was designed as a roofless chapel in the open air. Every time I pass between those bays, they give me a sense of purpose, protection, determination, and strength, all of which are welcome, whether I'm going in there to work or to pray. They were two of the first things I planted and are now nine feet tall. They cost 80 francs (about £8) each, but have since trebled their height and have justified my burst of extravagance beyond reckoning. Spiritually, they are a perfect example of the way in which plants can encourage prayer on more than one level.

The bay tree and its associations with success and reward can lead to a simple prayer for God's blessing on our gardening labours and for a good harvest, or it can remind us to transfer that supplication to every aspect of our lives. But whether one is clipping bay, arranging it in a vase, or sitting quietly by the growing tree, if there is time to meditate further it will most certainly lead to a reflection on the nature of true success, victory, and reward in Christian life and death. The bay tree in its strength and protection is a reminder to me of the One to whom I may turn with confidence in my weakness and vulnerability: 'He gives power to the faint, and to him who has no might he increases strength' (40:29). And as Isaiah continues, the Advent theme is there again: 'They who wait for the Lord shall renew their strength, they shall run and not be weary, they shall walk and not faint' (40:31). Christ himself reinforces this: 'Come unto me all you who labour and I will give you rest' (Mt. 11:28). Each of us must fight the battle and run the race of life, but Christ will prevent us from fainting and raise us when we fall; each of us must labour, but Jesus assures us that if we take his yoke upon us we shall find it light.

Isaiah, who forms such an instructive, inspirational backbone to the Advent liturgy, is careful to warn against falling into the trap of pride in any success we achieve, whether it is in the garden, in our other work, or even in the life of prayer, if ever we dare to think we have made a little progress in it. True success in any of these areas, particularly the last, comes from God. The disciples are left in no doubt that they must put themselves last and that the greatest must be the servant of others. And so we too must dig, fight, compete, serve, and pray in the certain knowledge that, if we 'run the race' in humility and in love for others, Christ, through his life, death, and resurrection, has opened the gates of heaven to us. His is the greatest victory of all for he has conquered death itself.

The bay tree with its long history of being given as a reward, must lead us also to reflect on the reward we ourselves may expect to receive. Paul sees death as the end of the battle, the end of the race, but also as the beginning of the eternal reward won for us by Christ in his First Coming amongst us. But at his Second Coming, we know there will be a sorting of sheep from goats and that we will be judged by our deeds towards Our Lord himself in the person of any of his 'little ones'. If we act accordingly, we will be able to sing with confidence, 'Where is death's sting? where, grave, thy victory? / I triumph still, if thou abide with me' (H. F. Lyte, 1793–1847, 'Abide with Me').

Bible Readings
Isaiah 40:25–31: The Lord gives strength to the wearied
Isaiah 25:6–26: Success is from God
Isaiah 2:11: Human pride will lower its eyes
Isaiah 12:2: The Lord has become my salvation
Acts 10:43: All who believe in him will have their sins forgiven
Romans 8:35–7: Yet in all this we are conquerors
1 Corinthians 4:5: There will be time for each one
2 Timothy 4:7: I have fought the good fight. I have kept the faith
Hebrews 12:6: Let us run the race with patience
Matthew 11:28–30: My yoke is easy and my burden light
Luke 14:7–12: Everyone who exalts himself will be humbled
Matthew 10:42: Whoever gives even a cup of cold water

Intercessions
For all school students preparing for examinations; for undergraduates
and medical students; for laypeople who have chosen the celibate life; for
single people who are unhappy without a partner; for God's blessing on
our work and gardens and for strength, perseverance, and patience in our
endeavours; for the avoidance of undue pride in our achievements; that
our faith may be strengthened; that we may use our gifts to the benefit of
others; for more awareness of the ways in which plants can turn our minds
to God.

Thanksgiving for the redeeming death of Our Lord, and a prayer that
we may always turn to him if we grow faint and weary as we wait for his
coming.

Place of Spiritual Retreat
Listening to Jesus' conditions for discipleship, as in Mattthew 10

THURSDAY WEEK TWO IN ADVENT

LEEK *Allium porrum*

Cultivation Notes
Leeks appreciate a rich loam but are not fussy and will grow more or less
anywhere. Sowing time is mid-March. When plants are six to eight inches
tall, usually in late June, plant out in open, well-dug ground, freed of any

stones. All should be in their final position by early July. The books say you should have eighteen inches between the rows and nine between the plants. I set closer than this because leeks are useful from the time they become no thicker than a little finger. Necessary thinnings are always appreciated in my kitchen, leaving room on the leek patch for the development of fat winter specimens. They do better for me in a squarish plot rather than in long rows. For some reason I find the task of planting leeks one of the most satisfying of the gardening year. It certainly cannot be rushed. First trim off any yellow or wispy ends, then make holes with a dibber just a little less deep than the length of the plants. Drop a plant into each hole and water in as you go. This keeps the hole firm whilst you work on the next one and encourages the roots to take. The secret in planting out is to find a day when the soil is neither crumbly nor waterlogged; if the former the dibber won't hold a shape; if the latter it will just make a claggy mess. Either way you will have no holes at all. Unless you are very hard-handed wear gloves, or you will have a blistered palm. Lift the mature leeks as required through the autumn and winter. They are extremely hardy and can be left in the open ground even in the severest winters.

History and Lore
The word 'leek' comes from Old English *leac* and this underrated, subtle, and wholesome vegetable was tremendously important to the Anglo-Saxons. A homestead garden was called a *leac*, somewhat as we refer to a 'cabbage patch' today (cf. gar-*lic*, char-*lock*, hem-*lock*). *Allium porrum* is the cultivated species of the wild leek, which grows in Iran and is cultivated in Israel today. In Britain, 'to eat the leek' came to mean the taking back of one's words. In Shakespeare's *Henry V*, Act 5, scene 1, Fluellen is taunted by Pistol for wearing a leek but turns the tables by forcing the mocker to eat it.

Any leeks left in the ground at the end of the season can be taken up for making soup to freeze, or you can let the stems run up but nip them off before flowering. This will produce 'leek bulbs', which are a handy substitute before shallots are ready. Alternatively, you may wish to let some go up to seed for flower arrangements. (Naturally, the leek will reappear in these pages on David's day, 1 March, and its Welsh connections will then be explored.)

Towards Meditation

'Behold the farmer waits for the precious food of the earth, being patient over it until it receives the early and late rain' (Jas 5:7–9b).

In Numbers 11:5 the leek is mentioned as one of the foods the children of Israel missed in the wilderness when they became tired of the Manna. We are more fortunate as we have the leek and the spiritual food of Holy Communion. However, these days the leek is often disparaged as the rather coarse, poor relation of the onion. To me it is the onion, although equally valuable, that is the brash and demanding garden resident. The leek on the other hand is patient and independent in the earth, a willing, versatile servant in the kitchen, and endowed with much more subtle flavour.

Gathering the fully-grown leeks in all their green and creamy glory, I reflect on the long period of patience required in growing them. Sown in March, they can take as long as nine months to reach full maturity. In this they draw a gentle line under truths of faith and lead me to think of the long wait between the prophets and the First Coming, of the way in which Christians today wait to celebrate it, and of their seeking and yearning for God. Isaiah as usual puts the latter feeling into strikingly beautiful language (26:7–23), and Peter Chrysologus (died *c*. 450) meditates on it in one of his sermons: 'Love cannot bear not to have sight of what it loves.' He also warns against replacing the loved one with other things whilst we wait.

The leek is patient in the ground, and so must we be as we grow to greater maturity; the leek is an easy servant, and so must we be as we try to follow Christ. The leek is long in the ground and presents a pale symbol of the dead awaiting resurrection. 'Many of those who sleep in the dust of the earth shall awake' (Dan. 12:2); 'O dwellers in the dust, awake and sing for joy' (Is. 26:19). Leeks will reward careful digging and meticulous planting; in this they mirror a proper preparation for the Lord's coming. As time passes, he continues to cast his influence over the leeks we have set and at the same time constantly nurtures the response we show towards the seed he has sown in our souls. He is present in the darkest, coldest night of midwinter, even though at times he seems to have removed himself utterly. But he is ever present, and all along, like the leek, we are growing under his hand. It is in the winter of nature that we harvest our leeks and in the winter of nature that we have sight of his glory: 'You also be patient. Establish your hearts, for the coming of the Lord is at hand' (Jas 5:8).

Bible Readings
Isaiah 26:7–23: The Promise of the Resurrection
Daniel 12:2: Those who sleep in the dust
Isaiah 46:13: I will give salvation to Sion
Matthew 11:11–15: The prophets and the law prophesied until John came. Let anyone with ears listen!

Intercessions
For commercial leek growers; for patience and meticulousness in our work; for the ability to listen more to others.

Thanksgiving for unsung good things of earth; for a lessening of prejudice in the world and an increase in acknowledgement of God's power and sovereignty; for a constant focus on the true meaning of Christmas and that we may not be led astray by satisfaction in earthly substitutes for joy; that we may approach our spiritual preparation for Christmas with minds uncluttered by material concerns.

Place of Spiritual Retreat
With Jesus as he preaches and teaches through the cities as in Matthew 11

FRIDAY WEEK TWO IN ADVENT

CHINESE LANTERNS *Physalis alkekenji/franchetti*; bladder cherry; winter cherry (not to be confused with the pot plant *Solanum capisastrum* also called winter cherry)

Cultivation Notes
You can buy Chinese lanterns in early autumn but it is much less expensive to sow seed under glass in early spring or in a warm spot in open ground in early summer, where it may take several weeks to germinate. In well-drained soil it will form an extensive rooting system, so make sure there is space for the plants to spread and become a large clump about two feet in height. The insignificant white flowers are followed by ridged and papery lantern-shaped seed-pods. These are green at first, later turning to the familiar bright orange-red. You can sow seed from the lanterns or propagate by division the following spring. *Physalis* is a deciduous perennial and dies back in winter. Change the site every three to four years to maintain quality.

History and Lore

The Greek *physa* relates to bellows and explains the name bladder cherry. The plant is found growing wild from South East Asia to Japan. Dioscorides mentioned the fruits as a cure for epilepsy and in European folk medicine they were taken to relieve scarlet fever (see 'Doctrine of Signatures' under daisy, p. 49 and lungwort, p. 283). The foliage was used in the treatment of anaemia and malaria. Nowadays it is not popular as an internal medicine because the foliage and unripe fruits are harmful when eaten. However, the leaves can be picked in summer and used in poultices to reduce skin inflammations.

The long-lasting vibrant red seed-heads are a firm favourite with flower arrangers. They mix well with eucalyptus, honesty, and wild clematis, and individual lanterns are effective as natural Christmas tree baubles. Cut the stems in autumn before frost, rain, or winds threaten. Remove the leaves and air-dry the lanterns. Lay them in open boxes or stand in a well-ventilated warm place until needed.

Towards Meditation

'Hasten, as he commanded, to meet him with lamps alight' (from the Collect of Mass for the day).

As we approach the third weekend in Advent, haste may perhaps be the operative word, at least in the worldly sense. Budget is much on the mind and I go around saying, 'I don't feel very "Christmassy"' and wishing the Feast were not so near. Friends groan agreement and I am relieved not to be the only one who is behindhand. Magazine articles entitled 'How to enjoy Christmas on a shoestring, without lifting a finger' are no help at all. There is no time to read them. Besides, some ethic instilled in childhood makes an attempt at economy *de rigueur*. Another perversely contradicts it and forbids any cutting of corners or omission of time-honoured family customs. And so every year there is the attempt to cram into each day more than is humanly possible, every year the wish for more time, and every year the moment of irony, when I realize that I am contradicting my daily Advent prayer, 'Come Lord, do not delay!' And I steady myself in remembering that he will come in his own way and in his own time.

Chinese lanterns are today's subject because this weekend will be a good time to plan, and perhaps even make, some of the Christmas flower arrangements. The red glow of the lanterns will provide a first real splash

49

of festive colour in a dark season, and as I work with them, they will evoke all the scriptural references to light already mentioned in these pages. Later I may reflect more deeply on our Lord's castigation of those to whom the light was shown but who failed to acknowledge it (Mt. 11:16–19); and I may study the passage from Irenaeus (*c.* 130–200) in today's Office of Readings. Here we see the First Coming of Christ in terms of his lighting up his own creation by becoming visible in it. The extract contains an examination of the role of Mary in the divine plan and since the red lanterns seem to bring Christmas nearer, it is appropriate that Our Lady should be considered now. The Gospel shows her in direct contrast with those criticized by Christ in the Matthew text. But even she, according to the Divine Office responsary 'began to fear the light' when Gabriel appeared to her. Fortunately for the whole of humanity her fear proved momentary and she went on in perfect faith to fulfil the destiny for which she was made: 'Thy word is a lamp to my feet and a light to my path' (Ps. 119:105).

Bible Readings
Isaiah 48:17–19: The Lord himself is the lamp
Matthew 11:1–19: We piped to you and you did not dance
John 8:12: I am the light of the world

Intercessions
For sufferers from epilepsy, anaemia and malaria; for the peoples of South East Asia and for the Church there.

That we may make time for prayer during this busy build-up to Christmas and that we may continue to focus our minds and hearts on the true meaning of the approaching feast; for an avoidance of extravagance and waste; for those who live without the light of faith, or who have not heard the Good News; that we may be open to the Light of the World and seek his guidance on the path we tread.

Place of Spiritual Retreat
In the crowd to whom Jesus said, 'I am the light of the world', as in John 8

SATURDAY WEEK TWO IN ADVENT

GLADDON *Iris foetidissima*; stinking iris; glad-win; gladyne

Cultivation Notes

Gladdon is an evergreen perennial and grows in thick tufts reaching a height of up to twenty inches. It propagates readily from seed and tolerates quite heavy shade. The flowers, which are an ashy slate-grey purple, appear from June to August. Later, the seed capsules split to reveal bright orange berries inside. Do not be put off by *foetidissima* (stinking). Gladdon releases an unpleasant odour only if its roots or leaves are bruised.

History and Lore

The etymology of the English gladdon is obscure, but it is mentioned in the *Épinal Glossary* (*c.* 700). The dark green spear-like leaves have led to the theory that it comes from *Lilium gladina*, in itself an altered form of *Lilium gladiolus* or sword lily. Gladdon is found in ancient churchyards, notably the one at Saint Margaret's Tilbury-juxta-Clare in Essex, which is surrounded by a circular hedged bank and ditch. Gladdon flowers are rather drab but can be dried in summer and kept for Advent, and the bright berries add greatly to the plant's decorative value at Christmas. Cut the stems just after the pods have split and hang upside down to air-dry. The berries will shrivel later but will retain their strong colour and last all winter in an arrangement without water.

Towards Meditation

'Your voice shall come from the ground like the voice of a ghost and your speech shall whisper out of the dust' (Is. 29:4b).

Today, a third candle will be added to the arrangement begun two weeks ago, and with it a single bloom of gladdon, ghostly pale and delicate, but hinting with its ashy gleam that the penitential violet of Advent is beginning a transformation into the joyful white light of Christmastide. One thinks again of John the Baptist, the beacon, as yet dim, in the dusty wilderness, who will grow stronger by degrees until he becomes the 'burning and shining lamp' described by Our Lord in John 5. In Matthew 19 he refers to John as 'the Elijah who is to come'. Both texts emphasize his exasperation with deliberate blindness to the light, with obdurate deafness to the Word, and the Church drives this home by having the same reading from Matthew as the Gospel on two consecutive days.

The smell of bruised gladdon is akin to that of burning rubber and this reminds me of Ecclesiasticus 48, where Elijah is praised as a type of John. His 'word burned like a torch. ... Three times he brought down fire. ... How glorious you were, Elijah, in your wondrous deeds' (48:1–4). In his prophecy of the Second Coming Isaiah tells of its suddenness and that it will be accompanied with a 'flame of devouring fire' (29:6).

But the red berries of gladdon will turn my mind back to the Incarnation and to the image of Christ as the fruit of the land, the glorious plant of the Lord, the righteous branch of the stock of Jesse. And here I will probably wish to continue my reflections on Mary, the mother of the Lord, and the example she sets of openness to God. Blessed Isaac of Stella (c. 1100–c. 1169) writes with great clarity on her role as an ark, a place of nurture for the Lord, and compares it with that of the Church and of the individual soul. Christ, he says, lived for nine months in Mary's womb, but he abides until the end of ages in the tent of the Church's faith, and forever in the knowledge and love of every faithful Christian. If only we will hear and see, we may become, as Paul says, 'the temple of the living God'.

'I will make my abode among you, and my soul shall not abhor you. And I will walk among you, and will be your God' (Lev. 26:11–12).

Bible Readings
Isaiah 29:4–6: Then deep from the earth you shall speak
Ecclesiasticus (Sirach) 48:1–4: The prophet Elijah rose like a fire
Isaiah 4:2: The plant that the Lord has grown
2 Corinthians 6:16: I will live in them and move among them
John 5:32–40: You sent to John and he has borne witness to the truth

Intercessions
That we may open our eyes and ears to receive Our Lord; that our souls

may be ready to welcome him whenever he comes; that the coming of God's Son may dispel darkness and reveal us as children of light; that the hearts of those who rule may be open to God's Spirit of wisdom, counsel, and justice.

Place of Spiritual Retreat

With Jesus as he testifies to John and himself as in John 5

THIRD SUNDAY IN ADVENT

EUCALYPTUS *Eucalyptus gunnii*; Tasmanian cider gum

Cultivation Notes

Eucalyptus thrives on good average soil. The young tree, even though evergreen, will need protection during its first two winters. It will respond well to hard pruning and if treated as a bush will be less top-heavy and continue to produce juvenile leaves which are small and almost circular, forming little rosettes round the stem. These may suffer in a hard winter, but if a frost-damaged tree is cut down, it will re-shoot from the base. Eucalyptus flowers between September and December and fruits between January and March. It is fast growing, up to 100 feet, and is an open graceful addition to the garden. The only disappointment is that the leaves of *E. gunnii* are virtually scentless when crushed. For a lemon-scented variety try *E. citridora*.

History and Lore

The name 'eucalyptus' comes from the Greek *eu*, good, and *kalyptos*, covered. It is native to Australia and was introduced to Britain for its ornamental qualities. The young leaves are popular with flower arrangers and certainly provide the prettiest foliage in my garden. I love the silvery-green with its tinges of mauve, pink, and white, so suitable for this season, and yet available all year round. If you do not have room for a tree you can buy branches to preserve. The glycerine method is recommended. The leaves should retain a greyish-green if kept in the solution for up to 48 hours. Immersion for a longer period brings out the violet, which may even turn to purple. This could be a desirable result for Advent and Lent. Alternatively you can hang branches upside-down in bunches and allow to dry naturally. Slow drying is necessary to avoid leaf curl.

The lemon-scented variety is the richest known source of citronella and has traditionally been used for perfumery and in sachets for freshening linen cupboards; it deters insects, especially cockroaches and silver fish, and I have found it effective against a type of wood flea that in certain summer conditions can infest houses in south-west France. Commercial production of eucalyptus was begun in Victoria, Australia, in 1866 by Joseph Bosisto, a Yorkshire entrepreneur. Its timber and bark are valued and 'kino', a resinous gum that exudes from incisions in the bark, contains tannin. The Aborigines use bark, kino, and leaves to treat sores and dysentery. The bark charcoal is antiseptic, and kino is recommended in powders and tinctures for athlete's foot.

Percy Grainger wrote the 'Gum Sucker's Waltz', a title singularly lacking euphony from one whose trademark is tunefulness. (But then the humour is in character. I remember his bowling briefly into Ken Russell's BBC film about Delius, bringing a shaft of sunlight into the drear and blighted days of the dying composer.) Apparently the idea for the waltz came from the antipodean habit of sucking eucalyptus leaves to quench thirst. But be warned: the oil is toxic and subject to legal restrictions in some countries, and all parts of the plant can irritate sensitive skins.

Towards Meditation

'As a hart longs for flowing streams, so longs my soul for thee, O God. My soul thirsts for God, for the living God' (Ps. 42:1–2).

Today, whilst cutting small sprays of pink- and white-tinged eucalyptus, I will reflect on this beautiful text and on the frequency with which Scripture uses the figure of physical thirst to express a spiritual yearning for God. It is imagery that would have been particularly significant in the wilderness and desert experience of the children of Israel. Isaiah invites us as their heirs, to come to the waters, and Christ himself promises us that 'whoever believes in me shall never be thirsty' (Jn 6:35). Only by drinking at the well of faith in him will our parched souls be satisfied and refreshed: 'With joy you shall draw water from the wells of salvation' (Is. 12:3). We are blessed if we thirst after righteousness. In an earlier meditation I considered how, in Matthew, the Lord makes it plain that this thirst involves action on our behalf, and we are warned against neglect of the physical and spiritual thirst of others. Before I leave the garden today, I shall pray for an increase in love and faith and give thanks for the waters of Baptism. The hymn 'As pants the hart for cooling streams' will be offered, whether I sing it aloud or not.

Later, as the eucalyptus and heather are added to the Advent arrangement, the pink and silvery-white will turn my mind to the increasing joy and suggestion of light that feature strongly in today's liturgy. Advent gloom is beginning to lift. This is *Gaudete* Sunday, so named from its Mass Introit, 'Rejoice in the Lord always, again I say, rejoice'. The whole Mass takes up the theme. Isaiah prophesies future glory; the responsorial psalm is the *Magnificat*; the second reading exhorts us to be happy at all times, to pray constantly and to respect prophecy; and in the Gospel we are shown John the Baptist as a lamp witnessing to the Light.

The Divine Office enters into the glory and mystery of Christ's two Advents and includes a reading from St Augustine of Hippo (354–430) in which he meditates on the role of John the Baptist, who knows himself as a voice for the time and eventually knows Jesus as the Eternal Word whom he has heralded. John understands himself as the lamp prophesied by Isaiah and does not allow himself to be 'quenched by the wind of pride'. Those around him think he is the Christ, but it is as if he cries out to them and to us, 'My mission is to lead Christ into your hearts, but he will not come unless I prepare the way.' Later today, the Office reminds us that from his prison cell John sends two of his followers to Jesus, asking him if he is the One. It is of comfort to know that before his death, John has his mission both confirmed and vindicated by the message Jesus sends back to him.

Three candles will be lit after it has gone dark, and they will burn throughout the evening, representative of the Light for whom we wait. *Gaudete* Sunday will draw towards its close with Vespers, the concluding prayer of which asks for happiness as our Advent preparation nears completion, and true joy in our celebration of Christmas. It is a prayer that always seems to be granted before the candles are blown out after Night Prayer. Whatever material concerns may plague me, on this night I have always felt a deep contentment and faith in God's Word, so soon to quench our thirst, so soon to bring us 'a garland instead of ashes, the oil of gladness instead of mourning' (Is. 61:2).

Bible Readings
Isaiah 29:13–24: The coming judgement
Isaiah 55:1: Come you to the waters
Isaiah 61:11: For as the earth brings forth its shoots
1 Thessalonians 5:16–24: Be happy at all times

2 Thessalonians 1:6–10: Christ will be glorified and seen
2 Thessalonians 3:12–13: Love is the way
Revelation 7:16: Neither shall they thirst anymore
Matthew 5:3ff.: Hunger and thirst after righteousness
Matthew 11:1–5: John heard in prison about the deeds of Christ
Matthew 25:35: I was thirsty and you gave me to drink
John 1:6–8; 19–28: The one who is coming after me
John 6:35: Whoever believes in me shall never be thirsty

Intercessions

For the peoples of Australasia; for those involved in the commercial use of eucalyptus; for laundry workers and athletes; for the peoples of drought-stricken countries, that the richer nations may organize effective relief; for greater love, faith, gratitude and humility; that we may wait in joyful patience for the coming of Christ.

Place of Spiritual Retreat

With John the Baptist at Bethany as he explains his identity and mission to the priests and Levites, as in John 1

MONDAY WEEK THREE IN ADVENT

CEDAR *Cedrus libani*; cedar of Lebanon

Cultivation Notes

A young cedar is conical. Only in maturity does it put out its branches horizontally to form the familiar flattened, spreading shape. Male and female flowers appear in the same tree, and the barrel-shaped cones eventually ripen above the flat plates of needle-dense foliage. They can be up to six inches long and grey or pinky-brown in colour, each one concealing two winged seeds per scale. Cedar of Lebanon can reach a height of 150 feet, and should not be confused with western red cedar of the *Thuya* genus, which grows only in the West.

History and Lore

The cedar of Lebanon is thought to have been introduced into Britain for ornamental purposes around 1680, and in the eighteenth century 'Capability Brown' planted it on many of the estates where he was employed to redesign gardens. Many still grace the countryside and will continue to do so as cedar is slow-growing and long-lived. The wood is dense, durable, and sweetly scented, and to the Victorians it came to symbolize incorruptibility. The timber has long been valued in carpentry for veneers and inlay work, not merely because of its strength and fragrance but because it is resistant to rot and woodworm. The oil is used in perfumery but is repellent to insects. Carpet shops were sometimes lined with cedar wood to deter moths, and it is used in products for storing textiles. Oil is obtained from chipped branches to make decoctions for the external treatment of dandruff, or inhalations to ease bronchitis and nervous tension.

In earlier civilizations the Ancient Egyptians used the oil in their embalming process and the Tibetans burned it as temple incense. The Old Testament mentions the cedar frequently, notably as 'trees of the Lord' (Ps. 104:16). Psalm 92:12 alludes to its strength and height, as does Ezekiel (17:3); and Joshua uses it as a symbol of power in his message to Amaziah (2 Chr. 25:18). Earlier, Hiram had sent cedar wood to David for housebuilding (2 Sam. 5:11). In 1 Kings 5:10 Solomon makes peace with Hiram in the exchange of wheat and oil for all the cedar wood he needs to build the Temple and his palace. His felling went on for 25 years and used up most of the cedars on Mount Lebanon. Later, as we read in Ezra 3:7, his example is followed in the rebuilding of the Temple. Fortunately today the few remaining groves on the Mount are the subject of conservation. In *Bible Teaching in Nature* (1878), the Reverend Hugh Macmillan wrote:

> But what a magnificent relic the one grove of Kedisha is! Each huge trunk, scarred and hoary with the elemental strife of hundreds of years, still spreads out its great gnarled boughs laden with emerald foliage and exquisite cones, 'full of sap' in the freshness of undying youth ... no temple of nature can be grander than the interior of that grove, where ... Mass is celebrated annually in June. It is a spot unique on earth. The sacred associations of thousands of years crowd around one there. In the fragrance of the cedars comes up the richness of Bible memories; each sight and sound suggests some incident alluded to by psalmist or prophet, and a feeling of awe and reverence, such as few other scenes can inspire, fills the soul to overflowing. There, at an elevation of six thousand feet, with their roots firmly planted in the moraines of extinct glaciers,

with their trunks riven and furrowed by lightnings, with the snows of Lebanon gleaming white through their dusky foliage, with the stillness of earth's mightiest powers asleep around them, who can fail to feel the force of the Psalmist's words, 'The trees of the Lord are full of sap; the cedars of Lebanon, which He hath planted.'

Towards Meditation

'My steadfast love shall not depart from you, and my covenant of peace shall not be removed, says the Lord, who has compassion on you' (Is. 54:10).

On a slight rise to the west of our house lies the village cemetery, and in it grows a cedar that must be at least two hundred years old. Whether in flesh or spirit I will, during the mild, cloudless clarity of a brief afternoon, make my way up the straight road from the house carrying tools for grave tidying and a bouquet of rosemary, bay, eucalyptus, and tricolour sage.

The heavy iron gates now closed behind me, the intermittent noises of the outside world are muffled and distant. In more ways than one I stand at the boundary separating two worlds. Ahead of me lies a wide gravelled avenue with the cedar in a central circular clearing. To my right and left are the graves, ornate and simple alike, strewn with the faded tributes placed on them at All Souls by faithful families. I pass across the ground beneath the cedar branches, bone-dry and comforting whatever the weather has been. As I approach my mother's grave it seems to me that the tree is breathing out strength, security, and tranquillity. I settle to the work I have come to do, the prayer I have come to offer, and even though my sorrow for her sufferings is undiminished, there is no morbidity in my regret, nor desolation in my loss. A habitual memory comes of visiting the cemetery with my mother in the early 1990s. She confided that during my long absences at work in London, she would often come here after a hard stint of gardening, to rest and think, sitting on the bench in the lee of the cemetery wall. She had been a widow fifteen years, and I asked her if she did not find the place depressing. 'No,' she said, 'I think of happy times with Daddy and you. The cedar makes it so peaceful. There is nothing upsetting here.' As I hugged her I am certain we both knew she would be buried here, close to the cedar. The thought was unspoken, but she seemed contented in the acceptance of this place as the edge of her eternity. We were happy together that day, and I feel it is then that we said goodbye, not seven years later, when her mind had been destroyed by disease, nor when she could no longer swallow, nor just before she sank into a final coma. Her grave now tidy, I rest on the bench and, looking towards the cedar, as she so often did, begin the day's meditation.

The first prayer is of thanksgiving for the love of my parents for each other and for me, which like the cedar was strong, wholesome, and unshakeable. And then, what else has the tree to say on this late Advent afternoon? It speaks of Balaam's poem in Numbers 24: 'The tents of Jacob … like cedar trees beside the waters! … A hero rises from their stock, he reigns over countless peoples.' And Balaam prophesies, 'I see him, but not in the present. I behold him, but not close at hand – a star from Jacob takes the leadership, a sceptre arises from Israel' (24:6, 17). Balaam's eyes are opened, albeit dimly, but later, in Matthew 21, it seems that those of the chief priests and elders are deliberately closed. They will not see and will not accept the authority of Jesus. He exposes the chicanery in their questioning and they are left in the dark. William of Saint Thierry (c. 1080–1148), in his Treatise *On Contemplating God*, shows how we should contemplate him in love, not interrogate him in arrogance. We should not ask Christ, 'What are your credentials for authority?' but, 'How are we to be saved?' He loved us first, and although he is stern against obduracy, he is gentle if we respond to his sacrifice with love. I began by thanking God for human love, which is good, and capable of withstanding much, but the cedar has reminded me that it is but a shadow of the love God proclaims through Isaiah, and the merest tiny reflection of the love shown to each one of us in Christ's redeeming death.

It is time to go. I pause beneath the tree and reflect that even the 'incorruptible' cedar will eventually know decay. But the decay of our dead is temporary. My mother has not fallen into a bottomless cavern of oblivion. She is somewhere sentient with all the dead waiting for this 'corruptible to put on incorruption, and this mortal to put on immortality.' As I reluctantly reopen the iron gates, my heart echoes Isaiah and sings with joy for the living and the dead, 'He will not hide himself. Your eyes shall see him, your ears hear him. Blessed are they who wait.'

Note: Not long after I wrote this entry, the news came that there had been a freak tempest, which had done tremendous damage in the village and surrounding area. Returning to France after my three-year exile, I discovered to my sorrow that the storm had been so powerful as to sweep away the cemetery bench, but worse, it had uprooted and destroyed the beloved cedar. In its absence the cemetery feels exposed and vulnerable. (The Commune has replaced it with two or three cypresses. It will never be the same again. Why could they not have been patient and planted another cedar?) But always, always when I visit the cemetery now, I close my eyes and remember the lessons taught by that old lost friend, and imagine it is still there. And each time I promise myself, God willing, a visit one day to Kedisha.

Bible Readings
Isaiah 30:18–26: Promise of happiness and prosperity
Isaiah 54:10–13; 48:17: My love for you will never leave you
Isaiah 61:1–2; 10–11: I exult for joy in the Lord
Numbers 24:2–7; 15–17: A star from Jacob takes the leadership
Philippians 3:20b–21: If we look expectantly
Matthew 21:23ff.: This was the Lord's doing and it is marvellous in our eyes

Intercessions
For carpenters and ornamental woodworkers, and those in the carpet and perfumery industries; for sufferers from scalp disorders, bronchitis and nervous collapse; for Alzheimer's patients and stroke victims; for wise husbandry of trees throughout the world; for greater effort against arrogance, pride, greed, and selfishness, that as we enjoy the exchange of presents this Christmas, we may remember both practically and spiritually those who are alone and giftless.

For our beloved dead.

That we may be open to the light of Christ, learn his way, proclaim the Word and walk under the authority of his love.

Thanksgiving for human love and for Christ's love for us.

Place of Spiritual Retreat
With Jesus, the Chief Priests and Elders, as in Matthew 21

TUESDAY WEEK THREE IN ADVENT

SHEPHERD'S NEEDLE *Scandix pecten-veneris*

Cultivation Notes
Scandix is an annual weed of the cow parsley family and grows on cultivated land. It appears from spring to late summer, has finely-cut

bright green leaves, bears its small conical white flowers on simple umbels, and grows to a maximum height of about nine inches.

History and Lore

Shepherd's needle is simply a translation of the Greek and is named after its fruit, usually eight long beaks. It is apparently becoming rare, particularly in Wales and Scotland. In my experience it is an innocent angel in comparison with the insidiously virulent mare's tail, against which I waged constant war in Devon, and the rank, trunk-rooted dock, and the suffocating, crafty bramble, which are the bugbears in my present garden.

Years ago, in between assaults on the mare's tail, my father and I used to amuse ourselves by reading aloud, in sermonizing tones, from the moralistic didacticism of the Suttons' *Culture of Flowers and Vegetables* (1936) in which the punishment for neglect of weeding is too spine-chilling to contemplate:

Weeds will be troublesome to the overworked and the idle
gardener, while the best-kept land will be full of seeds blown
upon it from the sluggard's garden and the first shower will
bring them up in terrific force. All that we have to say about
them is that they must be kept down for they not only choke
the rising crops in seed-beds and spoil the look of everything,
but they very much tend to keep the ground damp and cold,
when, if they were away, it would get dry and warm, to the
benefit of all the proper crops upon it. Neglect will make the
task of eradication simply terrible, and in the meantime,
every crop on the ground will suffer. The two great months
for weeds are May and September; but often the September
weeds triumph, because the mischief they do is not then so
obvious to the casual eye.

Indeed, *Messieurs* Sutton, you spoke truth, and we could do worse than
apply your strictures to spiritual life, but I am not now growing for an
Edwardian kitchen; I am not pressured to produce exotic novelties in the
depths of winter and do not have a brigade of boy under-gardeners to
whip out the merest wisp of willow herb. The perfect 'look of everything' is
not the same for me as it was for you. Unless a weed is truly unsightly or
hindering the growth of something I treasure and need more, it is left
alone. My French neighbour is something of a latter-day *Suttoniste*, whose
patch is rather more of a production line than a garden. He seems to do
everything by machine. In fifteen years, I have never seen him actually
touch the earth or hand-dig a single spit of it. Even his hoe is motorized!
He regards herbs as dangerous and once called over the fence, 'I hope you
know what you're doing with those things.' I am sure he thinks I am
slightly dotty if not actually a witch. I would not be surprised if he thinks I
ignore some of the weeds out of laziness, which in fact has nothing to do
with it. His mechanized perfection intimidates me and I do my hard
labour while he is out at work. When he is there on the other side of the
fence in May evenings and at weekends, I will deliberately stand admiring
my carpet of Virgin's-blue speedwell while he judders to and fro on one or
other of his contraptions. And I smile to myself, thinking of Browning's
'Soliloquy in a Spanish Cloister' 'Sst, there's Vespers! Plena gratia / Ave
Virgo! Gr-r-r – you swine!' I would as soon grub up the speedwell as the
bronze fennel under which it creeps.

As for shepherd's needle, I have not seen it for some years, and to discover it on my patch or in the arable fields around would be delightful rather than offensive. I search for it each late summer in the hope of being able to dry some of its fruits. But for today a mental image of the plant will suffice to remind me of my mother, who was a needlework teacher and dressmaker, and of my father lovingly teasing her by quoting Thomas Hood's 'Song of the Shirt' whenever, as frequently happened, she was working against the clock to finish some garment. Between stitches she would give him a quick smiling glance that said, 'Get away with you, foolish, fanciful fellow whom I love.' And we all three would laugh in the warmth of the moment. But nostalgia aside, shepherd's needle will also remind me to make a garden inspection and a list of outstanding mending and maintenance tasks; to check defences and perhaps sketch some plans for next season. The boundary fence belongs to my neighbour and is therefore not my responsibility, but I must constantly make sure that nothing on my side is likely to straggle into his. Robert Frost's 'Mending Wall' strikes a very personal chord here.

Towards Meditation

'I myself will be the shepherd of my sheep, and I will make them lie down, says the Lord God. I will seek the lost, and I will bring back the stray, and I will bind up the crippled and I will strengthen the weak, and the fat and the strong I will watch over; I will feed them in justice' (Ezek. 34:15–16).

We recognize these promised loving actions of God as the marks of a good shepherd, and if we substitute plants for sheep, of a good gardener. But none of us is *the* Good Shepherd or *the* Good Gardener. Anything we do well, we do by the grace of God, and by following his example.

As I conclude my list of tasks and make plans for the proper organization of my plot, or 'fold', I arrive again at the corollaries expressed earlier. I am protector and protected, meant to imitate the Shepherd, but also a member of his flock; I should care for plants, but am a plant myself. So now I must look at whether I have gone astray or allowed gaps to develop in the defences, which as a result, need application of the 'darning needle'. I must probe the state of my roots and the quality of my fruit. A Catholic may turn to a spiritual director to ensure objectivity in the examination before embracing the Sacrament of Reconciliation, but I firmly hold that grace will be poured out on anyone who undertakes self-assessment in the light of the two greatest commandments. The post-Communion prayer of today's Mass asks God to teach us to weigh carefully the things of earth and to love the things of heaven. So I begin today's reflections by asking: How are my relationships (love of others); how is my prayer life (love of God)? Impossible to predict from year to year what the result of the second examination will be. As to the first, I have been somewhat facetious about my neighbour and have exaggerated my feelings of irritation towards him. I certainly do not hate him, as poor Brother Lawrence is hated in the Browning poem. My neighbour and I do not argue. We simply let each other alone to make progress as each sees fit. But we and the two Spanish monks have much to tell about living in a community. Although the poem is humorous, it is darkly so, and shows how mere dislike can escalate into hatred if there is no escape from the chafe of daily living together. In other circumstances I would have to fight harder to prevent irritation from developing into the venomous fury of Browning's imagined monk.

So much for neighbours and colleagues. What about friends and family? Three years ago, in Advent, I was nursing hurt feelings over the inexplicable rupture of a twenty-six-year-old friendship and fretting over my relationship with my mother during her last years. In taking these wounds into Confession, I made every effort to spare myself nothing. I did not want to make excuses. Why did I experience a healing that would not have been possible at the hands or word of a counsellor or psychiatrist? I believe it was because I was not expecting a mere human to solve my problems or anaesthetize my pain. If forgiveness were necessary, it was not his I sought, nor his to give. The healing came because the priest and myself both knew we were involved in a sacrament; our joint action was a prayer for grace; and grace was given. The facts were not changed, but acceptance and balance were somehow achieved. The confessor is the listening ear of Christ and the face of his mercy; he is the Shepherd's needle in the mending of souls.

For years, I shared the attitude of many pre-conciliar Catholics, that Confession was simply a matter of going into the 'box' and getting it over with. Nowadays some people find carpets and cushions in 'reconciliation rooms' helpful, sometimes essential. But – and this is not just 'good old Catholic guilt' speaking – I don't think it can ever be easy if properly done. My present experience is that preparation is the hardest part, and if I have made a real effort over that, then any seat is comfortable for the actual sacrament. On the first occasion I went to my present confessor, he, not knowing my previous practice, offered me 'the box' but seemed less surprised than I was myself when I preferred a couple of chairs in front of the Seven Sorrows altar. I thank God for him, as he helps steer my course through the thickets of doubt and struggle for acceptance that characterize middle age. Nor do I forget the two priests who helped during the last harrowing years of my long-since-annulled first 'marriage'. I pray for more priests in the Church like these three, who are wise and gentle in their rigour, sensitive to the individual needs of their penitents, and who are not hidebound by either dead tradition or modernity for its own sake.

However, preparation for Advent Reconciliation immediately suggests that poor time-allocation and lack of patience should be on the list yet again this year. Perhaps I have digressed, but the liturgy today does concentrate on God's protection, on the salvation of the poor in spirit and of sinners, and on the necessity for kindness and humility. A passage from *The Imitation of Christ*, Book 2, by Thomas à Kempis (*c.* 1380–1471) rewards study and includes the difficult injunction, which is as applicable to life in the world as it is to life in the cloister, 'Accuse yourself, excuse your brother. If you wish to be borne with, bear with others.'

Bible Readings
Isaiah 30:27–33; 31:4–9: The Salvation of the Holy City
Jeremiah 23:6: In his day Judah shall be kept safe
Ezekiel 34:15–16: I myself will pasture my sheep
Zephaniah 3:1–2: Salvation promised to the poor in spirit
Zechariah 7:9: Show kindness and mercy each to his brother
Matthew 21:28–32: Salvation of sinners

Intercessions
For shepherds, gardeners, tailors, and dressmakers; for good humour, kindness, and tolerance; for good neighbourliness; for greater harmony in our homes, workplaces, and communities, and between nations; for a throwing down of the walls of hatred and for peacemakers; for greater commitment to the practical demands of our individual calling; for humility and the grace to examine our consciences.

Thanksgiving for our sense of humour, and for those who bring the joy of laughter into our lives.

Place of Spiritual Retreat
Listening to Jesus teach the parable of the servants, as in Matthew 21

WEDNESDAY WEEK THREE IN ADVENT

DAISY *Bellis perennis*; bairnswort

Cultivation Notes
Botanical books give flowering time as March to October, but Nicholas Culpeper, in *The English Physician Enlarged, or the Herbal*, (1653), is more realistic, telling us that the daisy can appear all year round. It is not at all unusual to see it in December and I find it particularly cheering then.

History and Lore
The daisy is native to Europe, the Mediterranean regions, and West Asia. The word comes from the Anglo-Saxon for *day's eye*, so the flower was almost certainly named from its habit of opening its petals to the light of day and closing them at dusk. It is frequently and delicately depicted in the borders of medieval Books of Hours, and there is a portrait of Chaucer with a daisy in the corner usually reserved in medieval painting for the subject's coat of arms. (Chaucer extols the 'eye of day' in the Prologue to his *The Legend of Good Women*.)

In 1730 John Bartram, a Pennsylvanian Quaker, was sitting under a tree, idly pulling a daisy to pieces, when he became aware that he was destroying a small miracle. He immediately rode into Philadelphia, found a bookshop, and emerged with tomes of Latin grammar and botany. Later he was given Parkinson's *Theatrum Botanicum* (1640), and exchanged plants with foreign visitors. Later still he made North America's first botanical garden at Schuylkill, for which the daisy that had perished at his hand was indirectly responsible and surely did not die in vain.

In European folklore the daisy has long been the white symbol not merely of childhood in general but of the innocence of the Christ Child. Its northern name is bairnswort, sometimes the childing daisy. In German it can be *Marienblümchen*, Mary's little flowers, or *Tausenschönchen*, a thousand prettinesses. In France and Italy as well as England it acts as a love measure, and many of us have memories not only of alternate petal counting ('He loves me, he loves me not') but also of the intricate business of making daisy chains. Katherine Mansfield remembered a childhood game of being married wearing a daisy chain with the 'service' read from a seed catalogue. She wrote to her sister, 'People say I love flowers because I spent my childhood among all those gorgeous tropical trees and blossoms. But I don't seem to remember us making daisy chains out of magnolias –

do you?' And Sylvia Pankhurst wrote of 'the great lawn of daisies, the dearest of childhood's flowers'.

The daisy has a long history of use in folk medicine. Lotions and ointments were made for minor eye troubles such as sore eyelids. This use was probably encouraged by the Doctrine of Signatures, a somewhat risky belief that a plant's characteristics were God's indication of the parts of the body it should be used to treat. Paracelsus, the German-Swiss alchemist (1493–1541), is believed to have fathered the theory, but its greatest exponent was Giambattista della Porta, who laid it down as a serious doctrine in 1588. 'Signature' notwithstanding, the daisy also had a strong reputation as a general healing herb, and its leaves were crushed and applied to wounds and bruises. Indeed, in some parts of Britain it was known as bruisewort. Tinctures were made for the treatment of skin troubles and boils. In our time, it has recently been under investigation for use in HIV therapy. In the kitchen young daisy leaves and flower buds add a pleasant sour flavour to salads. Harvest them in spring and use fresh.

Towards Meditation
'Let the earth open, that salvation may sprout forth and let it cause righteousness to spring up also; I the Lord have created it' (Is. 45:8).

After my previous comments about weeds, no one will expect me to disparage the daisy as an unwelcome nuisance. Quite the reverse. May it never be weeded out of existence:

> Trampled under foot,
> The daisy lives and strikes its root into the lap of time:
> Centuries may come
> And pass away into the silent tomb,
> And still the child hid in the womb of time,
> Shall smile and pluck them, when this simple rhyme
> Shall be forgotten, like a churchyard stone
> Or lingering lie, unnoticed and alone.
>   (John Clare, 1793–1864)

No, Clare, your melancholy rhyme is not forgotten. Better still, it makes me happy, for as long as there is grass, there will be daisies.

This book could be described as a 'doctrine of signatures' for the soul, and I have yet to find the plant that does not, through its symbolism, have a helpful bearing on spiritual life. Some plants – and the daisy is an example – suggest more than one possible theme for meditation. Today, as we draw ever closer to Christmas, its message is threefold. First, in its innocent, humble springing out of the earth in midwinter, it reminds me of Christ himself. When it closes its mauve-tinged petals at the end of a brief December day, it hints at the Passion that the Child in the crib will endure for us. And because so many gardeners regard it as a nuisance, it calls to mind 'To him shall come all who were incensed against him' (Is. 18:21–6) and the fulfilment of that prophecy when, in Luke 7, at the end of his confirmatory message to John the Baptist, Jesus adds the words, 'And blessed is he who takes no offence at me.' At this point I may reflect on the lowly circumstances of Christ's birth and on those who showed no offence at them; and on the reasoning in this part of the divine plan, which inspired such perfect co-operation in Mary, such unrestrained joy among the angels, such awed belief among the shepherds, and such reverent homage in the Magi. And of course Herod is there, his offence against the Lord taking the form of murderous intent. The earthly king jealous for the wrong kind of power is the forerunner of those who later in Jesus' life would also wish to do away with him.

When I was teaching at primary school in mid-sixties London, we still had a Christian morning assembly and one of the children's favourite hymns was, 'Daisies are our silver, buttercups our gold. This is all the treasure we can have or hold' (Jan Struther, 1901–53). In those days London children still knew what the flowers looked like. Sadly I am not convinced the majority do now, but the point here is that the daisy has value, not to be measured against material possession. Those children, Christian or not, had innate understanding of 'laying up treasure in heaven' and I am certain that is why they loved the hymn.

The second theme the daisy offers is connected with faith. As anyone knows who has tried to get rid of daisies, they cannot be completely eradicated. A glance at their masses of fibrous roots will explain this tenacity and lead to a consideration of the state of our 'roots'. Is the 'soil' we are offering conducive to indestructible establishment of the 'plant' of faith? How much do we pray for the 'water' of grace to nourish its roots and keep them healthy and strong?

Last, for today, I think of the similarity between what the daisy automatically does and what we should try to do and be. The daisy opens to the light; it is not destroyed by being trampled on; it does not care what gardeners say about it but just goes on in small humility, living in the light and looking towards it. But *we* know where that light comes from. *We* know that the light we look for is God. In his treatise *Against the Heresies*, Irenaeus muses on our desire to see God. In respect of God's greatness and glory, he reminds us, no one shall see God and live. But God, in his love and mercy, does grant a glimpse of himself to the pure in heart who love him. He was seen by the prophets through the Spirit; he is seen in his Son whose birth we await, but he will only be seen in Heaven as the Father. The light is shed on those who recognize the Son, through whom they partake of God's splendour. God's splendour gives life; those who see God in this way partake of life.

'Then the eyes of those who see will not be closed and the ears of those who hear will hearken' (Is. 32:3).

Bible Readings

Isaiah 18:21–6: From my mouth has gone forth in righteousness a word that shall not return
Isaiah 31:1–3; 32:1–6: The reign of true righteousness and integrity
Isaiah 45:6–8: I form light and create darkness
Luke 7:19–23: Jesus replies to the message of John the Baptist

Intercessions

For writers and poets whose work celebrates plants and their Creator; for botanists past and present and for those who created public parks and gardens and who work in them today; for people with eye problems and those who work in that area of medicine; for sufferers from AIDS and HIV, and for those researching for a cure; for an increase in tolerance and humility; that we may not be daunted but turn more often to God's counsel and mercy in our trials and difficulties; that we may approach the celebration of Christ's birth in a spirit of greater co-operation, joy, awe, faith and homage.

Place of Spiritual Retreat

With Christ when he speaks of those who take no offence at him, as in Luke 7

THURSDAY WEEK THREE IN ADVENT

MISTLETOE *Viscum album*

Cultivation Notes

Mistletoe is an evergreen parasitic shrub that flourishes in warm damp
climates where there are soft-barked trees inhabited by berry-eating birds.
It will grow on hazel, poplar, maple, ash, willow, rowan, and hawthorn,
but seems to favour lime, apple, and oak. Male and female plants appear
on the same tree in spring, and the berries ripen in winter. These contain a
sticky juice, which the birds carry away on their beaks. Pliny thought that
mistletoe seed would not germinate unless it had first passed through a
bird. However, Philip Miller, an eighteenth-century curator of the
Chelsea Physic Garden, discovered that smearing sticky seed on a suitable
tree was enough to establish it. And, as he observed in *The Gardener's
Dictionary* (1737), this was only to imitate the mistle thrush,

> for the viscous Part of the Berry, which immediately
> surrounds the seed, doth sometimes fasten to the outward
> Part of the Bird's Beak; which to get disengag'd of, he strikes
> his beak against the Branches of a neighbouring Tree, and
> thereby leaves the Seed sticking by viscous Matter to the
> Bark; which, if it light upon a smoothe part of the Tree, will
> fasten itself thereto, and the following Winter will put out and
> grow.

If you have a suitable host tree you may like to crush berries into a crevice
and see what happens.

History and Lore

Mistletoe is believed to have been first found in Europe and was held in
great veneration by the druids, in whose New Year celebrations it played
a significant part. Only oak mistletoe was used, after it had been cut from
the tree with a golden knife. They must have learned by experiment what
we now know from botany, namely that the quality of mistletoe's
constituents varies according to the minerals it is able to draw from the
host tree. The oak is still considered to bear the best mistletoe.

Viscum is the Latin both for birdlime and mistletoe, and *album* must be
descriptive of the white berries. The Anglo-Saxon *misteltan* is derived from

mist, meaning manure, and *ten/tan*, meaning twig or shoot. It must have been regarded as an exudation or excrescence from its host. The Welsh word is *uchelwydd*, meaning upper tree, from its place of growth. But the Gaelic *an t'uil ioc'*, meaning 'that which heals all', brings us closer to ancient belief in its supposed supernatural and protective powers. In European lore mistletoe was thought to evoke dreams that revealed the secrets of eternal youth, and if hung over a baby's crib, it was believed to prevent mischievous sprites from exchanging the human baby for a fairy one.

In *Titus Andronicus* (Act 2, scene 3), Shakespeare mentions the 'baleful mistletoe'. This may refer to its poisonous berries or to its association with druidic human sacrifice. There was also a tradition that the cross of Christ had been formed by it. This may have been a transmutation of the myth of Baldur, the Scandinavian god of peace who was killed by the jealous god Loci with an arrow made from mistletoe. Baldur was resurrected by other deities, and although the plant was banished to the tree tops by Frigg, Baldur's grieving mother, it was later entrusted to the goddess of love, who made it a custom that anyone passing beneath it should receive a kiss and her special blessing. So it seems that our tradition of kissing under the mistletoe is Nordic in origin. In what was probably a revival of this pre-Christian custom, the mistletoe bough came much to the fore in the early seventeenth century, with the further accretion that the man should pick a berry for every kiss – and when all the berries were gone, no more kissing!

To the medieval mind mistletoe, with its lack of roots in the ground, seemed to represent supernatural generative power and continuing life in midwinter. With characteristic earthiness they interpreted the white berries between splayed leaves as the signature of a potent charm against human infertility. Perhaps even more 'biologically', the substance in the berries reminded them of the way in which seed is carried to the human womb. In any case, women who wished to conceive would tie a sprig of mistletoe to their wrists or waists. One would think that these pagan associations are behind the continuing tendency to exclude mistletoe from Christmas decorations in church. The Reverend C. S. Tyack, in his *Lore and Legend of the English Church* (1899), thinks this distaste and caution go back as far as the dawn of English Christianity. 'Our Saxon forefathers,' he says, 'so far clung to their ancestral myths that they would not use the death symbol of Baldur at the birth of the White Christ.'

In the eighteenth century a fad for druidism affected the eccentric Reverend William Stukely to such an extent that he regarded the druids as heralds of British Christianity and built a druidic temple in his garden, at the centre of which was an apple tree overgrown with mistletoe. More than a century later members of the Woodhope Naturalists' Field Club, a third of whom were clergymen, collected mistletoe from an oak near Aymestrey, Herefordshire, and distributed the 'heaven born plant, unpolluted by any touch of earth' among the ladies present at one of their gatherings (*Transactions of the Woodhope Naturalists' Field Club*, 1870). It may be noted that the druids of the time were not much impressed by the goings-on!

There are occasional carvings of mistletoe in churches, but they are conspicuous by their rarity, and, in spite of the Reverend Stukely and the clerics of Woodhope, the Church has shown an aversion to architectural representation of mistletoe. In 1893, Oklahoma made the mistletoe its emblem, the first time a plant had been so adopted. Possibly it was chosen because of its meaning: 'I surmount all difficulties.'

As to the practical uses of the plant, it was formerly a constituent in birdlime for trapping birds. In modern homeopathic practice there is a tincture of mistletoe for the treatment of cancer, and in herbal medicine it is used to strengthen the heart and reduce blood pressure. Decoction of mistletoe has been claimed as effective in the control of epilepsy. However, all parts of the plant are toxic, and there are restrictions on its sale and use in some countries. It can be used externally to relieve chilblains, ulcers and varicose veins, but the advice must be against dabbling with it. Most mistletoe is deliberately cultivated to satisfy the Christmas market, and most of that sold in Britain comes from Northern France, but it can also be seen from the TGV high up in trees all the way down from Tours to Angoulême. At first sight I thought the rounded clumps were birds' nests. I did not realize what it was until I later saw it at closer quarters in the Charente and Dordogne. Many French and British apple-growers encourage it in their trees as a catch crop when their orchards are resting from their main purpose. Herefordshire is the traditional British region for mistletoe production, and at Tenbury Wells there is still an annual Mistletoe and Holly Market. It is a relief to know that in spite of the voracious seasonal demand, the mistletoe, even when old orchards are grubbed up, seems to find new hosts without any difficulty.

Towards Meditation
'And by your descendants shall all the nations of the earth bless themselves, because you have obeyed my voice' (Gen. 22:16).

Since mistletoe is such a familiar part of our celebration of Christ's birth, its association with human fertility and growth in the barrenness of midwinter turns my mind to the occasions in the Bible when God intervenes in the lives of childless women. Sarah, wife of Abraham, compensates him for her own barrenness by giving him the concubine Hagar, who bears a son. In her old age Sarah, long resigned to childlessness, laughs in disbelief when she overhears the 'visitors' telling Abraham that she too will bear a son. Then she denies that she has laughed and is afraid. But God visits her as he has promised, and Isaac is born. 'God has brought laughter for me; everyone who hears will laugh with me' (Gen. 21:6). It is not surprising that Abraham chooses the name Isaac, which indeed means 'laughter'. Later Sarah becomes jealous of Hagar and her son Ishmael and asks Abraham to send them away. This he does, but only after being told by God to obey Sarah, 'for through Isaac shall offspring be named for you' (21:12). Sarah seems a mere instrument throughout the events, unaware of their deeper meaning, or of the Divine purpose behind them. God speaks to Abraham either directly or through angels, not once to Sarah. Nowhere is she offered a choice. We are not told whether she knows of God's demand for the sacrifice of Isaac, or of how close she came to losing her son. That ultimate sacrifice is not demanded of her. It is not the faith and obedience of woman that God wills to test at this point. The history of Abraham and Isaac hints at the later salvific sacrifice of God's own beloved Son. And in that phrase from Genesis 22:18 'all the nations' is another glimmer of the New Covenant.

From Sarah, my mind goes to the wife of Manoah, mother of Samson; to Hannah, mother of Samuel; and to Elizabeth, mother of John the Baptist. But the liturgy will unfold their stories during the remaining days of Advent, and so I leave them for the time being and turn to a more general consideration of childlessness. Three types suggest themselves. First, that of young women who desperately wish for a child but fail to conceive. Hannah's only hope of relief from anguish lay in prayer. Nowadays the subject leads us into most difficult areas of moral theology and medical ethics, but lack of qualification in these disciplines by no means exempts me from the responsibility of praying about the issues raised by modern fertility treatments. My prayer for women who submit to medical intervention is based in deep compassion, and it is not my place to stand in judgement. But I worry constantly that we have already trespassed too far on God's prerogative.

However, it is the other types of barrenness that particularly concern me today. The second is that of a woman who has borne children and, having lost them, failed to conceive again. I write as one who falls into this category. To have experienced travail and yet remain childless is a peculiarly agonizing thing, and I sympathize profoundly with women who share it, either from miscarriage, stillbirth, crib death, adoption, accident, or disease – to say nothing of women who as I write are losing their children to starvation and the gun in so many parts of the world.

Without faith I would not have been able to come to terms with my losses. I was still young, and hope made them a little easier to endure. But as middle age crept nearer, I faced a final acceptance. How would I manage resignation without bitterness? How would faith help then? Now that chasm in the pilgrimage has been crossed, it is possible to attempt an answer. Today's liturgy encourages me to believe that it was God who gave me, first the opportunity, and then the grace, to take on, in a very small and belated way, the third type of barrenness, namely the freely chosen physical childlessness of the religious life, in other words to accept it in retrospect as part of my vocation, as something I could offer up wholeheartedly; and together with it, forty years as a teacher, during which I have been able to 'spread the tent' unreservedly in the love and nurture of other people's children.

As for women who from their youth consecrate themselves entirely to God, I am told that many of them sooner or later have a crisis in which they realize the enormity of what they have given up. Not until this point is the sacrifice truly offered; not until then is the nun truly made. Further I am told that the women who thus embrace childlessness are the ones who make the most balanced, feminine, and indeed, motherly nuns. In this way they are anything but barren, and I have found this particularly true of members of contemplative Orders. Perhaps this is because they cannot avoid their crises in a plethora of good works in the world. This isn't the place to reflect on the value of what they *actually* do, but I have found their motherliness completely free of the self-indulgent sentimentality some biological mothers display. Nuns themselves will tell you with a candour and conviction impossible to doubt, 'What need have I now of a human son when I have Christ? He is my portion and my cup, and he has made me free to love all his children equally.' This is movingly conveyed in the French film noir, *Thérèse*, when the Carmelite saint of Lisieux and her community welcome the Christ Child to his crib. For brief moments each sister holds the doll to her breast as if she were Mary holding the Son of God. But for them this is not merely a time of personal fulfilment. Christ is the promise of hope to all believers, and, as the documents of Vatican II press home, he completes the whole revelation begun in Genesis. God speaks to us by his Son, 'the Word who enlightens all men ... there will be words, works, signs, miracles, death, resurrection, sending of the Spirit.' This is how John the Baptist was to recognize him (Lk. 7:22). For John, that message must have meant vindication of his whole life and been perfect consolation. Far beyond our desserts, it is the same for each of us and for the whole of Christ's Church. 'He maketh the barren woman to keep house and to be a joyful mother of children' (Ps. 113:9).

Bible Readings
Genesis 18:12–15: Sarah laughed to herself
Genesis 21 and 22: Through Isaac offspring shall be named for you
Isaiah 32: A promise of hope for believers
Isaiah 54:1–10: Sing, O barren one
Luke 7:18–30: Go and tell John what you have seen

Intercessions
For commercial producers of mistletoe; for French and British apple growers.

For all sufferers from cancer, heart disease, epilepsy, ulcers and varicose veins; for childless women; for progress in medical science that is pleasing to God; for newly bereaved mothers; for teachers; for consecrated women and thanksgiving for their lives.

That we may be healed from past sin and open our hearts to a wider world both in prayer and action.

Place of Spiritual Retreat
With Jesus when John's disciples come to him, as in Luke 7

FRIDAY WEEK THREE IN ADVENT

POINSETTIA *Euphorbia pulcherina*; fire flower of the Holy Night

Cultivation Notes
Poinsettia is of South American origin but has achieved popularity in Europe as a Christmas plant. The modern varieties are bushier and much less delicate than earlier specimens. But it is unfortunate that chemicals

are used to keep the plants small for the domestic market. The 'flowers' are actually coloured bracts and should last two to three months. When buying, look at the tiny yellow central flowers. They should be unopened for maximum life in the house. Reject any plant you suspect has been in a cold atmosphere. Put your chosen poinsettia in a well-lit spot away from draughts and keep reasonably warm. Avoid over-watering; wait until compost is moderately dry. If you want the plant to bloom again next Christmas, the following procedure should work. When the leaves have fallen, cut back to stumps five inches high. Keep the compost almost dry in a mild, shady place. In early May, water and re-pot. Continue careful watering, and shoots should appear. Feed and remove some of the new growth leaving four or five strong stems. (Prunings can be used as cuttings.) From September you must cover your poinsettias with black polythene from dusk to early morning. About fourteen hours of darkness is essential each night. Do this for eight weeks and then treat as before. This system replicates the plant's natural habitat as nearly as possible. It should blossom at Christmas, but will be taller than in the previous year.

History and Lore
Poinsettia was discovered by the American Minister to Mexico J. R. Poinsett (1779–1853) and named after him in 1867. Its older name, fire flower of the Holy Night, originates from a Mexican folk story about a little girl who was so poor that she had nothing to offer at the Christmas crib. Sad and alone, she watched the procession winding its way to church and then followed it, but only as far as the churchyard. There she came across a carved stone angel whose face was almost completely obscured by tall grasses and weeds. As she knelt to clear some of them away, she suddenly heard a voice saying, 'Pick these weeds, take them to the church and offer them to the Christ-Child.' Obediently, the little girl carried an armful of the weeds into church and nervously approached the crib. As she did so, the top of each weed turned a bright flame-red, like tongues of fire. The poinsettia was born that night and has been grown especially for Christmas ever since.

Towards Meditation
'Your eyes will see the king in his beauty' (Is. 33:17).

I will always try to have at least one poinsettia in the house by today because its legend serves two purposes. The first is that it reminds me of the poor and oppressed, particularly in South America. In the specific case of Mexico, I think not only of present conditions but also of a past in which it was plundered by the Conquistadors, and long before that, when thousands of humans were sacrificed annually to Mextli, the ancient god of war, who was supposedly born fully armed and who gave his name to the country. As Isaiah foretells, 'your mind will muse on the terror' after it is over. At Mass today we pray with the psalmist that when the King comes he will bring protection, deliverance, and justice for the poor. The Gospel reminds us that at his First Coming, although he was of royal descent, the King himself was born in lowly conditions. In today's Office of Readings Isaiah paints a desolate picture of a world where greed reigns supreme, where treaties are broken and where there is no respect for human life, where there are no travellers on the roads, and where the land has become an unproductive desert. Not for the first time, the prophet's vision chills my heart, so accurately does it describe our modern world. He goes on to say that although there will be reward for the righteous, it will be reserved only to those who despise the profits of oppression, who speak honestly and behave justly, who take no bribes, and who cannot bear war and bloodshed. These alone are the people who 'will dwell on the heights', whose bread and water will be secure, and whose sins will be forgiven. Their eyes will see Jerusalem and 'the king in his beauty'.

The second value of the poinsettia legend is that it can be seen as a metaphor for prayer. The poor little girl with nothing to give represents anyone who desires to pray but feels a woeful inadequacy; her clearing of foliage from the angel's face, our first efforts in prayer; and the message she hears, God's test of our obedience and faith, but also his encouragement. Our attentiveness and obedience should mirror hers when we try to pray; her gathering of the weeds and taking them into church should remind us of the gift of faith; and her nervousness of how often that faith is shaky, always through our own fault. 'I believe; help my unbelief' (Mk 9:24). Finally the turning of the weed tips into tongues of flame reminds us of the working of the Holy Spirit in us when we pray. 'Progress in prayer' is not the right phrase because it has the sense of our pushing forward as the result of our own efforts. I prefer to think that the soul automatically responds to the gravitational pull of God when he chooses to touch it with his Spirit. It is not up to the soul to say, 'I have done this and that, and now God should do this for me, or to me.' It is not its business to question God's timing. Each successive Advent reminds the soul of its business throughout the year, which is to be alert and waiting with lamp alight.

Today's Office of Readings includes an extract from St Augustine of Hippo's *Discourses on the Psalms*. I have found it helpful in times of consolation and aridity, for we are assured here that the very desire to pray is in itself a prayer, and I am reminded also of Blaise Pascal (1623–62): 'You would not be seeking me if you did not already possess me. Therefore do not be anxious.' Augustine goes further and says that if the desire is constant then the prayer will be constant too and 'never absent from the ears of God'. Even if we are going through a bad patch and God seems to have absented himself, we can be sure that he hears and sees everything in our secret souls and will 'repay' us for our continual prayer of longing. Wisely the saint does not say *when* the reward will be given, and does not imply that it will be easily earned. God takes each one of us and rears and prunes us for heaven in the way he chooses. And the rearing and pruning can be uncomfortable or downright agonizing. St Jane Frances de Chantal (1572–1641) responded thus: 'O my Lord, I am in a dry land, all dried up and cracked by the violence of the north wind and the cold; but as thou seest, I ask for nothing more; thou wilt send me both dew and warmth when it pleaseth thee.'

After Christmas, when I cut back my poinsettias, I will remember that when they bloom next December they will be plants of greater stature. In the meantime, 'I groan because of the tumult of my heart. Lord, all my longing is known to thee, my sighing is not hidden from thee' (Ps. 38:8b–9).

Bible Readings
Psalm 38: Lord, all my longing is known to thee
Psalm 63: O God for you I long
Psalm 72: In his days may righteousness flourish
Isaiah 33:7–24: The Lord is our king; he will save us
Matthew 1:1–17: The genealogy of Jesus Christ
Mark 9:17–27: All things are possible to him who believes

Intercessions
For the peoples of Mexico; for a more just distribution of the world's resources; for openness to the Holy Spirit; for perseverance in prayer whatever our spiritual state; for deeper and stronger faith; for the mentally ill; for those enduring aridity.

Thanksgiving for graces granted in prayer.

Place of Spiritual Retreat
At the healing of the demoniac boy, as in Mark 9

17 DECEMBER

SWEET CHESTNUT
Castanea sativa

Cultivation Notes
There are usually one to three
nuts encased in the familiar
spiny autumnal husks. In
Britain they are often blown
down in October gales, but
if they do reach full ripeness
on the tree, home-grown
chestnuts are crisper and
sweeter than imported varieties.
They are reputed to be at
the peak of flavour after the first
frosts. However, British summers
are generally too cool to provide a commercially viable crop, and most of
the nuts sold at Christmastide are imported from the south of France or
Italy. The sweet chestnut can grow to 100 feet and its trunk may attain a
girth of 50 feet. The mature bark develops long spiral fissures that make
the tree easily recognizable. The male catkins are long and pale yellow,
and appear in midsummer on the same tree as the female. Many British
chestnuts have germinated in the wild and are well established in woods,
but they have also frequently been planted for ornament in parks and
gardens. Varieties recommended for keeping quality and ease of peeling
are *C. sativa* 'Marron de Lyon' and *C. sativa* 'Paragon'. The latter produces
a single kernel and is preferred for commercial growing.

History and Lore
The tree is named after Castanea in Thessaly, which was renowned for
chestnuts. It was probably introduced to Britain by the Romans, who
made a form of porridge by slowly drying the nuts over an open fire and

then grinding and mixing them with milk. This *pollenta* is still eaten in poorer regions of southern Europe and it is ironic that in wealthier areas of Europe and North America the chestnut is the basis of luxury sweetmeats such as marrons glacés. Chestnut leaves, gathered and dried in summer, can be infused to make an effective gargle for sore throats and coughs.

Chestnut wood is similar to oak in weather resistance and is used in panelling, beams, and rough fence paling. Kent and Sussex are major areas for chestnut coppicing. Thousands of acres, mainly planted in the nineteenth century, are managed for wood production. The sweet chestnut is noted for longevity and there is a famous example in Tortworth, Gloucestershire. Standing by St Leonard's church, its trunk measures 30 yards in circumference. Collapsed branches at its side have taken root and are sending up new growth. The tree is surrounded by a fence on which is a plaque bearing the legend:

> This tree is supposed to be
> 600 years old 1st January
> 1800
> May Man still Guard thy Venerable form
> From the Rude Blasts and Tempestuous Storm
> Still mayest thou Flourish through
> Succeeding Time,
> And last, Long Last, the Wonder of the Clime.

The King James Bible is almost certainly wrong to render 'chestnut' in Genesis and Ezekiel since the tree is not indigenous to the Holy Land, but I somehow prefer it to the 'plane tree' of other translations. 'And the chestnut trees were not like his branches; nor any tree in the garden of God was like unto him in beauty' (Ezek. 31:8).

Towards Meditation
'May he defend the cause of the poor of the people, give deliverance to the needy' (Ps. 72:4).

One Friday morning last year, during the usual protracted wait for London Transport, thoughts of the sweet chestnut tree transported me to a glen on the western outskirts of Sheffield just inside Yorkshire's boundary with Derbyshire.

It is October 1945. A man and a woman walk, shoulders touching, down the wide brake leading to the burnished cavern of the woods. Each has a hand on the pushchair in which their two-year-old daughter is strapped. They are just another couple in love, but their happiness is of the order experienced only when a man has returned safely at the end of a war; when against all her dread a woman has not been widowed, her child not been made fatherless. They grieve for the many less fortunate. Their Christmas will be a frugal affair, but it will be the first the man has spent with his baby daughter and truly a festival of joy, peace, and security. Evacuation to Melton Mowbray, terrible partings on dim railway stations, pregnancy and birth under threat of the 'telegram' for her; Scapa Flow, the Battle of the Atlantic, and the sweeping of the English Channel before D-Day for him – all these are things of the past. They enter the wood. The man begins to examine the abundance of fallen chestnuts. He knows each tree, its age, position, and fruiting potential. This is because, as the child in the pram will later learn, he had explored these woods, boy and man, until the war came.

The train arrives at last; there are no seats, and so I stand gazing through the carriage window at the cabled and grimy tunnel wall, thanking God for a childhood of Sunday mornings during which my father tutored me in woodland lore. In the autumns of the 1940s and 1950s, Ryecroft Glen always produced more ripe chestnuts than we could carry home. So much for what the books say about our British climate. They are right, though, about the superior flavour of the English chestnut. I fear that unless I go back to the Glen I shall not taste it again, and even then perhaps not. The place is probably a part of urban sprawl by now. Depressed by this thought I close my eyes and linger over the memory of fireside conversations with my father as we waited for roasted chestnuts to pop from the grate into the hearth. On one such occasion he asked me if I had heard of the expression 'to pull the chestnut from the fire'. I confessed not and was told that it means to save the situation for someone and comes from the fable of the monkey who persuaded the cat to extricate chestnuts from the fire for him.

The train stops, and more people crowd in. I am jolted back to the here and now, and reflect on today's poor, who have not even *pollenta* to eat, and on the very few chestnuts we pull out of the fire for them. I see the chestnut tree as symbolic of the good things of earth, dropping its fruits in a circle beneath its branches, not favouring north, south, east, or west. A children's fable begins to spin: 'Once upon a time, there were some fine sweet chestnut trees growing on the boundary between a rich man's land

and a poor man's land. The trees dropped nuts equally on both sides, but the rich man was greedy and sent his servants to plunder the poor man's share. Sometimes he would pay the poor man for the chestnuts, but only a fraction of what they were really worth. This was a terrible thing because the chestnuts were the poor man's staple food, whereas the rich man wanted them only as a luxury. Some of the people who lived on the rich man's land believed his behaviour was against nature and against God's will, but they had no power and there were not enough of them to change things. . . .'

I continue in this vein until it is time to change trains. No power, insufficient numbers, but the responsibility is personal as well as collective. How can I, how do I answer it? Life is a constant struggle to pay bills, to make ends meet. I conduct a mental survey of my tutor group at school: one Israeli who knows his Judaism but admits he cannot believe in God, two Baptists, one Roman Catholic, one avowed atheist, and the rest floundering agnostics. None, however, is indifferent to religion. Discussion of it frequently breaks out among them, into which they will drag me if at all possible. They know I will contribute informatively in Christian terms without any attempt to convert them. Increasingly they ask for explanations and solutions. They know all about vested interests; they refuse to buy Nike or Gap products because of the way those companies use sweat labour in South-East Asia; they would immediately understand the metaphor of the chestnut tree. They seem conscious of the spiritual poverty in modern life and express awareness that in spite of technological advances a worse world is being handed on to them than the one inherited by my own generation. In a way they are asking to be given faith, which of course is not possible. But I cannot remain silent in the face of their desire to have my Christian response. They deserve more than a story on the failure of Christians to obliterate material and spiritual poverty from the world. And so my constant answer is that too few people, of all religions, have loved enough, too few have prayed enough, too few have lived their calling to the full. As a result an unstoppable monster of greed and selfishness has free rein over the earth. My students have not yet asked whether this neglect and failure is redeemable. In the tube I pray that if they ever do, God will grant me the right words to express the Christian faith that an affirmative answer is possible only in the death and resurrection of Jesus Christ: 'With you is wisdom, she who knows your works. . . . Send her forth from the holy heavens, and from the throne of your glory send her. . . . For she knows and understands all things, and she will guide me wisely in my actions and guard me with her glory. Then my works will be acceptable. . . .' (Wis. 9:9–12).

Leaving the train, I begin the fifteen-minute walk to school. The poor remain firmly in mind until I come to the chestnut tree a few yards from the playground gate. This morning I do not walk straight past it but stand for a few moments tracing the bark spirals with my fingers and remembering that to the Victorians the tree had the meaning, 'Do me justice.' Turning from the tree I silently anticipate the first great Advent *Magnificat* antiphon, *O Sapientia:* 'O Wisdom, which came from the mouth of the Most High, and reaches from one end to another, powerfully and sweetly ordering all things; Come and teach us the way of prudence.' And then as I enter the school gate, the voice of the Spirit speaks to me through the Psalmist, 'I will instruct you and teach you the way you should go. I will counsel you with my eye upon you' (Ps. 33:8).

Bible Readings
Psalm 32: Blessed is he whose transgression is forgiven
Psalm 72: May he defend the poor of the people
Isaiah 4:2: The branch of the Lord shall be beautiful
Isaiah 11:1–3: There shall come forth a shoot from the stump of Jesse
Isaiah 11:10: The root of Jesse shall stand as an ensign to the peoples
Wisdom of Solomon 9: With you is wisdom
Matthew 1:1–17: The genealogy of Christ
Luke 1:32: His name shall be glorious
Luke 16:19–31: Dives and Lazarus
Luke 18:18–30: The rich young ruler

Intercessions
For those who manage chestnut woodland and work in the fencing industry; for biblical scholars and translators; for teachers and their pupils; for orphans; for those whose childhood was unhappy or who suffered parental divorce; for the poor throughout the world, and for the work of aid agencies.

That the hearts of those who govern may be moved to a fairer distribution of food.

Thanksgiving for natural woodland and for the trees in our parks, gardens, suburbs, and cities; thanksgiving for the loving marriage of parents, happy childhood memories, and for the safe return of parents after the war; for wisdom and a greater devotion to prayer; for those who dedicate themselves to prayer in the contemplative life.

Place of Spiritual Retreat
With the rich young ruler being counselled by Jesus, as in Luke 18

FOURTH SUNDAY IN ADVENT

BLUEBELL *Scilla non scripta*; *Endymion nutans* (lit. bent downwards, nodding/waving)

Cultivation Notes
If you are lucky enough to have space for a woodland section in your garden, now is a good time to plant bluebell bulbs and be cheered in the anticipation of their loveliness next spring.

History and Lore
Scilla comes from the Greek *skyllo*, to annoy, possibly because the fresh bulbs are poisonous. Linnaeus, the great eighteenth-century Swedish botanist, added the tag '*non scripta*' because, unlike those of wild hyacinth, bluebell petals are not marked with dark spots and are therefore 'not written upon'. *Endymion* must refer to the beautiful shepherd grandson of Zeus, with whom Selene, the moon goddess, fell in love, and to whom she bore fifty daughters. Having been allowed by Zeus to choose his own fate, Endymion elected an eternal sleep in which he would remain forever young. Every night Selene would visit him in his cave on Mount Latmus to gaze on his beauty, sometimes awaking him to satisfy her passion. Even though Shakespeare's Juliet begs Romeo not to swear by the *inconstant* moon, Selene was certainly constant to Endymion. The bluebell, once established – and *left unpicked* – mirrors the constancy of their love and also the fecundity of Selene. At the time of the Boer War, it was the emblem for constancy and was used to commemorate the heroes who had died in battle. Two postcards were published, one showing a soldier saying goodbye to his sweetheart: 'Your tears are falling; / Bluebell, we two must part.' On the second card the same man is wounded and delirious, and there is an inset of his loved one at home: 'There on the hillside lying, / There mid the guns' loud roar, / Bluebell, your true love's dying; / Calling for you once more.'

The bluebell is native to Northern Europe. Nowhere else can its gentle and fragile beauty occur naturally. For those of us fortunate enough to have first encountered bluebells in childhood, the memory will be of delighted enchantment. But we all have to learn from experience that our natural desire to keep the magic and take it home, cannot be satisfied. The wonderful blue fades to a dull grey very soon after picking and, what is worse, torn leaves do irreparable damage to the plants. The birthday after I learned this lesson, my disappointment was greatly assuaged by the gift of a painting of a Bluebell Wood for my bedroom. It was one of a nature series and probably by Margaret Tarrant or Racey Helps. It hung on my wall for years but was sadly 'lost' in a house move after my departure to teach in London. Oh, how I wish it was with me today so that I could relive with more piercing immediacy that moment when I first saw, in Tennyson's phrase, bluebells 'that seem the heavens upbreaking through the earth'!

Towards Meditation

'I will not leave you desolate; I will come to you' (Jn 14:18).

The fact that I have as yet been unable to plant bluebell bulbs does not prevent their constancy from leading to a reflection on the constancy of God. I am helped in this by the day's liturgy, in which this is a major theme. In the first reading at Mass we find him promising, 'I will find a place for my people Israel: I will place them there and they shall dwell in that place and never be disturbed again; ... I will give them rest from all their enemies.' Then the Psalmist celebrates his certainty of God's everlasting love as expressed in his covenant with David: 'I will keep my love for him always; for him my covenant shall endure.' But this is the Old Covenant. In the Office of Readings, we find Isaiah strongly hinting at the New: 'I am God, declaring the end from the beginning and from ancient times things not yet done, and I will accomplish all my purpose. I have spoken and I will bring it to pass.' In the second Mass reading Paul speaks of this predicted purpose as a mystery kept secret for endless ages, but now fully revealed in Jesus Christ. In the Gospel, Luke begins to tell the detail of how God brought this about and of the involvement of a young woman who had been in his mind from the beginning. At Mass today a bright shaft of light pierces the Advent gloom.

In the second Office reading the *Epistle to Diognetus* provides a more extended reflection, speaking of God's plan as having been darkly hinted at by the prophets in figures and types, but kept secret until John the Baptist. God had always been long-suffering as well as loving towards us, but only in his giving of his Son could we possibly be made aware of the full magnitude of his love. We would have had no hope of entering the kingdom without this gift, and through it alone could we begin to realize the marvel of God's patient constancy, or to grasp the amazing fact that he has not rejected us. Instead, he bears with us through his Son who takes our sins upon himself.

My bluebells will eventually be planted in the herb garden at the foot of the statue of Our Lady, because God chose to make his loving constancy fully manifest through her. And they are also entirely appropriate because their colour is hers. Nor will I forget the human constancy of Joseph, which had its part in the human upbringing of our supremely constant Saviour, to whom highest thanksgiving is due, and who left us this promise: 'Lo, I am with you always, to the close of the age.' Adding the fourth candle to the Advent arrangement today I will remember this and pray the second Great Advent *Magnificat* antiphon: 'O Adonai, and leader of the house of Israel, who appeared to Moses in a flame of fire, and gave him the Law on Sinai: Come and deliver us with an outstretched arm.' And for music today, Christopher Tye's setting of *Rorate Coeli* strikes just the right chord of confidence in God.

Bible Readings
2 Samuel 7:1–5; 8–11: I will find a place for my people
Psalm 89: God's covenant with David
Isaiah 46:1–13: In your old age I shall still be the same; my purpose shall last
Romans 16:25–7: The mystery is now made clear
Luke 1:28–36: In the sixth month the angel Gabriel was sent from God

Intercessions
For all bereaved during successive wars; for artists who paint plants and natural scenes, and for poets who draw word-pictures of them; thanksgiving for their work; for a world in which children have greater access to the natural environment and grow up with a knowledge and love of it; for constancy in our relationships, in our work, and in our prayer; thanksgiving to God for his constant love and for the birth of his Son.

Place of Spiritual Retreat
With the disciples listening to Christ's promise, as in Matthew 28 and John 14

19 DECEMBER

HOLLY *Ilex aquifolium* (lit. having pointed leaves)

Cultivation Notes

Holly does not like wet soils but is otherwise tolerant of poor and harsh conditions. However, it tends to be sterile in shade. In good light female trees will produce flowers from late spring to early summer and the familiar red berries from autumn to March. Those that escape looting by the birds and humans stay on the tree throughout the winter. The tree attains a height of between 10 and 70 feet. It is conical in shape but may become straggly with age. Holly is a good subject for a clipped hedge. I pass a fine example on my way to an annual meeting at Regent's College near Baker Street in London. It borders the lawned and wooded college grounds and I come upon it after crossing a bridge over a stream where ducks paddle. Fortunate the citizens who study in such a place! But despite this I walk on, preferring and missing the ancient coppiced holly I saw many times during the 1970s, in Yarner Wood, South Devon, a few miles from where I lived.

History and Lore

Holly is native to west and southern Europe and to western Asia. Its name comes from Anglo-Saxon *holegn*, a word related to the Welsh *celyn* and Gaelic *cuillean*. The Middle English *hollin* means a grove of holly trees. Many British place names and surnames speak of its widespread growth through the ages. The wood is white, hard, and dense, sometimes with a greenish streak. It has been used for inlay work, woodcuts, the manufacture of sea groynes, in the craft of chimney sweeping, and sometimes in water divining as an alternative to hazel or willow. During the Industrial Revolution thousands of Staffordshire holly trees were felled to provide bobbins for the Lancashire cotton mills. The leaves have a high calorific content and it is thought that their use as winter fodder for sheep may have originated in pre-history. There is certainly evidence that the practice was once prevalent in the Pennine foothills. The berries are poisonous to humans and have a violently emetic and purgative effect. The leaves do have some therapeutic qualities, and in flower essences are supposed to calm destructive emotions.

The popularity of holly at Christmas has led to illegal poaching and to whole trees being chain-sawed for their berries. But despite such violent plunder the holly is still spreading, for reasons partly to do with changes in grazing practice. Its domestic use in winter decoration is ancient and may derive from the Roman Saturnalia or from old Germanic custom. Pliny tells us that its branches were thought to protect houses from lightning and witchcraft. The belief persisted into medieval times with the added superstition that it invited bad luck if brought into the house before Christmas. Another belief was that to cut down a holly tree was unlucky. This is probably why they are seen in hedgerows that have grown up around them, and also why they are retained if those hedgerows are cleared. The pragmatist who says they are left merely as landmarks for the ploughman is not entirely convincing. Yet another tradition is that a good crop of berries forecasts a hard winter. Knowing of this in advance, God has provided the thrushes with an extra supply of their favourite food. Perhaps the idea accounts for the holly's meaning 'foresight' in *The Language of Flowers*. However, a heavy crop of berries is in fact merely the result of a good summer just past. On the Isle of Man it was the custom to keep the Christmas decorations up until Shrove Tuesday. Holly wood generates a fierce heat in the cooking-range fire. Perfect for pancakes perhaps.

Holly water was sacred to the Druids, and in pagan times it was sprinkled on newborn babies to keep them safe and happy. It was supposed to ward off evil and destruction and was associated with eternity, perhaps because of its long-lived berries and affirmation of continuing life during midwinter dormancy. Christianity was not tardy in applying its own symbolism, and, as the ever-popular carol testifies, the holly has for centuries represented both the spirit of Christmas and the Passion of Christ. In the Middle Ages people wrongly thought of the berry-bearing holly as male and cannot therefore have looked very closely. Long may *she* brighten the gloom of our Advent landscapes and find a place in our homes as we celebrate the Saviour's birth.

I do not bring greenery indoors until Christmas Eve, not out of superstition but because in town there never seems time to deal with it before then. In the country we collect it in the pine woods above the village and spend the afternoon, in between kitchen tasks, decorating the house and Christmas tree. But in town or country, by 19 December the Christmas rush has gathered speed and I must at least think about the decorations. As with the chestnut, meditation will most probably be 'on the hoof' today.

Towards Meditation

'Behold they are like stubble; the fire consumes them; they cannot deliver themselves from the power of the flame. No coal for warming oneself is this; no fire to sit before' (Is. 47:14).

This text comes to mind because of the fierce heat thrown out by burning holly. Isaiah is talking about the destruction of Babylon in a world he knows, but as with so much Old Testament prophecy, there are other interpretations. Here are conveyed both the impossibility of our salvation before Christ came the first time, and the way it will be before he comes again. Only because of his First Coming can we join in Isaiah's exhortation, 'Sing for joy, O heavens, and exult, O earth; break forth, O mountains into singing! For the Lord has comforted his people, and will have compassion on his suffering ones.' Only through him can we say with Paul, 'But our commonwealth is in heaven, and from it we await a Saviour, the Lord Jesus Christ who will change our lowly body to be like his glorious body, by the power which enables him even to submit all things to himself.' In today's Office of Readings an extract from Irenaeus (Treatise, *On the Redeeming Incarnation*, Book 3), the point is underlined that we can only be rescued from the 'fire' by God in the form of his Son.

If we consider holly as an emblem of foresight, it will still lead to a reflection on the prophets as interpreters, for their own generations, of the mind and will of the all-foreseeing God. But often their God-inspired foresights were to be fulfilled in circumstances not known or understood by them. Isaiah's Messianic prophecies, which form the Old Testament backbone of the Advent liturgy, were given in a very different situation from the one Jesus himself was to know. At seventeen years of age, while studying for 'A-level' Scripture, I spent several wonderfully enlightening months discovering that Christ is so frequently and inescapably recognizable in Old Testament prophecy. Ever since, this fact has been one of the strongest bedrocks of my faith.

During a recent Advent our London church held a special evening service to celebrate prophecy. Readings and hymns were arranged so as to remind us of the medieval *Bibliae Pauperum*, books in which pairs of images related Old Testament prophecy to New Testament redemption. In an age when illiteracy was common they were valuable educational tools. Here is Gregory the Great (*c.* 540–604) on the genre: 'We do not worship the pictures that enable us to learn in depth a biblical tale. What Holy Writ makes present to the reader, pictures make present to the illiterate, for whom pictures are the equivalent of reading.' In my own library is an early nineteenth-century *Book of the Rosary*, which for each mystery has two engravings, one of the New Covenant mystery and one of its Old Covenant prefiguration. Be we never so sophisticated we can still benefit from the type of instruction offered by this genre. Indeed, our parish notes for the Advent Prophecy celebration concluded thus:

> In our church we can enter the historical process of the *Bibliae Pauperum* in a unique way. In the sanctuary we have [frescoes of] the Annunciation and the Visitation in the apse, and the High Altar and Tabernacle in the centre, conveying our redemption in Christ. Above them, between the arches supporting the clerestory windows are [further frescoes of] six prophets: Moses, David, Isaiah, Jeremiah, Ezekiel, and Daniel, foretelling that same redemption. Moses is given a proleptic vision of the crucifixion by an angel.

Each Advent now at around this date thoughts of holly will ensure I make time to meditate a while, if possible beneath those frescoes, thanking God for the faith-strengthening influence the prophets have had on my pilgrimage.

I have written elsewhere about Christian transmutation of pagan practice. Sometimes I think this is to look at things through the wrong end of the telescope. For instance, the heathen sprinkling of new-born babies with holly water is so reminiscent of Christian Baptism as to suggest humanity groping blindly for the Sacrament which God would reveal in his own good time. It is as if by instinct we knew our need for it, and even guessed its form. But we could continue only to sprinkle our infants with holly water until Christ came to give us the holy water of Baptism, vivified through his Spirit.

The Mass readings for today relate the births of Samson and John the Baptist, taking me back to an earlier theme. In both cases God reverses barrenness in a married woman; an angel announces the births; there is fear on the part of the parents; both boys are to be vowed to God. But there are many important differences in the history and character of the two. These throw into sharp relief John's role as the immediate precursor of the Saviour, whose Incarnation was essential in God's saving plan. Samson's nameless mother has only partial understanding of events, her husband Manoah almost none at all. By the time he utters the *Benedictus*, the initial fear and disbelief of Zechariah and his wife Elizabeth are completely dispelled in a shared understanding of God's will and meaning. Samson's name, derived from the Hebrew for sun, is chosen by his mother; God himself chooses John's name, which means God's gracious gift. Samson does not distinguish himself spiritually and is by no means a prophet. Endowed with great physical strength, he is sexually self-indulgent, a fault that leads to his downfall. He is no martyr. John on the other hand, is not only born of priestly parentage but abandons traditional priesthood to begin the foundation of a new rite and is a prophet from the beginning. He matches physical hardihood with spiritual strength. Although chaste, he too comes to grief at the hands of an amoral woman. Thus he attains martyrdom. Samson begins to save Israel in his own time; John heralds the One coming to save all people for all time, the One of whom he would testify, 'The one who sent me to baptise with water said to me, "He on whom you see the Spirit descend and remain is the one who baptises with the Holy Spirit." And I myself have seen and have testified that this is the Son of God' (Jn 1:33). 'O Root of Jesse, which stands as an ensign for the peoples, before whom kings are silent, to whom the nations shall entreat, come and deliver us and tarry not' (Third Great *Magnificat* antiphon).

Bible Readings

Judges 13:2–25: Samson's birth is announced by an angel
Isaiah 13:22: Its time is close at hand
Isaiah 14:1: The Lord will have compassion
Isaiah 47: Behold, they are like stubble
Isaiah 49:13: Sing for joy, O heavens
Philippians 3:13: Our commonwealth is in heaven
Luke 1:5–25: Gabriel foretells the birth of John the Baptist
John 1:15–34: John the Baptist bears witness to Jesus

Intercessions

For carpenters, foresters, and those who construct sea defences; for workers in the textile industry; for ploughmen, and for sheep farmers and their flocks; for those whose surnames, or the names of the places where they live, which derive from the word holly; for all whose homes have been destroyed by fire.

Thanksgiving for places such as Regent's College grounds and Yarner Wood, and that we may preserve them for our well-being; for the maintenance of our bird sanctuaries; for a lessening of destructive emotions; thanksgiving for our churches, books, paintings and music which assist us in prayer; for those about to be baptized; thanksgiving for our own baptism; thanksgiving for the Word spoken through the prophets and for the Incarnation of Jesus and for a deeper grasp of its meaning; for greater faith; for the courage to bear stronger witness to Christ; for his compassion on our weakness.

Place of Spiritual Retreat
With Elizabeth and Zechariah as they celebrate the birth of John the Baptist with their friends, as in Luke 1

20 DECEMBER

ANGELWING BEGONIA *Begonia coccinea*

Cultivation Notes
Angelwing Begonia is cane-stemmed and a houseplant. It belongs to a group of giants among flowering evergreen types but is more compact than some, which can reach six feet if not pruned. Staking and a springtime pinching-back are recommended. The flowers appear in summer and are waxy, red, and pendulous. The shape of the leaves accounts for its household name. Avoid too much water and sun. Keep the compost moist from spring to autumn but be sparing with water in winter. To propagate, take cuttings from the plant's lower branches. Begonias are particularly susceptible to botrytis (grey mould). This can be cured by removing affected parts, changing
the compost, reducing moisture, and improving ventilation. Root rot, on the other hand, is fatal, unless you spot the problem early. If the roots prove to be mostly rotten, the plant has probably had its day. If there are sufficient firm white roots, cut away all the dead ones, and leave the plant out of its pot for a couple of days before re-potting in new compost. Keep away from direct sun and water sparingly when new growth appears.

History and Lore

The begonia family has grown to huge proportions and is difficult to sort out. Some came from India, some from the Andes, but all seem to have responded brilliantly to the hybridizer's art. An Angelwing Begonia is a lovely gift for a houseplant enthusiast, made especially personal if you have reared it yourself. I have also found that plant-lovers very much appreciate the set of instructions, background notes, and literary or biblical quotes, which I include with the gift. If space is at a premium there are four other begonias whose foliage and names make them seasonally appropriate: *B. rex* 'Merry Christmas' has yellow leaves with a broad edge of green and a centre that lightens from deep red to a pinkish-red blush; *B. rex* 'Silver queen' has silver leaves with a dark green edge and centre; *B. rex* 'Yuletide' has golden-centred leaves spreading through a pinkish-red blush and yellow to a golden edge; and the plain *Rex begonia*, which is anything but plain, has beautifully Christmassy red leaves with a broad greenish-gold border edged with a tinge of red. Watering must again be judicious and the leaves must never be wetted. *B. rex* begonias should last a couple of years and new plants can be propagated from leaf cuttings.

Towards Meditation

'In the sixth month the angel Gabriel was sent from God to a city of Galilee named Nazareth, to a virgin betrothed to a man whose name was Joseph, and of the house of David; and the virgin's name was Mary' (Lk. 1:26).

There is an ancient tradition that, before the Annunciation, Mary had already vowed herself to God in perpetual virginity, and although this is obviously not an article of faith it would perhaps explain why Joseph, traditionally an older man, should have agreed to undertake a protective and celibate marriage with her. In any case she can hardly have been hoping for a child at the time of Gabriel's visit. A pregnancy at that point would have brought disgrace on both herself and Joseph. Mary, knowing Joseph's innocence, would expect him to cast her off, as indeed he almost did. She would be a disowned, possibly homeless outcast. How much of this ran through her mind when Gabriel spoke is not ours to know. In the Old Testament angels are often unrecognized by the people they visit; they are only partially understood and sometimes cause fear. In the New Testament, Zechariah is troubled at the very sight of an angel. 'Fear fell on him,' says Luke. The old man seems pole-axed, even before Gabriel speaks to him, and his doubting response is punished by dumbness until his son is named. Mary on the other hand does not seem much frightened. Perhaps in the very economy of his language Luke intends to make it clear that her recognition and acceptance of the angel are immediate and calm. Has God already led her so deeply into contemplation that she is able to react in such a still, receptive way? She *is* troubled by the *terms* of Gabriel's greeting, but only because she cannot at first comprehend *how* they can apply to her. She ponders them rationally in the silence. Gabriel reads her mind and explains. Her response is totally different from Zechariah's. His had the flavour of, 'What you say is not possible.' Mary's conveys, '*How* will what you say be *made* possible?' She offers no argument against God's ability to make this amazing thing happen, but gently enquires how it will be so. Everything we know of Mary, the Mother of Jesus, marks her as the complete antithesis of her forebears. She does not, like Sarah, laugh at God's plan; she has no jealousy of another woman and her son, no dynastic ambitions. She stands, the perfect opposite of her ancestors whom God had castigated: 'I know you are obstinate, and your neck is an iron sinew and your forehead brass' (Is. 48:4). And so whilst Gabriel tells Mary of Elizabeth's pregnancy, we and the whole world, as St Bernard of Clairvaux so effectively puts it, wait for Mary's decision in regard to her own. Can she have known, he continues, what actually hung on her answer? Did she know that Adam, Abraham, Daniel, all the prophets, and all of us await it? Did she know that our salvation depended upon it? God knew of course, 'Therefore the Lord himself will give you a sign. Behold, a young woman shall conceive and bear a son, and shall call his name Immanuel, which means God is with us' (Is. 7:14).

Given Mary's circumstances, and whatever the answers to Bernard's questions, her *fiat mihi*, despite its familiarity to us now, is eternally stunning. She was no passive instrument but accepted God as Master of the future and made the act of perfect compliance with his will to effect our freedom through the redemptive incarnation of his Son. She spoke the word and received the Word.

But Jesus was Mary's son in the flesh as well. Maisie Ward, in her *Splendour of the Rosary*, mentions the medieval vision of Sister Eulalia, during which Mary, described as 'the Mother of all Nature', tells of the deep thrill of joy she feels when we linger on the words 'the Lord is with thee' in our repetitions of the angelic salutation. Then it seems to her that Jesus is within her even as he was during his preparation to come into the world to save sinners. She knew unutterable bliss at the time, and remembers it whenever the *Dominus tecum* is said with proper attention. The historicity of the vision may be doubtful, but it enshrines an insight that has profoundly affected my own praying of the Hail Mary. In the country, three times daily, the village church across the road sends the notes of the *Angelus* resounding through our house and garden, thus punctuating all activity with thoughts of the Annunciation. In town, the urgent little bell of our parish church is heard twice a day amid the roar of central London. Its small and poignant voice is in many ways more effective than that of its big country cousin, with whose loud sonority no human clamour or traffic noise is there to argue. On Saturdays in town the *Angelus* is rung at noon, immediately after Mass; this means we repeat the *Dominus tecum* three times, while Christ is still present in us through the Holy Communion just made. These occasions are therefore very special indeed.

On 20 December two favourite paintings of the Annunciation come to mind. Both are frescoes: the first, and the greater, is that of Fra Angelico; the second is the one already mentioned, in the apse of our parish church, by an unknown late nineteenth-century artist. The first is also more suitable for today, seeming to catch a moment before Mary's *fiat*. The second strikes me as a portrayal of the moments immediately following that event. March 25th will be the occasion for a meditative comparison between the two frescoes. There is no time today. Martha's voice has become insistent. And so I close with a Hail Mary and offer thanks for Mary's part in enabling us to pray the fourth Great Advent *Magnificat* antiphon, *O Clavis David*, 'O Key of David that opens and no man closes, and shuts and no man opens, come to lead out the captive from the prison, and he who sits in darkness and the shadow of death.'

Bible Readings
Isaiah 48:1–11: I know you to be obstinate
Isaiah 7:10–14: The Lord himself will give you a sign
Jeremiah 23:5–6: Behold the days are coming
Luke 1:5–25: How shall I know this, for I am an old man?
Luke 1:26–38: Let it be with me according to your word

Intercessions
For all horticulturists and house-plant enthusiasts; for the peoples of India and the Andes; for the disowned, homeless, and outcast and that in our

seasonal exchange of gifts we shall not forget them; for prisoners whether through crime or injustice; for prison chaplains and all who work in the prison service.

For the souls in purgatory; for those who find the circumstances of their lives difficult to bear.

Thanksgiving for the angels, and for church bells and their messages; that we may find a proper balance between 'Martha' and 'Mary' in the expression of our Christian living; for perseverance in spiritual aridity and thanksgiving for the privileged moments in prayer; that following Our Lady's example we may be still in prayer, our hearts open to receive the Lord in humble compliance with his will.

Place of Spiritual Retreat
With Our Lady, journeying to visit Elizabeth, as in Luke 1. (Mary has no companion in the biblical account, but many artists have depicted her with one. Metaphorically at any rate, we should all go with her.)

21 DECEMBER

SOWBREAD *Cyclamen*

Cultivation Notes
Autumn-flowering sowbread is the only type of wild cyclamen in Britain, but the many cultivated varieties provide pleasure almost all year round. For sweet scent in summer plant *C. europaeum*; for crowns of pink or white flowers in autumn, *C. hederifolium* is the usual choice; and in winter the small rosy jewels of early *C. orbiculatum* will shine bravely in the Christmas garden. All prefer a dry place, partial shade, and lime in the soil. Plant the corms several centimetres deep. Cyclamen is perennial and naturalizes easily. At fruiting time the seed-case stalk lies on the ground in a spring-like coil and then eventually buries the seed in the ground. Ants can move the seeds and plant them in rock or wall crevices, a fact that evokes, 'O my dove, in the clefts of the rock, in the covert of the cliff, let me see your face, let me hear your voice, for your voice is sweet, and your face is comely' (Song 2:14).

C. persiculum decora is lovely as a Christmas house-plant with deep pink flowers and silver, green-centred leaves. In autumn buy a plant that has plenty of closed buds. It will enjoy a fairly cool windowsill out of direct sunlight, should bloom for several months, and can be kept for the following winter. When flowering is over reduce already careful watering and feeding. Place the pot on its side and keep dry until summer. Then re-pot in new compost to half the depth of the pot. Keep cool and well lit and water sparingly.

History and Lore

The name *Cyclamen* is probably from the Greek *cyclos*, meaning a circle, because of the spiralling fruit stalks. Linnaeus claims that the common name, sowbread, comes from the fact that it was the main food of the wild boar in Sicily! To humans it is a drastic purgative, and although a homeopathic tincture is made from the corm to treat migraine, the plant is best avoided in domestic medicinal use.

Cyclamen bravely withstands adverse weather. Two years ago Advent imprisonment in London was cheered by a pink cyclamen growing in the courtyard flowerbed of our apartment block. It had appeared in mid-autumn and was joined in late October by a white relation. The season was mild, but November brought gales and rain. Well-established 'Pink' was hardly affected. 'White' was dashed, but not fatally. Passing by at least twice a day, I marked their state of health, hoping they would still be there on 21 December. They were, although 'White' was struggling.

I was, and remain, grateful for these two courageous little cyclamen, which gave me perhaps greater pleasure than a carpet of their like would have done in a country garden. What is more, each day that Advent they served to remind me of God's providence, and that plants and people need the right conditions for health and growth: 'They shall feed along the ways, on all bare heights shall be their pasture; they shall not hunger or thirst, neither a scorching wind nor sun shall smite them' (Is. 49:9b–10a). And there is the famous text from the Song of Solomon (2:8–14), normally associated with spring, but which for me that Advent yielded a new significance: 'Arise my love ...'. And Mary sets out to visit Elizabeth; the winter that is past is the one eternally ended by the incarnation; the little cyclamen are the flowers that appear; the time for Mary to sing *Magnificat* has come. There is a tradition that the small blood-red splash in the centre of the cyclamen flower dropped from Mary's heart when it was pierced by the sword of Simeon's prophecy. But today I prefer to focus on the fact that, in *The Language of Flowers*, the brave cyclamen represents diffidence. These characteristics remind me of Elizabeth, who is also brave, as well as diffident in the sense of being retiring and modest. I will think of her especially today.

Towards Meditation

'They were both righteous before God, walking in all the commandments and ordinances' (Lk. 1:6).

Thus Luke introduces the parents of John the Baptist. When in her 'old age' Elizabeth conceives, she regards it as the divine lifting of a social stigma. And yet she hides herself for five months, until neither she nor anyone else can doubt her condition. Until then she would probably have been disbelieved and an object of derision. Luke's 'advanced in years' need not necessarily mean that she was ancient. In her own historical setting, she need only have been in her fifties to be described as old. But whether she was fifty or eighty, the prospect of childbirth cannot have been easy to face. I imagine she spent a great deal of time in prayer as she made the usual antenatal preparations. Yet again, by not saying much, Luke seems to convey an atmosphere, this time of gravely serene resignation. There is none of Sarah's 'well fancy that' laughter here. Elizabeth knows the heavy responsibility her child will bear, its importance far exceeding that of Isaac. Apart from one remark, there is silence until Mary's arrival. Then Elizabeth and the baby within her are filled with the Holy Spirit and immediately recognize Mary as carrying the Son of God, the long-promised Holy One of Israel. Then from the hitherto almost taciturn Elizabeth is wrung the 'loud cry' of recognition and welcome. But buried in her remarkable words there is a deep modesty and lack of self-importance: 'And why is this granted me, that the mother of my Lord should come to me?' How amazing it must have been for such a woman. She knew her Scriptures, and Luke makes it clear that Zechariah, despite his temporary dumbness, has shared with her his knowledge that their own son is to herald the Messiah. And now, here in front of her *is* that Messiah hidden in the flesh of her own kinswoman.

Yet again I am reminded of two paintings. The first is in the *Hastings Book of Hours*, and the second is a fresco in the apse of our parish church, opposite the *Annunciation* mentioned yesterday. The first shows a middle-aged, healthily plump Elizabeth, who seems to have run from her house in order to honour her visitor. A much older Zechariah is hobbling up, some distance behind his wife, and if a man can be painted to look dumb, he looks dumb! The domesticity of the scene gives it truth. The apse fresco, on the other hand, depicts a much older and frail Elizabeth, at a later moment during the arrival of Mary. No third figure of Zechariah distracts the eye from Mary and her cousin. Both 'Elizabeths' express profound respect for Mary and a most earnest need for confirmation and reassurance from her. The 'apse Elizabeth' is kneeling but is about to be raised by Mary, whose hands rest with gentle firmness on the older woman's arms. One can almost feel, with her, Elizabeth's fragile, thin, and aged bones beneath the poor cloth of her robe. Compassion streams from Our Lady here. This is not all by any means, and both pictures will reward deeper consideration on the Feast of the Visitation (31 May). I am reminded now that the Visitation is not merely a meeting; it lasts three months. If Luke's dates are accurate, Mary stays with Elizabeth almost until the birth of John. But today concern is with the earth-shattering exchanges he records as taking place between Mary and Elizabeth, and with the identity of their unborn babies.

In Book 2 of his *Commentary on Saint Luke's Gospel*, St Ambrose of Milan (339–97) draws attention to a very important aspect of the mystery of the Visitation. Everyone who has believed, he says, both conceives the Word and recognizes his (God's) works. And so before going Christmas shopping, and of course inspecting the cyclamen, I again conclude with a Hail Mary and the fifth Great *Magnificat* antiphon, *O Oriens*: 'O Day-Star, Splendour of everlasting light and Sun of Justice: come to illumine those who sit in darkness and the shadow of death.'

Note: Going into Mass two days before Christmas in the year of the cyclamen described above, I encountered Michael, our green-fingered Master of Ceremonies, planting up the tubs outside church with cyclamen and related primulas. On Saint Stephen's day, courtyard and church cyclamen survived the sudden plunge in temperature and attendant snow. In the New Year, 'White' looked happier than 'Pink'. On Epiphany however, I was horrified and almost wept to see from our sitting room window that the landlord's 'gardeners' were busy grubbing up everything that had been growing round the edge of the flowerbed. 'My' cyclamen were no more. Happily, the church ones lived on, Michael having more sensitivity and knowledge of what he is about, than our meddling destroyers in the courtyard. If I could believe they had taken the cyclamen to plant in their own gardens, their vandalism would have been easier to forgive, but as someone once said, 'You must not blame people for not knowing what they do not know.' Well, and I am delighted to report it, someone must have redressed the ignorance of the 'meddlers', or the cyclamen managed to cast seed when they dug it up, because as I write, there is quite a colony of cyclamen where 'Pink' and 'White' first appeared.

Bible Readings
Song of Solomon 2:8–14: Arise my love, my fair one and come away
Song of Solomon 2:14: O my dove in the clefts of the rock
Isaiah 49:9b–12: Neither scorching wind nor sun shall smite them
Luke 1:5–7, 24, 39–45: He looked upon me to take away my reproach among men; Elizabeth was filled with the Holy Spirit

Intercessions
Thanksgiving for the way in which plants naturalize, especially for those whose flowers cheer our winters; for church gardeners, florists, sacristans, and all who serve at Mass; thanksgiving for God's providence and that we may co-operate with him in the establishment of a more just world; that we may *follow* Elizabeth's example, and that this Christmas her astonished joy may live anew in us; that the Lord will visit and free us from every trace of sin; that he may bring the dead into unquenchable light.

Place of Spiritual Retreat
With Elizabeth as she prepares for the birth of John, before, during, and after the Visitation

22 DECEMBER

VIRGIN'S BOWER *Clematis*; traveller's joy; old man's beard

Cultivation Notes
The wild clematis is perhaps too rampant for the garden. However, its symbolism can be brought to mind by planting one of its cultivated climbing relatives. If your soil is not naturally limy dig in some lime rubble at planting time and make sure the roots are in shade. *C. flammula* (little flame or banner) is a deciduous native of southern Europe and was introduced to Britain towards the end of the sixteenth century. Its popular name is Fragrant Virgin's Bower and it produces a mass of gently almond-scented white flowers in August, which is important because of the feasts of the Assumption and of the Queenship of Mary. It grows up to fifteen feet, and the mature shrub tends to make a top-heavy confusion while the stems remain bare, so under-planting will be advisable. *C. flammula* will grow into established trees and shrubs. If support needs to be provided it should be remembered that clematis, being a leaf-stalk climber, cannot grasp

thick things. Second choice would be the hybrid *C. x violacea rubro-marginata*. This also flowers in August and has fragrant white blooms edged with pink.

History and Lore

Clematis is thought to derive from the Greek *klema*, meaning 'twig' or 'vine shoot'. The deciduous and perennial *Clematis vitalba* is the 'old man's beard' of British hedgerows. It must have been so named because of the feathery cloud of silver-grey fruit, borne on stems that loop and twist their way to the top of the host plant. Attractive to bees and hoverflies, this fruit often lasts well into winter. In France it is known as *l'herbe aux gueux* (beggars' weed), because the plant can have a blistering effect and beggars used it to simulate sores. In pre-Reformation England the name 'Virgin's bower' marked the legend that it had sheltered Mary on her various journeys. John Gerard, in *The Herball* (1597), was responsible for changing this. Having seen it, 'decking and adorning waies and hedges, where people travell [...] thereupon I have named it Traveller's Joy.' This is one example of early Protestant de-Marianization of plant names. However, to a Catholic who knows the original legend, 'Traveller's joy' will have much the same connotation as 'Virgin's bower'. And the bearded old man has to be Saint Joseph.

Filial love and safety are the meanings given to clematis in *The Language of Flowers*. The first reminds us that Jesus, in his death agony, lovingly commended his mother to the care of John the Evangelist. I will dwell awhile on this before turning to the second meaning and allowing it and the domestic names of clematis to stimulate further reflection on Mary's visit to Elizabeth.

Towards Meditation

'Lift up your heads, O gates! and be lifted up, O ancient doors! that the King of glory may come in. ... Who is this King of glory? The Lord of hosts, he is the King of glory' (Ps. 24:7, 10).

Today the gates of the psalm become the door lintel of Elizabeth's house as Mary enters beneath it, and in sheltering her, that house becomes 'the fragrant Virgin's Bower'. When Luke tells us that Mary arose in haste to go into the hill country, he conjures the urgency familiar to all of us who, like Mary, have dropped everything and made that sudden journey when even joyful family matters are so complex that we cannot stay away. Even husbands and fiancés must be left to fend for themselves and explanations given later. But our joy and urgency on these occasions bear no comparison with those of this traveller. She knows that the Son of God is in her womb and must confirm this as soon as possible to Elizabeth. Not only that, but Elizabeth needs the physical care and moral support of her young kinswoman. Mary's journey, in its spiritual and practical motivation, shows her obedience to the two greatest commandments, which her son would later emphasize: 'Love God and your neighbour as yourself.'

I like to think that the words of the *Magnificat* formed in Mary's heart as she journeyed. She would almost certainly have been familiar with the story of Samuel's birth and with the words of his mother's song of thanksgiving. Perhaps Mary searched her store of scriptural knowledge for a hymn that would approximate to her own feeling. This is a natural impulse in spiritual people. Whether or not she thought comparatively of Hannah's case and her own is not our business, but it may prove instructive for us to ponder the difference between them. Hannah is constantly provoked by Peninnah, her husband's other – child-bearing – wife, who used 'to irritate her, because the Lord had closed her womb' (1 Sam. 1:6), and her prayers for a son are coloured with a desperate desire to stop being humiliated and to 'get her own back' on her tormentor. When she makes the vow to give any such son to God, it is a child-like attempt to bargain with him. Hannah's outward demeanour at prayer so lacks control that Eli thinks she is drunk. There is no angel involved, and when God remembers her prayer and promise, Samuel is conceived in the natural way, and his name is chosen by his mother. Hannah keeps her promise and dedicates him to God, but the feelings and events in her story are of the natural order.

Mary is betrothed to a man whose only wife she will be; she is not involved in some squalid domestic competition with another woman for Joseph's respect and gratitude; she has not prayed for a child; she is honoured by an archangel, and throughout his visit her mien is serene and rational. Mary is told the divinely-chosen name she must give to her child. Hers not to make promises about his destiny. He cannot be promised to God as were Samson and Samuel, for he *is* God. She does not even mention the fear of worldly humiliation. Hers is complete humility. Her promise is also a prayer, but it has no strings attached. 'Behold the handmaid of the Lord. Let it be with me according to your word' (Lk. 1:38). She will keep it throughout Christ's childhood, ministry, death, resurrection, and ascension. She will keep it on the day of Pentecost. She has kept it ever since and keeps it still. Of all women she is the most blessed, not only because of her virginity; not only, as The Venerable Bede (673–735) remarks in his *Commentary on Luke*, because the blessings attendant on the reversal of Eve's fall spring from her; and not only because of her perfect compliance with God's will, which can almost be described as 'superhuman'. Perhaps most importantly, she is the most blessed because the conception of Christ was effected by God's action through his Holy Spirit. It was a totally supernatural event.

I have heard it said that Mary's *Magnificat* was merely her own poorly remembered copy of Hannah's song, and even that Luke put the words into her mouth for the sake of scriptural continuity and dramatic, literary effect. I do not accept either view. Rather, Hannah's song is an imperfect type of Mary's. It is like a photograph in a darkroom tray, showing partial definition of contours that will change, emphases that will shift when the full picture finally emerges in the *Magnificat*. Hannah's terminology and tone belong firmly in her own time, and to the Old Covenant; Mary's most definitely to all time, and to the New.

Hannah triumphs in the Lord, Mary extols him. Hannah says her strength is 'exalted'. There is no mention of her lowliness or servantship in relation to God. Mary's *spirit* rejoices, for her holy and mighty God 'has regarded the low estate of his handmaiden', and she glimpses with wonder her own part in the divine plan: 'from henceforth all generations shall call me blessed'. Hannah is firmly locked in her own situation and tradition. She is grateful for salvation from barrenness, and she derides her enemies. God is holy, but is set in competition with the false gods of the heathen: 'There is no rock like our God.' It is almost childlike again: 'My Dad's stronger than your Dad.' Hannah speaks of revenge and judgement, and it is hard to believe she is not addressing her former rival. 'Talk no more so very proudly, let not arrogance come from your mouth'; 'actions are weighed'; 'the adversaries of the Lord shall be broken to pieces'; and 'the Lord will judge the ends of the earth'. She speaks of seats of honour, the trappings of relative social position. The poor will be raised up to temporal relief from want, but by a mighty warrior God who is concerned to give strength to his king, and to exalt the power of his anointed. We may put a prophetic gloss on Hannah's words, but I doubt she had any long-term vision of the future.

Mary, on the other hand, speaks of God's mercy on those who fear him. She refers to it twice. And it is a mercy that stretches throughout history, 'from generation to generation'. She, I believe, is speaking of the mighty, the rich, and the poor throughout time. And the hungry who come are fed spiritually as well as physically. The rejected ones are not violently cut off but simply 'sent empty away'. There is sadness for these lost ones in Mary's phrase, not vengefulness against them. And because God has remembered his mercy, salvation is open to all. In her final words, Mary places the forthcoming incarnation as the most important event in the whole of time, going back in the past to Abraham, and forward to the future, 'and his posterity for ever'.

At the Annunciation God pulled his people one huge step along the path to redemption, and in Mary's mouth at the Visitation God offers us the chance of a wider, deeper understanding of himself and his action up to that point and beyond. If Mary did not understand it fully at the time the Spirit spoke through her, I find it hard to believe that she did not later perfectly well know the significance of the difference between Hannah's song and her own. And so, as Christmas approaches, the *Magnificat*, in its deep spirituality, its earthly universality, and its application to eternity, offers to every receptive soul a wonderful strengthening of faith, hope, and love. It is therefore most appropriately enclosed, at Vespers today, by the sixth great Advent antiphon, *O Rex gentium*: 'O King whom all the peoples desire, you are the cornerstone which makes all one. O come and save man whom you made from clay.'

Bible Readings
1 Samuel 1:24–8: Hannah gives Samuel to the Lord
1 Samuel 2:1–10: Hannah's song
Psalm 27: The Lord is my light and my salvation
Isaiah 49:14–50: God compares himself with a mother
Micah 5:4–5: They will live secure
Haggai 2:6–9: The new glory of this temple
Luke 1:46–56: Mary's song

Intercessions
For beggars; for the poor and homeless and those for whom travelling is a way of life; for pregnant women and the safety of those we love and for whom we are responsible.

For greater love and wisdom within families; for those who will spend Christmas travelling and away from home; for an end to arrogance, materialistic self-seeking, derision, and vengefulness.

Thanksgiving for Our Lady's promise, and for her protection of us; that we may mark her example in our prayer; thanksgiving for God's mercy; that we may pay deeper attention to the Liturgy of the Word; and that our Christmas joy may light up the darkness of the world around us.

Place of Spiritual Retreat
In the vicinity of Elizabeth's house during the Visitation

23 DECEMBER

OUR LADY'S BEDSTRAW *Galium verum*; cheese rennet; maid-hair

Cultivation Notes
Our Lady's bedstraw is a hardy perennial and likes dry well-drained soil. It grows up to three feet and flowers in July and August. It has needle-like leaves and golden heads of four-petalled blooms. Sow ripe seed in summer or propagate by division in autumn or early spring.

History and Lore
Galium most probably comes from the Greek *gala*, meaning milk. It is native to Britain and was formerly used as a substitute for rennet to coagulate milk in the cheese-making process. The foliage yields a yellow dye, and this was used in the colouring of cheese and butter. When the plant is dried it smells pleasantly of new-mown hay, and it is said to discourage fleas. No wonder it was used for loose bedding and mattress stuffing. Nowadays, the symbolism of its name is sufficient to warrant a place in the garden and in flower arrangements. For the best results, cut and dry while the plant is in flower.

At home today in my garden workshop, as I select some dried Our Lady's Bedstraw to put in the crib tomorrow, it will suggest two threads for meditation. One concerns Elizabeth's pregnancy, from Mary's arrival to the birth and naming of John the Baptist, and the other 'the milk of the Word'.

Towards Meditation

'Behold I will send you Elijah the prophet before the great and terrible day of the Lord comes' (Mal. 4:5).

Jesus alludes to this verse of Malachi when he confirms the identity of John the Baptist in Matthew 11:14. And all four Gospels make the *connection* between John and Elijah – Matthew, Mark, and Luke in their first chapters and John in his third. But it is Luke to whom we are indebted for the precious details of the '*birth* narratives'. How much we should have lacked without Luke. And imagine Lauds without the *Benedictus*, Vespers without the *Magnificat*, or Compline without the *Nunc Dimittis*, not to mention the music settings of these canticles, which would never have been written. These are just three of the reasons why Luke is my favourite synoptic evangelist. At this time of year my Bible falls open naturally at his first chapter and obliges me today as, led by Our Lady's Bedstraw, I turn to verse 56: 'And Mary remained with her about three months.'

For any pregnant woman in ordinary circumstances, the physical and emotional support of a beloved female relative can be a tremendous consolation. But these were no ordinary circumstances, and the caring helper was the most extraordinary female in creation. Elizabeth, alone among women, has the mother of her Lord as antenatal nurse. Bedstraw makes me think of the palliasses on which they may have slept. Anyone who has experienced the immobility and discomfort of later pregnancy will easily imagine Elizabeth's gratitude as Mary helped her to lie down at night and get up each morning. But I have absolutely no doubt that to Mary and Elizabeth, and indeed to Zechariah, the spiritual significance of what was happening to them was of paramount importance. All three, because of their background and the fact that Zechariah was a priest, would have been steeped in the law and prophecies of the Old Covenant, and in the genealogy of their families. During the months of Mary's stay, it is hard to believe that they did not re-read and discuss these things, Zechariah communicating by sign language and writing; impossible to think that they did not pray, privately and together over the texts. If they considered Isaiah 51, they must have known that the prophet speaks of the salvation of Sion by the son Mary will soon bear. And if these God-chosen, God-inspired people saw any political relevance to their own time in the prediction, it would have been of secondary importance. But prophecy is a prism. What you see depends on how you turn it to the light. And today, holding this particular jewel of Isaiah's in the palm of my hand, I see

Mary, and even Elizabeth: 'He will comfort all her waste places, he will make her wilderness like Eden, her desert like the garden of the Lord. Joy and gladness will be found in her, thanksgiving and the voice of song' (Is. 51:3).

Luke implies that Zechariah's muteness was a punishment for doubting God. But *hysterical aphonia*, that is the state of being dumbstruck by shock, is now a recognized medical condition. Zechariah had a bad case of it, caused not only by actually seeing an angel but by what the angel said. He was humble and holy; he had believed all his life that the Messiah would come; but the idea that he and his wife could have anything closely to do with his coming was simply too much. At the naming of John the Baptist, it is not absolutely clear whether Elizabeth knows John's name because Zechariah has previously informed her, or because she is divinely inspired at the moment. But during the previous three months he would have communicated with Mary and Elizabeth through sign language and writing on tablets, and he would have contemplated them as they went about their daily round. For five months before Mary came he had been silent, and his wife had stayed hidden. The increased comprehension and belief wrought in Elizabeth and Zechariah by Mary's presence is unknown and incalculable. And yet Zechariah remains speechless until after she has gone. Surely by now the purpose and meaning of his silence has deepened. His time spent with the mothers of Jesus and John constitutes the silent retreat to end all silent retreats. At the naming of John, Elizabeth, no longer hidden or diffident, speaks up bravely, and Zechariah, after writing the name John on the tablet, at last comes out of retreat and gives utterance to that glorious blueprint of salvation history, the *Benedictus*. In silence he has come to understand the Advent of the Word, and only now does the Spirit inspire his human voice to express that Advent and its significance in human words.

And so, eventually, to the second thread suggested by today's plant, namely, the milk of the Word: 'Like newborn infants, long for the pure, spiritual milk' (1 Pet. 2:2). Mary, Elizabeth, and Zechariah certainly did. Hippolytus (died 235) elaborates on Peter's text in chapter 9 of his *Treatise Against the Heresy of Noetus*. We must, he says, look at things as God has chosen to reveal them in Scripture. For prior to the beginning of the revelation within it, the Word had only been visible to God. Now, with the Incarnation, the world will see him too and be saved. 'The Word is the mind of God shown forth as his Son.' This is the God of the law and the prophets, who spoke by the Holy Spirit and proclaimed God's purpose and will. In Scripture we find continual and enduring evidence of God's desire that we should believe and that we should glorify his Son, and of his will to bestow his Holy Spirit. Then let us believe in him, let us glorify him, and let us receive him: '*O Emmanuel*, O God with us, our King and Law-giver; whom all peoples await, and their salvation, come and save us, Lord, our God' (seventh great *Magnificat* antiphon).

Bible Readings

Isaiah 9:6–7: For to us a child is born, to us a son is given
Isaiah 35:10: They shall obtain joy and gladness
Isaiah 51:1–11: He will make her wilderness like Eden; the just one is near
Jeremiah 29:11–13: I know the plans I have for you
Jeremiah 30:21–2: A ruler shall appear, and of themselves
Malachi 3 and 4: Behold I send my messenger to prepare the way
1 Peter 2:2: Like newborn infants, long for the pure, spiritual milk, that by
    it you may grow into salvation
Luke 1:57–66: The birth and naming of John the Baptist
Luke 21:28: Your liberation is near at hand
John 1:1–5: In him was life

Intercessions

For dairy workers and bedding manufacturers; for nursing mothers, midwives, and obstetricians; for the dumb and those with communication difficulties; for courage to speak up for our beliefs; for an increase in faith in a world weighed down with unbelief; for greater fervour in preaching and listening to the Word; for an end to self-seeking and pride.

Thanksgiving for the Scriptures, for the liturgy, and for the music that assists our prayer.

Place of Spiritual Retreat

Amongst the friends of Elizabeth and Zechariah celebrating the birth and naming of John the Baptist

CHRISTMAS EVE

NORWAY SPRUCE *Picea abies*; Christmas tree

Cultivation Notes

A rooted tree planted out after the festivities may grow to 50 feet and spread for 20, so even if you have the space it will be wise to consider whether it will later block light from windows or have an adverse effect on nearby plants. Your own age could determine whether you live to see it produce cones. Having been told that this may not happen for up to 35 years, I was surprised when my tree, five foot at planting, produced cones only five years later. The Norway spruce has a rather shallow root system, so guard against wind and waterlogged soil.

History and Lore

The word spruce comes from German *Sprossen* (young shoots). *Sprossen bier* came into English as pruce-beer, later Prussian beer. The tree is not considered native to Britain, and although it did grow here before the last ice age, it was not reintroduced until about 1500. It is most important in building and carpentry and in the manufacture of packing cases, pit props, telegraph poles, chipboard, and paper pulp. The timber is sometimes known as 'violin wood' because of its use in making soundboards to transmit vibrations from strings to the wood of the sides and back of the instrument.

Norway spruce is of course best known as the Christmas tree, and it is a rare Londoner who does not know and appreciate that the tree that stands in Trafalgar Square at Christmastide is sent by the people of Norway in commemoration of war-time solidarity between the two countries.

The subject of tree dressing takes us into the pagan past. Certainly, there is evidence that the practice of bringing decorated greenery into our dwellings at the winter solstice dates back to the Iron Age. There is however, a biblical precedent for the use of evergreens as decoration, at least in church. 'The glory of Lebanon shall come to you, the cypress, the plane, and the pine, to beautify the place of my sanctuary' (Is. 60:13). This text satisfyingly quells any worries about paganism and supports one of the major premises of these pages: if you bring a branch into your house for the sake of mere superstitious ritual it is worse than useless; if you do it for God it is a form of prayer.

The prototype of the first Christmas tree in England is supposed to have been an evergreen branch decorated with golden oranges and almonds, for the royal children's party in 1821. Another twenty years were to pass before Prince Albert and Queen Victoria brought his native custom to life in Windsor Castle, when they hung lights and decorations on a tree there. The habit must have been taken up widely and rapidly, for in 1850 we find Dickens referring to the Christmas tree as 'the new German toy'. He had published 'A Christmas Carol' in 1843, and his reaction seems incongruously 'Bah! Humbug!' for a man widely accepted as having created our modern image of Christmas tradition and conviviality. Perhaps he resented Albert's treading on his territory. And he was very wrong about the newness of the Christmas tree. The Prince Consort could no doubt have told him the legend of St Boniface, the Devonian monk who left Crediton around 719 to evangelize Germany. The story goes that one day whilst on his travels he came upon an oak tree that had been the scene of pagan human sacrifice. Boniface* symbolically cut down the tree, and as it fell a little fir tree began to grow in its place. The saint subsequently used the miracle as a metaphor in his preaching. Some time later a legend arose, also in Germany, that as the cattle bowed their heads on Christmas Eve, the forest trees put out green shoots at the same time. After that, evergreens, particularly fir trees, were taken into houses and called Christmas trees, but decoration of them apparently only began to take hold after about 1530. Another German legend holds that one frosty Christmas Eve, Martin Luther was so moved by the seemingly millions of stars in the sky that he placed lighted candles on a fir tree to symbolize the light of the Incarnation in Bethlehem.

For many years it was customary to decorate the trees where they grew and not to bring them indoors. Later, greenery was used to decorate the outside of houses. Stowe's *Survey of London* (1598) tells us 'that against the feast of Christmas everyman's house, as also their parish churches, were decked with holme, ivy, bayes, and whatsoever the season of the year afforded to be green'. This outdoor adornment continues in squares and village greens throughout Britain, although most of them go up even before Advent has begun, and I am afraid this exposes commercial rather than religious motivation. In south-west France almost every house and shop has a decorated tree or fir branch outside its front door or drive entrance. Until recently trees indoors were uncommon, and their

---

* St Boniface seems to have been a plantsman; there is evidence in extant correspondence in which he is asked to send back certain plants from the Continent.

decoration was a rather paltry, half-hearted affair. Gradually though, French children would be brought into the houses of their British expatriate neighbours on Christmas Eve, to admire *le sapin anglais*. Very soon the French succumbed to its magic, so that now in the weeks before Christmas French *hypermarchés* are banked high with the familiar baubles, garlands, and gewgaws. There are cribs, stars, and angels, in greater profusion and variety than you would find even in London stores. (This is strange since declining Mass attendance and shortage of priests are even greater problems for the Church in France than they are in Britain.) There is also, as in Britain, a tremendous range of deceptively magnificent artificial trees.

When I was a child, a *pretend* tree was 'not quite the ticket' – an expression I suspect derives from 'not quite etiquette'. My mother rebelled against the taboo and moaned about the impossibility of getting rid of 'real needles' afterwards: 'You two won't be on your knees *then*, will you!' But every year my father and I united against her; every year we prevailed; and every year she gave in with good humour. I am sure she secretly agreed with us. There *is* something pathetically soulless about an artificial tree that, deep down, even my practical, overworked mother had to acknowledge. Then there were the metal clip-on candle-holders that my father had brought back after the war. (They were German and had somehow found their way into the wardroom of his minesweeper.) In the interests of safety they and the real candles they held were eventually replaced by electric *fairy lights*. However pretty these were, they could not recreate the aura of those early Christmases when the tree, its branches warmed by natural flame, would release into the room the most glorious scent of pine. This is the smell that evokes Christmas for me above all others, even though it does so now only through the power of memory.

During the time when my husband and I ran Christmas house-parties in France, the collection of greenery from the pine-woods on Christmas Eve afternoon was one of the most popular activities among our guests. After they had tramped off, I would bring out the decorations and spread them on the library floor. On their return, seemingly with half a forest, the guests, fortified with seasonal refreshments, would decorate the room, its overlooking gallery, and finally, the tree. After a rest we would reassemble in the now dark library, someone would play the portable organ and we would have our house carol service. During this the crib would be blessed and the tree lights switched on. Then, after a simple sustaining supper, there would be another rest until the cars arrived to take everyone to

Midnight Mass in the medieval fortress town two kilometres away. They were happy and fulfilling times.

Towards Meditation

'Rouse yourself, rouse yourself, stand up O Jerusalem. Hark, your watchmen lift up their voice, together they sing for joy; for eye to eye they see the return of the Lord to Zion. Break forth together in singing, you waste places of Jerusalem' (Is. 51:17; 52:8–9a).

Today is especially the day for answering Isaiah's call, both spiritually and practically. However few the guests at tomorrow's feast, and however well I have prepared, there are always those culinary tasks that family tradition dictates must be left for today. As I perform them, I am doing exactly as my mother, grandmother, great-grandmother, and great-aunt did before me. An early start is essential and time must be allowed at least for the Office Readings. Here I find St Augustine, in his *Sermon 185*, 'Truth sprang from the earth', also telling me to wake up. It was, he says, for all of us that God was made man. We are to awake from sleep and Christ will give us light. We could not have come to life again, had he not come to die our death. Peace on earth can spring only from Truth coming out of the earth and being born of flesh. Christ, the Word, born of a virgin, is that Truth and the Light. Thus fortified I go about my work.

Wherever I am, the turning on of the tree lights is for me the moment when Advent ends. It is the moment when I offer a prayer for absent loved ones, alive and dead, and when I give thanks for the Christmases they made for me, or that I shared with them. When did I first appreciate the symbolism of the lighted tree and the bright star? 'Christmas is for children': so runs the cliché. But 'unless you become as little children, you shall not enter the kingdom of heaven'. And if we take heed of Our Lord's warning, we must surely realize that it is for us all, particularly for those who are blind to its light. There was a Christmas Eve (during parental opposition to my Catholic conversion) when I had insisted on watching a televised Mass by the light of the tree alone. My father exercised his considerable wit at the expense of vestments, incense, and church Latin. A fierce and noisy argument broke out, during which we did not notice the end of the Mass, or the beginning of the Nativity play that followed it. Suddenly the voice of a male child cut across our discord with the simple imperative, 'Look at that bright light.' His tone conveyed an awestruck, almost peremptory urgency, totally devoid of artifice or sentimentality. It won our silence, and we turned to the screen. There stood the boy shepherd, gazing up at the distant star. And there stood we, our anger, fear and recrimination all vanquished in the utter purity and honesty of the moment. Our views on religion would always differ, but we were never again acrimonious about denomination. Every Christmas Eve when the tree lights are turned on, I hear that boy's voice. And at every Midnight Mass I feel to my depths the truth of Isaiah's words, 'the people who walked in darkness have seen a great light; those who dwell in a land of deep darkness, on them has light shined' (Is. 9:2). And as Zechariah predicted, the 'dawn from on high' has broken upon us. Jesus Emmanuel – God is with us.

Bible Readings
Psalm 96: All the trees of the wood shout for joy
Isaiah 4:2: On that day the plant the Lord has grown
Isaiah 9:1–7: The people that walked in darkness have seen a great light
Isaiah 11:1–2: A shoot shall spring from the stock of Jesse
Isaiah 51:17; 52:7–10: The Good News is brought to Jerusalem
Isaiah 61:11: As a garden causes what is sown in it to spring up
Matthew 1:18–25: Joseph, son of David, do not be afraid
Luke 1:67–79: Zechariah was filled with the Holy Spirit
Luke 2:1–14: There were shepherds out in the fields, keeping watch over their flock by night

Intercessions
For the peoples of Norway and Germany; for those who work in industries where spruce is used; for violin makers, orchestral and solo string players, choristers and church musicians; for children and teachers involved in Nativity plays; for children everywhere, particularly the sick, homeless, and starving; for parents and children who are estranged; for absent friends and relations; for those close to us who work unstintingly, and make sacrifices to give us a happy Christmas; for those whose wounded, scarred experience puts the joy of Christmas beyond their reach; that amid the glitter and tinsel, we may not lose sight of the true meaning of Christmas and may find time to ponder it.

Place of Spiritual Retreat
With the shepherds in the fields, as in Luke 2

CHRISTMASTIDE

CHRISTMAS DAY

CHRISTMAS ROSE *Helleborus niger*; Christmas bloom, Holy Night rose

Cultivation Note

The leaves of this well-known perennial rise from the roots, which it does not like to have disturbed. It grows well in the shade of shrubs or under walls. The seed is slow to germinate, so it is best to buy young plants in autumn. The plant's country name witnesses to its usual flowering time. These are a little like single roses and have pale yellow centres and five white petals, which sometimes are purplish towards the edges. Mulch with organic compost after flowering.

History and Lore

The Christmas rose is a native of European alpine regions. However, it has grown in Britain for a long time. Culpeper mentions it, and in medieval times it was also known as the flower of Saint Agnes, possibly because it was still blooming on her feast-day (21 January). I have chosen it to celebrate Christmas, not only because of its name and because it will bloom for the feast, but also because of the charming legend of its first appearance on earth. The story goes that while the shepherds were offering gifts and adoring the Christ Child in the stable, a little shepherd girl stood weeping nearby. It was freezing cold, she was poor and had nothing at all to offer him. But God took pity on her and the Archangel Gabriel descended. Stooping to the ground, he threw aside the blanket of snow and revealed the first Christmas roses blooming underneath. The little girl picked some and took them into the stable to lay at the crib. (The legend of the poinsettia seems to be an echo of this legend.)

From a church point of view Christmas Eve is lovely in town, but for Christmas Day I much prefer the country. It is still dark when I rise after not much sleep. The tree is lit up first and will afford the sole illumination in the library until much later. At the crib, I offer a first prayer of welcome to the Lord and then open a window to assess the weather. In the pre-dawn gloom I leave the house and go down the garden. In the herb garden, where the inspiration for this book first came to me, I seek out the Christmas roses, whose white petals gleam in the fast receding night. Already two natural things have pierced the darkness and turned my mind to the Light of Bethlehem and of the world. It is time for the Office, and as much of a meditation as can be managed before breakfast and the tasks and feasting of the day take over. I think enviously and gratefully of the Benedictine nuns of Stanbrook in England and of the Cistercians of Echourgnac, nearby, over in the Dordogne, who will probably by this time be singing Lauds in full. Approaching the slumbering house, I look up at the library windows and see the warm glow cast from the tree. I hurry inside and upstairs to our little chapel at the end of the gallery above the library, where there is a smaller tree. By its light, I offer my Office of Readings and Morning Prayer. Thus in the silence interrupted only by the turning of pages and occasional muffled sounds from the sleepers in bedrooms below, I join in the prayer of the Universal Church.

Towards Meditation
'Light dawns for the righteous and joy for the upright of heart' (Ps. 97).

The symbolism of light is everywhere, penetrating the dark hours and brightening the short daylight ones. In the house, in the Christmas tree; in the garden, in the Christmas roses; and perhaps most of all in the fabric of the liturgy, shot through with images of light. But the little shepherd girl of legend leads me to concentrate on details of its weave. First there is the thread of constant confirmation that Christ comes to save *all* people. No one is excluded: 'The Lord has bared his holy arm before the eyes of all the nations and all the ends of the earth shall see the salvation of our God' (Is. 52:10); 'All creation rejoices today' (Ps. 47); 'the joy of all the world' (Ps. 48); 'his vindication in the sight of the nations' (Ps. 98). In the Gospel of the third Mass of the day, John hails Christ as the 'true light that enlightens every man that comes into the world'. All of us are enlightened, be we humble or exalted, as the first visitors to the stable show in the Gospel of the dawn Mass. The Christmas rose legend is simply an underlining of this truth. The Christmas rose represents light. But it leads me to consider a second thread in the fabric, that of joy. The little shepherdess had nothing, and therefore her joy was the greater. Without Christ we have nothing, are nothing. So we pour out our joy in the psalms of the Office, not only in response to the Saviour's birth, but because, like the shepherdess, we have been given something to give. The Christmas rose represents the faith he has given us and the light of our joy in that faith, which must shine out in the dark world around us. The next thread is an intertwining of strength, gentleness, and peace. Shepherds are carers, and the Office draws our attention to the fact that Christ will conquer with the word and not the sword. Isaiah foretells, 'He shall smite the earth with the rod of his mouth' and goes on to describe a kingdom in which there is no aggression, rapacity, or fear of hurt.

The shepherdess is ennobled and enriched when Gabriel provides her with something to give back to the Infant Christ. She is made special. 'Behold your salvation comes, and you shall be called Sought Out, a city not forsaken' (Is. 62:11–12). I see the favoured little girl as the Church, and the Christmas rose as symbolic of Christ's coming to found her. But it can also signify our individual baptisms and callings, and what each one of us chooses to make of them. This is the fourth thread for attention today. The last is the need to meditate, to contemplate constantly. As we follow the little girl into the stable bearing our own 'Christmas roses', Mary's example in prayer is set before us. Thanks to Luke it is there for all posterity to learn: 'But Mary kept all these things, pondering them in her heart.'

In the Office of Readings St Leo the Great, in his *Sermon 1*, 'The Nativity', draws together all these threads. He stresses that there are no outsiders. Since no one is without sin, no one is beyond redemption. He holds up the joy of the angels at the incarnation. How much more greatly should we rejoice? He exhorts us to be aware of our nobility as Christians. In Christ we are made a new creation, the new work of his hand. At baptism each one of us was made a temple for the Holy Spirit and should not drive away the 'Indweller'. We must think of the Head, and of his Body of which we are members. We have been rescued from darkness, transferred to the light of God. And so Leo brings us back to the Light that is Christ. Without him we should be nothing and could do nothing. As Paul remarked to Titus, our salvation is made possible, not by deeds of righteousness but by the compassion of Christ. Today is the birthday of that saving compassion. It is the birthday of life, the birthday of the Light: 'In him was life, and the life was the light of men.' This is the moment, the realization for which we have been preparing throughout Advent. It is at the heart of this book. Everything has been leading to it, and I have faith that everything after it will be vivified and enlightened by it.

It is time to go downstairs to the kitchen, snatch a hasty breakfast and let the bustle of the day take over. I cannot attend all the Masses, may not even return to the other Offices, but I carry their words in my heart. And as night falls, I will thank God for the Christmas rose and remember: 'The light shines in darkness and the darkness has not overcome it' (Jn 1:5).

Bible Readings
Psalms 47 and 48: All creation rejoices; joy of all the earth
Psalm 97: Light dawns for the righteous
Psalm 98:1–6: His vindication in the sight of the nations
Isaiah 11:1–10: He shall smite the earth with the rod of his mouth
Isaiah 52:7–10: The Lord has bared his holy arm
Isaiah 62:11–12: Behold your salvation comes
Titus 3:4–7: We are saved by the compassion of Christ
Hebrews 1:1–6: He reflects the glory of God
Luke 2:15–20: The shepherds hasten to Bethlehem; Mary kept these things in her heart
John 1:1–18: The life was the light of men

Intercessions
For shepherds, both of sheep and of souls; for peace on earth; for musicians, particularly those who will assist at the liturgy today; for music in contemplative Orders; that our Advent preparation and Christmas celebration may increase our understanding of their mysteries.

Thanksgiving for Holy Mass and the Divine Office; that our joy may be reflected in our deeds, and that we may spread light, hope, and peace around us.

Place of Spiritual Retreat
Outside the stable at Bethlehem

28 DECEMBER

The Holy Innocents

GLORY-OF-THE-SNOW *Chionodoxa luciliae*

Cultivation Note

This early spring bulb can grow to a height of nine inches. The flowers are usually a lovely sky-blue with white centres, but both white and violet varieties are available. These are respectively *C. luciliae alba* and *C. luciliae gigantea*. The flowers are star-shaped and carried in delicate sprays on upright stalks. Outdoors they make an excellent edging plant, even in a window box. They are also effective between shrubs, or in the rock garden, and will naturalize if left undisturbed for several years. Plant in autumn, two inches deep, in groups, three or four inches apart. If in window boxes, water until foliage dies down. Normally they will flower in February, sometimes as early as January, but try the following procedure if you hope for an indoor display on Holy Innocents' Day.

The previous September, buy bulbs that have been specially prepared for early flowering. They are worth their dearer price. Plant straight away, making sure they do not touch each other, or the sides of their containers. Put them in the garden and cover with black polythene or a four-inch layer of peat. Avoid any warmth at this stage. Leave them for about ten weeks, checking occasionally that the compost is still moist. Bring indoors between the middle and end of November when the tips should be one to two inches high. Keep the bowls in shade at first, and move to a windowsill after a few days. A few weeks later, buds should appear. Move again to a draught-free and bright, but not sunny, spot. Certainly they should be kept away from fires or radiators. Keep the compost moist and continue to feed until leaves have withered. Remove bulbs, dry and remove dead foliage, and store in a cool dry place. They will not provide a second indoor display, but can be planted in the garden or window boxes next autumn. (This method can be tried with most popular spring bulbs.)

History and Lore

'They shall walk with me in white, for they are worthy' (Sixth Response at Matins, Old Roman Breviary).

'Glory-of-the-snow' is a translation of the Greek *chion* meaning snow and *doxa* meaning glory. The beautiful colour of the flowers and their early arrival are obvious reasons for the name. But there is also significance in the six-petalled blooms because tradition has it that there were at least six baby boys in Bethlehem whose age destined them for death in Herod's blood-bath. The highest estimate of their number is twenty-five, but, however many, they are truly, 'the glory of the snow'. Their feast has been kept in the West since the fourth century. Childermas was its early English name, and there was for a time a nasty practice of whipping children who had been naughty during the previous year. It must have gone on in Italy as well, because the custom is the basis for some of the stories in the *Decameron* of Boccaccio.

In English literature we have the Chester, York, and Coventry Cycles, in all of which Herod appears. These plays are a wonderful example of how the medieval mystery play can lurch, at the turn of a page, from knock-about comedy to a horribly violent and bloodthirsty cruelty, and then to tender pathos, and still be dramatically convincing and enjoyable. Our theatrical forebears dealt with evil characters by making them ridiculous, over-blown figures, at whom we love to laugh. But *because* we have been laughing at Herod's antics, our shock is all the greater when the buffoon turns murderer and the massacre of the Innocents takes place. The language of the plays is harsh and coarse in Herod's scenes, but becomes lyrically spiritual in those involving the Holy Family. And the Coventry *Nativity* contains the painfully beautiful carol *Lully Lulla*, sung by the traumatized, mourning mothers of the Innocents. It seems to me that the anonymous composer, by writing a dotted crotchet followed by a quaver on the word 'little' before 'tiny child', has put a tiny sob in the throat into the tune, indicative of the struggle to sing through the depth of a terrible grief.

The Holy Innocents are classed as martyrs, and therefore their liturgical colour should be red. But a white flower seems more appropriate for them. First, there is plenty of red about the house at this time of year. One can always look at holly berries, for instance, if one needs reminding of the babies' blood spilt by Herod's soldiers. But in my heart today, I will be thinking 'white'. I was first taught about the Holy Innocents in Sunday

School at St Mary's Walkey in Sheffield, and I have the teachers there to thank for the fact that ever since I have thought of Herod's victims when singing 'Once in Royal David's City': 'Then like stars his children crowned / All in white shall wait around.' Another reason for choosing a white *Chionodoxa* is the sublime *O Quam Gloriosum* motet by Tomás Luis de Vitoria, that Spanish jewel in the crown of the Renaissance, whose music is so powerfully and intensely spiritual that to sing it makes one realize the truth of the choristers' motto *They that sing pray twice. O quam gloriosum* – 'O how glorious is the kingdom wherein all the saints rejoice with Christ: Clothed in white robes they follow the Lamb wherever he goes.' In the motet the altos, tenors, and basses introduce the phrase *Amicti stolis albis*; they repeat it, this time with sopranos, while the basses drop out, and then a final time, all four lines woven together in such a softly delicate radiance that one can almost feel and see the glorious texture of the shining white robes. 'All the saints', says the motet, but at those eight bars I would always have a special thought for the Holy Innocents. My choir years are over but this motet reminds me to thank God for the privilege I had for so long of knowing, from the inside, music of such a high order. Today, although I cannot sing the motet, those eight bars will be in my heart.

Towards Meditation

'My eyes are spent with weeping; my soul is in tumult; my heart is poured out in grief ... because infants and babes faint in the streets of the city' (Lam. 2:11).

The Massacre of the Innocents happened because Herod was incapable of seeing things spiritually. He saw kingship in terms of his own miserable share in worldly power. He did not understand the nature of Christ's Kingship. He knew the Scripture that foretold the coming of one who would take the throne of David, but, like many of the Jews at the time, interpreted it literally. The Messiah would have the trappings of earthly kingship and would rout the oppressors of his people in conventional battle and with political might. Under that kind of regime, Herod would have expected to retain high position.

God came into the world at a time when it was impossible for Herod to think in any other way. But this petty puppet of the Roman rulers was right to fear Jesus, not because he would take the earthly throne of David but because he would subordinate all earthly thrones under his own heavenly kingship. The babies died because of Herod's fear and lack of understanding. However many infants were killed, the figure is as nothing compared with the numbers of babies who have since been done to death – and are still being done to death in the interests of politics and greed or as a result of our bad stewardship of the earth. Herod was ignorant. Christendom is not, and collectively it has no excuse before God for its continually allowing children to be massacred and starved to death. We have even created a society in which children torture and kill each other. In such a state of affairs we have no right to demonize Herod. No wonder Our Lady in her appearances has spoken of being unable to stay her Son's hand for much longer. With the profoundest respect to the Blessed Virgin, we should not need her warnings. Everything we know of Christ's attitude to children should tell us that retribution will be exacted. I tremble with fear at the thought. What can the majority of us, as politically and financially powerless individuals, with the responsibilities of our own vocations, do about this? We can deny ourselves more, we can squeeze more out of the household income to give to charity. But most of all we can pray. We can try more nearly to obey Paul's injunction to 'pray without ceasing' (1 Thes. 5:11). As I get older and feel that we are careering ever closer to wilful self-destruction, increasingly nothing less than prayer without ceasing seems to have any chance of changing our course.

Why, since the Innocents died before Christ, does the Church celebrate them as martyrs? How could they wash their robes in the blood of the Lamb, when the Lamb's blood had not yet been spilt? Groping for answers, I think that perhaps it is because our measurement of time, what occurs in it and when, is not God's. The Innocents are special martyrs because they died not only for Christ but instead of him. Human sin caused their deaths, not God. God sent the angel to Joseph in a dream to make sure of Jesus' escape to Egypt and, in response to human sin, took the infants to himself as a ransom for that escape. By naming the infants as martyrs, the Church implies a belief that they were taken immediately into heaven and did not have to wait, with the patriarchs and prophets, for Christ's descent into hell on Holy Saturday to burst open its gates and lead those whom he loved to the light.

Also, on a very human level, the defencelessness of these victims stirs the Church's deep maternal compassion, and makes her want to honour them in this way. Both the old and new Breviaries include passages that support this view. In the modern Office of Readings, St Quodvultdeus (died 439) salutes the Innocents because, although they could not even speak, they confessed Christ. Even though they were helpless to fight for him they still carried off the victory. The Christ Child made babies like himself, through our fault, a fitting witness. In the old Office of Matins we find 'They are rightly called the flowers of martyrdom; hardly had these buds of the Church shown their heads above the soil, in the winter of unbelief, when the frost of persecution nipped them' (Sixth Response at Matins, once attributed to St Augustine, but now uncertain). And the hymn at Lauds took verses from Aurelius (348–c. 404):

> All hail! you infant Martyr flowers.
> Cut off in life's first dawning hours,
> As rose-buds snapped in tempest strife,
> When Herod sought your Saviour's life.

> You, tender flock of lambs, we sing,
> First victims slain for Christ your King:
> Beneath the altar's heavenly ray,
> With martyr palms and crowns ye play.

I love the image of the Holy Innocents blithely playing about the throne of God and using their martyr crowns and palms for toys. So apparently did the Church, until the new Divine Office was compiled.

When I am in France for this feast, I place a bowl of Glory of the Snow under a painting of the *Flight into Egypt* that hangs in our chapel, and I remember a further verse from Aurelius:

> What is the gain of such a sin?
> What doth his crime for Herod win?
> Saved only from so many slain
> Away uninjured Christ is ta'en.

Last year, beneath the picture, the horror of the plight of children in my own time hung over me, an ever-present and terrible cloud. Prostrated by impotence to affect anything at all, I prayed for counsel. Eventually, I heard, above the noise of Ramah, 'Keep your voice from weeping and your eyes from tears, for your work shall be rewarded ... there is hope for your future, says the Lord' (Jer. 31:16–17a). I spent a long time with Jeremiah that day, praying for the work of children's aid agencies and for increased faith in the Word.

Bible Readings

Psalm 124: The snare is broken and we have escaped

1 John 1:5–2:2: The blood of Jesus purifies us

Matthew 2:13–18: Joseph's dream; the slaughter of the Innocents and the Flight into Egypt

Jeremiah 31:15: A voice is heard in Ramah ... Rachel is weeping for her children

Hosea 11:1: Out of Egypt I called my son

Exodus 1:8–16: The killing of the Hebrew children in Egypt

Lamentations 1:16: For these things I weep

Lamentations 2:11: Infants and babes faint in the streets of the city

Jeremiah 31:16–17a: Your work shall be rewarded

Revelation 21:4–5: There shall be an end to death and mourning

Place of Spiritual Retreat

Following the Holy Family on the road to Egypt, as in Matthew 2

SUNDAY WITHIN THE OCTAVE OF CHRISTMAS

(or 30 December if Christmas fell on Sunday)

Feast of the Holy Family

LAVENDER *Lavandula*; elf-leaf; rabbit tobacco

Cultivation Notes

Lavender is an evergreen perennial shrub. There are two main types, *L. latifolia*, which is mainly cultivated for commercial use, and *L. angustifolia*, the usual choice for garden planting. From the latter group you can stick with the species or try one of the many varieties. *Nana alba* (white), *rosea* (pink), or 'Royal Purple' are recommended. Height will vary according to your choice, the average being 18–24 inches. Although lavender is hardy once established, seedlings should not be put out until there is no danger of frosts. Plant in a well-drained sunny site, and prune established plants in spring to encourage sturdiness and longevity. Flowering time is from late spring to early autumn. Do not dry lavender in the sun: the oils evaporate from the flowers and leave them scentless. Cut early just before buds open. Dry in trays, or hanging bundles.

Handle gently after drying, as it tends to be brittle. For pot-pourri, harvesting can be slightly later.

History and Lore

It is generally accepted that lavender is so called because of its long association with laundry and the Latin *lavare*, to wash. Some have argued that it could be from *lividus*, medieval Latin meaning 'bluish', after its flower colour.

One reason for the choice of lavender for today is the legend that the Virgin Mary, looking for somewhere to hang out her baby's clothes, draped them on a lavender bush, which up to that point had been scentless. After she took in her laundry, the bush was found to be imbued with the wonderful perfume that it keeps to this day. There *is* a type of lavender growing in the Holy Land, but our lavender originated in southern Europe. The Ancient Greeks and Romans used it as an antiseptic and to sweeten bath water and laundry. T. W. Sanders, in *The Encyclopaedia of Gardening* (1875), claims that it first arrived in Britain in 1568, but surely he can only be half right. It is hard to believe that the Romans did not introduce it during their occupation. Probably like so many other herbs, it simply died out after they left. Today it is grown all over the world, either in gardens or for commercial purposes. In France, for instance, whole regions are devoted to the production of lavender oils.

In medieval times lavender was an essential strewing herb and valued for its medicinal, refreshing qualities. It was an ingredient of 'Four Thieves Vinegar': robbers would douse themselves in this concoction before burgling houses whose occupants had died of the Plague. And the glovers of Grasse in the hills north of Cannes used oil of lavender to scent leather. The oil could well have been supplied by the twelfth-century Cistercian abbey of Senanque at nearby Gordes in Provence. The community produces lavender essence to this day, and there are perfumeries at Grasse and a lavender market at Forcalquier.

Gerard recommended lavender to bathe the temples of sufferers from 'light migrain or swimming of the brain'. Over the centuries it has been used to treat hysteria, fainting, palpitations, sprains, stiff joints, halitosis, and wounds. Izaak Walton, of *The Compleat Angler* fame, wrote, 'I long to be in a house where the sheets smell of lavender.' It was also used in diluting paint to produce the gentle tones needed in hand-painted china and to clean the artist's brushes. Today, in some quarters, lavender is thought to awaken spiritual sensitivity, integrity, and stability. This may be true in the sense that it clears the brain and therefore may assist concentration and receptivity in prayer. *L. angustifolia* is an ingredient in scent and aromatherapy products, while *L. latifolia* is employed in the manufacture of cleaning materials, insect repellents, and air fresheners. At home, you may: take a blissful lavender foot bath after a heavy session of gardening; carry a lavender-soaked cotton-wool ball as an insect repellent (mosquitoes hate it); wear a sprig in your lapel to combat headaches and lift the spirits; sprinkle a few drops on your pillow against restlessness; bathe your temples with lavender water as a tonic or use it to refresh your skin and hair; place in wardrobes and drawers against moths; keep some in the medicine cabinet to treat bruises, stings, and bites; make pot-pourri and lavender baskets to keep or give away. (Lavender baskets are easily made from bunches of lavender: tie just below the flowers and then pull the stalks upward over them to form a ball, which can then be hung up.) Small dried bundles can be used to throw on an open fire to scent a room, and individual stalks can be used as lighting tapers.

The compilers of *The Language of Flowers* seem to have been arbitrary in some of their attributions, and it is hard to understand why they should have applied 'mistrust' to this lovely plant, which offers so much practical help and aesthetic delight. Versatility, purity, tranquillity, or love, would all have been more apt. A worthier memorial is given by Dion Clayton Calthrop in his *The Charm of Gardens* (1911):

> Here lies
> Imprisoned in this grey bush
> LAVENDER
> It is renowned for a simple purity
> A sweet fragrance and a subtle
> strength, it is the odour of
> the domestic virtues and the
> symbolic perfume of a quiet life
> Rain
> Shall weep over this bush
> Sun
> Shall give it warm kisses
> Wind shall stir the tall spikes
> Until such a time as it is required
> When it shall flower and so
> Yield to us its secret.

Those compilers were more interested in romantic love. Had they been able to read Calthrop's tribute, I doubt they would have recognized in it a beautiful extended symbolism for Mary, the Mother of Jesus, of the love they bore each other, and the love that we bear them both.

Another reason why I will lay lavender before the crib on the feast of the Holy Family is the familiar little rhyme: 'Lavender's blue dilly dilly, / Lavender's green, / When you are king, dilly dilly, / I shall be queen.'

Both lavender- and dill-water were once used to lull children to sleep and the song most probably had its origins in this custom. The image it raises for me is one of a mother, comforting her baby, singing him to sleep as the donkey pads on towards the safety of Egypt. It brings home, with sudden enlightening force, the divine and human reality of the birth we have just celebrated. The divine reality can never be understood. But the human reality can only put me beside myself with concern and love for Jesus and his mother. If it can have this effect on a mere mortal, what must Joseph have felt? Quite aside from the danger, the angel had told him that their exile must last until Herod died, but the possessions they had abandoned were as nothing to them because they knew God had given them charge, until Jesus came to maturity, of the most precious possession the world had ever known, or would ever know. The words of 'Lavender's blue' apply so well to Mary because when she would at last behold Jesus not as the vulnerable human baby on the road to Egypt but as the King of Glory, he would make her Queen of Heaven.

Towards Meditation
'Mary kept all these things pondering them in her heart' (Lk. 2:19).

In his accounts of the Annunciation and Visitation, Luke has already shown us the depth of Mary's prayerful, loving, and contemplative temperament. He has underlined it after the departure of the shepherds. He has shown Joseph as obedient, God-fearing, responsible, and protective of his charges. He is the first foster father in Christendom, and the supreme example to all who have the care of other people's children. Our only other glimpses of the domestic life of the Holy Family before Jesus came to manhood, are also found in Luke. The Presentation narrative shows us their absolute adherence to the laws of religion, despite their poverty. Later, when Jesus is lost in Jerusalem, we recognize their anguished parental panic. How much worse for them, because surely they could not have forgotten the identity of the one lost. And yet when Jesus is found in the Temple, neither Mary nor Joseph at first understands his saying, 'Why were you searching for me? Did you not know that I must be in my father's house?' (Luke 2:49). After the incident Jesus goes down to Nazareth with them and is 'obedient to them'. But his mother does not forget. She ponders things in her heart.

John's account of the wedding at Cana is richly symbolic and prophetic, but I leave these aspects for pondering during Epiphanytide. *Today*, I remember that Christ's first recorded public miracle is performed at Mary's behest. It is clear that by now she knows a great deal more about her son – so much, it seems, as to make her certain that he can turn the water into wine if he chooses. His response seems to imply her knowledge that she is asking for a miracle prematurely, that she knows he had not intended to begin his public ministry just yet; but as a loving son he relents, and in so doing shows us that within family life love should dictate action, and that sometimes young adults should adjust their career timetables to accommodate the wishes of their mothers. Christ's childhood subjection to Mary and Joseph exemplifies and sanctifies family life, as does his granting his mother's wish at Cana. And his very presence at the wedding sanctifies marriage itself.

Leaving the lavender by the crib tonight, I remember how I used to regret that we know so litttle of Christ's early life. Now I believe that in the Gospels, if we will only look deeply enough in the light of the Spirit, God has given us everything he wants us to know and understand. My reflections today, for instance, have merely scratched the surface of the lessons this feast holds about the way he wants us to conduct our family lives.

Bible Readings

Sirach 3:2–6: Mutual respect in the family upheld by God
Psalm 127:1–5: Your wife is a fruitful vine
Psalm 83: The beauty of the Lord's dwelling
Luke 2:16, 19: The shepherds find Jesus; Mary ponders
Matthew 2:13–15: Joseph's dream and the flight into Egypt
Psalm 84: As they go through the bitter valley they make it a place of springs
Luke 2:22–40: Presentation in the Temple; Simeon's prophecy
Luke 2:51b: Early days after the return from Egypt
Luke 2:41–52: Loss and finding of Jesus in the Temple
John 2:1–11: The miracle at Cana
Colossians 3:12–21: Husbands, wives and children; love the bond that makes us perfect

Ephesians 5:21 – 6:4: Married and family life
1 John 3:1–2: God's love for us, his children

Place of Spiritual Retreat
In the Temple with Simeon and Anna, as in Luke 2

1 JANUARY

Solemnity of Mary, Mother of God

MARIGOLD *Calendula officinalis*; husbandman's dial; Mary bud; sun's bride; sun's herb
MOTHERWORT *Leonurus cardiaca*

Cultivation Notes
Marigold is a hardy annual. Sow in spring in a sunny position on open ground or singly in pots, and again in late summer for autumn and winter

flowering. Outdoors, space plants at 18-inch intervals, or grow them among roses to protect them from nematode worm and near tomatoes to discourage white fly. Marigolds attract bees, and help to keep the ground healthy. They grow to a height of between 12 and 20 inches. Deadhead to encourage continuous flowering. Choose dry conditions to pick flowers and young leaves. Dry at a low temperature or macerate in oil to preserve colour. There is an interesting and popular variant, *C. prolifera*, sometimes known as hens and chickens because it produces several smaller flowers from the base of the main flower head.

Motherwort is a hardy perennial that appreciates sun, and it can be planted in spring and autumn. It likes moist but well-drained conditions, self-seeds frequently, and can be divided in late spring and October. White to pinkish-mauve flowers appear from summer to mid-autumn, but motherwort is often grown for the attractive foliage, at its best in spring. The plant can reach a height of four feet and spread for two feet, so it is effective as a background for lower-growing subjects with less distinguished foliage. Cut when flowering, but before the seed sets.

History and Lore

The Latin name *Calendula* was probably given because the plant blooms throughout the year. Like the sunflower, it follows the sun, which explains the English name husbandman's dial. Shakespeare knew of this allegiance to the sun, and in *The Winter's Tale* (Act 4, scene 3) he has Perdita say: 'The marigold that goes to bed wi' the sun, / And with him rises weeping.' In Britain we think of marigold as a flower of warmth, but in German folklore it was called *Totenblumen*, meaning 'flowers of the dead'. And in Mexico there is a legend that the marigold sprang from earth stained with the blood of native Americans who had fallen victim to the treasure-lust and cruelty of early Spanish settlers.

In England, the marigold has long been valued as a culinary and medicinal plant, and its dye was once used to colour cheese and butter. In *The Herball* (1633), John Gerard wrote that 'no brothes are well made without it'. During Queen Anne's reign (1702–14), marigold pudding was a favourite. Charles Lamb (1775–1834) may have been partially responsible for the later decline in the culinary popularity of the plant. Recollecting his meals at Christ's Hospital, he describes 'Boiled beef on Thursday with detestable marigolds floating in the pail to poison the broth.' However, the marigold never fell from favour as a health remedy, and it was reputedly used by field doctors as an immediate wound treatment during the American Civil War. It has definite properties as an antiseptic and is particularly good for chilblains and broken or chapped skin. The ointment is helpful for nursing mothers and is non-toxic to the baby. It is also effective in the treatment of measles, ulcers, varicose veins, in-growing toenails, and insect stings. For a gentler treatment, bathe the affected area with marigold petal tea. The dye can be used as a saffron substitute, and gives a soft corn yellow to wool.

Of all the names given to marigold, the tender Mary bud is surely the most appealing. Before the Reformation it was a favourite in monastery gardens, no doubt because of its efficacy in kitchen and infirmary, and it is thought that some monk or nun coined the name, having noticed that the plant was in bloom on every one of Mary's feasts. It remained in common usage for some time, as Shakespeare proves, this time in a song from *Cymbeline* (Act 2, scene 3): 'Hark! hark! the lark at heaven's gate sings / And winking mary-buds begin / To ope their golden eyes.'

The Reverend Johns suggests that the Latin *Leonurus* for motherwort is derived from the Greek for 'lion's tail', 'because of some fancied resemblance in the plant'. The English name definitely comes from its use in Ancient Greece, where it was prescribed to reduce anxiety in pregnancy. Research has proved that it calms the heart and reduces the risk of thrombosis, thus vindicating Culpeper, who claimed that 'there is no better herb to take away melancholy vapours from the heart and strengthen it.' Today it is still respected as a sedative, for its anti-bacterial, anti-fungal effects, and as a stabilizer of menstrual pain, hot flushes, and blood pressure. Its dark green dye can be used to colour wool. In England, motherwort can be found growing wild on roadside verges and waste ground, as an escapee from old herb gardens. Look for it in late summer and dry it to make tinctures. If your search fails, plants can be bought from specialist suppliers (see Appendix 3).

Note: Motherwort is *not* now given to pregnant women.

Historical Note on today's Solemnity: The dogma of Mary's Motherhood of God was defined at the Council of Ephesus in AD 431, but it was not until fifteen centuries later that Pius XI instituted an official feast, to be observed in the universal calendar on 11 October. After Vatican II – whose Constitution on the Sacred Liturgy had declared that feasts of Mary were to be emphasized, as she is 'joined by an inseparable bond to the saving work of her Son' – it was decided that a date closer to Christmas would be more logical and fitting.

Towards Meditation

'Behold a virgin shall conceive and bear a son, and shall call his name Immanuel' (Is. 7:14b).

Each feast of Our Lady encourages us to meditate on a different aspect of her relationship with the Persons of the Holy Trinity, and all draw attention to her function in God's plan for our salvation. We know from Christ's words to the good thief that nobody who genuinely desires to be a member of his family will be turned away. At the foot of the cross Mary received John as her son, and with him all of us. Today, the liturgy invites us to an overview of Mary, from her Immaculate Conception to the Presentation of Jesus in the Temple. Realizing the impossibility of considering all of this in any depth on one day, I made a list of the characteristics that today's plants share with Mary and so found a way of meditating on different aspects of her significance during the time between now and Epiphany.

Marigold

Obedience: follows the sun, symbolically God's will

Fecundity/Fruitfulness: it is called *prolifera*

Nourishment: physical and spiritual – maternal responsibilities

Warmth/Tenderness: maternal characteristics

Health-giving: protection of other plants, symbolic of Mary's protection of Christ, and of ourselves

Death: plant's sorrowful lore symbolic of Mary's sorrows and the redeeming death of Christ

Motherwort

Life enhancement: support and enhancement of other plants, symbolic of Mary's rearing of Jesus and concern for us

Serenity: Calming properties point to Mary's serenity

Joy: plant conquers melancholy, reminds us of the joys and sorrows of Mary and the joy she brings to us

Strength of Heart: medicinal properties of plant symbolize Mary's strength of heart, even when pierced

Cleansing: property of plant symbolic of Mary's purity

Survival: plant has spread its seed in the wild, symbolizing the Word born of Mary through the Holy Spirit, and spreading to all nations

Healing: Soothing properties in marigold and motherwort symbolic of Mary's concern for us in our pains and troubles
Change: Dyeing properties of both plants symbolize the changed destiny of the human race at the Annunciation

Obedience
(a) Mary's obedience to God's will and the example she sets us.
(b) Her obedience was loving and unquestioning and through it God took our flesh in order to redeem us. As a result of Mary's perfect compliance, the Word could be brought to all nations.
(c) Mary's obedience brought her joy, both in her own personal situation, and in the far-reaching effects it would have.
(d) Christ himself, in becoming a human child, although he was always about his Father's business, was obedient to Mary and Joseph. This is an even more amazing mystery than Mary's obedience. At the Annunciation God submitted himself to human beings in order to save them.

As I leave the pot of marigold and motherwort leaves before Our Lady's statue, I will again thank God for all the plants that help me to meditate and pray. My final prayer today will be even more deeply felt than usual. The Hail Mary is one that trips too easily, and without due reverence or attention, from Catholic lips. It is printed below in such a way as to make one linger over each phrase in love, wonder, gratitude, and entreaty. The name of Jesus is breathed rather than spoken in the central line, but we have total confidence that the Mother of God will hear and take our prayer to him.

Hail Mary
Full of grace,
The Lord is with thee.
Blessed art thou among women,
And blessed is the fruit of thy womb
Jesus.
Holy Mary,
Mother of God,
Pray for us sinners,
Now,
And at the hour of our death. Amen.

Bible Readings

Psalm 24: Let him enter, the King of glory

Sirach 24: Like a vine I caused loveliness to bud, and my blossoms became
glorious and abundant fruit

Micah 5:3–5a: Only so long as a woman is in labour ... He shall appear

Zephaniah 3:14–15b: The Lord is in your midst

Zechariah 9:9a: Your king comes to you

Baruch 5:3–4: In you God will manifest the splendour of his presence

Galatians 4:4–7: God sent his son born of a woman

Hebrews 2:9–17: Christ became like his brothers in every way except for
sin

Luke 1:28: Blessed are you, Virgin Mary

Luke 2:16–21: He was called Jesus

Luke 2:40–52: The boy Jesus in the Temple

EPIPHANYTIDE

6 JANUARY

Solemnity of the Epiphany of the Lord

Note: This entry covers Epiphanytide, which lasts from now until the Feast of the Baptism of the Lord. If 6 January falls on a Sunday, or the Epiphany is celebrated on the Sunday nearest that date, there will be six days between the Solemnity and the Feast. If Epiphany is celebrated on a weekday, the number of days reduces accordingly, so that if it is a Saturday, the next day will be the First Sunday of Ordinary Time, and the Feast of the Baptism of the Lord.

STAR-OF-BETHLEHEM *Ornithogalum*; Betty-go-to-bed-at-noon; shame-faced maiden; *La Dame de l'onze heures*

Cultivation Notes

This perennial bulb produces plants that reach a foot in height and flower between April and June. There are two main types, and the distinction between them is important. *O. angustifolium umbellatum* is reasonably hardy and manages in quite poor soil. It naturalizes and can be divided in summer. Store in dry warmth over the winter, or protect until March if left in open ground. This is the common 'star-of-Bethlehem' and has star-shaped, sky-facing flowers. *O. angustifolia nutans* (nodding) has about a dozen pendant flowers on each stem. *O. thyrsoides* is tender and has to be raised indoors, either as a houseplant or for planting in the garden in late spring. Put bulbs in cutting compost in February. Keep in the dark for six weeks and then place in full sun. Water once a week. *Thyrsoides* is Greek for 'stalk', and this type bears about twenty-five flowers on wand-like stems. I have long wanted to have star-of-Bethlehem in the house chapel on Epiphany. Next year, as well as growing in the normal way, I will try both types, using the forcing method suggested for glory-of-the-snow on Holy Innocents' Day.

History and Lore

The Latin *angustus* means narrow, and *angusticlavius* denoted the plebeian tribune, who was marked out by a narrow stripe of purple on his tunic. The botanical description of star-of-Bethlehem therefore comes from the fine central streak of white along the front of its long narrow leaves, and probably from the fact that the plant reverses this pattern on the back of its petals, each of which has a thin green vein from base to tip. So *O. angustifolium umbellatum* translates as 'striped, parasol-shaped bird milk'. The flower is composed of three petals and three sepals, and in the centre there are six glistening, yellow-headed stamens. The chalice-shaped seed case has six vertical ridges. Six is unusual in flower formation, five occurring far more frequently.

Star-of-Bethlehem is extremely sensitive to light, closing its petals after midday, before that if the weather is dull. This habit explains the English and French country names. The flower is 'of Bethlehem' because it has grown in the Holy Land since Old Testament times. Linnaeus identified it with the foodstuff sold during the siege of Samaria: 'the fourth part of a kab of dove's dung for five shekels of silver' (2 Kgs 6:25), i.e. 300ml for 57 grammes of silver. The plant still grows in the Holy Land. William Salmon, writing in 1679, refers to its edibility when cooked: 'the root serves for meat or food being roasted in embers, mixed with honey', and

John Parkinson described it as 'sweeter than a chestnut'. In 1954 Professor Tackhom pointed out that our European species is poisonous and could not have been eaten. (It is also poisonous to cattle.) It seems that Salmon and Parkinson were describing the biblical star-of-Bethlehem, *O. narbonense brachystachys*, which is edible, but only when roasted or boiled. Perhaps this was brought to England by pilgrims returning from the Holy Land. In appearance it resembles our *O. thyrsoides*, but obviously it is safer not to eat any of the *Ornithogalum* species. *O. angustifolium* grows in profusion in the Breckland area between King's Lynn and Ely.

History of the Feast of the Epiphany

Epiphaneia is Greek, meaning 'Manifestation'. The feast was known to the Greeks as the *Theophaneia* (Manifestation of God), or the Day of Holy Lights, and it celebrated three different ways in which Christ's glorious light was made manifest. The first is his showing of himself to the Magi, who have ever since been seen as the first fruits of the Gentiles, and as showing that salvation is open to all the peoples of earth; the second is God's proclamation of Jesus as his Son at his baptism; and the third is when Jesus changed water into wine at Cana, showing the glory of the miraculous aspect of his public ministry and himself as Lord of the Universe. There is also a very ancient tradition that lights appeared over the Jordan at Christ's baptism. In the rites of several eastern sects water was blessed at first Vespers of the Epiphany, and then sprinkled on the people. There is a ritual for the purpose in the old Roman Rite, and the day was long regarded as a special day for baptism. We know from Gregory Nazianzen (*c*. 329–90) that sometimes only the baptism of Christ was celebrated at the Epiphany. In some places the clergy would bless the local river and, whatever the weather, the faithful would plunge into the hallowed water. (In our own times, on the Sunday nearest Epiphany, Greek Orthodox clergy dip a cross three times into the sea at Hastings. A similar service is held at Margate, but here the cross is thrown into the sea, to be retrieved by a chosen swimmer.)

The feast of the Epiphany was introduced at Rome during the second half of the sixth century, but the Office hymn at Lauds, composed by Prudentius (fourth century), proves that the three-fold commemoration within the feast is ancient in the West as well as the East. The hymn has moved to the First Vespers in the post-Vatican II Breviary, and the liturgy for today and the following week makes it clear that the Church does not wish us to limit our Epiphany reflections to the star, the Magi, and the gifts.

In England the custom of blessing the plough on the Sunday after Epiphany has survived at Chichester and Exeter Cathedrals and at several country parish churches. It was also the tradition on the Monday after Epiphany for the ploughboys to rope themselves to a festooned plough and trail it round the villages collecting pennies for the 'plough light' in church. If a household refused to give, the ground in front of the doorstep would be ploughed up! 'Plough Monday' was also the day when the ploughmen took on new apprentices. In Cambridgeshire the lads' noses would be rubbed underneath a horse's tail, or more pleasantly their shoes tapped with a stone. Thus initiated, they could join the team of ploughmen. Our custom of taking Christmas decorations down on Twelfth Night has an indirect ecclesiastical connection. At home the trees, candles, garlands, and ribbons came down on 5 January, but in church not until Candlemas, the practice no doubt symbolizing that we continue in the dark of winter until the last great feast of light before Lent begins. In our region of France there is still a tendency to leave the Christmas decorations in place until 2 February.

Towards Meditation
'He was revealed in flesh' (1 Tim. 3:16).

Star-of-Bethlehem is an obvious choice for Epiphany because of its name, but there are deeper reasons. The plant has to be searched for in the wild and is adorable when found, thus symbolizing the long journey of the Magi and their eventual finding of Christ, who is hidden from Herod. Without sufficient light star-of-Bethlehem will hide its face, much as we are in darkness until Christ, through his miracle at Cana, lets us glimpse his Light. In *The Language of Flowers* the plant represents purity, and reminds us of the purity of Christ and his Mother, and of the cleansing waters of baptism. The hexandrian nature of the plant's separate parts signifies the maximum six days of liturgy needed between the Epiphany and the Baptism of the Lord. As usual in this book, I have accommodated the longest period, but however few days there are in a given year, and however busy we may be, it should be possible to reflect briefly on all the aspects of the plan below, or to select one for concentrated attention.

Note: The word 'theophany' first appeared in English in 1633, and 'epiphany' in 1667. 'Hexandrian' was coined by Linnaeus to denote plants with six stamens.

Epiphany of the Lord

When I contemplate the whole flower, closed and open, and observe its response to light, it will lead me to reflect on the salvation for the whole world manifested at Bethlehem in the form of a speechless, swaddled infant.

Bible and Office readings

Isaiah 63:19b – 64:11: Prayer for God to visit his people
Isaiah 9: The people that walked in darkness have seen a great light
Micah 5:2: You, Bethlehem of Ephratha
Ephesians 5:13–14: Christ shall give you light
Matthew 2:1: Jesus is born at Bethlehem
John 1:1–18: The light shines in darkness and the darkness has not overcome it
John 2:3–11: The miracle at Cana
Hymn at Evening Prayer, 'Bethlehem of noblest cities'
'God has appointed a strong bulwark to our faith ... Christ was born with the very nature of man ... this makes saints of sinners, even to believe that in one and the same our Lord Jesus Christ, there is very Godhead and very Manhood' (Leo the Great, *5th Sermon on the Epiphany*).

7 January, or first day after Epiphany

The star shape formed by the flower's three petals and three sepals cannot fail to remind me of the star that led the Magi to Christ, the infant Lord of the Universe.

Bible and Office readings

Psalm 2: The nations his heritage, the ends of the earth his possession
Matthew 2:2–9: We have seen his star in the east
Matthew 4:12–25: The kingdom is near
John 3:22 – 4:6: Test the spirits
Office hymn at Morning Prayer, 'Songs of Thankfulness and Praise'
Office hymn at Evening Prayer, 'Fairer than the sun at morning'
'It was not the young Child who followed the star, but the star which followed [him] ... the young Child ruled the star instead of the star ruling him ... there is but one who rules the destiny of man, even He who made man; neither was man made for the stars, but the stars for man; and if we say that they rule his destiny, we set them above him for whose service they were made' (Gregory the Great, *10th Homily on the Gospels*).

8 January, or second day after Epiphany

I concentrate more closely on the way in which the three sepals and three petals surround the central six stamens and think of the petals as the Gentiles (symbolized by the Magi) and the sepals as the Children of Israel. The shining stamens remind me of our hope to behold Christ's glory.

Bible and Office readings

The Magi and the Gentiles:

Isaiah 60:1: The Gentiles shall walk in thy light and kings in the brightness of thy rising

Psalm 71: All nations shall fall prostrate before you, O Lord

Psalm 46: The princes of the peoples are assembled

Psalm 85: All nations shall come

Ephesians 3:2–3: Pagans may now share in the inheritance

Revelation 14:4: All the nations will come

Second reading at the Office of Readings, Monday after Epiphany, 'God did not wish us to be ignorant of him' (Peter Chrysologus, *Sermon 160*).

'The wise men teach us a great lesson in that "they depart into their own country another way." That which they did … we ought to do. Our country is heaven; and, when we have once known Jesus, we can never go there by returning on the way we walked before we knew him. We have left our country far, by the way of pride, and disobedience and worldliness. Let us then depart into our own country another way' (Gregory the Great, *10th Homily*).

The Magi and the Jews:

Isaiah 4:2–3: Everyone enrolled in the book of life shall be called holy

Matthew 2:1–18: The Magi and Herod – 'When Jesus was born he was manifested to the believing, but hidden from his enemies.… Herod's infamous act served to spread wider abroad the heaven-told news of the birth of the Lord' (Leo the Great, *5th Sermon*).

'God, in the Old Testament had commanded the first-fruits to be offered to himself, being born of man, [he] consecrated to his own worship the first fruits of the nations. The Shepherds were the first-fruits of the Jews, and the wise men, of the Gentiles' (Fulgentius, *5th Sermon on Twelfth Day*).

9 January, or third day after Epiphany

The three petals or sepals on their own call to mind not only the gifts of the Magi to Christ but Christ's gifts to each one of us. The way we use these gifts will determine the quality of our own humble offerings to him.

Bible and Office readings
Psalm 95: Bring offerings and enter his courts
Isaiah 60:6b: They shall bring gold and frankincense
Matthew 2:11: Then opening their treasures they offered him gifts
'The wise men set forth three things concerning him ... by the gold, that He was King; by the frankincense, that He was God; and by the myrrh, that He was to die ... He who cannot suffer as touching His Godhead, was made capable of death as touching the manhood which he shares with us.'
'There is another signification.... Gold is a type of wisdom as said Solomon: "In the mouth of the wise abides a treasure to be desired." Frankincense, which is burnt in honour of God, is a figure of prayer.... "Let my prayer be set forth as incense before Thee." By myrrh is represented the putting to death of the body.... "My hands dropped myrrh" (Canticle, v. 5).
'Let us ... make offering out of what treasures we have ... whatever we have is not our own, but Christ's' (Ambrose of Milan, *Homily on the Gospel of Luke*, Book 2).

10 January, or fourth day after Epiphany
When I hold a seed case of star-of-Bethlehem in my hand, its six ridges represent the joyful Church, receiving, enclosing, and protecting the Seed of the Word and then spreading its Light. With her, I look forward to the event of Christ's manifestation to the Magi, and I celebrate the continual epiphanies he makes through the vivifying waters of Baptism and the nourishment of his presence in the Blessed Sacrament.

Bible and Office readings
Isaiah 60:1–22: Arise, shine out Jerusalem
Isaiah 65:15–23: A new creation
Isaiah 66:10–23: Rejoice Jerusalem
Zechariah 2:11: He will make his dwelling with you
Titus 3:4–5: He saved us
Mark 6:34–44: Feeding of the five thousand
Second reading at the Office of Readings, Wednesday after Epiphany: Proclus of Constantinople, *Oration 7 on the Theophany*, 'Sanctifying the Waters'

'We are instructed by the tradition of the Fathers, to keep ... this Solemnity in honour of several joyful events ... On this day our Lord Christ was, first, manifest to the Gentiles by the loading of a star; second, that being bidden to a marriage, He turned water into wine; and, third, that He received baptism from John, whereby He hallowed the waters of the Jordan ... He has given us to drink of the cup of his blood of the New Testament; and ... hath hallowed for us that saving Fountain wherein we are born again' (Maximus, *First Sermon on the Epiphany*).

11 January, or fifth day after Epiphany

The six central golden-headed stamens remind me of the Trinitarian aspects of Epiphanytide liturgy. In it there are two manifestations for each Person: the Father speaks to the Magi in a dream and then at the baptism of Christ; the Son is shown as the Lord of Creation and as the Word; the Spirit conceives the Word and witnesses to the divinity of Christ at his baptism.

Bible and Office readings
Matthew 2: The dream of the Magi
Matthew 3:17: This is my beloved Son
Luke 5:12–16: Jesus in the synagogue
Mark 6:45–52: He came towards them, walking on the lake
Luke 5:12–16: Jesus cures the leper
Luke 1:35: And the Holy Spirit will come upon you
Matthew 3:16b: And he saw the Spirit of God descending
1 John 5:5–13: The Spirit, water, and blood
'It behoves us ... to keep holy ... this the birthday of his wonderworking ... these three anniversaries are rightly preached to us, who acknowledge the unspeakable mystery of the Trinity under the name of one God. By these miracles the Lord Christ our Redeemer willed to manifest some of the power of that Godhead, which in him lay hidden under the Manhood' (Maximus, *First Sermon*).

12 January, or sixth day after Epiphany

As I ponder the way in which the three petals and three sepals are joined at the centre, I think of the rejoicing Church as she receives the Light of Christ her Bridegroom; of John the Baptist, the self-described 'best man'; and of the fact that the Lord takes delight in his bride, the pilgrim Church.

Bible and Office readings
Psalm 149: The Lord takes delight in his people
Isaiah 49:6: I will give you as a light to the nations
Isaiah 63:7–11: God's love for his people
John 2:1–11: Wedding at Cana
John 3:22–30: The bridegroom's friend is glad when he hears the bridegroom's voice
John 3:1–11: He will baptise you with the Holy Spirit and with fire
1 John 4:7ff.: God is love; love one another
1 John 4:4–21: Whatever we ask, he hears
Second reading at the Office of Readings for Tuesday after Epiphany, St Hippolytus (attributed), 'Discourse on the Holy Theophany, Water and the Spirit'
Second Reading at the Office of Readings for the Thursday after Epiphany, Cyril of Alexandria on St John's Gospel, 'The Outpouring of the Holy Spirit'
Second Reading at the Office of Readings for the Saturday after Epiphany, Faustus of Riez, *Sermon 5 on Epiphany*, 'The Marriage of Christ and the Church'

At the end of the time before the Baptism of the Lord, one can only be amazed that Star of Bethlehem, a largely unregarded, hidden, even plebeian plant, should have led so thoroughly into the mysteries of the Epiphany. In God's plant creation, it is one of those that underline Christ's lesson, that the greatest shall be least and the least the greatest. I love it, above all because it has led me to deeper understanding of Paul's words to Timothy: 'Great indeed, we confess, is the mystery of our religion: He was manifested in the flesh, vindicated in the Spirit, seen by angels, preached among the nations, believed on in the world, taken up in glory' (1Tim. 3:16).

Places of Spiritual Retreat
With the Magi, as in Matthew 2; at the wedding at Cana, as in John 2; on the banks of the Jordan at the Baptism of Jesus, as in Matthew 3.

THE BAPTISM OF THE LORD

(First Sunday in Ordinary Time)

WATERCRESS *Rorippa nasturtium aquaticicum*; *Nasturtium officinale*
LAND CRESS *Barbarea verna*

Cultivation Notes

Watercress grows wild in the rivers and streams of British chalklands. If you are fortunate enough to have a freshwater stream running through your garden, propagate the plant by seed or root cuttings in semi-shade, either in the water or on the margin. It can grow to a height of two feet, and is a natural trailer, so pinch out for bushiness and to delay flowering. Tiny white flowers normally appear in summer. The oldest leaves and stems have the strongest flavour. It is possible to grow watercress in very moist pots, but this necessitates changing the water at least once a day and is too time consuming for most of us to consider. However, the 'streamless' gardener can replicate the flavour of watercress by growing land cress. This biennial should not be confused with mustard and cress, or with *Barbarea vulgaris*. Land cress has glossy green leaves, loves moisture, but will grow in fertile and damp conditions. It runs to seed quickly if not watered thoroughly in hot weather, and the flavour becomes coarse and strong. Sow in spring for summer picking, and in early summer for autumn and winter. Pick about two months after sowing. Leave some to run to seed and they will self-seed easily for transplantation later.

History and Lore

The habitat and flavour of watercress is reflected in its botanical name, which means, 'river water nose-twister'! (The common garden nasturtium has nothing to do with watercress and was probably named because of its pungent smell.) Watercress is an ancient plant and was highly valued by the Greeks, who recommended it for those whose wits appeared to have deserted them and gave it to children to increase their strength and stature. Pliny gave the Latin name and mentioned its use in the treatment of brain disorders. It is native to Britain, and its richness in vitamin C, iodine, and calcium led to its use in the prevention and cure of scurvy. Traditionally it was taken as a tonic in spring and as a digestive. I always make sure it is available at Christmas, to counteract the richness of seasonal menus. If you find it in the wild, be careful not to pick near stagnant or polluted water, or in streams that run through sheep pastures. In these places the plant can harbour liver fluke eggs.

Nicholas Meissner of Erfurt in Germany is believed to have begun commercial cultivation in Europe, and a flourishing trade began in England around 1808. It has been popular ever since as a salad and garnish plant and as a sandwich ingredient. The English took it with them wherever they went and are believed to have transported it to America in jars of water. An infusion of watercress leaves and raspberries in a compress helps to clear spots, and applied to the forehead it eases headaches. The juice is also used to treat warts. The seventeenth-century poet Robert Herrick praised it, although he is of course talking about much more than the virtues of the plant:

> Lord, I confess too when I dine
> The Pulse is Thine,
> And all those other bits, that Bee
> There placed by Thee;
> The Worts, the Purslain, and the Messe of
>   Watercresse
> Which of Thy kindness Thou has sent;
> And my content.

One of our favourite family walks when I was growing up was to Monsaldale in Derbyshire. Arriving at Monsal Head via Monyash, we would make the steep, wooded descent into the dale and wander along by the gently waving beds of watercress growing in the pure and sunlit flowing water. I never eat watercress without remembering the place; it is forever associated in my mind with a bright and wholesome cleanliness.

The Feast of the Baptism of the Lord in the Roman Rite

After the division of Eastern and Western Christendom in the mid-fifteenth century, the Greek emphasis on Baptism remained in the liturgy of Epiphanytide for more than five hundred years. During that period, however, Western Christianity came more and more to concentrate, at least at Epiphany itself, on the Manifestation of Christ to the Gentiles in the symbolic Magi. But it was not until 1960 that Pope John XXIII presided over and sanctioned revisions to the Breviary and the Mass. The octave of the Epiphany was abolished, thus leaving a Sunday on which the whole Church could properly commemorate the Lord's baptism. After the

Second Vatican Council the feast was kept, but with an almost completely different set of liturgical readings. Nevertheless, the period after Epiphany has retained a strong baptismal element, with the wedding at Cana suggested in the Office of Readings for the Friday after Epiphany. The result is that the Church has provided a system in which we meditate on all three aspects of Epiphanytide, but in a much more balanced way than before.

Towards Meditation

'Jesus came from Galilee to the Jordan to John, to be baptised by him. John would have prevented him, saying, "I need to be baptised by you, and do you come to me?" But Jesus answered him, "Let it be so now; for thus it is fitting for us to fulfil all righteousness." Then he consented' (Mt. 3:13–16).

One can well understand John's initial reluctance to baptize Christ in a rite that was one of repentance for sin. The sinless One he had foretold could surely have no need of it. The watercress of Monsaldale helps me to approach the huge significance of Jesus' answer to John, and to know why John submitted without further argument.

Watercress requires running water to flourish. John's rite of penance, although godly and great, was stagnant in the sense that it could not save. Its waters could flow nowhere until, by opening the fountain of life, Christ transformed them into a sacrament of regeneration, so that our baptism could be by water and the Spirit.

Watercress has strengthening properties. The Baptism of Jesus strengthened John's resolve, vindicated his prophecy, and gave God's approval of his mission. The beginning of our own strength as Christians lies in our baptism. Furthermore, in the voice from heaven and in the dove, God testified to the identity of Jesus. This was strengthening to John's faith by the Jordan, as it is to ours by our fonts today.

Watercress cleanses and purifies the system. Jesus came up from the Jordan having sanctified its water, and the one who baptized him; he came up having made sanctification possible for the whole world. Through our baptism we are given a fresh start and it becomes possible for us to enter into salvation. The heavens opened at Christ's baptism. As a result, they are open to us.

Watercress was supposed to encourage growth and increase stature. At Christ's baptism, the Divine plan unfolds and grows a stage further before our eyes. In being baptized Christ seals a sacrament through which the Church grows, and through which each one of us has the opportunity to increase in stature.

Watercress quenches thirst and nourishes the body. Only through our baptism are we able to drink at the fountain of life; only through it may we be spiritually nourished by the Body and Blood of Christ.

Bible Readings
Psalm 28: The Lord's voice resounding on the waters

Psalm 113: Today the heavens opened, the waters made sweet, earth is glad

Isaiah 55:1–11: Oh come to the water all you who are thirsty

Isaiah 42:1–9: Here is my servant in whom my soul delights

Isaiah 61:1–2a: The Spirit of the Lord is upon me because he has anointed me

Isaiah 12:2–6: With joy you will draw water from the wells of salvation

Acts 10:34–8: God anointed him with the Holy Spirit

1 John 5:1–9: There are three witnesses, the Spirit, the water and the blood

Mark 1:7–11: He will baptize you with the Holy Spirit

Matthew 3:16–17; Luke 3:22: Today heaven opened when Jesus was baptized

Place of Spiritual Retreat
On the banks of the Jordan, as in Matthew 3, Mark 1, and John 1

ORDINARY TIME BEFORE LENT

FROM FIRST MONDAY OF ORDINARY TIME TO SHROVE TUESDAY

The Gardener's Journey towards Lent

Until Epiphany the Church allowed us to linger near the crib of Christ, but then she prised us suddenly away from Bethlehem to the banks of the Jordan: Christ has grown up and so must we. For yet another year she has reminded us that we cannot come to Christian adulthood without our baptism, which in its turn would not have been possible without the baptism of Christ. Unless we go with the Church to the river Jordan, we cannot join the vast and joyful throng that now sets off again, this time on the road towards Lent.

This period of the Church's year can last up to eight weeks. Horticulturally and spiritually, it is steadily and quietly busy. Roses, lilies, bulbs, pinks, heathers, herbs, fruit, vegetables, hedges, shrubs, and house plants all require our attention. There is new planting, and greenhouse and pond work for some of us. The problem is how to achieve everything during the few days when the weather does not keep all but the most intrepid and hardy gardener indoors. Someone once said that gardeners garden during three seasons of the year, and in the fourth they read about it. In my experience, this does not tell the full story. The truth is rather that I plan mentally all year round. The winter weather gives me *time* to examine the previous seasons' hastily scribbled notes, to make an assessment of failure and success, and to haul back unrecorded ideas. From this, a coherent plan emerges for the new season. Finance will also be a factor for most of us, and there always seem to be things that must wait another year. The poorer you are, the more does gardening teach patience and acceptance. But it is comforting to remember that even a rich person cannot make a leek grow any faster.

While we are laying the foundations of a new season in the garden, the Church, through her liturgy, prepares us for Lent by making a thorough examination of the faith that is her safe pilgrim tent on earth until she reaches her true and eternal home with God. During the coming weeks she will, if we will only listen, guide us in some focused and thorough Bible study. Up to now I have dedicated a plant for each day and used it as a springboard to meditation. In this section I have identified eight seasonal liturgical themes and suggested plants whose symbolism makes them appropriate for inclusion in a pre-Lent garden. Some of the plants have already been dealt with in earlier entries, some feature in Part Two (and yet others are planned to appear in future books). Full details of their cultivation and history therefore appear on days when they are being considered exclusively. In any year the themes are amenable to selection according to the time available. Alternatively, one could take any one of the themes and spend the whole season meditating on it, but they all encompass each other in some measure.

THEME 1: CHRISTIAN LIFE AND DESTINY

We are a chosen people set apart; in our work and witness we are 'a letter from Christ to the world'; he has said that he regards us as his brothers and sisters; as members of his family we are in fraternal fellowship with him and with each other, in the loving freedom of the New Covenant and Law. God wants us to strive to be fully developed: that is, to have the fullness of Christ in us so that we may find rest in our prayer on earth and eternal rest and joy in heaven. The measure we achieve will depend on the measure we put in.

Plant	Significance
Mock orange	Fraternal love
Buckbean	Calm repose;
Everlasting flower	Eternal life

Bible Readings
Genesis 1:20ff.: God makes man and woman
Genesis 3:1–24: The Fall and Expulsion from Eden
Proverbs 15:33: Man in the sight of God
Psalm 33:12: People chosen as his heritage
Zephaniah 2:3; 3:12–13: A humble and lowly people
1 Peter 2:9–10: A people set apart
Romans 12:5; 1 Corinthians 12–13; Ephesians 4:7: The Body of Christ
2 Corinthians 3:1–6: You are a letter from Christ

Hebrews 2:14–18: He became completely like his brothers except for sin
Hebrews 3:7–14: Keep encouraging one another
Hebrews 4:1–11: We must do all we can to reach this place of rest
1 James 1:1–11: You will become fully developed
Mark 3:13–19: He summoned them to be his companions
Mark 3:31–5: Whoever does the will of God is my brother, sister, and mother
Mark 4:21–5: The measure you put in is the measure you will receive
Matthew 5:13–16: You are the light of the world, the salt of the earth

Place of Spiritual Retreat
Resting in Christ's words, as in Mark 3:35

THEME 2: HOW WE MUST SHOW OUR LOVE FOR GOD AND OUR NEIGHBOUR

The plants listed below are reminders of Christ's new commandment, 'Love God, and your neighbour as yourself.' They underline the fact that the better we love God the better we shall love our neighbour, and the better we love our neighbour the better we shall love God.

Plant	Significance
Violet	Penitential colour
Passionflower	Belief
Mallow	Formerly used to treat deafness
Bulrush	The written Word
American cowslip	You are my Divinity
Canterbury bell	Gratitude
Agrimony	Thankfulness
Raspberry	Remorse
Snakeshead lily	Persecution
Wood anemone	Sickness, poverty
Cape jasmine	Joy
Box	Stoicism
Oxeye daisy	Patience
Clove-scented pink	Dignity
Ivy	Clinging
Adder's tongue	Venom
Chamomile	Humility

Prayer plant	Prayer
Moneywort	Economy
True Service tree	Duty
Yarrow	Battle
Vernal grass	Poverty
Trefoil	Unity
Scarlet verbena	Church unity
All good	Unite against evil
Thuya	Unchanging friendship
Thrift	Sympathy

Bible Readings: What we must do to achieve the goal

Love
Deuteronomy 4:1: What God requires
Deuteronomy 24:1–25: Commandments concerning our neighbour
Deuteronomy 6:4–25: The law of love
Psalm 18: I love thee, Lord my strength
Romans 13:8–10: The whole law summed up in love
Hebrews 10:19–25: Stir a response in love
1 John 4:7–19: Anyone who lives in love, lives in God
1 Thessalonians 3:12–13: Loving one another and the whole human race
1 Corinthians 12:31 – 13:15: Love defined
1 John 2: He who loves his brother abides in the light
Mark 12:32–3: Loving God and our neighbour
John 13:34: A new commandment I give you, that you love one another

Repentance and forgiveness
Deuteronomy 30:1–20: Promise of pardon
Jeremiah 29:13–14: I will restore your fortunes
2 Samuel 1–17: I have sinned against the Lord
Ecclesiasticus 17:24–9: Abandon sin, return to God
Psalm 51: In thy mercy blot out my sin
Psalm 32: Confession and forgiveness
Mark 1:14–20: Repent and believe
Mark 2:1–12: The Son of Man has authority on earth to forgive sin
Mark 2:13–17: I did not come to call the virtuous, but sinners to repentance

Faith and trust in God

Psalm 57: In the shadow of thy wings I will take refuge
Psalm 112: His heart is firm, trusting in the Lord
Isaiah 63:8–9: We put our faith in God's love
Jeremiah 17:5–8: Trust in God
Ecclesiasticus (Sirach) 11:11–28: Trust in God alone
Galatians 2:11 – 3:14: Faith brings life to the just
James 4:13–17: If the Lord wills we shall do this or that
John 9:14–29: Lord, help the little faith I have
Matthew 6:24–34: Do not worry about tomorrow
Mark 6:24–34: The lilies of the field

Listening to the Word

Deuteronomy 4:1: Write the precepts of the Lord in your hearts as in a book
1 Samuel 3:1–20: Speak Lord, your servant is listening
Deuteronomy 18:15–20: I will put my word in his mouth
Hebrews 11: God speaks through the prophets and through his Son
James 1:19–27: Be doers, not just hearers
Mark 4:1–20: The sower is sowing the Word

Joy, praise, and thanksgiving

Psalm 19:9: The heavens are telling the glory of God
Psalm 34: Glorify the Lord with me
Psalm 100:2: Make a joyful noise unto the Lord
1 Samuel 2:1–8: Joy in the Lord
1 Peter 1:3–9: You are filled with joy
Psalm 18:47: Shout to God with loud songs of joy
Psalm 81:2: Sing aloud to God our strength
Psalm 68:27: In festive gatherings bless the Lord
Tobit 4:19: Praise the Lord at all times
Tobit 12:6: Praise God and thank him for his mercy
Ecclesiasticus (Sirach) 42:15–43: Praise God in his creation

Hardship, poverty, persecution and illness

Deuteronomy 31:2–8: Be strong, stand firm
Psalm 55:23: Cast your burden on the Lord
Tobit 2:9–14: Tobit did not complain
Hebrews 12:1–2: We should keep running steadily in the race we have begun
2 Corinthians 6:4–5: We prove ourselves by fortitude in times of suffering

Prayer
Daniel 47:2–11: Put your heart into your love for God
Hebrews 4:14–15: Let us be confident in approaching the throne of mercy
Psalm 73:21–8: There is nothing on earth that I desire besides thee
Psalm 84: How lovely is thy dwelling place
Psalm 61: For God alone my soul waits in silence
James 5:13–20: Heartfelt prayer is powerful

Compassion and love for the poor
Deuteronomy 7:6–8: You have been given mercy
Isaiah 58:7–10: Share your bread with the hungry
James 2:14–26: Faith without works is dead

Honesty and control of the tongue
Proverbs 30:8: Keep falsehood and lies far from me
James 3:1–10: Nobody can tame the tongue

Friendship and welcoming strangers
1 Corinthians 1:10–17: Make up your differences
Ecclesiasticus 6:5–17: A faithful friend is beyond price
1 Kings 8:41–5: If a foreigner comes

Civic duty and service
1 Peter 4:7–12: Service of others
Mark 12:13–17: Render unto Caesar the things that are Caesar's and unto God the things that are God's

Places of Spiritual Retreat
Resting in Christ's words, as in Mark 2:13–17
With Christ and the man born blind, as in John 9, or listening to Christ's teaching on trust in God, as in Matthew 6
Listening to Christ's explaining the parable of the sower, as in Mark 4

THEME 3: HOW THE HOLY TRINITY HELPS US TO ACHIEVE OUR GOAL

(a) God the Father helps us through his love, expressed in the Scriptures, and his sending us his Son to redeem us.

Plant	Significance
Watercress	Baptism
Hazel	Reconciliation
Wheat and vine	Holy Communion

Bible Readings

Isaiah 63:8–9: We put our faith in God's love

Proverbs 9:5: Come, for all is now ready

Daniel 9:4: God keeps his covenant in steadfast love with those who love him

John 3:16; John 4:10: God loved the world; this is what love is

Luke 14:16–17: A man once gave a great banquet

Isaiah 11:1–2: The spirit of the Lord shall rest upon him

Galatians 3:27–8: The baptized have put on the person of Christ

1 John 2:20, 27: You have been anointed by the Holy Spirit

(b) God the Son helps us through his bringing in of the New Covenant, through his teaching and healing love, and through the sacraments, but above all through his redeeming death.

Plant	Significance
Willowherb	Pretension
Bairnswort (Daisy)	Children's flower
Down of cotton thistle	Formerly used to treat rickets
Barley	Food
French marigold	Jealousy
Polyanthus	Pride of riches
Tuberose	Dangerous pleasures
Lucern (alfalfa)	Life
Basil, Ginger, Goldenseal, Angelica, Anise, Peppermint, Sage, Clover, Rosemary, Linden (lime) blossom, Chamomile	Aids to digestion
Garlic, Horseradish, Pumpkin, Tansy seeds, Thyme, Dog-rose hips	Good to combat and expel internal parasites
All good	Cure all
Trefoil	Unity

Scarlet verbena	Unite against evil; Church unity
Pine	Pity
Juniper	Protection

Bible Readings
1 Corinthians 15:12–20: If Christ had not risen our faith would be in vain
Ephesians 5:2: Christ loved us and gave himself for us
Matthew 5:1–12: The Beatitudes
Mark 10:13–27: Humility; sell everything you have
Mark 9:41–50: It is better that you should be lame
Luke 6:17–26: Happy are the poor; alas for the rich
Mark 7:14–23: It is not what you eat that counts
Isaiah 53:5: He was wounded for our transgressions
Romans 5:9: We are justified by his blood
Galatians 3:13–14: Christ was accursed for our sake
Hebrews 5:1–10: He learned to obey through suffering
Hebrews 9:15, 24–8: He sacrificed himself to do away with sin
Hebrews 10:1,14: Christ has perfected for all time those who are sanctified
John 6: The mystery of the Blessed Sacrament

Places of Spiritual Retreat
Listening to Christ's teaching, as in John 6
Resting in the Beatitudes as in Matthew 5

(c) God the Holy Spirit helps us, through the sacraments; through his love, comfort and inspiration, and through the bestowing of his gifts.

Plant	Significance
Angelica	Root of the Holy Spirit; inspiration
Camellia 'Inspiration'	Inspiration
Climbing roses: 'Breath of life' and 'Danse du feu'	Pentecost
Bittersweet nightshade	Truth
Quake grass	Agitation
Heartsease	Consolation
Prayer plant	Prayer
China rose	Beauty ever new
Hart's tongue fern	The soul's thirst for God
Red double pink	Pure and ardent love

Borage	Courage; gladness
Box	Stoicism
Snowdrop	Consolation
Swallow-wort	Cure for heartache
Everlasting sweet pea	Lasting joy
Coriander	Hidden merit
White lily	Pure offering

The presence of these plants in the garden is a daily reminder that from the Holy Spirit comes the grace to overcome sin, to recognize true and false prophets, to discern good from evil, and to find the way we should walk. His presence calms our fretful, fearful spirits, which can never be securely at peace until they rest in God. The Holy Spirit opens our senses to God's will, and to the beauty of his dwelling place. He inspires a yearning thirst for God; he awakens our love for God, so that prayer is heartfelt and powerful; he inspires courage and fortitude; he consoles us in spiritual and temporal difficulties; and he inspires our joy and exultation in God. Any pure offering of our spiritual and apostolic lives can only come about through his working in us.

Bible Readings
1 Kings 3:4–13: Prayer for ability to discern good from evil
1 Corinthians 12:13: In the one Spirit we were all baptized
1 Corinthians 12:4–11: The Spirit distributes gifts

Place of Spiritual Retreat
With the disciples as they receive power to heal and cast out devils

THEME 4: WISDOM

Plant	Significance
White mulberry	Wisdom

The traditional significance of the white mulberry comes from the fact that it never buds until there is no danger of frost. Paradoxically, its botanical name is *Morus alba*, and *morus* is Greek for 'fool'. And so it symbolizes the wisdom of God and the foolishness of humans. *Morus alba*, contrary to the impression given in the old rhyme, 'Here we go round the mulberry bush', is a tree that can grow to a height and spread of twenty feet. Most of us will not have the space for it. But its very absence should remind us that at the end of our earthly lives, we will be fortunate if we have even begun to plumb the depths of God's wisdom.

Bible Readings
Isaiah 11:1–2: A spirit of wisdom and understanding
Psalm 36:30: The mouth of the righteous utters wisdom
Psalm 19:8: The testimony of the Lord makes the simple wise
Proverbs 1:1–33: Choose wisdom
Proverbs 3:1–20: How wisdom is found
Proverbs 8:1–36: Praise of eternal wisdom
Proverbs 9:1–18: Wisdom and foolishness
Proverbs 10:6–32: Various wise sayings
Proverbs 15:33: The fear of the Lord is instruction in wisdom
The Wisdom of Solomon, and the Wisdom of Jesus son of Sirach
  (Ecclesiasticus): The nature of wisdom and how it is to be found
Isaiah 11:1–2: A spirit of wisdom and understanding
Job 12:1–25: God's dominion over all human wisdom
Job 28:1–28: Wisdom rests with God alone
Romans 12:16: Do not think yourselves wise
1 Corinthians 1:23–4: The world's wisdom
1 Corinthians 1:26–31: God's wisdom
1 Corinthians 2:7–10: The depths of God's secret wisdom
1 Corinthians 3:18–19: Christ, the wisdom of God
John 6:56: The wisdom of Christ

Place of Spiritual Retreat
Listening to Christ's teaching on the mystery of his body and blood, as in John 6

THEME 5: TITLES OF CHRIST

(a) The Word

Plant	Significance
Bulrush	The written Word

Bible Readings
1 Thessalonians 2:13: The very Word of God

Mark 4:1–20: The sower is sowing the Word
John 1:1–17: In the beginning was the Word

Place of Spiritual Retreat
Listening to the Sower sowing the seed, as in Mark 4

(b) The Lord of the Sabbath and of nature

Plant	Significance
Balm of Gilead, thyme, marjoram, fenugreek, lemon, barley, lovage, motherwort, sorrel	Healing: all used in modern herbalism to treat fever
Pennywort	Being researched for the treatment of leprosy
Melilot, sun-spurge, wallflower	Formerly used to treat paralysis
Chamomile, mullein	Used in modern herbalism to treat ear complaints; cure of deafness
Clary sage, eyebright, damask rose, borage, chamomile, cucumber, fennel, goldenseal, tansy, thyme	All traditionally used in eye treatment
Comfrey, goldenseal, marshmallow, raspberry, blackberry, clover, marigold	All used in modern treatment of mouth complaints
Paeony	Being researched for the treatment of convulsions
Chaste tree, raspberry, Our Lady's mantle, motherwort	Used to ease gynaecological, menstrual and menopausal problems
Soapwort	Symbolic association with cleanness of spirit
Peppermint, rose hips, sage, chamomile, clove, catnip, hop, lemon balm, lavender, lime flowers, feverfew, rosemary, valerian, borage	All used to refresh the spirit, clear the mind, ease headaches, insomnia, and nerve disorders
All heal, All good, holy thistle	Formerly believed to be panaceas against all physical, mental,

| | intellectual, emotional, and spiritual ill health |
| Alfalfa, watercress, lemon | Excellent as tonic cleansers of the whole system |

Bible Readings
Mark 1:29–39: He cured many diseases of one kind or another
Mark 2:1–12: The paralytic man cured
Mark 2:23–8: The sabbath is made for man, not man for the sabbath
Mark 1:40–5: A leper is cured
Mark 3:1–6: Cure of the man with the withered hand
Mark 3:7–12: Jesus heals many, and is recognized as the Son of God by the unclean spirits
Mark 3:22–30: Satan cast out
Mark 5:1–20: Come out, unclean spirits
Mark 5:21–43: The woman with the issue of blood cured, and Jairus' daughter raised
Mark 6:7–13: The disciples also cast out devils and heal many
Mark 6:53–6: All who touched him were healed
Mark 7:24–30: A Greek woman's daughter freed of a demon
Mark 7:37: He even makes the deaf hear and the dumb speak
Mark 8:22–6: A blind man cured
Mark 9:15–29: The dumb and deaf convulsive boy
Mark 10:46–52: Bartimaeus, born blind, receives sight
Luke 7:1–10: A centurion's servant is cured

Place of Spiritual Retreat
Each year, among the crowds at a the scene of a different cure, as in Mark or Luke

(c) The Good Shepherd

| **Plant** | **Significance** |
| Shepherd's needle | Symbolic of garden maintenance, care of one's charges, and good neighbourliness |

Bible Readings
2 Samuel 5:1–10: The shepherd of my people Israel

Psalm 23: The Lord is my shepherd
Hebrews 13:15–17: The great Shepherd of the sheep

Place of Spiritual Retreat
Resting in the love and compassion of Christ

(d) The Bridegroom

Plant	Significance
Meadowsweet	Traditional bridal flower; Christ as Bridegroom of the Church and the individual

Bible Readings
Hosea 2:16–22: I will betroth you to myself
Isaiah 62:1–5: The Bridegroom rejoices in his bride
Mark 2:18–22: The Bridegroom is with them

Place of Spiritual Retreat
Rejoicing in spiritual communion

(e) The Head of the Body, Lord of the universe

Plant	Significance
Masterwort	Symbolizes Christ as the Head of his Body, the Church, and the master of all his followers

Bible Readings
Psalm 77:14–16: Thou art the God who workest wonders
Proverbs 8:22–30: I was there beside him like a master workman
Job 12:1–25: God's dominion
Mark 1:21–8: He taught them with authority
Mark 4:36–41: Even the wind and waves obey him
Mark 2:1–12: The Son of Man has authority
Mark 11:27–33: Authority
Mark 8:1–10: All had their fill
Luke 4:14–21: Christ in the synagogue; this text is being fulfilled today
Revelation 1:18: I hold the keys of death

Ephesians 4:15; Galatians 5:1–25: Christ, who is the head
John 2:1–12: The miracle at Cana

Place of Spiritual Retreat
Listening to Jesus in the synagogue, as in Luke 4

(f) Son of Man

Plant	Significance
The apple tree	Christ as the tree of life and the Second Adam

Bible Readings
Matthew 24:30: The sign of the Son of Man will appear
Mark 2:1–12: The Son of Man has authority
Mark 8:27–33: The Son of Man must suffer
Mark 9:30–7; 10:32–45: The Son of Man will be delivered

Place of Spiritual Retreat
Preparing to enter Jerusalem for the Passover

(g) High Priest

Plant	Significance
Incense tree (Boswellia)	Prayer and sacrifice

Bible Readings
Psalm 110:4b: You are a priest for ever after the order of Melchizedek
Hebrews 7; 8; 9; 10: Dissertation on the old priesthood and the transforming eternal priesthood of Christ

(h) Christ the King

Plant	Significance
Kingcup	Christ reigning in glory

Bible Readings
Psalm 24: He is the King of Glory
Mark 9:2–13: The Transfiguration

THEME 6: VOCATION

(a) Holy Life

Plant	Significance
Holy grass	Smells of new-mown hay; sacred to the Blessed Virgin Mary
Holy thistle	Originally grown in monastery gardens, and regarded as a cure-all

These two plants symbolize the joy and the pain we experience in our efforts to follow Christ, whether we be lay or religious, active or contemplative.

(b) Celibate Life

Plant	Significance
Dame's violet (vesper flower, eyeweed)	Watchfulness (see Scholastica, 10 February, in Part Two)
Monk's pepper (chaste tree)	Chastity

Dame is the style given to fully professed Benedictine nuns. This flower makes me remember them with admiration, respect, and love. Named vesper flower because its perfume is strongest in the evening, its traditional meaning is watchfulness. This probably accounts for its third name, eyeweed. And indeed one has to be on guard to preserve chastity. Monk's pepper has long been associated with celibacy. Its botanical name, *Vitex agnus-castus*, means 'pure lamb', and its ground seeds are thought to have been used in monasteries in former times as a condiment for the control of the 'old Adam and Eve'.

(c) Married and Family Life

Plant	Significance
Linden tree	Conjugal love
Sage	Domestic virtue
Pink verbena	Family union
Oxeye daisy	Patience
Chaste tree	Celibate marriage, chosen or imposed by circumstance

These plants may lead us to meditate on our membership of Christ's family, or to examine the health of our marriages and family relationships.

Bible Readings

Deuteronomy 18:1–22: You must be entirely faithful

1 Thessalonians 4:1–18: A holy life, the hope of resurrection

1 Thessalonians 5:1–28: The way of life for the children of light

1 Corinthians 12:4–11: The Spirit distributes gifts as he chooses

Hebrews 10: Priesthood under Christ

Proverbs 31:10–31: The perfect wife

Ecclesiasticus (Sirach) 26: A modest wife, a twofold boon; the Lord is the beauty of a good wife

1 Corinthians 7:32–5: The unmarried woman

Genesis 2:18–25: Adam and Eve made one

Mark 10:1–12: What God has joined let no man put asunder

Hebrews 13:1–8: Married and family life

Place of Spiritual Retreat

Examining the state of one's calling in the light of Christ's teaching

THEME 7: PHASES OF LIFE/RITES OF PASSAGE

An inescapable and sombre thread of suffering runs through the liturgy during these weeks of Ordinary Time, and the closer we come to Lent the more appropriate this seems.

Plant	Significance
Watercress	Fresh running water (Baptism)
Spring crocus	Gladness, celebration
Oak	Bereavement of offspring (David and the death of Absolom; God, Our Lady and the death of Christ)
Moses acacia	Bereavement of an elder (Death of Moses)
Yew and harebell	Sorrow and grief (The Man of Sorrows; Our Lady of Sorrows)
Scabious	I have lost all (Job)
Wallflower	Fidelity in adversity (Job)

Wood/Field anemone	Sickness (Job)
Comfrey, fenugreek, houseleek, lupin, sage, Saint John's wort, teasel, walnut	All used in the treatment of Ulcers (Job)
False indigo	False peace (Job)
Valerian	Accommodating disposition, acceptance of change
Guelder rose	Winter of age
American starwort	Cheerfulness in old age
Lemon	Elixir of long life

Bible Readings

Feasting, gladness, and celebration
3:1–22: There is a season for everything
Deuteronomy 16:14–15: Rejoice at your feasts
Nahum 1:15: Keep your feasts

Sorrow, trials, old age, and death
Genesis 22:6: Abraham loads the wood on his son Isaac
Deuteronomy 32:48–52: Death of Moses
2 Samuel 18:9–19:3: Death of Absalom
1 Kings 2:1–44: Death of David.
Ecclesiasticus (Sirach) 2:1–11: Prepare for an ordeal
Job 1:1–22: Job deprived of his possessions
Job 2:1–13: Job afflicted with ulcers
Job 3:1–26: Job's dirge
Job 7:1–21: Job calls to God
Job 29:1–10; 30:1, 9–23: Job's lament in affliction
2 Corinthians 4:8–10: We are in trouble on all sides
Hebrews 10:33–9: Sufferings and trials
Psalm 27: He will hide me in the day of trouble
Ecclesiasticus (Sirach) 11:7 – 12:14: Reflections on old age
Psalm 71:9: Do not cast me off in the time of old age
Psalm 23: The valley of the shadow of death

Place of Spiritual Retreat
With Christ the Good Shepherd, as in Psalm 23

THEME 8: THE LAST THINGS

The Church balances suffering by reminding us once again of the purpose and meaning of our struggles, and she strengthens us with thoughts of justice, hope, and eternal reward in the presence of Christ.

Plant	Significance
Chestnut	Traditional meaning: do me justice
Mint	Virtue
Hawthorn	Traditional symbolism: hope
Hemlock	Represents death
Coltsfoot	Traditional meaning: justice shall be done you
Garland of roses	Represents reward
Stock	Traditional meaning: lasting beauty
Everlasting sweet pea	Symbolic of everlasting joy

Bible Readings
The Book of Job
Psalm 23: The valley of the shadow of death
James 5:9–12: The judge is already at the gate
Ecclesiasticus (Sirach) 36:1–17: Have mercy upon us O Lord, the God of all
1 Peter 1:18–25: Remember the ransom that was paid
1 Corinthians 15:54–8: Victory through Christ
Mark 10:28–31: Eternal life
Jude 17–23: He will bring you safe to his glorious presence

ENVOI

Final advice and help before setting out on the Lenten road

Plant	Significance
All Good	Reflect again on Christ's power to heal whenever he wills
Heartsease	Rest in the Lord
Violet	Repent
Traveller's joy	God loves you
Michaelmas daisy	Be cheerful; give with a smile

Bible Readings for the Monday and Tuesday before Ash Wednesday

Psalm 112: Happy are those who
  fear the Lord
Psalm 91: My refuge and my fortress,
  my God in whom I trust
Psalm 90: Lord, you have been
our dwelling place in all generations
Galatians 2:19–20: Christ lives
  in me
2 Peter 3:11–18: We are waiting
  for a new heaven and a new earth

All Good and Heartsease

Part Two

SOLEMNITIES AND SAINTS' DAYS

INTRODUCTORY NOTE

During Advent the Church is preoccupied with the first great stage of her annual journey, namely the dark road that leads to the true light of Christmas. Keeping our eyes focused on that goal, she leads us slowly but surely forward under the lamp of Old Testament prophecy. This she has kept trimmed over the centuries, and each year it comes unfailingly to her aid. Occasionally she halts on the march in order to show us some of the treasures in her scrip. These are the saints of Advent and its one great Solemnity, the Immaculate Conception of the Blessed Virgin Mary.

During Christmastide to Epiphany the Church rests joyfully and adoringly in Bethlehem, and then, after the Baptism of the Lord (the first Sunday of Ordinary Time, in early January), she resumes her journey, this time taking the road towards Lent. Once again she has a weekly plan of travel, but, as in Advent, she occasionally lingers to study some of the details that are embroidered on the basic cloth of her liturgy. These are the saints of Ordinary Time to Shrove Tuesday. The Church encourages us to pay attention to them, not only because of the countless numbers of souls they have already brought to the kingdom of Christ, but because by their teaching, example, and prayers they continually help us to attain it ourselves.

DECEMBER

3 DECEMBER

St Francis Xavier, Pastor (1506–1552)

JAPANESE MAPLE *Acer palmatum*

Cultivation Notes

This deciduous garden tree, popular because of its colour in autumn, grows to around ten feet in its first decade, and can reach an ultimate height of eighteen feet. It needs lime-free soil and shelter, and it can be susceptible to spring frosts, so choose the site carefully. A wide range of cultivars is available, but the more ornamental, the more sensitive it will be to the amount of sun and shade it receives. It will not thrive if it has too much of either. My Japanese maple is a thing of the future, but when the time comes, I will look for one as near to the species as possible. Even in my part of France the site factor cannot be ignored, and there may be a problem of space in the Advent garden. If this proves the case, a bonsai specimen will be the answer. Downy Japanese maple is attractive with autumn leaves that are golden-centred, deepening to red around the edge of the divisions in each one. The Japanese have been experimenting with the crossing of different varieties of the tree for over three centuries, and it is even more common in their gardens than in ours, both in full-size and in bonsai form. The idea of bonsai trees as house plants did not originate in Japan. A bonsai tree can be enjoyed indoors for a few days, but its natural home is in a pot or trough in the garden, where it will need the same consideration as its full-size relative.

History and Lore

Francis Xavier was a Spanish Basque and an early Jesuit missionary who worked in Goa and Sri Lanka. Ignatius of Loyola had only recently formed the *Society of Jesus,* in support of Counter-Reformation ideals, and Francis, as well as evangelizing, did much to reduce the scandal of bad Catholic example wherever he found it. He met with some success during a short spell in Japan, where he learned that sometimes pragmatism is

169

advisable in the furtherance of God's kingdom. He gained access to the Mikado by dressing sumptuously and offering rich gifts, and as a result obtained the use of a deserted Buddhist monastery. Remarkably, for a man who had difficulty in learning foreign languages, he translated a simplified Christian creed into Japanese, and it is estimated that by the time he returned to Goa in 1552 there were some two hundred Christians in Japan. After a short while he set out again, this time for China, and his ceaseless, tireless voyaging, particularly since he suffered badly from seasickness, is another sign of his apostolic commitment and determination. He was never to set foot on mainland China. During the journey he contracted the illness that would eventually lead to his death on an offshore island, in sight of his goal. His body is in Goa. Until recently it was incorrupt, but it is now showing signs of deterioration. His right arm is in the Gesù, in Rome. Bute's 1908 translation of the Roman Breviary reports amazing miracles, even while Francis was still alive. It claims the gift of prophecy for him but does not elaborate. He was canonized by Pope Gregory XV in 1622 and in 1927 was made Patron of the Foreign Missions by Pope Pius XI.

The Xaverian Brothers have their roots in Belgium in 1939, and reached a peak of membership in the 1960s. But after Vatican II vocations dried up, so that today they number only 265 worldwide, the majority being American. However, they maintain an international presence in Haiti, Bolivia, Bangladesh, Lithuania, Congo, Kenya, Sudan, Belgium, England, and the USA.

Towards Meditation
'The harvest is rich but the labourers are few' (Lk. 10:2).

In my garden a curry plant and annual chillies represent Francis Xavier's Goan years, but I look forward to planting a maple to commemorate his Japanese legacy on some not too distant 3 December. He was a prolific correspondent, and today, in the second Office reading, the Church invites us to ponder a passage from his letter to St Ignatius. In it, he describes an actual village and how the spiritual poverty of its people prevented him from eating, sleeping, or saying his Office until he had taught them the essentials of the Faith. He goes on to bemoan the lack of other missionaries and criticizes those who spend their time arguing theological points when they could be out and about helping Christ to save souls. Francis Xavier's conversion methods have been criticized, as have those of many missionaries, both Catholic and Protestant. My answer is that Christ can only come to us as we are, that is as creatures of our times. The efficacy of our response to the needs of those times will depend on how open we are to his Holy Spirit, and on how much we really desire him to move us forward and bring us closer to the doing of his will. The fact that we are sinful and unworthy to preach the word does not diminish the word itself. Through the Divine Office the Church enables Francis Xavier to continue preaching it almost half a millennium after his death. And 265 Xaverian brothers also preach it, in the places to which God still calls them. Truly, the Saint after whom they are named is the first illuminating halt on the Advent road.

'You will receive power when the Holy Spirit comes on you, and then you will be my witnesses to the ends of the earth' (Acts 1:8).

Bible Readings
Psalm 117: Praise the Lord, all nations! Extol him all peoples
1 Corinthians 9:16–23: Woe to me if I do not preach the gospel
Matthew 28:16–20: Go, therefore and make disciples of all nations

Place of Spiritual Retreat
With the eleven disciples on the road to Galilee after the appearance of the Risen Lord, as in Matthew 28

4 DECEMBER

St John Damascene, Doctor (657–749)

PENCIL CEDAR *Juneripus virginiana*

Cultivation Notes
This elegant, slow-growing conifer grows to about 45 feet and is the tallest member of the juniper family. It is hardy and adaptable, and likes a rather dry soil. The male flowers are round and yellow, the female small and green, opening on separate shoots in March. Pencil cedar wood is soft, aromatic, and resistant to insects and is used to make moth-proof linings in furniture. The English name probably refers to its popularity with the manufacturers of high quality pencils, and its very shape is reminiscent of a pencil. It was introduced to England as an ornamental shrub from

north-east America in 1664. For a smaller garden dwarf rockery forms are available, and it is a good Bonsai subject.

History and Lore

John Damascene, often known as the last of the Greek Fathers, was born in Syria and spent his whole life under Muslim rule. Before becoming a monk at the monastery of St Sabas near Jerusalem, he had followed in his father's footsteps and worked for the Caliph. He is remembered especially for his writings, the most famous of which is *Fount of Knowledge*. The third part of this work, *De Fide Orthodoxa*, is a comprehensive and systematic exposition of the teaching of the Fathers who had preceded him. It concentrates particularly on the Trinity, the Incarnation, and the person of Jesus Christ. In his three *Orations in Defence of Sacred Images*, he also wrote against iconoclasm, and after his death his views were sanctioned at the Council of Nicea in 787. St John Damascene has had a great influence in both East and West. He was a contemporary of the English historian monk, the Venerable Bede, and was made a Doctor of the Church nine years before him in 1890.

Towards Meditation

The second Office reading today is from the first chapter of *De Fide Orthodoxa*. In it John Damascene asks God to give him the right words and, through the tongue of fire of the Holy Spirit, to ensure that his language will be clear and fluent. This reinforces my own humble experience that such a prayer is essential every time one sits down to write about God, or on God's behalf. Every day the Holy Spirit must be invited to be the real author. It is essential constantly to implore his presence, guidance, and protection. We must 'put on the whole armour of God', for it is the business of evil to get in and do damage if it finds the slightest chink left open. In the commemoration of St John, I am struck anew by the marvel of language, and by how much the literate take it for granted. Our power to write and read is no accident. For us to receive oral tradition alone would have been insufficient for God's purpose. The Word had to be expressed and promulgated in written form, and moreover God endowed us with brains that could invent systems whereby the blind, deaf, and dumb could also receive and promote him.

The word 'pencil' is from the Latin *penicillum*, and the later Old French *pincel*, meaning an artist's paintbrush. Perhaps our modern pencil came to be so called because with it we can paint word pictures. So the pencil cedar reminds me of St John Damascene's association with words and sacred images. During Advent, I mentioned the medieval *Bibliae Pauperum*, in which pictures were used to teach the faith in an age of mass illiteracy. The idea and the practice go back much further than the Middle Ages, however. In his third *Oration in Defence of Sacred Images*, John Damascene says that what matters is the artist's intention. We must ask ourselves whether the work is for the glory of God and his saints, and whether it encourages virtue and works for the salvation of souls. Affirmative answers, he says, require us to value, revere, and love these images, and regard them as 'books for the illiterate'. And so when I look at my dwarf pencil cedar, it will call forth renewed gratitude to God for my own power to use and love words, and for the same but vastly greater power in his prophets and saints, which has enabled me to receive the Word.

Bible Readings
Psalm 19:7–14: Appreciation of God's law and prayer for protection from error
Ecclesiasticus (Sirach) 15:1–6: The spirit of wisdom and understanding
1 Corinthians 1:18: The language of the cross
2 Timothy 1:13–14: Follow the pattern of words you have heard from me
Mark 4:1–20: Parable of the sower

Place of Spiritual Retreat
At the feet of Christ, listening to the parable and reflecting on his words of explanation, as in Mark 4

6 DECEMBER

St Nicholas, Bishop (fourth century)

MONEYWORT *Lysimachia nummularia*; roving sailor; meadow runagates; herb twopence; creeping Jenny; *l'herbe aux écus*

Cultivation Notes
This creeping perennial resembles the yellow pimpernel, but, as its botanical name indicates, it is more closely related to the loosestrife family and is found in damp woodland. The yellow flowers, which never fully open, appear from May to early autumn. The plant throws out long stems

that run along the ground bearing small round coin-shaped leaves. It rarely produces fertile seeds, so propagate by division. Moneywort is a vigorous ground cover plant.

History and Lore
In the seventeenth century moneywort was believed to have pain-relieving properties, and in modern herbalism ointments and lotions are still made from it for application to wounds. Most of its names have obvious explanations, except perhaps for meadow runagates. 'Runagate' is a corruption of 'renegade' and has also come to mean vagabond or fugitive. As for the French name, an *écu* was an old silver coin considered as equal in value to the pre-decimal English half-crown. There were also gold *écus*, which were much heavier. Occasionally one still hears the now defunct five-franc piece referred to as an *écu*.

Little is known about the life of St Nicholas except that he was bishop of Myra, in south-west Turkey, now named Mugla. His cult was strong in the East from the sixth century and by the tenth was also known in the West. After the shrine at Myra was taken by the Muslims, in 1087 the relics were removed to Bari, and a new church built there to accommodate them. From then on Nicholas became universally revered in the West. Legends of him abound throughout Europe and he is supposed to have saved three unjustly condemned men from the death penalty; to have rescued three drowning sailors on a voyage to the Holy Land; and to have secretly thrown three bags of gold for marriage dowries into the house of a destitute family, thus saving its three daughters from the degradation of prostitution. (This is thought to be the origin of the traditional three golden balls outside pawnbrokers' shops.) From his shrine at Bari, there exuded a sweet-smelling manna-like substance, making the place a great centre of pilgrimage. These stories explain St Nicholas' patronage of sailors, unmarried girls, pawn-brokers, and perfumers, but he is best known as Santa Claus, the protector of children, and this patronage probably has its basis in the story that he raised from the dead three boys who had been murdered in a vat of brine by a butcher. The custom of giving children presents on his feast is well known in Holland, Belgium, and parts of France. In Holland on 6 December *Sinta Klaas* rides over the rooftops on a shining white horse, and children leave stockings or clogs filled with hay and carrots in the hope that he will take them for his horse and leave presents in exchange. The Dutch Protestants of North America combined legends of Nicholas with other Nordic folklore to produce a festival in which the presents were denied to children who had been persistently naughty during the previous year.

Towards Meditation

I often think that the position of saints close to each other in the calendar cannot be entirely arbitrary. Yesterday we were thanking God that John Damascene did not hide his light under a bushel. Today we consider a saint whose life is shrouded in mystery. If Nicholas did throw the gold through the sisters' window, he did it unostentatiously. But even if the legend is complete fabrication, when it is set against the achievement of John Damascene, it draws our attention, not to a contradiction in the teaching of Christ, but to the perfect balance within it. As far as the Word is concerned, we must proclaim it from the housetops and let the world see our good deeds, but to God's glory, not ours. These two saints together demonstrate that scholarship and charity in the service of the Kingdom must be characterized by humility and discretion. As St Augustine of Hippo (354–430) says in today's Office reading, if we love Christ, we will set about finding his sheep and feeding them, shepherding them for him and not for ourselves. A bishop is a shepherd, and in the legends of St Nicholas we see the misty outline of a very good one. Moneywort suits him, not only because of its association with gold *écus*, but because of its humility and secretiveness in hiding, yet spreading strongly, under the shadow of other plants. Today will be a day of prayer for bishops, and for reflection on my stewardship of the talents God has given me.

Bible Readings

Psalm 23: The Lord is my shepherd
Ezekiel 34:11–16: A shepherd keeps his flock in sight
Acts 20:28; 1 Corinthians 4:2: Trustworthy shepherds of the Church
Matthew 25:14–25: The parable of the talents
John 10:11–16: Christ, the Good Shepherd

Place of Spiritual Retreat
Listening to Christ teaching the parable of the talents, as in Matthew 25

7 DECEMBER

St Ambrose, Bishop (340–397)

BEE BALM *Monarda didyma*; bergamot; oswego tea-plant

Cultivation Notes
In late summer this hardy herbaceous perennial produces bright red
flowers with reddish-green bracts. It grows to a height of four feet and
relishes rich moist soil and sun. Sow the seed in spring or take softwood
cuttings in early summer. Mulch established plants in spring. Bee balm is
prone to mildew in dry conditions. It is particularly attractive to bumble-
bees, and honey-bees will not disdain it, even though they must reach the
nectar through holes made in the petals by other insects. Butterflies also
favour it, as do the humming birds of North America. The hybrid
'Cambridge scarlet' is recommended. Cut the leaves before flowering and
use fresh or dried to make tea. Dried flowers retain colour and are an
effective addition to arrangements or pot-pourri. Float the flowers on cool
summer drinks, but soak in water first as some of the insects already
mentioned may need to be evicted. The flowers soaked in milk make a
soothing drink to calm ragged nerves.

History and Lore
Bee balm is native to North America, and the botanical name honours the
Spanish botanist priest, Nicholas Monárdez, who discovered it and
included it in his book *Joyfull Newes out of the Newe Founde Worlde* (1571,
translated into English 1577). This work was almost certainly the first
European commentary on American medicinal plants, but Dr Monárdez
probably named it bergamot because its aroma is reminiscent of the small
Italian orange *Citrus bergamia*. It later became popular in Europe for
making tisanes, and after the 'Boston Tea Party' in 1773 it was a widely-
used substitute for tea. It is thought that the first seed to arrive in England
was sown by one Peter Collinson, who in 1745 had received it from friends
who had collected it on the shores of Lake Ontario, where it grew in
abundance. Several Indian tribes of the Oswego region used the plant to

treat colds and chest complaints, and it is likely that the settlers learned from them. Bee balm contains the powerfully antiseptic thymol, and it produces a good expectorant. It is also beneficial to the digestive system. The Omaha and Ponca Indians boiled the flowering tops to make hair oil. In England the National Collection of *Monarda* is in the Culpeper Garden at Leeds Castle, Maidstone, Kent.

Towards Meditation

There is a legend that a swarm of bees settled on the cradle of the infant Ambrose, which was taken as an omen of the eloquence he later proved to possess. But bees also symbolize industry and good organization, both of which qualities Ambrose exemplified in his calling as Bishop of Milan. Prior to this he had become a successful lawyer. Tradition has it that the voice of a child cried out in the electoral assembly, 'Ambrose for bishop!' He is supposed to have been baptized and consecrated within the week. At the time, Milan was the administrative capital of the Western Empire, and so Ambrose was able to exercise his considerable influence to strengthen and defend the Christian faith. He showed an unswerving purpose and was uncowed by secular authority. He showed this when his friend the emperor Theodosius had commanded the massacre of Thessalonians for having lynched the commandant of the town. Ambrose wrote privately to Theodosius telling him, in the most tactful, sensitive, but firm terms that until he had done public penance for the massacre he could not receive the Sacrament. The Emperor complied and the victory was won for the moral law of the gospel. It was an extremely important moment in Church history, and it reminds me that as Christians we must have the courage of our convictions and speak, yes, sensitively, but also firmly, even though what we say is unpopular or hard. He reminds me of the enjoyment inherent in duty assiduously performed, and of the fruits borne of toil. But St Augustine, whom he brought to the faith and baptized, called him 'Father' Ambrose, and there are in his life and writings threads of kindness, serenity, and absolute trust in God. Today's Office reading is an extract from one of Ambrose's letters, in which he speaks of the need for the faithful to be calmed and soothed by preaching, as well as to be energized by it. Freedom from anxiety is to be found in complete trust in Christ. He believed that as bishop he should be accessible to the flock, and in another letter to Theodosius he maintained that, above all, work must be founded on prayer.

Ambrosian chant cannot be ascribed exclusively to St Ambrose, but scholars seem fairly well agreed that he is, as Martin Luther claimed, the father of church hymnody. He had a talent for words and music and is thought to have written, with Augustine, the *Tonus Simplex* for the *Te Deum*, which is still in the Roman Gradual. Other beautiful hymns worth meditating on today are the Advent *Conditor Alme Siderum* (Creator of the stars of night); the Christmas *Veni Redemptor Gentium* (Come thou Redeemer of the earth); and *Deus Creator Omnium* (Maker of all things, God most high). This last is supposed to have comforted the grieving Augustine after the death of his mother Monica. Between them, these hymns encapsulate a great deal of Ambrose's teaching about living the faith and transmitting it to others. Not the least, that if we have a gift for words, we should use it to comfort others.

Bible Readings
Psalm 89:1 I will sing of thy steadfast love O Lord, forever
Ezekiel 34:11–16: I myself will search for my sheep
Ephesians 3:8–12: This grace was given to bring to the Gentiles the boundless riches of Christ
2 Timothy 4:2: Preach the word, be urgent, convince, rebuke, exhort with patience and teaching
John 10:11–16: Christ, the Good Shepherd

Place of Spiritual Retreat
Listening to Jesus' words to the Pharisees, as in John 10

8 DECEMBER

The Immaculate Conception of the Blessed Virgin Mary

A SELECTION OF OLD GARDEN ROSES

Gallicas
'Apothecary' (var. *officinalis*): Introduced before 1300; fragrant; pale crimson; three feet; bushy, tidy; small round hips; spray against mildew.
'Charles de Mills' ('Bizarre triomphant'): Origin unknown; fragrant; wine-red, small pink and white flecks; five feet; beautiful pattern of petals.
'Rosa mundi': Before 1500, slightly fragrant; pale pink, striped crimson; three feet; spray against mildew.

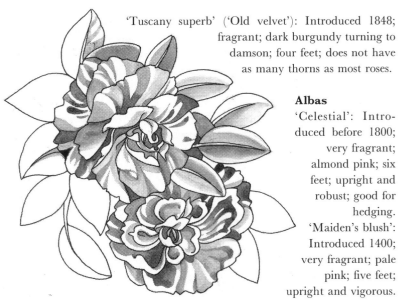

'Tuscany superb' ('Old velvet'): Introduced 1848; fragrant; dark burgundy turning to damson; four feet; does not have as many thorns as most roses.

Albas
'Celestial': Introduced before 1800; very fragrant; almond pink; six feet; upright and robust; good for hedging.
'Maiden's blush': Introduced 1400; very fragrant; pale pink; five feet; upright and vigorous.

'Queen of Denmark':
Introduced 1826; very fragrant, pink-scented; rose madder; silver, blue-green foliage; five feet.

Damask
'Ispahan': ('Pompon des princes'): Introduced before 1832; fragrant; pink; upright; R.H.S. award winner; five feet.

Centifolias
'Fantin-Latour': ('Provence' or 'Cabbage rose'): Introduced 1900; fragrant; delicate blush-pink; five feet; upright; R.H.S. award winner.
'Cristata' ('Chapeau de Napoléon'): Introduced 1826; fragrant; deep pink; five feet.

Bourbons
'Souvenir de la Malmaison': Introduced 1843; very fragrant; white, flushed pink; six feet; climbing form available, which does not flower as well as true bush type; unlike gallicas and albas is a repeat flowerer.
'Louise Odier' ('Madame de Stella'): Introduced 1851; fragrant; rose-pink; four feet; repeat flowerer; may need support.

179

'Madame Isaac Pereire': Introduced 1881; deep pink; very fragrant; huge flowers; six to seven feet; repeat flowerer.
'Zéphirine Drouhin' (thornless rose): Introduced 1868; very fragrant; carmine-pink; climber or bush; deadhead to ensure repeat flowering.

Rugosa
'Rosarie de l'Hay': Introduced 1901; fragrant; wine red; bushy; repeat flowerer; six to seven feet; will grow in poor soil and exposed conditions.

History and Lore
The rose is of great antiquity and the history of civilization can almost be traced through the history of the plant. The earliest domesticated roses are thought to have been types of deep crimson *Rosa gallica*, and to have originated in Iran. Carried by merchants, pilgrims, and possibly crusaders, the rose made its way to Greece through the Holy Land and Asia Minor. Drawings of roses from the sixteenth century BC have been discovered on the walls of caves in Knossos on Crete. The word 'rose' comes from the Greek *rhodon*, meaning red, and the island of Rhodes was most probably named because the 'queen of flowers' grew there profusely.

Fourteen of the roses in the above selection were introduced to Britain before the close of the nineteenth century, in the middle of which Pope Pius IX had defined the doctrine of today's Solemnity. Rosarie de l'Hay scrapes in because many people who heard or read the Pope's Bull would have still been alive when the *rugosa* arrived here. Further, it stands for all of us who have lived since then to honour the Immaculate Conception of Mary. And how could one leave out a rose with such a name? My list covers all shades of pink, from the palest blush to the deepest crimson. All are exquisite; all are fragrant. The rose has symbolized the Blessed Virgin Mary or been associated with her in the literature of Britain and Ireland for at least nine hundred years. There is an eighth-century Irish Litany that refers to her as 'the crimson rose of the land of Jacob', and the beautiful fifteenth-century carol praises her thus:

> Ther is no rose of swich vertu
> As is the rose that bare Jesu:
> Alleluya!

> Fior in this rose conteined was
> Heven and erth in litel space
> Res miranda.

By that rose we may wel see
That he is God in persones three,
Pari forma.

Two early Florentine paintings are among my favourites: the first, by Filippino Lippi, *La Madre Pia*, depicts a mystical garden fenced by a balustrade, beyond which is a rose hedge in bloom. The Virgin kneels in the middle adoring the Child, who has his finger to his lips, indicating that he is the Word. A kneeling angel is scattering rose leaves over him, the child John the Baptist also kneels, and four more angels complete the composition. In the second painting, *Madonna of the Rose-Trellice*, by Francia, Jesus is lying on flowery grass. Mary is standing, gazing down on him in tender devotion, her hands crossed over her breast. Jesus is holding up his tiny right hand in a divine *Ave Maria*. He had sent those words to her by the angel Gabriel. Now he is here, and as their eyes meet he is silently communicating them to her in his flesh, taken from her. This time the mystical garden is enclosed by a trellis of roses. Jesus and his mother are alone, to the exclusion of all other earthly relationships. There is no heavenly adoration or protection in the form of angels. This has a deeply poignant effect in that it stresses Jesus' vulnerability. God has put himself under the protection of his human mother.

History of the Solemnity of the Immaculate Conception
The emperor Comnenus (died 1180) mentions 9 December as the date for the Feast of the Virgin's Conception. In Western Europe England was among the first countries to celebrate it. Observance spread from England to Normandy, and by 1153, to Lyons. St Bernard of Clairvaux, who died that year, is said to have rebuked the canons of Lyons for celebrating a feast not officially approved at Rome.

St Bonaventure (died 1274) wrote that he did not dare to approve or disapprove of the doctrine of Mary's Immaculate Conception. In 1328 a letter supporting the doctrine, allegedly by Anselm, was discussed at a council in London. By the middle of the fourteenth century, it is clear that the feast of the Conception of Mary was established in the Roman calendar, but belief in the *Immaculate* Conception had not been made binding on the faithful. Towards the end of the fifteenth century Sixtus IV sanctioned a proper Mass and Office for the day, to be celebrated on 8 December. In the years that separate him from the final definition in 1854, successive popes hedged their bets, took one side or another, but on the whole managed to keep the disputants under control and avoid schism.

The crux of the debate was whether Mary had been made free of original sin at the moment of conception and had thus been in the mind of God since before the Creation, that is before time began. The opposition held that she had been sanctified in her mother's womb, or at some other point after her conception. They claimed there was not enough in Scripture, tradition, or revelation to justify making the Immaculate Conception an article of faith. Clearly the Roman authorities found enough in Scripture and tradition for inclusion in the proper Mass and Office. But what of revelation?

In 1830, a novice Daughter of Charity in the Rue de Bac, Paris (later St Catherine Labouré), had a series of visions of the Virgin Mary, who instructed that medals be struck, bearing round their edge the prayer, 'O Mary conceived without sin, pray for us who have recourse to thee.' Catherine's confessor, Abbé Aladel, showed Bonaventurian caution and did nothing to obey the Virgin's request. In 1831 Pius VIII died and was replaced by Gregory XVI, who was in favour of the doctrine. After the accession of the new pope, Abbé Aladel at last reported Catherine's visions to him via the archbishop of Paris, who was also a supporter of the Immaculate Conception. The medal was struck and miracles began to occur. Gregory developed a great devotion to it and sanctioned the feast of the Immaculate Conception, also allowing the appellation, 'Queen conceived without original sin', to be inserted into the Litany of the Blessed Virgin. Pius IX was elected in 1847, and it seems very likely that the prayer on the Miraculous Medal, as it had become known, together with several other factors, bolstered his nerve finally to issue a dogmatic Bull defining the doctrine on 8 December 1854. The Bull makes it clear that for the previous six years he had been praying and fasting for divine guidance on the subject. The visions of Catherine Labouré were not approved until sixty years after her death, so Pius could hardly put them forward in the Bull. But in 1858 Bernadette Soubirous of Lourdes had a series of visions of *Aquero*, a dialect word meaning 'that', used by the visionary to refer to the lady she saw, until, that is, she asked *Aquero* to identify herself and received the reply: '*Que soy er' Immaculata Concepciou*' (That which is the Immaculate Conception). The faithful took Bernadette's visions as a vindication of the Doctrine, and of Pope Pius' definition of it.

Towards Meditation

> Mystic Rose! that precious name
> Mary from the Church dothe claim
> (from an old medieval verse)

The Litany of the Blessed Virgin, or of Loreto, was approved by Pope Sixtus V in 1587. Much of it, however, is older than the foundation of the Sanctuary at Loreto, which dates from 1294. My reflections today are on Mary, the mystical rose, and on the meaning of the Immaculate Conception in relation to several other titles of Mary featured in the Litany. They take the form of a prayer to her. The appellation 'Queen conceived without original sin' seems to me to embody all the others. She could not be any of them unless she had been immaculately conceived, and she could not have been immaculately conceived unless she were all of them. But as well as honouring Mary, we love her. A friend said to me after we had listened to Lennox Berkeley's setting of *I sing of a Maiden* one 8 December that it was the most beautiful love song he had ever heard. In Latin, the words 'my rose' were a term of endearment, and so they are used to introduce my prayer:

Rosa mea

Mystical Rose, Morning Star, pray for us.
By being conceived immaculate in God's mind before time began, you were heralded as the one without sin, the thornless rose who would crush the head of the serpent and be the new Eve. As a human creature, you were redeemed by Christ outside time at the moment of your conception, before you bore him; we receive the fruits of redemption at our baptism. By your bringing him into the world, God began to carry out his plan to make our redemption possible.

Mystical Rose, Ark of the Covenant, pray for us.
Because of your Immaculate Conception before time began, the Old Covenant rested in you as the Word all the way through the wanderings of the Children of Israel; you were the receptacle containing the Old Law, kept in the holiest place in the Tabernacle; you were the temple of the Word, who would bring the New Covenant, and found the body of his Church of which we are members.

Mystical Rose, Mirror of Justice, pray for us.
By your being conceived immaculate, we see the distant hope of God's

justice. You reflect the justice of Christ's twofold exhortation, 'Love God and your neighbour as yourself'; you are God's example to us of unblemished human obedience to him, and of serene acceptance of his will. You are the perfect lens he chose through which to shed his light upon us.

Mystical Rose, Gate of Heaven, pray for us.
From your Immaculate Conception came your perfect obedience and faith; you agreed to God's plan to raise fallen humankind and became the means by which he passed through heaven's gate to earth, and also the instrument through which he would throw open that gate to us. By co-operating in his Incarnation, you heralded a new heaven and a new earth in which this became possible for all generations.

Mystical Rose, Vessel of Honour, pray for us.
Only your Immaculate Conception made your womb a fit vessel to hold the honour of Christ. No one conceived in original sin could come as close to him as you did. He could not have taken his flesh from imperfect flesh; you are therefore the most perfect human in his creation. There is no other like you.

Mystical Rose, House of Gold, pray for us.
By your Immaculate Conception you were fitted to shelter the King of kings in your womb, in your arms, and in the earthly home you provided for him. You were the treasure house of God, and as such, made of the richest materials in creation. We must be tested in the refiner's fire and be beaten into gold; you were gold before time began.

Mystical Rose, Tower of Ivory, pray for us.
By your Immaculate Conception you were able to provide a pure, gleaming bright, and impenetrable fortress for the shelter of Jesus before his birth; you soar above us, but through your intercession we are helped to become fit dwelling places for him.

Mystical Rose, O Mystical Rose, pray for us.
Your Immaculate Conception means that the fullness of grace in you is incomprehensible to our limited minds. The angel Gabriel said in his greeting that you were the highly favoured one, and thus marked your singularity of perfection among human beings. 'The Lord is with you,' he said. How then could you not have been full of grace? The function of the Holy Spirit was to conceive the Word in your flesh, not to make you immaculate. You were immaculate already, or, like Jesus himself, the

Holy Spirit could not have come to you in such a way. The Saints receive grace in varying measure, but you alone among humans were full of it. Aside from Jesus you are the most powerful mediator between us and the Father; and aside from the Holy Spirit, the most powerful support in our prayers for grace.

Mystical Rose, Queen of Heaven, pray for us.
Your Immaculate Conception made it possible for you to be crowned Queen of Heaven because you alone of all creatures had been worthy of this honour in the mind of God from the dawn of time. Therefore you are our Queen too.

Mystical Rose, Queen conceived without original sin, pray for us.
In your instructions and announcements to Catherine Labouré and Bernadette Soubirous, you confirmed the mystical nature of your identity. Bernadette had called you *That.* You supplied the missing definition, 'I am that which is the Immaculate Conception.' Our litany in your honour conveys through inadequate human image and metaphor the glimmerings of our understanding of your grace, privilege, and function in God's plan for our salvation. We offer it in love and humility.

> I sing of a maiden that is makeless*
> King of all kinges to her son she ches**
> He came all so stille there his mother was
> as dew in Aprille that falleth on the grass.
> He came all so stille to his mother's bowr,
> as dew in Aprille that falleth on the flowr.
> He came all so stille ther his mother lay,
> as dew in Aprille that falleth on the spray.
> Mother and maiden was never none but she;
> well may such a lady Godes mother be.
> (Anon, *c.* 1450)

Bible Readings
Genesis 3:9–15: I will make you an enemy of each other: your offspring and her offspring
Psalm 85: Surely his salvation is at hand

---

* makeless, without a mate
** ches, chose

Psalm 96: Sing a new song to the Lord, for he has worked wonders
Judith 14:18–20: You are the highest honour of our race
Isaiah 43:1: I have called you by your name, you are mine
Romans 5:11–21: When sin abounded, grace abounded all the more
Romans 8:29–30: All those who from the first were known to God
Ephesians 1:3–6: Before the world was made God chose us in Christ
Ephesians 5:25–7: Under the predestined plan of the one who guides all things
Galatians 4:4–5: God sent his Son, born of a woman
Luke 1:26–38: Hail O favoured one, the Lord is with you
Revelation 11:19–12:10: A great sign appeared in heaven; I saw a new heaven and a new earth

Place of Spiritual Retreat
Resting in the mystery of the Annunciation

12 DECEMBER

St Jane Frances de Chantal, Religious (1572–1641)

CLIMBING ROSE 'Gloire de Dijon'

Cultivation Notes
This rose has been popular in England since its introduction in 1853; it was probably the indirect result of the rose breeding done by the French Philippe Noisette, who lived in the United States, and of his American neighbour John Champneys. The fragrant blooms are large and buff-yellow, appearing early in the season and lasting until autumn. At the time of introduction it was the closest achievement in the quest for a yellow rose, and was much sought after for bridal bouquets. It does best in a sheltered site. Foliage can become sparse at the base, but this is easily disguised by under-planting.

ROSA GALLICA 'Old Velvet'; 'Tuscany Superb'

See Selection for the Immaculate Conception.

Note: Both these roses require vigilance against mildew.

MUSTARD *Brassica nigra*

Cultivation Notes

Black mustard is an upright annual with stalked leaves, bristly at the base and smooth higher up. It can reach a height of over six feet and flowers from May onwards. The yellow petals are double the length of the sepals, and the seed case is dark brown. Sow in April in finely raked ground. Thin to six inches apart if growing for the seed. Mustard is hardy, but likes well-drained soil and sun, though some shade is required to prevent bolting. Gather in late August or when the pods begin to darken. Dry to complete the ripening process. This prevents loss of seed to the ground from the brittle seed cases. The harvest can be stored indefinitely in a dry place.

History and Lore

Mustard has been used as a condiment in the West for over two thousand years, and the Romans are reputed to have pickled the leaves in vinegar. In the thirteenth century French cooks began to grind the seed and mix it with first fermentation grape juice, in French *mout*, in English *must*, both words being derived from the Latin *mustum*, meaning 'new wine'. The second part of the word comes from the Latin *ardens*, from which in turn come the French and English *ardent*, meaning 'burning'. So from the original *mustum ardens* to *mout ardent*, we arrive at *moutarde* and mustard.

I have chosen the two roses for Jane Frances de Chantal because of her beauty of soul, to which St Francis de Sales (1567–1622) and St Vincent de Paul (1581–1660) both attested. The former described her as the perfect woman, and the latter as one of the holiest souls he had ever met. She was an exemplary wife and mother for eight years before being widowed and taking a vow of chastity. The bridal association of 'Gloire de Dijon' and the fact that she was born in Dijon make the rose appropriate to her. Jane was of noble Burgundian stock, so the colour of 'Old velvet' is apt, and the dark damson of the older blooms calls to mind the many bereavements she suffered and also that, in later life, she was no stranger to spiritual darkness. Mustard is chosen not merely because her birthplace is famous for its production, but because of her single-mindedness and ardency. The prolific growth of mustard mirrors the rapid spread of the Visitation Order, which she co-founded with Francis de Sales.

Jane Frances de Chantal was widowed at the age of twenty-eight as the result of a shooting accident. Three years later, in 1604, she met Francis de Sales, who as her spiritual director at first counselled her in the responsibilities of her state in the world. By 1610, however, he must have come to believe that God had other plans for her, because in that year the first Visitation convent was founded at Annecy, with Jane as superior. The Order was to be particularly welcoming to widows, and to women who lacked the health to endure physical austerities. This caused objections, but the wish of Francis and Jane for their nuns to have a special vocation to visit the sick and the poor roused real opposition from Rome. This was probably the result of Counter-Reformation zeal to stamp out laxity and abuses in religious life. And so the Visitation Order lost one of its founding principles and became strictly cloistered. Sixty-five convents were established during Jane's lifetime. She managed the Order with wisdom and sensitivity, living herself according to St Francis' maxim that humility is the virtue from which all the others spring. In her later years she made visits to all the Visitation communities. She died in Moulins on a return journey from Paris at the age of sixty-nine. She was canonized by Clement XIII in 1767.

Towards Meditation

St Jane is my patron by accident, since I was named after Jane Austen. But it is a happy accident, and I have appreciated it more and more as life has unfolded. There is so much in her experience from which I can learn, and against which I can measure myself. Her day will be celebrated with an examination of conscience inspired by her life and example, and, like the sowing of mustard seed, it will be an annual exercise. Thus I may meditate today on one or several of the following concepts, experiences and virtues, as they have bearing on my own life: duty, responsibilities, spiritual direction, chastity, charity, sensitivity, bereavement, exercise of authority, humility, diligence, 'seed sowing', passion for God, openness to the Holy Spirit, acceptance.

I can conduct this process in the quiet of home or church, but in France my favourite place in future years will be near the roses dedicated to this very dear Saint because, no matter how inclement the weather, I will visit them on 12 December and ensure that they and I are firm in the soil.

Bible Readings

Psalm 131: Humility and quietness in God's will

Romans 8:26–30: We are called according to his purpose
Matthew 13:31–52; Mark 4:31–2; Luke 13:19: Parables of the kingdom of
  heaven
John 15:1–11: Christ the vine, we the branches

Place of Spiritual Retreat
Listening to Christ's explanation of the parables, as in Matthew 13

13 DECEMBER

St Lucy of Syracuse, Virgin and Martyr (died 304)

HONESTY *Lunaria biennis*; *Lunaria rediviva*; lunarie (Chaucer); penny flower;
moon flower; silver plate; pope's money

Cultivation Notes
L. biennis, as its name suggests, is a biennial, but it reappears quite readily
from self-seeding. *L. rediviva* (capable of renewal) is perennial, grows easily
from seed, and spreads freely. Both may reach a height of about two feet.
Sow in May and June in light soil and partial shade. The small purple
flowers are fragrant and attractive in groups, but of course honesty is more
prized for its silvery translucent seed-pods. To safeguard these do not
dead-head the flowers but harvest in August before there is any risk of
gales. Hang in a cool dry place until it is possible to peel away the outer
scales and reveal the silver 'moons' within. It is possible to buy honesty for
indoor arrangements, usually from early autumn.

MAHONIA JAPONICA

Cultivation Notes
This evergreen shrub is popular because of its yellow candle-like flowers
that appear in clusters from November to February. It likes some shade
and will grow in any reasonable soil to a height of about six feet. Cut back
in April. *M. media* 'Charity' is a good choice.

History and Lore
Both these plants are obvious choices for St Lucy, whose name of course,
means 'light'. Honesty was named for its transparency, and Mahonia

brings to mind the beginning of the Christmas season in Sweden. There the tradition is that Lucy was a brave young girl who took food to refugee Christians hiding in caves. She wore a crown of candles so that she could carry more and still see her way in the dark. On 13 December, the youngest Swedish girl in a family or community wears a white dress and a crown of evergreens and candles. In memory of St Lucy she carries a tray of *Lucia buns* to her parents and schoolmates and to the sick.

Towards Meditation

Little is known about Lucy except that she lived in Syracuse and was martyred there. As a virgin, she combined the greatest virtue with the ultimate faithfulness. The legend surrounding her death was perpetuated by the Englishman Aldhelm at the end of the seventh century, but he was working from sources unacceptable to the modern historian. However, in common with most legends surrounding the saints and martyrs, it underlines the virtues of clear-sightedness, honesty, and bravery in defence of the truth and therefore bears examination today.

Lucy is supposed to have been the daughter of a noble Christian family. She took her sick mother, Eutycha, to the tomb of St Agatha. When her prayers for her mother's recovery were answered, she requested that her own marriage dowry be distributed among the poor. The man to whom she had been betrothed against her will objected and accused Lucy before the prefect Paschasius of being a Christian. The prefect, having failed to make her renounce Christ, ordered her to be sent to a brothel, there to be violated, but they found it impossible to move her there. Oil and pitch were poured on her and set alight, but the fire did not harm her. Her eyes were torn out and miraculously restored. Finally, a sword was thrust through her neck, whereupon, before dying, Lucy prophesied the peace that would come to the Church after the deaths of Diocletian and Maximian. It is the conversation she allegedly had with Paschasius before the tortures began that is particularly instructive. The prefect had warned her that very shortly words would mean nothing. Lucy replied that God's servants never want for words and then quoted the Gospel: 'You will be dragged before kings and governors . . . do not worry about how you are to speak or what you are to say; for what you are to say will be given to you at that time; for it is not you who speak, but the Spirit of your Father speaking through you' (Mt. 10:18–20, Mk 13:9–11). Paschasius then asked her if the Holy Spirit was in her. She answered that those who live in chastity and piety are the temples of the Holy Spirit. It was then that the threat of the brothel was made, with the cynical intent of getting the Holy Spirit out of her. Lucy replied that her will could not be prostituted. If they caused her to lose her physical virginity, the crown of her spiritual purity would be made brighter by suffering.

If today is a working day, I shall pass two Mahonia Japonica shrubs on my way to school, but whatever the day and whether in England or France, I will make an arrangement of honesty and evergreens in memory of St Lucy, and meditate along the following lines: for the distribution of Lucy's dowry, read the proper allocation of my own resources; for the brothel, the world we live in; for her quoting the Gospel, reliance on the Holy Spirit; for her physical virginity, spiritual chastity and piety; for the fire that did not burn her, the protection of God; for her restored eyesight, the search for God's truth; for the sword, my opportunities to speak up for Christ.

Bible Readings
Song of Songs 8:6–7: Love as strong as death
Psalm 45:10–11: A love song
Hosea 2:16–23: God betrothes his people to himself
2 Maccabees 7: The horrific death of a family of martyrs
1 Corinthians 7:25–35: The single woman's opportunity for total devotion to God
1 Peter 4:12–19: Be glad if you share in Christ's sufferings
Matthew 25:1–13: Ten bridesmaids and their lamps

Place of Spiritual Retreat
Listening to Christ's teaching on what we are to say, as in Matthew 10 and Mark 13

13 DECEMBER

St John of the Cross, Doctor (1542–1591)

EGLANTINE *Rosa rubiginosa/eglanteria*; sweet briar rose

Cultivation Notes
Although it is known as the English wild rose, Eglantine is native to Europe. The leaves have sticky rust-coloured hairs on their undersides,

and the single blooms have bright pink petals with yellow centres. It likes dry conditions, grows to about eight feet, and the flowers appear in early summer. These are scentless, but Eglantine is distinguished by its foliage, which gives off a delightful apple perfume, particularly after rain. It is very thorny, hence its name, from the Old French *aiglant*, meaning 'needled'. The bright oval hips are a great attraction to birds, but they are full of vitamins, and tea made from them is extremely good for the human system. Eglantine is also attractive to bees, and parsley, garlic, mignonettes, and lupins make mutually beneficial growing companions. *Sauce églantine*, supposedly a favourite of Queen Victoria, was made from a puree of hips and lemon juice.

History and Lore

Eglantine is the medieval symbol of romantic courtly love, and Chaucer's naming of his Prioress in the *Canterbury Tales* is surely deliberate. Madame Eglantine, with her badge bearing the legend *Amor vincit omnia*, is more concerned with niceties, manners, and accents than with the spiritual love sought by a true nun. Chaucer's contemporaries would have immediately appreciated his irony. However, this rose is also the traditional emblem of poetry itself, which makes it eminently suitable for arguably the greatest poet-mystic that God has raised up in the Church. Moreover, as his appellation suggests, John had a great devotion to the cross and willingly accepted much suffering. The thorns of Eglantine remind me of this. Another reason for its choice is that in his commentary on his poem *The Spiritual Canticle* St John explains that the apple tree represents the cross, and the rose tree, the understanding, memory, and will of the soul.

Juan de Yepes y Alvarez was brought up by his widowed mother and joined the Carmelites in 1563. He studied theology at Salamanca and was ordained in 1567. His work with Teresa of Avila for the Discalced Carmelite reform is well known, and for most of the 1570s he was confessor to the nuns at her motherhouse. In 1575 he was captured and imprisoned by the Calced, unreformed Carmelites in Toledo. Here he is believed to have written, amongst other works, at least seventeen stanzas of *The Spiritual Canticle*. He escaped after less than a year. In 1575, after the two branches of the Order had finally separated, John became rector of Baeza College, which he had founded, and then prior at, successively, Granada, and Segovia. From 1588 onwards he suffered, even at the hands of his own discalced vicar general. In 1591 he was deprived of his offices, with the intention of sending him to Mexico. Instead he was sent to Ubeda in Andalusia. Here the prior is reputed to have cruelly mistreated him during his final illness. The old Roman Breviary claims that when asked by Christ in a vision what reward he would choose for his work, John asked for suffering and humiliation for the sake of his Master. Further, he is supposed to have frequently asked to die in a place where he was unknown. Whatever the truth of these stories, they do not excuse the fact that John was a victim of the jealousy and power struggles in the Order of his day. His seems to have been a bleak life, and yet, reading his work, one cannot fail to be struck by his warmth and passionate love for God in the person of Jesus. His gifts as a poet and mystic are remarkable, but he is even more special because his comments on his own work demonstrate his intellectual control, soundness of theological training, and deep biblical knowledge. John of the Cross was canonized in 1726. It is hard to understand why he was not made a Doctor of the Church until 1927.

Towards Meditation
Today, I will select a single fragment of *The Spiritual Canticle*. The poem, followed by minute commentary, takes the form of a dialogue between the bride/soul and the Spouse/Christ. It is full of imagery from the natural environment, from gardens, and from close physical contact. This last may be altogether too sensual for northern European spiritual sensibilities, but my own reservations slowly evaporated when I studied the commentary on each phrase. The poem has thirty-nine short stanzas, each one describing a subtle complexity in the soul's search for and relationship with the Beloved, at particular stages of its development. It is far too dense and complex a work to describe in detail here, but anyone who loves Christ and desires to be united with him should read it and its commentary. The second Office reading today is a salutary preparation. It is from St John's explanation of his sentence from the 36th stanza of *The Spiritual Canticle*, 'Let us enter farther into the thicket.' Referring to St Paul, John reminds us that all wisdom and knowledge lie hidden in Christ. No matter how learned or holy we may become in this life, we will never fathom his depths, and we cannot begin to reach his treasures without first passing through the thicket: that is, internal and external suffering. Many spiritual gifts and long experience are necessary even to begin, and these are not the same as knowledge of Christ's mysteries. They are essential, though, in making us want to fathom the

depths. Not only must we be prepared to enter the thicket of suffering, we must want to enter it and actually regard it as a consolation. John reminds us that his counsel is the same as that given by Paul to the Ephesians. If we really long for Christ we must long for a share in the thicket of the cross. We may long for the riches on the other side of the thicket, but are we prepared to pass through it? The thorns of eglantine now take on a deep significance.

Bible Readings
Psalm 119: Desire for knowledge of God's law and obedience to it
Wisdom of Solomon 7: The love of wisdom
1 Corinthians 2:1–10: Wisdom for those who have achieved maturity
Ephesians 1:15–23: The riches of his glorious inheritance
James 3:17–18: The nature of wisdom
Luke 22:24–30: You have continued with me in my trials

Place of Spiritual Retreat
Face to face with the thicket of the cross

26 DECEMBER

St Stephen, Deacon and first Martyr (died *c.* 35)

SNAKE'S HEAD LILY *Fritillaria meleagris*;
chequered lily
CROWN IMPERIAL *Fritillaria imperialis*
CROWN OF THORNS
Euphorbia milii/splendens

Cultivation Notes
The two perennial fritillaries are both members of the lily tribe, but are very different in appearance and symbolism. Plant bulbs of the snake's head lily in early autumn at a depth of two inches. The lantern-shaped purple-red chequered flowers appear from April to May and are

carried singly on stems that reach a height of up to eighteen inches. In the wild the plants grow in damp meadows, so it is wise to give them moist soil. They are quite hardy and do well under trees that provide light shade. They will naturalize easily into spreading clumps, but if planting in grass, make sure this will not need cutting before July, by which time the fritillaries will be dormant. Crown imperial bulbs should be planted in August under about four inches of soil and will produce yellow flowers the following May. These appear in pendent clusters on stately three-foot stalks, with an unusual 'crown' of leaves separating the top petals from the rest of the bloom. *Lutea maxima* is recommended. After a few years the plants may become cramped and need division in August. Plants may be dried for a display on the Feast of Stephen. Crown of thorns is a fairly easy houseplant, and more people will have access to it than to the rarer fritillaries. It will thrive in a sunny window and if the leaves drop in winter, they will soon be replaced. The stems are covered with long sharp thorns and bear circular clusters of tiny red flowers. These usually appear from spring to summer, but the plant can flower all year round in a brightly lit place. Re-pot every two years in spring. The sap is poisonous. Let it dry before planting stem cuttings.

History and Lore

Fritillaria are native to Britain but also indigenous to cool temperate regions in Central Asia and western Siberia. *Fritillus* is Latin for dice-box, although the flowers of *F. meleagris* rather evoke the chequered board on which the dice were thrown. 'Snake's head' is appropriate because of the shape and markings of the unopened blooms. There is a legend that the plant sprang originally from Danish blood spilt in battle on English soil. In *The Language of Flowers* it represents persecution, which makes it apt for Stephen. One is reminded too, of Christ's instruction to his disciples that they should be 'wise as serpents and innocent as doves' when dealing with the world (Mt. 10:16–19). 'Crown of thorns' clearly connotes not only the Passion of Christ but martyrdom in general, and 'crown imperial' is evocative of the dignity and glory of the martyr's crown. Between them, these plants cover three aspects of Stephen's story, and they will shape my meditation today.

Stephen was probably a Hellenistic Jew, and he was one of seven deacons appointed by the Apostles to oversee the distribution of alms, especially to widows, so there is a connection between him and the much later church tradition of opening the poor boxes on Chrismas Day and distributing the contents as 'dole of the Christmas box' on the next day. Apprentices would carry boxes to their masters' clients in the hope of receiving seasonal gratuities. The tradition was still very much alive during my northern girlhood and I remember the coalman, postman, milkman and paper-boy knocking for their Christmas boxes. The term 'box' was still firmly in use as a synonym for a money gift to tradesmen, and most of them made sure of receiving their dues before Christmas! Nowadays, in London, I only have the postman to reward for his faithful year's service. He finds the gift hanging on the front door in a small red felt Christmas stocking. In France too, the postman calls, as well as a representative of the local fire-brigade, each bringing a calendar in exchange for his *don*.

Probably because of the manner of his death, Stephen is patron of bricklayers, and invoked against headaches. Not surprisingly, he is patron of Deacons and, since the founding of the Archconfraternity of Saint Stephen in London around 1901, patron of altar servers as well. Many parishes in Britain, Africa, Australia, Malaysia, and the Caribbean have Guilds of Servers belonging to this society, and Stephen is mentioned in the Guild promise prayer. Members wear a medal bearing the palm and crown of the martyr's victory, and the Guild motto, *Cui servire regnare est* (To serve Christ is to reign). Up to the late 1960s the London parish where I was a chorister had a High Latin Mass on 26 December. In earlier years full-blown Victorian polyphony would raise the rafters on the feast; latterly, a choir much depleted after the rigours of the previous two days could manage only the plainchant proper of Saint Stephen.

Towards Meditation

He that once a little child,
Shivering in the manger lay,
Set on Stephen's blesssed head
A crown that fadeth not away.
>(Matins Invitatory from the old Roman Breviary, Bute translation)

Scholarship suggests Stephen's long speech in Acts was polished by later writers, but there is no doubt that the Apostles made a good choice in him. As we read, we know he is indeed 'a man full of faith and of the Holy Spirit'. He preaches with a forceful eloquence grounded in knowledge of the Scriptures; he justifies Jesus as the fulfilment of prophecy and attacks those who resist the Spirit. St Fulgentius of Ruspe (468–533) describes him as a soldier to whom Christ gave strength to fight and conquer. But it was a strength born of love that showed itself first in the king and then in his soldier. Stephen used it as a weapon against the anger of his hearers, and won the crown that is the meaning of his name. The love that brought Christ from heaven lifted Stephen from earth to heaven. It is the love that enabled him, like his King, to forgive his murderers; it is the love inherent in his prayer for those he had been unable to convert by argument and learning. Stephen, with his blend of wisdom and gentleness, perfectly follows Christ's instruction, 'Be wise as serpents and innocent as doves.' He is rewarded with the crown of martyrdom and just before death is blessed with a vision of heaven and his Lord in glory. Saul, who would become Paul on the road to Damascus, stood by, holding the coats of the men who were stoning Stephen, and approving their actions. Fulgentius takes delight that Stephen and Paul now rejoice together in the eternal presence of Christ. He presses home the point that love wrought Paul's conversion and made brothers of erstwhile adversaries. And he is especially engaged by the love and forgiveness shown by Stephen. He calls it a ladder set up by God, by which each Christian may reach heaven. He tells us to keep a firm grip on it, to show it to each other, and, by making progress up it, finally reach our goal.

Pondering today's liturgy, I am again made forcefully aware of my own petty irritation when I lose an argument and of how miserable is my lack of forgiveness of those who hurt me. If I cannot bear these tiny pinpricks to my pride, what hope is there for me? My meditation today is bound to end in self-loathing, and in a firm intention to use the forceful, eloquent side of myself to more constructive effect, and above all, to show more understanding, love, and forgiveness to those around me. Mindful of our Lord's saying that if we do not take up our cross and follow him, we are not worthy of him, I should make a much greater daily effort to embrace whatever my own infinitesimal martyrdoms may be, praying always for the help of the Holy Spirit: 'He who endures to the end will be saved' (Mt. 10:22).

Bible Readings

Psalm 31: Into thy hands I commit my spirit
Wisdom 3:1–2a, 3b: The souls of the just are in God's hands
Acts 6:1 – 8:3: The life, preaching and death of Stephen, and the involvement of Saul

1 Peter 5:10–11: You will have to suffer only for a little while
James 1:12: Blessed is he who endures under trials
Matthew 10:16–42: Behold I send you out

Place of Spiritual Retreat
Receiving the conditions of discipleship from Christ, as in Matthew 10

27 DECEMBER

St John the Evangelist (died late first century)

WINTER JASMINE *Jasminum nudiflorum*

Cultivation Notes
This hardy self-sufficient deciduous climber is normally planted in autumn or winter. It bears small golden star-like flowers from November to late February on long, whippy leafless green stems, made during the previous summer. It should be possible to have some for home or church display on the feast of St John. The small trifoliate leaves appear after flowering. This is the time for pruning. Light control seems to rejuvenate it. Stems trailing on the ground will root fairly easily. Winter jasmine is a most effective plant for brightening a north-facing wall. Mine is very happy in just such a place.

History and Lore
Robert Fortune discovered the species in Northern China, near Shanghai and Nanking. In 1844 it was introduced to Britain, where it was at first assumed to be tender. However, it very quickly demonstrated its hardiness and has become one of our best-loved winter shrubs, which is one of several reasons why I have chosen it in honour of 'the disciple whom Jesus loved', the first chapter of whose Gospel is so precious to Christians for its beauty and theology. We all have memories of beginning to understand it and of recognizing the profound difference between John's writing and that of the other three evangelists. In King's College, Cambridge, and elsewhere, John 1:1–14 is traditionally the last reading at countless Festivals of Lessons and Carols. Whenever I hear it, I am taken back to school, reading the cadences of the Cranmer version at school carol service. My voice does not tremor, but the knees behind the lectern are

knocking together in fright; the heart beneath the house captain's badge is thumping with joy in the Word, and in amazement at its owner's temerity in daring to speak it aloud. I fell in love that first time with the writing of John, and I am still in love.

Pre-conciliar Catholics will remember 'The Last Gospel' (Jn 1:1–14) being read by the celebrant at the end of Mass – and how they felt when it was abandoned. It was often gabbled to the point of sacrilege, but I mourn it, because the Church valued its theology so highly as to have put it there in the first place.

Towards Meditation

I have said there are several reasons why the winter jasmine is chosen for St John. The theme and tenor of my meditation today will depend on which of these I decide to concentrate on. I could for instance continue a reflection on the closeness of John to Jesus, and the special trust Our Lord invested in him. Time and again, John is a member of a select band of three who were permitted to witness major events or signs that demonstrated the identity of Jesus. John is there with Peter and James at the raising of Jairus' daughter; he witnesses the Transfiguration; he is next to Jesus at the Last Supper, and with him in the Garden of Gethsemane; he is present at the crucifixion, and Christ speaks to him from the cross. He is enjoined henceforth to treat Mary as his mother, and she in her turn is to treat John as her son. The Church has long taken this incident as symbolic of the way each Christian should regard Mary, and be regarded by her. But we should not lose sight of the deeply personal nature of Jesus' words. Here are arguably the two people he humanly most loved in the world, and he commends them to each other. Many of us will have received a similar charge from the lips of a beloved dying relative, and our feelings on that occasion may give a tiny insight into how John must have felt. It has been suggested that he was the son of Mary Salome, Our Lady's sister. If that was the case, Jesus was not simply asking his best friend to look after his mother. He was asking his cousin to look after the most special aunt in the world. The Church, then, is more than justified in putting his feast-day between the incarnation and the Feast of the Holy Family. John makes the meaning and significance of the former crystal clear at the opening of his Gospel, and his perpetual care for Mary after her son's death makes him an honorary member of the Holy Family, a sharer in its loving fellowship. He is at pains throughout his writings to show how we too can be welcomed into this fellowship and how we too must love one another within it.

In his *Commentary on the Epistle to the Galatians*, St Jerome (*c.* 341–420) writes: 'The Blessed Evangelist John ... was used simply to say, "My little children, love one another." The disciples and brethren were weary with hearing these words continually, and asked him, "Master, wherefore ever sayest thou this only?" Whereto he replied, "It is the commandment of the Lord, and if this only be done, it is enough"' (Matins Second Nocturn, Sixth Lesson, pre-conciliar Breviary).

The jasmine flowers early on bare twigs, careless of frost and impatient of its leaves. We know that John and his brother James could be impetuous. They wanted to call down fire from heaven on the Samaritans for not receiving Jesus. Even the beloved John was rebuked for this will to revenge (Lk. 9:54). And it is surely why Jesus 'gave [them] the name Boanerges, that is, sons of thunder' (Mk 3:17). On Easter morning, after Mary Magdalene has told them that the Lord's body has gone from the tomb, Peter and John race there in panic. John outstrips Peter and is first to look into the tomb and see the discarded grave clothes. Peter arrives, and they enter the tomb together. They go home uncertain of what has happened, but John privately notes that no one could steal a body and leave the grave clothes in such neat order. There is a lesson for us in John's impetuosity and haste and, on Easter day, in his calming down sufficiently to actually see what he was looking at. First we should examine our consciences for the slightest impulse to revenge and root out any that we find. If in the past we have acted in a vengeful spirit, we must beg forgiveness, or we too will deserve a rebuke from the Lord. As for John's initial haste and eventual observation before he leaves the tomb, we should examine our own approach to God. How well do we prepare to meet him in prayer, or in the Blessed Sacrament? How sadly wanting will we find ourselves, and in view of this, how great and undeserved are his gifts to us in prayer and at the altar steps. All of this must call forth greater determination to seek Christ in quiet, unhurried serenity and a deeper gratitude for the graces we receive.

The Mass introit today describes John as 'robed in glory', and on his feast the winter jasmine is robed in glory too. It bears witness to life and light in the gloom of winter, and likewise John's written legacy shines as a beacon, testifying to the Life and the Light, not just in this dark season but throughout the Christian year and throughout each Christian's pilgrimage. John's is the record of a man who actually saw, heard, and touched

Jesus. Few were privileged to know him so well, and John often presses this home, not out of pride, but because he knows that his personal contact with Christ has great power to bring readers to faith. Further, John does not merely report events. Mostly he assumes our knowledge of these. His concern is to expound the meaning and significance of Christ's life and death and thus to help us enter more deeply into their mysteries. Not surprisingly, in English tradition he is known as John the Divine, or John the Theologian. Stephen was eloquent, but his arguments were primarily for a contemporary audience, the major purpose of his existence being the witness of martyrdom. John, on the other hand, having overheard Jesus' conversation with Peter about his destiny, knew he would not be martyred. And his comments on Jesus' words about him indicate that he understood their meaning better than anyone else (see John 21:20–4). Stephen laid down his life for Christ. John, in the long life allowed to him, set down as much as he could of his knowledge and understanding of Christ. He closes his Gospel with the acknowledgement that 'there are also many other things which Jesus did; were every one of them to be written, I suppose that the world itself could not contain the books that would be written' (21:25).

Traditionally we are told that Jesus loved John, 'because his singular gift of purity made him loveable' (pre-conciliar Breviary). Whilst accepting that John's virginity was a special reason for Christ's love of him, I find it hard to think it was the only one. On a human level, John was a loving soul, and love responds to love. More importantly, the divine, all-seeing eye of Jesus would have known in advance the magnitude of the contribution his beloved disciple would make to the furtherance of his kingdom.

So, immediately after Christmas, the Church places the feasts of the first martyr and of – arguably – the first theologian. Through them we celebrate the two great ways by which the faith has been spread, interpreted, and defended down the ages. As I gather the winter jasmine, the words light, life, love, fellowship, and joy will be engraved in my mind. They are at the heart of what, and indeed why, John wrote. 'That which we have seen and heard we proclaim also to you so that you may have fellowship with us; and our fellowship is with the Father and with his Son Jesus Christ. And we are writing this that our joy may be complete. This is the message we have heard from him . . . that God is light and in him is no darkness at all' (1 Jn: 3–5).

Bible Readings

Psalm 97: Rejoice in the Lord, O you righteous

Luke 8:49–56: He permitted no one to enter with him except Peter, John and James

Mark 9:2–9: Jesus took with him Peter and James and John and led them up a high mountain apart by themselves

Mark 14:32–42: And he took with him Peter, James, and John, and began to be greatly distressed and troubled

John 19:25–7: When Jesus saw his mother and the disciple whom he loved

John 20:2–8: The other disciple outran Peter

John 21:20: Peter turned and saw following them the disciple whom Jesus loved

Acts 4:19–20: We cannot but speak of what we ourselves have seen and heard

1 John 1:1 – 2:3: That which was from the beginning

John 1:1–18: In the beginning was the Word

Place of Spiritual Retreat

With the disciples after the Transfiguration, as in Mark 9; or in the Garden of Gethsemane, as in Mark 14; or at the foot of the cross, as in John 19; behind Peter and John as they race to the tomb, as in John 20; or with John following Jesus and Peter, as in John 21

29 DECEMBER

St Thomas Becket, Archbishop and Martyr (1118–1170)

PINK *Dianthus*
RASPBERRY* *Rubus idaeus*

Cultivation Notes

Pinks are short-lived perennials that will survive frosts in well-drained soil. Select a sunny position and propagate by layering or root division in late summer. Now is the time to order plants for setting out next month.

---

*   Raspberry contains frangarine, which is a relaxant to the uterus and therefore should be avoided in any form during pregnancy, until the onset of labour.

There are summer- and autumn-fruiting varieties of raspberry. The former need support. Although raspberries are a thirsty crop, they hate being waterlogged. Plants are sold bare-rooted or in containers, and spineless types are also available. A month before planting, prepare trenches in a sheltered spot where they will enjoy full sun in spring and summer. Dig the trenches eighteen inches wide and nine inches deep. Exterminate as many weeds as possible, and before returning the soil, fork in compost or rotted manure. Supports should go in next. There are many methods, from a single post system to elaborate wire and wood fence arrangements. I used the former last time, as I was only planting one row of canes. Posts should be buried to a depth of two feet.

Space the plants at eighteen-inch intervals, and leave six feet between rows. New plants can be raised from your own canes, as long as they were bought from a respectable source and are no more than two years old. Simply remove and plant suckers in October or November.

History and Lore

I have chosen two pinks for St Thomas. First is the variegated 'Alice'. The red centre signifies the blood of martyrdom, and the white outer petals the purity of intention that Thomas Becket struggles to attain in T. S. Eliot's play *Murder in the Cathedral*. In *The Language of Flowers* the variegated pink is symbolic of refusal, here Thomas's refusal to accept the encroachment of Henry II into the rights of the Church. (The 'Laced monarch' variety would also be apt, in view of the public penance by flogging that Henry voluntarily underwent after Thomas's murder.) Any self-coloured pink represents love, so my choice is between 'Brympton red' and the white 'Mrs Sinkins'. Here they would symbolize Thomas's love for God and his flock. The word carnation has the same root as coronation, and is therefore appropriate for any martyr.

The Ancient Greeks and Romans regarded pinks as flowers of divinity and gave them a place of honour in the garlands they awarded. They were floated in the drinks of engaged couples and so became known as flowers of love. In art, by medieval times, they had come to represent betrothal. The spicy perfume of pinks is unmistakable and they have long been used for flavouring sauces, cordials, syrups, oils, and vinegars. They can be air-dried for pot-pourri, infused in wine, and taken as a tonic. Hilary Spurling's edition of *Elinor Fettiplace's Receipt Book (1570–1647)* gives a helpful recipe for crystallizing flowers. The modern carnation is descended from an Elizabethan gillyflower, *D. caryophyllus*, while most 'old fashioned' pinks come from *D. plumarius*. The *Allwoodii* pinks are named after the man who first crossed the two.

Traditionally, the raspberry signifies remorse, and here it represents the remorse of Henry, and the remorse of Thomas for the life he led before becoming Archbishop of Canterbury. Fossils have shown that the raspberry was part of human diet from early times, and it is mentioned by the Latin poet Propertius (*c.* 50 BC–16 AD). We know that by the mid-sixteenth century it was being cultivated in England. It was taken to North America by the colonists and eventually crossed with *R. occidentalis* to produce dark red or purple raspberries. Several tribes of native North Americans used indigenous varieties such as *R. odoratus* (thimbleberry) to treat dysentery or to flavour medicines (as do modern commercial pharmacists). The raspberry is probably named from the Old French verb *rasper*, meaning to scratch or scrape, which came into English in the sixteenth century as 'rasp' (as the raspberry is still called in Scotland). In the previous century there had been a kind of wine known as raspis.

We know from Luke 6:43 that Jesus was familiar with the fruiting bramble. There were probably two types growing in the Holy Land during his time. *R. sanclus* and *R. ulmifolius* grow in thickets, and both, somewhat like raspberries, propagate by underground stems and by suckering. The grape and the fig were the superior fruits in Our Lord's culture, and he would have known of the bramble's vicious propensity for spreading as a weed. Hence he characterizes it as not just an inferior tree but as a bad one. You would not look for grapes on a bramble bush, he tells us, making the point that only the person of good heart bears good fruit. 'Thus you will know them by their fruit' (Mt. 7:20). Nevertheless, I feel he must be pleased when we control the bramble in its raspberry form. But he wants us to fight for the same control over the bramble of sin in our lives, and bear fruit for his kingdom. The raspberry *is* a culinary delight, but its association with remorse makes working with it in the garden a reminder of the need to recognize our sins and ask forgiveness. In both ways it is God's gift and I thank him for it.

Towards Meditation
'You have observed what persecutions I endured; yet from them all the Lord rescued me' (2 Tim. 3:11b).

The pink and the raspberry have led me to consider the life and martyrdom of Thomas Becket, and as a result to devise a plan for examination of conscience. It consists of a series of paragraphs about Thomas, each one followed by springboard words or phrases to be applied with a question mark to myself. You may say that the plan could have been made without Thomas or, indeed, the pink and the raspberry. Of course it could. But the point is that I might not have done it at all without the saint and the plants. It is an example of just how much can come from gardening with God. Furthermore it remains for future use quite independently of them.

It also led me to heed Pope Leo's warning in his *Ninth Sermon on Christmas*: 'He comes nearest to the knowledge of the truth, who, the farther he advance, sees all the more clearly that he can never overtake it. For he that imagines that he has ever attained the goal, has not found it, but has altogether missed it.' And to put into words my own prayer to the Holy Spirit with which to begin: 'O Holy Spirit, beloved of my soul, totally unworthy, I seek your comfort and indwelling. Humbly, I beg your gifts of counsel, understanding, knowledge, truth, and fortitude. Please help me to make this examination with such rigour and honesty that I may come to a recognition of my faults and sins, and to a true sorrow for them. I pray that you will give me grace to root them out so that I may become a more acceptable dwelling place for you.'

Raspberry – remorse

1. Until Thomas Becket was made Archbishop of Canterbury in 1162 he had led a self-indulgent life, and he later described himself as having been 'a proud vain man, a feeder of birds and follower of hounds'.

Questions:
Self-indulgence; time-wasting; laziness; undue frivolity; extravagance; pride; conceit (physical, intellectual, or spiritual); vigilance against them; prayer to the Holy Spirit for discernment, knowledge; remorse; prayer for mercy?

2. 'Will no one revenge me of the injuries I have sustained from one turbulent priest?' This remark of Henry II to his knights is famous in oral tradition. Said in unguarded anger, it was responsible for Thomas' murder. Remorse must have been at least part of the King's reason for having himself flogged as a penance. But Thomas was popular. The people 'canonized' him almost immediately after his death. Maybe Henry's motives were not impeccable.

205

Questions:
Careless speech in anger; a cause of pain to others; apology; sincerity; action or inaction, speech or silence to avoid unpopularity?

Variegated pink – refusal
3. Thomas and Henry clashed over the rights of the Church, not over a point of doctrine. They argued bitterly about taxes, and over which courts should try whom. Thomas held that in defending the worldly rights of the Church, he was also defending her Faith. Anything that reduced her purse or influence reduced her power to spread that faith.

Questions:
God and Caesar; civic duties; taxes; bills; efficient household budgeting; the Offertory plate and charitable giving?

4. Both Thomas and Henry were intransigent. The king was hot-tempered; Thomas took offence easily. They played a game of quite spiteful recrimination. Henry isolated Thomas and seized his lands, so that finally he had so few supporters that he was forced into exile in Cistercian abbeys in France. Finally he and Henry patched up a superficial peace. Thomas came back to find that Henry had, in defiance of the privileges of the Archbishop of Canterbury, been crowned by other bishops. The returning Primate immediately had them excommunicated.

Questions:
Refusal to listen to another point of view; ignoring other people's opinions; incomplete attention to others; bitter, hurtful, vengeful speech or action, however petty; exclusion of others; sincerity of peace-making efforts; irritability; hot-temper; readiness to take offence; forgiveness of slights, criticism and insults; trying others beyond endurance; insensitivity to others, oversensitive oneself; cutting people with sarcasm and enjoying it; petty point-scoring?

Self-coloured pink – love
5. Thomas had always been thorough and efficient, and he continued to be so when, in his own words, he became 'a shepherd of sheep'. In the Office of Readings on his feast, he speaks to us of the nature and responsibilities of the episcopate. Zeal in a pastor is of paramount importance, to the extent that he repeats his consecration oath every day and regrets before God that he

does not always live up to the vow. He describes the Word as a plant that must be watered, and many are needed to reap and store its harvest in God's granary. But whoever sows, waters, or reaps, God will give increase only to those who do so in the faith handed down by Christ through Peter. Thomas' death caused outcry not only in England but throughout western Christendom, which speaks of his good reputation as a loving shepherd. For this reason and because he had so forcefully defended their legal rights, he is the patron of English secular parish clergy.

Questions:
Insufficient thanksgiving for bishops and priests, my own in particular; prayer for them; demonstration of support and affection toward them; prayer for more shepherds; speaking up for the Church and the faith; how much sown and watered in prayer and action; duties of my state; care and efficiency at home and work; failure to love; outbursts of anger, exasperation, impatience; joining spiritually in the Pope's sorrow for the Church's global and social sins, past and present; gratitude to God for faith, the sacraments, and all the other blessings he showers on me; insufficient time in preparation for Holy Communion; effort against distractions in prayer; when was my last retreat?

Pink (carnation) – coronation
6. Thomas must have returned from exile knowing that his peace with Henry was unsound. He came back only when God had given him the faith and courage to face the possibility – perhaps those Cistercians had something to do with it. T. S. Eliot presents us with a Thomas who wrestles with the devil almost to the moment when Henry's knights plunged their swords into his body. Earlier in the play Eliot has put into Thomas' mouth a superb definition of a martyr, and then just before death he has the saint tell us that he is facing the last, the worst temptation, namely to accept martyrdom for the wrong reason. Eliot's Thomas has achieved detachment but is still struggling for purity of intention.

Questions:
Flawed intentions for apparently good acts; selfish motives; self-aggrandizement; self-deceit; spiritual pride; prayer to the Holy Spirit for vigilance and protection against them?

Raspberry again – fruit

7. Thomas Becket was martyred in Canterbury Cathedral, on 29 December, barely a month after his return from France. He was canonized three years later. During the following years many miracles reputedly took place at his tomb in the crypt. In 1220 his remains were moved to a splendid new shrine in the cathedral. Canterbury became one of the richest and most important places of pilgrimage in Christendom. Chaucer's description of the pilgrims is famously, if gently incisive, and it is interesting to reflect that he wrote some two hundred years after Thomas's death, that is, half a century further away from the events at Canterbury than we are from those at Lourdes. Anyone who has been to the French shrine will know that the range of spiritual depth in the pilgrims has not changed since Chaucer's time. Lourdes, like Canterbury before it, has been criticized for its commercialism, but the spiritual soul senses the intrinsic holiness of the place. Chaucer's archetypal Parson, and his Ploughman brother, would have been among the *brancardiers* at Canterbury. In many like them, St Thomas bore his fruit, as does Bernadette among the crowds at Lourdes today.

But the Host in the *Canterbury Tales*, in his dismissal of the Pardoner and his refusal to kiss the supposed breeches of St Thomas, makes clear some of the abuses that had crept in by Chaucer's time. Eventually Erasmus was to criticize the cult of Thomas, and Henry VIII finally destroyed his shrine. Images of Thomas were torn down or defaced, and his name expunged from the liturgy. It is hard to believe, however, that the Mass of St Thomas was not said again in England until the emancipation of Catholics in 1829. Before that the blood of many martyrs, both Protestant and Catholic, would be sown with that of Thomas in England's earth. Other souls escaped to America and planted the Word there.

Questions:
Intolerance; prejudice; right and proper attention to liturgy, sacramentals and devotional objects; thanksgiving for them; the sign of the cross made always with due thought and reverence; ritual for ritual's sake; thanksgiving for the martyrs and recusants; and for the music of Byrd and Tallis; when was my last pilgrimage?

By now a fairly clear picture will have emerged of my state of preparedness to meet God, and of whether I am likely to bear fruit in the end. It may have taken a week on and off, because of the demands of secular living, or a concentrated period of no less than an hour can be enough. In the silence afterwards I wait for the synthesis, usually a list of three or four horrors that have been exposed. These are written down to be taken to the sacrament of Reconciliation. A last wordless prayer to the Holy Spirit concludes the examination.

Back again in the world of work, I thank God again for the pink, the raspberry, and for St Thomas Becket, who, though he may not always have lived like a saint, was enabled in the end to die as one. Like that of many a saint before and since, his youth was less than holy, and therefore he is perhaps more encouraging than the ones who seem 'squeaky clean' from the outset. At any rate, he is among the heavenly throng, to whom he refers in today's reading. The Church, he says, in spite of her sufferings and blemishes, continually sends saints to God, and the company will go on increasing until the end of time. Only redemption through Christ, and taking up the cross daily, make it possible to believe that eventually you and I may stand with St Thomas and know the reality of Christ's words at the Last Supper: 'You are those who have continued with me in my trials; and I assign to you, as my Father assigned to me, a kingdom' (Lk. 28:28–9).

Bible Readings
Psalm 34:2–9: From all my terrors, Lord
Colossians 1:24–9: I became the servant of the Church
2 Timothy 2:8–13; 3:10–12: You have seen what persecution I have endured
Hebrews 5:1–6: Every high priest
Matthew 16:24–7: Whoever would keep his life will lose it
Luke 22:24–30: You are those who have stood by me
John 10:11–16: I am the Good Shepherd

Place of Spiritual Retreat
Listening with the disciples to Christ's promise, as in Luke 22

31 DECEMBER

St Silvester, Pope (died 335)

COMMON MARSH PENNYWORT *Hydrocotyle vulgare*; white foot-rot

Cultivation Notes

This perennial can be found in fens, marshes, and other damp places. It is recognizable from its rounded blue-green leaves and small pink flowers, which appear in midsummer. It is also known as white foot-rot, because it is supposed to cause that condition in sheep. The true culprit is probably the liver fluke that abounds in similar conditions. For humans it is emetic, purgative, and diuretic and can cause headaches or even coma. However, it once had the reputation for being an effective treatment for leprosy, and research is being done into this claim. The closely-related Indian pennywort, *Centella asiatica*, grows in rice fields. It has similar kidney-shaped leaves and produces pink flowers beneath its foliage. It reaches a height of six to eight inches, with an indefinite spread. It has long been used in India as an aid to meditation and is known as *Brahmi*, meaning 'bringing knowledge of "Supreme Reality"'. It is also traditionally used in India and Africa to treat leprosy, and knowledge of this use came to Europe via Madagascar and France. Research so far has shown that it does reduce scarring, improve circulation, and speed healing. It can however, irritate some skins, so care should be taken when handling it. It is quite tender and likes partial shade. Sow seed in spring.

History and Lore

Pennywort is the choice for St Silvester not because

I believe the legend that he cured Constantine of leprosy but because he presided over the Church at a time when she was grappling with the disease of two heresies. The first, Donatism, held that the validity of the sacraments depends on the moral character of the minister and, while not denying the Church's power to re-admit penitents, that sinners could not be members of the Church unless their sins were secret. Silvester became Pope in 314, the year Constantine summoned the Council of Arles, which decided against Donatism. Eleven years later, the Council of Nicaea anathematized Arianism, which denied Christ's consubstantiality with the Father and so effectively his true and eternal Godhead. It believed there had been a time when Christ was not, and that he was created out of nothing. Constantine was again involved, having recently become emperor of the East as well as of the West. Silvester was not present at either council but sent legates to both. He was Pope for twenty-two important years in the Church's history, but he seems to have made remarkably little theological contribution. Several Roman churches claim him as their founder, and the old Roman Breviary lists some innovations he is supposed to have made. Most of these have more to do with the etiquette of altar and sacrament than with the doctrine concerning them. It claims for instance that he settled the dress of deacons at Mass and reserved to bishops the right to consecrate the holy chrism. It is therefore the achievements of the councils during his papacy that I commemorate today, particularly giving thanks, as I repeat it, for the mighty Nicene Creed and the Fathers who composed it.

Towards Meditation

The leprosy legend, though spurious, calls to mind that the disease is still prevalent and warrants the existence of the Roman Catholic St Francis Leprosy Guild. In the Church of England there has been a minor success story in the Rufiji district of Tanzania. It is worth recording as an example of how much can be achieved by the prayer and action of a relatively small group of Christians.

At the end of the nineteenth century Kindwitwi village was a leper colony. Its desperate situation continued to 1961, when Canon Robin Lamburn retired from his post as Archdeacon of Masasi, where he had lived since 1926. Under the auspices of the diocese he took over the running of the leprosarium. He did the fund-raising himself and managed to support the village using his own pension and help from within Tanzania and abroad. Assistance was continually received from the

International Schools of Tanganyika and of Munich. In 1981 Alex de Waal, Chairman of the Trustees, spent his gap year in Kindwitwi. This was at the instigation of the Headmaster of the King's School in Canterbury, Canon Peter Pilkington (now Lord Pilkington of Oxenford). The Canon had himself been a missionary in Tanzania and was aware of the acute needs of Kindwitwi. Alex liaised with Fr Lamburn and returned to Canterbury with a report showing what was needed immediately. A charitable trust was set up to raise the £30,000 that would buy the essential land-cruiser, tractor, fuel, food, and drugs. Since then the trust has raised almost a million pounds and has continued to provide steady support. The treatment of leprosy throughout 6,000 square kilometres of the Rufiji district is now under the control of the Trust. In 1993 Kindwitwi was registered as a normal Tanzanian village, and the people started to elect their own leaders under the government system. Ninety per cent of the leprosy sufferers have been cured, but it is estimated that it will be a further decade before Kindwitwi villagers are completely self-reliant, and so the appeal continues with this as a major goal. The other aim is to provide full care and support to the elderly and totally disabled patients who have no family to look after them.

The attraction to support this charity lies in its being concerned with a specific place and group of people, who can be contacted direct (see Appendix 3, Useful Addresses). It is not swallowed up in a huge amorphous organization that has to spend a high proportion of donations on administrative costs. A simple quarterly newsletter keeps supporters informed of developments. Father Lamburn died at Kindwitwi in 1993. I have met several people who knew him, and I am convinced that the success of the Rufiji project is rooted in the prayer and active love of this holy priest. It shows that even if we are not wealthy, even though we may feel powerless, we *can* make a difference if we put our minds to it. That is, if we follow the motto of Father Lamburn, carved on his gravestone: Pray and serve, and leave the rest to God.

After a reflection on Father Lamburn's life, today's meditation will continue with a re-reading of the Bible texts involving leprosy, and the identity of Christ as the Lord of Nature.

Bible Readings
Leviticus 14:1–32: God's regulations concerning lepers
Matthew 8:1–4; Mark 1:40–5: Jesus heals the leper by touch
Luke 17:11–19: The ten lepers, only one of whom said 'Thank you'

John 5:1–29: The healing at the pool of Bethzatha and its aftermath

Place of Spiritual Retreat
With the one leper who went back to Jesus to say 'Thank you', as in Luke 17

JANUARY

2 JANUARY

SS Basil the Great, Bishop and Doctor (*c.* 330–379), and Gregory Nazianzen the Divine, Bishop and Doctor (329–389)

BLACKBERRY *Rubus ulmifolius/fruticosus*
APPLE *Malus sylvestris* var. *domestica*

Cultivation Notes

The bramble is a deciduous semi-evergreen. It does not flower until May or June, so there is no need to worry about frost. If you have no easy access to the countryside for the delightful autumn pastime of blackberry picking, compact hybrids and thornless varieties are available for garden planting. They can yield ten kilos per plant, so even if the birds appropriate a share, there should still be plenty for the kitchen. Do not plant where blackberries or raspberries have grown during the past several years. Put in bare-rooted plants in November, early December or March, and pot-grown ones at any time. Planting and support processes are much the same as for raspberries (see 29 Dec.; St Thomas Becket). The blackberries that grow wild at the bottom of our drive and along the lane are sufficient to our needs. From mid-August for a few weeks they give some recompense for the trouble they have caused me over the years. They come so early in France that I do not have to worry about the English warning never to pick in October because the devil may have spat on them. In Devon they say he may do something even more unpleasant!

The selection of apples for domestic growing is a more complex business. It will depend on space and pollination group, so the novice grower will have to seek a professional opinion. The all-time English favourite cooker, 'Bramley's seedling', is too large for the small garden and needs to be near three compatible pollinators. However, more and more of the best fruit trees are becoming available in dwarf form, so you may be lucky. I once heard it said that a garden is incomplete without at least one apple tree. My own lack will eventually be remedied with espaliered varieties, and the list of possibilities includes my second favourite, 'Grenadier', as well as 'Arthur Turner' and 'Reverend W. Wilkes'.

History and Lore

If the culinary relationship between raspberry and redcurrant is a sublimely happy marriage, then that between blackberry and apple is perhaps more a friendship that endures in spite of differences in nature. For this reason they seem perfect to commemorate Basil and Gregory. The 'orchard' of the Church in which they grew up was under dire threat of being choked by the weed of Arianism. Their friendship began when they met as students at Athens University. Today's second Office reading is an extract from Gregory's 'Oration 43', and in it he goes so far as to say that they became so close that it seemed as if one soul enlivened two bodies, each man regarding the achievements of the other as his own. Their agreement on Nicene doctrine was total, and before devoting their lives to fighting Arianism they grounded themselves in the monastic life together at Pontus. After this period, it seems, their differences in temperament began to show. Basil's talents as an active organizer demanded that he ramble, albeit with purpose, and penetrate as many corners of the 'orchard' as he could. He became an exemplary Archbishop of Caesarea, preached, wrote his famous monastic *Rules*, worked tirelessly for the poor and sick, and conducted an extensive correspondence. Gregory too was a preacher, but he was never happier, it seems, than when expressing his faith and opposition to Arianism through writings of great depth and eloquence. He liked to stay in one place in the 'orchard', and – the *Rules* notwithstanding – it is at least possible that he was more naturally contemplative than Basil. It is perhaps right that the latter should be called 'the Great', while for Gregory is reserved 'the Divine' or 'the Theologian'. The tension between their temperaments led Basil figuratively to pierce his friend's flesh with a thorn. As Archbishop, Basil found himself with an Arian rival at Tyana, and he had Gregory consecrated Bishop of Sasima so that he could more effectively wield his orthodox influence in the area. This caused a rift between the friends, Basil accusing Gregory of dereliction of duty, and Gregory refusing to be shunted into an insalubrious and hostile place or to have anything to do with ecclesiastical power-play. He never went to Sasima, and so the thorn was removed, but one wonders whether its scar ever entirely healed. Gregory stayed as assistant bishop to his father in Nazianzus until the latter's death. A year afterwards, when he was only forty-five, Gregory's own health broke down. But he was not to be left in peace and still had an important contribution to make to the return of orthodoxy in Constantinople before retiring in 384. He was poor and prematurely aged, but he was able to live on his family estate and write poetry and an autobiography. Basil, whom Gregory survived by a decade, had died at the age of forty-nine, worn out by illness, hard work, and the harshness of his life. News reached him shortly beforehand of the succession of Gratian after the death of the Arian emperor Valens. As well as being Doctors of the Universal Church, Basil and Gregory are two of the three Holy Hierarchs of the Byzantines, the other being John Chrysostom (386–407). St Benedict regarded Basil as the father of Eastern monasticism and acknowledged his inspiration in the drawing up of his own *Rule*.

Towards Meditation

Basil and Gregory are remarkable for their actions and writings in the service of Christ, and one stands in awe of their achievements, but the very fact that men of this stature were human enough to fall out makes them approachable, even loveable. They are convincing as real people and are not mere ciphers from the ancient past. Sometimes hagiography, when it whitewashes the Saints, takes away from the lessons they can teach us and makes us despair of attaining even the beginnings of wisdom and holiness. The quarrel between Basil and Gregory does not diminish their achievements. And I must not give up because at times I have tried to manipulate friends, and at others have dug in my heels, refusing to compromise my principle or be manipulated myself. But the question is, did my righteous resistance hide laziness? How did I react to unjust accusations of slackness? The test is to ask whether those failings have interfered with God's work. What were my true motives? Have I yet learned from experience to ask these questions before I act? Today, as (thanks to the freezer) I make a blackberry and apple crumble for dinner, the rupture in the friendship between these two most respected Saints will lead me to reflect on friendship and forgiveness. The deeper and warmer a friendship, the greater the pain when it is damaged or ended altogether. I will examine the health of my own friendships. Am I the cause of pain in any of them? Have I truly forgiven lost friends who have caused me pain? Do any traces of resentment or bitterness remain in me? Grace tonight will include a prayer for lost and absent friends, living and dead, and will end with thanksgiving for the happiness they have brought into my life.

Bible Readings
Daniel 2:21–2; 1 Corinthians 12:11: The Spirit gives a different gift to each
  person
Sirach 15:5–6: God finds the words
Ephesians 3:8–12: The work of building up the body of Christ
Ecclesiasticus (Sirach) 6:5–17: Friendship
John 12:1–8: Jesus at Bethany

Place of Spiritual Retreat
In the house at Bethany with Jesus and his friends, as in John 12

13 JANUARY

St Hilary of Poitiers, Bishop and Doctor (*c.* 315–368)

RED CLOVER *Trifolium pratense* (literally 'of a meadow')

Cultivation Notes
This clover has narrow pointed leaflets with a pale V band at the base,
and the tubular flowers appear from late spring. The plant is erect to
sprawling and grows to a height of up to two feet. Both red and white
clover grow in my grassed French courtyard without any help from me,
but if you have space for a crop 'Susan Smith' is an ornamental hardy
variety. It likes moist well-drained soil in sun. Propagate by seed or
division in spring. Dead flowers will stay on the head and conceal the seed
pod. Unusually, clover can turn the nitrogen in the air into nutrient salts
for plant growth. This is why for centuries it has been used as a ploughing-
in crop to enrich the soil. It is also the most important forage crop in
northern Europe, and the agricultural cultivar 'Broad red' has been
grown since the seventeenth century. It also flourishes throughout North
America as an immigrant from the Old World.
  Long-tongued insects are attracted to its flowers, but its main
pollinators seem to be bumble-bees. Honey-bees may prefer white clover,
but they will not disdain red if it is growing near their hives. It is
sometimes referred to as 'bee bread'. Harvest young flowers and upper
leaves in summer, de-stalk, and spread on trays. Put in a warm airy place
until completely dry. After about four to five days store in jars away from
light. A potent wine can be made from the flowers of red clover, and they

were once used in syrup to treat whooping cough. In modern herbalism red clover is taken to ease eczema, psoriasis, and ovary, breast, and lymph cancers.

History and Lore
Hilary of Poitiers, as a pagan convert to Christianity, was described by Jerome as a cedar that had been transplanted into the Church, and so one could grow a bonsai form of cedar to honour him. However, I feel happier with a plant that he most probably observed growing in his native soil. The trifoliate form of clover is also apt because one of Hilary's major works was a treatise on the Holy Trinity. When Basil and Gregory were born Hilary was fifteen. He later married and had a daughter. At the age of thirty-five, after long intellectual enquiry, he converted to Christianity. About three years later, in about 353, he was made Bishop of Poitiers, and he spent the rest of his life fighting the Arian heresy. An early effect of his orthodoxy was banishment to Phrygia in 356. After the Council of Seleucia in 359 Hilary went to Constantinople and saw for himself the grip of Arianism with which Gregory was to grapple some two decades later. Hilary's reaction was to petition the Emperor for a public debate with the Arian bishops, but they were unwilling to meet someone who had already ably refuted them in writing and had him removed from the scene. Hilary was sent back to Poitiers, but this did not prevent him from refuting the Arian bishop Auxentius in Milan in 364. Hilary's influence had great bearing on the eventual denunciation of Arianism by the Church in Gaul, but it was not until 1851 that Pope Pius IX made him a Doctor of the Church.

Towards Meditation
The second Office reading for today, marked in my breviary with a pressed red clover from the courtyard, is from the first part of Hilary's treatise, *De Trinitate*. Preparing to write in defence of orthodoxy, he addresses God rather than the reader. The reading therefore provides an excellent prayer for any Catholic writer about to set to work. The paraphrase below sets out the points he makes. I shall ponder them today and on many other days in the year:

> Almighty God and Father, it is my first duty to make you the subject of all my speech and thought.
> My ability to speak is a gift from you, and I want to use it

in your service by writing about you. This wish is only my will, and so I plead your aid and mercy, and that your Spirit may breathe the truth into my expression of faith, in the writing I have begun. Christ promised that if we knock, it will be opened to us, and I have faith in that promise.

I pray for things I lack and in their pursuit will read the Scriptures assiduously. But all must be according to your will. I am held back by my slowness and lack of intellect and hemmed in by my ignorance of you, but I am taught that eagerness for your teaching is the beginning of my training. Obedience to the faith pulls me on beyond my natural ability. Prompt my faltering steps; strengthen me to go on. I beg for the Spirit to enlighten me as to the meaning of the prophets and apostles and to enable me to understand their complexities.

I avow you, the Most Holy Trinity.

I pray for the right words, the right understanding, an appropriate style, and loyalty to the truth. Grant that I may succeed in proclaiming Jesus Christ to the world as true God.

Bible Readings
Psalm 119:9–14: Teach me, Lord
1 John 4:2–3, 6, 15: How to discern a spirit of truth from one of falsehood
John 14:1–17: Who has seen Jesus has seen the Father

Place of Spiritual Retreat
Resting in Christ's words, as in John 14

17 JANUARY

St Antony of Egypt, Abbot (*c.* 251–356)

POTENTILLA 'Abbotswood'

Cultivation Notes
This dwarf shrubby cinquefoil grows to a height of about 30 inches. It is not spectacular but is distinguished for other reasons. The flowering period is long, from May to September; it grows in any soil and requires little attention; it does well in sun or light shade. Remove unwanted or

damaged branches in spring, and cut back new growth by a third. It is chosen for St Antony because of its name and character.

History and Lore

Antony gave up worldly possessions at the age of twenty and went to live among the local ascetics. When he was about thirty-five he went into the desert and lived in solitude for the next decade. Here he experienced the constant onslaughts of the devil, which he overcame through prayer and fasting but also, as he is alleged to have said, because the devil cannot bear to witness a person's love for Christ or to behold Christ's cross. Antony supported his physical needs mainly by gardening and making mats. Eventually he left his solitary life and laid the foundations of monastic life by grouping his disciples around him, guiding them with the mature fruit of his own experience. He tempered extreme austerity with common sense, caution, and – most importantly – with love of God. For these reasons he is known as the father of all monks. But his hermit life did not prevent him from being aware of the Church at large. He went to Alexandria, first in 311 to support it during the persecution under Maximian, and again in 355 to help in the battle against Arianism. He was 105 years old when he died, reputedly with all his faculties intact. Athanasius, who was his friend, wrote a biography, which made him known in the Western Church. Antony had asked to be buried in an unknown place, but relics were eventually found and taken to Alexandria. St Antony was responsible for many conversions and also had a reputation as a healer of humans and animals. In 1100 the Order of Hospitallers of St Antony was founded in La Motte, a place which claimed his relics. It became a centre of pilgrimage for sufferers from 'St Antony's fire', ergotism caused by eating fungally-infected rye.

Towards Meditation

As we have seen, at this time of year the Church is giving us a 'refresher' course in the Faith, preparatory to Lent. It is interesting that at the same time she presents us with a group of saints who all lived during the time when she was fighting to preserve her belief in the divinity of Christ. They represent a rich variety of talent, charism, and calling, and since the beginning of the year we have been shown how these were effectively put to the Lord's service. These, the Church is telling us, are some of the men and women whom God raised up to protect the faith we hold today. Be thankful to him and to them.

The desert hermit life seems remote and impossibly severe to most of us, but this brief summary of the life of St Antony can lead to a profitable consideration of our personal state of materialism and worldliness; of the place of solitude, prayer, and self-denial in our lives; of the use we make of our talents in the defence and proclamation of the Gospel; of the guidance and help we give to others in our family or community; of what is, or should be, our approach to our own death; and, as an encapsulation of all these, how much we truly love God.

Bible Readings
Psalm 130: The soul waiting for God
Galatians 6:4–16: The world crucified to me, and I to the world
Matthew 19:16–26: Sell your possessions
Mark 10:17–22: The rich young man
Luke 14:33: You cannot follow me unless you give up everything

Place of Spiritual Retreat
With Christ and the rich young man, as in Mark 10

20 JANUARY

St Fabian, Pope and Martyr (died 250)
St Sebastian, Martyr (died around end of third century)

HONEYSUCKLE *Lonicera periclymenum*; woodbine

Cultivation Notes
This fragrant deciduous perennial grows wild in woods, hedgerows, and thickets. It climbs by twining round other shrubs, or trails near the ground. The leaves are dark green and the stems red to purple. These become woody with age. The stamens extend beyond the petals of the long yellow to orange tubular flowers, which deepen in colour after pollination. Different garden varieties are available to flower in every month except March and April. Honeysuckle is easy to grow in moist soil. It appreciates sun and some shade, and can reach a height of twenty feet. In early herb lore the flowers were used in potions to ease headaches and in the treatment of pulmonary and asthmatic conditions. It is emetic, diuretic, and laxative and is rarely used internally today. It is, however, one of

thirty eight ingredients used in Doctor Edward Bach's remedies, and the flowers are an important addition to pot-pourri for their perfume and colour. Harvest the flowers in the morning before they open. There is an old superstition that if sprays of honeysuckle are brought into the house, a wedding will soon follow. Honeysuckle particularly likes to twine itself around hawthorn, and since both Fabian and Sebastian embraced the thorny thicket of martyrdom, it is a suitable plant to commemorate them. Furthermore, it traditionally represents generous, devoted affection and both today's saints allegedly possessed these characteristics.

History and Lore
For most of Fabian's fourteen-year pontificate, the Church enjoyed relative respite from persecution. He seems to have been a man of administrative ability and vision, reputedly dividing Rome into seven regions and placing deacons over each one. Sub-deacons were also appointed with responsibility for collecting and recording the acts of the martyrs of their separate districts. He also arranged for the bodies of previously exiled Christians to be brought back to Rome and given honourable burial. Not much else is known of him except that he was one of the first to die in the persecution that resumed when Decius became emperor in 250. Eusebius (*c.* 260–*c.* 340) records the story that immediately before Fabian's election a dove had alighted on his head, showing that the Holy Spirit had chosen him. In today's second Office reading, Cyprian of Carthage, in his *Letter to the Church of Rome*, speaks of Fabian's life and martyrdom with profound reverence and appreciation. He was first buried in the cemetery of Callistus, where the stone covering his relics was found in 1854. These were later removed to the church of St Sebastian.

Sebastian is thought to have been a Roman soldier who had been made a captain of the Praetorian Guard by the emperor. At that stage Diocletian had not known of Sebastian's Christianity. However, the latter's consistent support of martyrs, including the brothers Mark and Marcellian, came at last to the notice of Diocletian, who ordered him to be shot to death with arrows. Sebastian survived to reproach the emperor for his cruelty. He was finally beaten to death with clubs, and, so the story continues, his body was thrown into the sewers. As the result of his appearance in a dream to a woman named Lucina, the body was found and buried in the catacombs. The church of Sebastian-without-the-Walls was later built over the site. Not surprisingly Sebastian is the patron of archers and soldiers, and, perhaps because of the association with sewers, he was invoked against the plague. It is possible that on some unrecorded occasion the plague was stemmed as the result of an appeal for his intercession. This may also have been the reason for his inclusion as one of the *Fourteen Holy Helpers*, a group of saints who became popular in the Rhineland from the fourteenth century onwards, and who were invoked against every type of disease.

Towards Meditation

The immediate lessons to be drawn from today's saints are the value of diligence and organization in our work; that it is our duty to respect the dead; that even though our trials and tribulations may not be of the violent physical kind endured by Fabian and Sebastian, we must embrace them and submit peacefully to the will of God; that we should offer kindness, support, and encouragement to the victimized; that we must have the courage of our convictions, whatever it may cost; and that we must pray constantly for the sick. In today's Office, St Ambrose, in an extract from his *Commentary on Psalm 119*, draws attention to the inner and outer persecution of the Christian soul by the devil and his human agents. He reminds us of New Testament texts that warn of the assaults that we must expect from those quarters. I will reflect again on these texts to strengthen my resolve and guard.

Bible Readings

Romans 8:31–9: Nothing can separate us from the love of Christ

2 Timothy 2:8–13; 3:10–12: All who want to live in Jesus Christ will be persecuted

Matthew 10:17–33: Declare for me on earth and I will declare for you in heaven

Place of Spiritual Retreat

Pondering, in his presence, Christ's words in Matthew 10

21 JANUARY

St Agnes, Virgin and Martyr (died *c.* 350)

LAMB'S LETTUCE *Valerianella olitoria*; corn salad; priest's or canon's salad

Cultivation Notes

The botanical name of this annual means 'little Valerian of the kitchen garden' and was given by one John Miller in the eighteenth century. Previously, it had been *lactuca agnina* (lamb's lettuce), perhaps because it appears at lambing time, or because lambs like to eat it. It will grow in any soil but prefers a dry, open position. If allowed, it will produce tiny five-petalled lilac-blue flowers from April to June. These appear in a cluster at the tips of stalks that can grow to a height of ten inches, and they are often hidden by green bracts. Lamb's lettuce, once common in cornfields, is now rare because of crop spraying. However, a search for it in south-west England may be rewarded. Look under hedges, and along footpaths or waste ground. Seed can be bought and sown in late summer until the end of September to supply winter salads through to the next spring. (It grows well with thyme.) Harvest in the same way as spinach by removing separate young leaves. They are rich in mineral salts and vitamins. The Reverend Johns records lamb's lettuce as a salad plant, and it is described in the Suttons' *The Culture of Flowers and Vegetables*, as 'a most refreshing episode in the routine of a good dinner'. I recommend a dressing made with walnut oil and nibbed walnuts.

History and Lore
Probably because her name means purity and is close to the Latin *agnus*, the lamb has long been the emblem of St Agnes. On her feast-day, at the church dedicated to her in Rome, two lambs are blessed. Wool is taken from them and sent to the nuns of Torre de'Specchi, who weave the *pallia* for new or 'translated' archbishops. The *pallium* is a band of white wool worn on the shoulders. It has two strings of the same material, and four purple crosses worked into it. Within three months of his confirmation, every new archbishop must beg his *pallium* from the Pope, and before it is sent to him it lies for a night on the tomb of St Peter. Strictly speaking, he may not exercise his full episcopacy until he receives it, normally from the hands of another archbishop. Nor may he hand it on to his successor, for it will be buried with him.

Towards Meditation
St Agnes is thought to have been only thirteen when she was martyred by the sword for consecrating herself to Christ and consequently refusing to marry. Although little is known for certain, her existence is verified by her inclusion in the Roman canon, and by the praise accorded her in the writings of other saints, notably Ambrose, during whose lifetime she was martyred. In his *Treatise on Virgins* (Book 1, chapter 2), he marvels especially at her extreme youth. This should have meant she could be only a learner, but through her chastity and faith she becomes our teacher. She is perhaps the supreme demonstration that age and erudition do not automatically bring wisdom. Like all the saints, she shows the way to the door beyond which it is to be found. Without humility we cannot even reach the door.

Bible Readings
Psalm 126: Sowing in tears and reaping in joy
Wisdom 3:1–9: God accepts them as a holocaust
Wisdom 8:21: Insight to know whose gift she was
1 Corinthians 7:25–40: Christian virginity
Revelation 19:6–7: The marriage feast of the Lamb; the bride prepared
Luke 14:7–14: Christ teaches humility
Matthew 10:34–9: Not peace but the sword

Place of Spiritual Retreat
With the disciples listening to Christ's teaching, as in Luke 14 or Matthew 10

22 JANUARY

St Vincent of Zaragoza, Deacon and Martyr (died 304)

SPANISH GORSE *Genista hispanica*

Cultivation Notes

This deciduous, shrubby plant has wiry stems and tiny leaves. From May onwards it produces masses of yellow flowers on cushions of springy branches. It favours sun and light soil. It can reach heights from two to twelve feet, depending on the variety, and is a favourite hedge plant. It is chosen for St Vincent because he is the protomartyr of Spain.

History and Lore

As a deacon at Zaragoza, Vincent allegedly read out the sermons of his mentor, the bishop, who had a speech impediment. He was martyred during the persecution of Diocletian. Relics were later claimed by Valencia, where he died, and by Zaragoza, Paris, and Le Mans. The English twelfth-century abbot Faricius also acquired relics for Abingdon. There was a time when Vincent was so revered as to be placed third (after Stephen and Laurence) in the list of martyrs invoked in the Litany of the Saints.

Towards Meditation

The traditional details of Vincent's death and the fate of his body smack strongly of exaggeration, but they do symbolize the impossibility of quenching Christ's truth. The story goes that Vincent was imprisoned, starved, scourged, racked, roasted, and had hot metal applied to his wounds. He was then returned to prison and made to lie on a bed of broken earthenware. His dead body was eventually thrown out unburied. A raven protected it from other birds and wolves that came to prey on it. Later, it was thrown into the sea, but it was washed up, found by Christians, and given reverent burial.

St Augustine of Hippo, writing of Vincent in his 'Sermon 276', gives a wonderful example of how an almost certainly embroidered legend can, through sound theology and biblical knowledge, be turned to good account in God's service. Vincent's belief and endurance, we are told, were divinely given. We, who live under no immediate threat of persecution, can learn the lessons Augustine draws from this, just as profitably as his contemporary readers. If we are able to speak effectively for Christ, we must not believe it is through our own unaided ability. If we overcome trials, the courage to do so must come from God. Next we are reminded of Christ's warning about persecution (see Bible readings for 20 January), and of his promise to come to the rescue. Vincent overcame because he knew and believed these things. Again, Augustine applies the lesson to all Christians. We must resist attacks by the devil from within and without. We must not give in to the lure of vanity nor let the world frighten us with its cruelty, because Christ has conquered it for us. Throughout the extract, Augustine stresses Vincent's eloquence, particularly at the height of his passion. This he tells us, returning to his first point, was the Holy Spirit speaking from the tortured body of the martyr. Vincent's speech is therefore a fulfilment of Christ's promise, the same that St Lucy (13 December) is supposed to have repeated to the prefect Paschasius.

Bible Readings
Job 23:10–11: Tested in the crucible I have become gold
Psalm 118: Call to the Lord in distress
John 12:24–6: The dead grain of wheat and its rich harvest
John 17:11–19: The world hated them
Gospel readings as for SS Lucy, Fabian, and Sebastian

Place of Spiritual Retreat
With Philip and Andrew pondering Jesus' words, as in John 12; or listening to his prayer for the Church, as in John 17

24 JANUARY

St Francis de Sales, Bishop and Doctor (1567–1622)

A MOIST POT-POURRI of rose (hybrid tea 'Crimson glory'); pinks; jasmine; mock orange; rosemary; thyme; dried orange peel
(Cultivation Notes are not given today as the plants are dealt with elsewhere)

History and Lore
My choice for Francis de Sales involves a long-term plan beginning in the

summer of 2002 and, God willing, coming to maturity on 24 January the following year. There are several reasons for my going to so much trouble in his honour. As the mentor of my patron, Jane Frances de Chantal, he has had considerable influence on me. His idea for a daily place of spiritual retreat is probably the best way I know of staying in God's presence, whatever the distractions of daily life and work, and I cannot recommend it too highly. Through his writings he has led countless laywomen along the narrow path with kindness, understanding, and love but above all with sanity. He wrote for specific individuals, and this is probably why the reader feels he is addressing her personally. He is patron of writers and journalists, and, I believe, has watched over all I have done for many years. During exile, I found myself attending a church that was dedicated on the Feast of the Visitation, and I have since been drawn more deeply into the mystery St Francis chose to name the Order he founded with St Jane. All the saints command admiration, gratitude, and respect, but there are a few whom one can dare to love as well. For me, St Francis is such a one.

St Francis is also dear to me because of his frequent use of plant imagery to underline points about the spiritual life. He once said that meditation is like sniffing the flowers and herbs in my planned pot-pourri separately; contemplation is being able to appreciate them all at the same time. This may seem whimsical, but it is supported by the mechanics of making a successful moist pot-pourri and by its eventual attributes. If it is stoppered while you are not there to appreciate it, it will keep its perfume for years. It takes longer to prepare than dry pot-pourri and is not visually so attractive, but the perfume is deeper and more mellow. Similarly we retain the insights and privileges given us during patient, concentrated prayer and meditation. Their beauty and value cannot be seen or touched but remain hidden in the soul for future reflection and enrichment. The analogy continues with the packing-down of layers of petals and spices; with the subsequent fermentation; with the fact that at this stage the scent is not striking; and with the eventual breaking up of the 'wodge' that has formed. Later, for beginners, an essential oil of only one of the ingredient flowers must be added. Blending is for the more experienced and unless you have a particularly keen sense of smell the result will be a blur of fragrance. Lastly a 'fixing' agent is added to hold the perfume. When St Francis' pot-pourri is finished it will be stored in sealed jars and not opened until his feast-day.

Francis de Sales was ordained in 1593, and before being made Bishop of Geneva in 1602 he brought back to the Faith over seventy thousand Haute-Savoie Catholics who had gone over to Calvinism. He survived this dangerous enterprise and achieved his goal through preaching character-ized by patience, gentleness, discretion, and love. These were to mark all his writings, but let no one be deceived: the glove may be velvet, but the hand within is one of firm discipline. St Francis de Sales was canonized only 43 years after his death and declared a Doctor of the Church in 1877.

Towards Meditation

Today, the Church turns her attention to one of her greatest spiritual directors, and concentrates on him as a champion of the devout life for lay people. The second Office reading is from Part 1, chapter 3 of his *Introduction to the Devout Life*. Here he explains that true devotion can be practised in any state of life. Using the analogy of a bee sucking nectar leaving the flower undamaged, he explains that if our devotion is true it will not conflict with the duties of our state. Rather, it will improve our performance of them and enhance our own lives and those of people around us. I have found this an invaluable yardstick against which to measure every aspect of my life, and I apply it at least annually on St Francis' day. The Office extract concludes with his firm conviction that although a purely contemplative life cannot be achieved in the world, there are other ways in which lay people can pursue perfection. Before opening the pot-pourri, I shall select for meditation an extract from his writings that is appropriate to my spiritual state and need at the time. This is easy to do as he presents his material under clear headings within his chapters.

Bible Readings

Wisdom of Solomon 7:13–14: Wisdom is an inexhaustible treasure
Ecclesiasticus (Sirach) 39:1–10: Wisdom from the study of the scriptures
1 Corinthians 2:10–16: We have the mind of Christ
Ephesians 32: Be friendly, kind, and forgiving; try to imitate God as a child that he loves
1 Timothy 4:16: Watch yourself and watch your teaching
James 3:17–18: Wisdom recognizable by its purity and peacefulness
Matthew 5:14–16: You are the light of the world
Matthew 11:29: Take my yoke and learn from me. I am humble and gentle of heart

Place of Spiritual Retreat
Resting with Christ in his words from the verses of Matthew 5 and 11

25 JANUARY

The Conversion of
St Paul the Apostle (died *c*. 65)

EYEBRIGHT
Euphrasia nemorosa

Cultivation Notes
This fascinating little plant
is parasitic on red clover,
greater plantain, rat-tail
plantain, and some grasses.
It is hardy and accepts
most soils and conditions.
From summer to late autumn
it produces white flowers, often purple-
veined, with a yellow throat and three
lobed lower petals. It grows to about a foot
in height. Scatter the seed near host plants to
which the roots of eyebright will attach themselves.

History and Lore
The botanical name comes from Greek and means 'to gladden'. Its use to
strengthen eyesight was known to the poet Edmund Spenser (*c*. 1552–99),
who wrote of it: 'Yet Euphrasie may not be left unsung / That gives dim
eyes to wander leagues around.' In 1855 Anne Pratt saw it in a shop in
Dover and was told that it was good for weak eyes, and in 1888 William
Thistleton, Director of Kew Gardens, confirmed that it was still in use for
treating eye complaints. It remains popular in herbalism to ease
conjunctivitis, eye injuries, weeping eczema, and hay fever.

Towards Meditation
I begin today by looking again at Albrecht Dürer's painting of St Paul

with St Mark. The great apostle stands in front of the evangelist. He is side-on to our view and conceals all but the head and shoulders of the much shorter Mark. His face is half turned to us so that we see the piercing gleam in his left eye. The zeal it expresses is startling and forbidding, and I found it quite frightening when I first saw it. But now I have come to think that perhaps Dürer is showing the fierceness of Paul's love for Christ and his young Church and his willingness to endure anything and everything on their behalf. He stands in impregnable defence of the written gospel in the person of Mark, who is looking at him in what seems a mixture of awe and confidence. Indeed no one would dare attack him with Dürer's Paul in the way. It is a work of tremendous power, and my initial fear has evaporated with repeated viewing. Paul is not repulsing me: rather I can get behind him and, with St Mark, feel the security of his protection against a hostile world.

After the painting, the reading of Acts 9:1–22 and Acts 22:1–21. The first is a third-person description of Paul's conversion; the second, Paul's own account of the event that changed his life and, because of God's purpose for him, that of every gentile who has since embraced the Christian faith. The Church celebrates this today and invites us to enjoy its dramatic, faith-strengthening elements, but she also wants to draw us more deeply into knowledge of Paul's missionary activity and into his theology. If we have time, it would be good to start a systematic reading of his letters. This would fit well with suggestions made for an approach to Lent outlined in Part One of this book.

Bible Readings

1 Thessalonians 4:13 – 5:11; 2 Thessalonians 2:1–12: The Second Coming of Christ

Romans 1:18 – 8:39; Galatians 1:6–24: Paul's gospel preaching

1 Corinthians: Paul sorts out disorder of various kinds

2 Corinthians 1:8–14; 3:1 – 6:10: Paul's love and endurance in ministry

Ephesians 1 – 3: The divine plan

Colossians 1:15 – 2:5: Christ, and Paul's task

Philippians 1:12–26; 4:1–20: Imprisonment and living in Christ

Philemon: A private letter to a convert and friend

1 Timothy 1:12–16: I acted in ignorance and unbelief

1 Corinthians 15:9: I persecuted God's Church; I am the least of the apostles

Acts 26:16b–18: You must tell others what you have seen

Galatians 1:11–24: God made Christ known to Paul so that he could preach his gospel

Mark 16:15–18: Proclaim the good news to the world

John 15:16: I have chosen you. Go out and bear fruit that will last

Place of Spiritual Retreat

On the road to Damascus with Paul and his companions, as in Acts 22

26 JANUARY

SS Timothy, Bishop and Martyr, and Titus, Bishop
(first century)

STONECROP *Sedum acre*; wall pepper; houseleek
DITTANY OF CRETE *Origanum dictamus*;
hop marjoram

Cultivation Notes

Stonecrop grows on walls, rocks, and sand dunes and produces mats of succulent leaves and star-like flowers. The stalks grow to a height of up to four inches, and do not all produce flowers. Suggested garden varieties are the bushy *S. tartarinowi*, which bears pale pink flowers in August and September, and the earlier-blooming *S. spathulifolium* with its purplish-blue foliage and deep yellow flowers. In former times Stonecrop was believed to have protective powers against thunder and lightning and was grown on housetops. Take care when handling, as it can cause blistering on sensitive skins.

Dittany of Crete is a very pretty spreading sub-shrub with woolly grey-white rounded leaves, and small pink pendant flowers. It grows to a height of about six inches, is extremely rare in the wild, and is not easy to rear domestically. Dittany dislikes the wet of winter and needs the special conditions for alpines. Theophratus (370–285 BC) recommended it to help women in labour, but it has no place in modern herbal medicine. It has, however, been used to flavour vermouth.

History and Lore

Timothy was born at Lystra, the child of a Jewish mother and a Gentile father. He became a much-loved disciple and companion of Paul and occasionally represented him at Thessalonica, Corinth, and Ephesus. Tradition has it that he was the first bishop of the Ephesians. Not by nature a man of heroic courage, he benefited constantly from Paul's bolstering, support, and love. He was martyred by pagans, probably for his opposition to the festivals of Dionysus. Stonecrop is chosen to commemorate him because he is alleged to have been beaten to death with stones and clubs.

Titus was a Greek Gentile who became close to Paul as companion and secretary. He undertook missions to Corinth and Dalmatia and was deputed by Paul to organize the Church on Crete. For this reason Dittany of Crete is chosen in his honour. The authenticity of the New Testament *Letter to Titus* has been the subject of much debate, but it is extremely critical of the Cretan character at the time and instructs Titus to handle the islanders firmly (Tit. 1:10–16). He is supposed to have lived to the age of ninety-four, and is celebrated by Cretans as their first bishop. His body was supposedly buried on Crete; his head was taken to Venice in 823.

Towards Meditation

Before Vatican II, Timothy appeared in the universal calendar on the day before the Conversion of St Paul and Titus not until 6 February. It makes much more sense to celebrate them together the day after we have concentrated on their mighty friend and master. By reading the pastoral letters Paul wrote to them, we gain tremendous insight into the problems they faced and into Paul's skill in marshalling, advising, and encouraging his troops. Furthermore, 2 Timothy, thought to be Paul's last letter, written when he was in prison facing imminent death, is perhaps the most moving of all his testimony. I will read it again today and extract from it Paul's teaching and example on gratitude to God; on endurance in the face of fear, suffering, and loneliness; on staying the course; on humility; and on the desire and duty to inspire the fearful with confidence. In giving us these two Pauline days, the Church reminds us that any summary of the Christian faith must include acknowledgement of the importance of Paul's apostleship.

Bible Readings
Psalm 92: God gives us strength
Acts 20:28: Watch over the flock
1 Corinthians 4:2: Trustworthy stewards
2 Corinthians 3:1–6: The qualifications of Paul and his companions to administer the New Law are God-given
Hebrews 13:7–9a: Remember those who preached the word to you
1 Peter 5:1–4: The sufferings of the Church
Matthew 28:16–20: Make disciples of all nations
Mark 1:14–20: Fishers of men

Place of Spiritual Retreat
By the Sea of Galilee at the calling of Simon, Andrew, James, and John, as in Mark 1

27 JANUARY

St Angela Merici, Foundress (*c.*1470–1540)

LOMBARDY POPLAR *Populus nigra*; 'Italica'

Cultivation Notes
This familiar deciduous tree is thought to have originated in Asia and was introduced to Britain from northern Italy in the eighteenth century. In Britain it has long been used to screen factories and other ugly buildings with its tall grandeur. A rapid and thirsty grower, its roots can sometimes break and block drains in the quest for water. There is a line of the trees behind my school, and one of them caused problems and extra expense during the digging of footings for a new annexe. Nevertheless, we are glad of them because, together with sycamores and elders and the allotments, they attract a variety of birds and other wildlife our pupils would otherwise never see or notice. Most Lombardy poplars are male and produce reddish catkins in April. Apart from their narrowness and height of up to 100 feet, they are recognizable by almost diamond-shaped leaves.

These are translucent at their toothed edges and a delightful pale green in spring. At home in France there is a fine avenue of them near the local river, but lack of space in my garden dictates the Lombardy poplar as another subject for the Bonsai collection.

History and Lore

I have chosen the Lombardy poplar to honour Angela Merici because she was born near Lake Garda in northern Italy and founded the Ursulines, the oldest unenclosed teaching order of nuns in the Church. At school it is impossible to watch the poplars swaying, yet strong against the winter gales, without thinking of her independence and resilience and of the work of present-day Ursulines.

Angela Merici was orphaned when very young but received a good education. As a Franciscan Tertiary, with several companions, she began charitable work among poor girls. At first this was conducted in lay dress and without vows, and the Church disapproved of the departure from the ideals of religious habit and enclosure. In 1565, however, the Rule was confirmed. The sisters were named *Ursulines*, because they were under the patronage of St Ursula, then thought to have been a fourth-century virgin martyr, but now removed from the universal calendar. They were confirmed as an Institute in 1572 at the request of St Charles Borromeo (1538–84), who had always taken a fatherly interest in them. St Angela often said that societal disorder is the result of dysfunction in the family, itself a symptom of there being too few Christian mothers. This comment on her times, possibly coupled with the lack she felt from the early loss of her own mother, was the driving force behind her life's work. Unfortunately, in today's 'developed' world at least, it is a saying that increasingly applies.

Towards Meditation

Today's second Office reading, from St Angela's *Spiritual Testament*, is about the teaching, care, and control of young people. Every year on her feast-day I measure my own practice against her counsel. First and foremost, she says, all our care and governance should be inspired by love of God and of our charges. If they are, our pupils and we shall not go wrong. In support of this conviction she reminds us of Christ's saying that a good tree cannot bring forth evil fruit. If our motivation is love, we cannot do other than good. Her next point is that we must treat our pupils as individuals and really get to know them inside out. This will not be difficult if we really love them. The more children there are in our charge, the more should this individual attention be given. As teachers we are spiritual mothers, and spiritual love is very powerful. In support of her next plea, for kindness and gentleness, she cites Our Lord's exhortation to learn of him, for he is meek and humble of heart. His yoke is easy, his burden light. So must be the constraint we lay upon our charges, and force must not be used. As God does to us, so must we to our pupils, by pointing things out, by invitation, and advice. There will be times when restraint of various levels of severity will be necessary, but even then it should be applied totally out of love and concern for the welfare of the individual concerned. I have to say that during a teaching career spanning forty years, spent mostly in inner-city schools, my best results (and I am not speaking merely of examination successes) have been achieved when my relationship with the pupils has developed according to St Angela's principles.

Bible Readings
Zephaniah 3:12–13: God will leave a humble people with us
Psalm 127: Unless the Lord builds the house
Proverbs 1:9: Do not reject your mother's teaching
Proverbs 5:1–2: Listen to my wisdom and understanding and learn discretion
Proverbs 23:26: Give me your heart and observe my ways
1 Corinthians 12:31 – 13:13: Love
Ephesians 3:14–19: The love of Christ is beyond all knowledge
Philippians 4:8–9: Think on these things
Mark 10:13–16: Let the children come to me

Place of Spiritual Retreat
Bringing all my pupils individually before Christ, as he commands in Mark 10

28 JANUARY

St Thomas Aquinas, Priest and Doctor (*c.* 1225–1274)

OXEYE *Leucanthemum vulgare*; moon daisy
BRISTLY OXTONGUE
Picrus echinoides

Cultivation Notes

Oxeye is perennial and reaches a height of up to two feet. It flowers from June to August and grows in any reasonable soil. The single blooms have white petals surrounding a central golden cushion up to two inches across. Juice of oxeye was once used to treat chest and liver complaints, or in drops to clear watery eyes. The botanical name is derived from the Greek *leukos*, 'white', and *anthos*, 'flower'.

Bristly hairs grow from little white spots on the leaves of Oxtongue. In southern England and Wales it is found under hedges and on field boundaries. The stalks can grow to a height of three feet, and the bright yellow flowers are borne at the top of the stem. They are surrounded by several narrow bracts, which in turn are surrounded by three to five broader ones. When fruiting it resembles a small dandelion 'clock'. Formerly used in pickling, bristly oxtongue is said to be quite pleasant-tasting after boiling. I have never tried it, preferring to let it grow wild amid the grass and clover of my courtyard, where it usually flowers until at least early November.

History and Lore

These plants are chosen to commemorate Thomas Aquinas, because

Albert the Great (1206–80), his one-time teacher, is supposed to have prophesied of him that, although he was known as the 'dumb ox', his lowing would one day be heard the world over. The 'eye' and the 'tongue' celebrate the monumental achievement, through insight and word, of his relatively short life. Educated first by Benedictines and then at Naples University, his decision to become a Dominican friar met with opposition from his family, who captured and imprisoned him. The old Roman Breviary tells the story that his brother sent a woman into his room to tempt him. Thomas drove her out with a firebrand. He then fell asleep praying before the crucifix and dreamed that angels girded his loins. He was never again troubled by the slightest sexual urge. Whatever the truth of this, all his future power was certainly concentrated in his mind, and his innocence earned him the title of 'angelic Doctor'. Another story of Thomas and the crucifix is that he was again praying before it when he heard the voice of Christ asking what reward he would like for having written so well of his Saviour. Thomas answered simply, 'Lord, yourself.' A Brother Reginald said of him that his great erudition was due more to the quality and efficacy of his prayer than to his genius. Apart from his gargantuan *Summa contra Gentiles* and *Summa Theologica*, which resulted in his sometimes being called 'Universal Teacher', he was also a gifted poet. In his sequence *Lauda Sion*, for the Mass of Corpus Christi, and the hymn *Pange lingua*, for the procession and Office of that feast, he combines theology and love for God into works of art in his honour. It is worth learning Latin to appreciate the originals fully! But even the translations show Thomas's mastery. The *Summa Theologica* was never completed. In 1273, the year before his death, he had a mystical experience while saying Mass, explaining afterwards that he would write no more, because compared with what he had seen, all his previous works seemed like straw. He died on 7 March 1274, on his way to Lyons to take part in the Fourteenth Ecumenical Council. He was canonized in 1323 and made a Doctor of the Church in 1567. His feast was observed originally on the anniversary of his death, but since 1970 it has been moved to the anniversary of his reburial at Toulouse in 1368.

Towards Meditation

Thomas Aquinas found time to preach and write commentaries for the laity. The second Office reading today is from his *Conference 6 on the Creed*, and deals with the passion and cross of Jesus. A brief summary shows its clarity and excellence as a basis for meditation:

It was necessary for Christ to suffer and die for us: (a) to redeem us; (b) to give us a perfect example of the virtues. The cross on its own is sufficient to instruct us in them.

1. Love: Christ loved us and laid down his life for us. We therefore should not regard the trials and tribulations we bear for his sake as a burden or imposition.

2. Patience: It is found in its noblest form on the cross, not only the endurance of a terrible thing but endurance of it when it could have been avoided. Jesus spoke no words of threat from the cross. We should run our own course, as he did, despising the shame, and bearing all for the sake of the joy that lies ahead.

3. Humility: God himself willed and allowed Pontius Pilate to judge and to put him to death in the Person of Christ.

4. Obedience: Jesus was obedient to the Father, even unto death. The New Adam atones for the sinful disobedience of the old Adam.

5. Poverty: We must show contempt for worldly wealth, honour, power, wisdom, knowledge, reputation, fine clothes, food, and drink. We should follow after the true King, who was mocked, spat upon, buffeted, crowned with thorns, stripped of all dignity, and given vinegar to drink.

Bible Readings

1 Kings 3:11–14: A heart wise and shrewd
Psalm 19: The laws of God are true and just
Wisdom 7:7–8; James 1:5: I prayed and received understanding
1 Corinthians 2:1–10: The hidden wisdom of God is taught in our mysteries
2 Timothy 1:13–14; 2:1–3: Keep the precious with the help of the Spirit
Matthew 19:21: The camel and the eye of the needle
Matthew 5:1–16: Spiritual poverty and true happiness
Matthew 10:3–8: Take up your cross

Place of Spiritual Retreat

With the disciples listening to Christ's words, in a chosen text from Matthew, as above

31 JANUARY

St John Bosco, Priest (1815–1888)

WILD MUSHROOM *Agaricus campestris*
TWINFLOWER *Linnaea borealis*

Cultivation Notes

The wild mushroom is found throughout Britain, Europe, and North America. When I was a girl growing up in Yorkshire my father frequently conducted early-morning expeditions to pick them in the warmth and damp of autumn. And from time immemorial mushroom gathering has been a favourite pastime in our area of France. My mother was often part of the select band of village *grandmères* who tramped off into the fields and woods just after dawn in late September, each bearing a *baton* walking stick, cut from the hedges, and singing '*ron-ron-ron petit pat-a pon*' as they marched along. She was honoured to be shown where the *cèpes* grow, for this is a fiercely guarded secret, revealed to no one under seventy.

Of course one must know how to distinguish edible from poisonous fungi, and novices should accompany the experienced gatherer until they have thoroughly absorbed this lore. *Never pick or eat a mushroom with white gills.* The gills of edible mushrooms are pale beige or pink at first, deepening to chocolate and finally black as they grow older. The Death Cap, for instance, has white gills throughout all its stages, and a bag at the base of the stem.

Twinflower

The twinflower is a rare creeping evergreen with paired pink flowers. It blooms from June to August and grows to a height of three inches. It is known to grow in eastern Scotland, and I have a photograph of it in Maine on the eastern seaboard of the USA. Its rarity may mean that I shall never have it in my garden to honour John Bosco, and unless I succeed in finding a plant, he will have to share the Lombardy poplar with St Angela Merici. I do not expect either will mind, as three centuries before him she had done for girls what he would do for boys.

History and Lore

John Bosco was a native of Piedmont, and the wild mushroom is one of the gastronomic delights of his region of Italy. He was born in the diocese of Turin, to the north of which now lies the *Parco Nazionale del Gran Paradiso*. Here the delicate twinflower is housed in the Alpine garden.

John Bosco knew poverty throughout his childhood. His mother brought him up single-handed, having been widowed when her son was only two. He is supposed to have arrived at the seminary wearing charity clothes. After ordination he was at first attracted to the missionary life but abandoned the idea in favour of work among the poor and homeless youth of his own locality. He began by living with his mother and some forty destitute boys, eventually opening workshops to train them in specific crafts. By 1856 there were over six hundred boys in his charge. A group of priests had joined him and helped to teach them in various small schools or 'oratories'. The boys were often taken on day retreats into the countryside, during which there would be a picnic and games in addition to religious instruction. I like to think that St John may have seen both twinflowers and wild mushrooms on these outings. He believed that deprived city boys benefited from contact with natural surroundings and from the spiritual power of music, and he seems to have had particular success with 'problem' boys. He developed a reputation as a gifted preacher, fund-raiser, and miracle-worker. He built several churches, including one dedicated to St Francis de Sales. His Society of Don Bosco, formally approved in 1874, was more commonly known as the Salesians from about 1854. John Bosco died at the age of seventy-seven, worn out from his labours but leaving behind a Congregation of over seven hundred priests and brothers, in more than sixty houses in the Old World and America.

Towards Meditation

The life of St John Bosco was marked by zeal, simplicity, and joyful trust in God, even in the face of a variety of obstacles. These qualities are reflected in today's Office reading from one of his letters. Like the extract from the writings of St Angela Merici, it is salutary reading for teachers. Another summary makes a good basis for reflection:

The Guiding Principles:

St John agrees with St Angela that love and concern for the happiness of each individual should be our driving force. As teachers, we prepare pupils to fulfil their potential, while they are in our charge and after they have left it. We are *in loco parentis* and must love them as if they were our own sons and daughters.

1. Impatience, anger, and threats: It is much easier to give in to these than to employ a firm gentleness in the handling of difficult pupils. St Paul's attitude of love for inattentive, unresponsive, and unruly converts is recommended. Above all, Paul prayed for them.

2. Punishment and authority: The administering of these must be calm, and not a venting of anger, or an assertion of authority in revenge against someone who has flouted it. Christ did not domineer but came to serve.

3. Ignorance, and slow learners: Christ treated his sometimes dull disciples with patience, kindness, and friendship and gave them the courage and confidence to ask forgiveness.

4. Contempt and hurtful words: These must be avoided. There should always be compassion if we need to correct faults.

5. Serious matters and long speeches: In grave circumstances we should pray rather than use words that wound the innocent and have little effect on the intransigent guilty.

Perhaps John Bosco found it easier than ordinary mortals to suppress anger in the face of obdurate bad behaviour and refusal to learn. Perhaps not. But for many of us, his deceptively simple advice is far from easy to practise. The more difficult we find it, the more does his final exhortation to prayer appear helpful and wise. Humbly, I venture to add that prayer for one's students and colleagues is efficacious in any case.

Bible Readings and Place of Spiritual Retreat
As for Angela Merici, with:
James 2:14–17: Faith without works is dead

FEBRUARY

2 FEBRUARY

The Presentation of the Lord (Candlemas)

SNOWDROP *Galanthus nivalis*; Candlemas Bell; Our Lady's Taper; Eve's Tears; Fair Maid of February; *Perce-neige* (snow piercer)

Cultivation Notes

A small leaf-like sheaf protects the tip of the flowering stem and enables the snowdrop to force its way up through the earth and snow. Its three inner petals are green-tipped and the three outer ones all white. Plant the bulbs as soon as they come to hand: dried-out bulbs are useless. Plant indoors in September at a depth of half an inch. Outdoors, a moist spot in light shade is best. Planting depth is about four inches, with a similar space between bulbs. Snowdrops can appear as early as January and will almost certainly have arrived by Candlemas. They normally grow to a height of 4–10 inches and provide an early mini-banquet for the bees, which search for nectar inside the green-tipped petals.

History and Lore

The botanical name was given by Linnaeus, from the Greek *galanthus*, meaning 'milk-flower', and the Latin *nivalis*, 'snowy'. 'Eve's Tears' probably has its origin in the legend that, as Eve sat weeping outside paradise, an angel came to comfort her. She had not seen a flower since the Fall, and the snow had fallen incessantly. As the angel spoke to her he caught a snowflake in his hand, breathed on it, and let it fall to earth as the first snowdrop. It blossomed each February until the birth of Mary, the second Eve, and every Candlemas it continues to do so in her honour. There is also a German story that at the Creation everything was given a colour, except the snow, whose total absence of colour made it invisible. It complained to God, who sent it to beg colour from all the flowers. They all refused, until the snowdrop offered its whiteness if it would be of any use. And so the snow became white and in gratitude protects the snowdrop bulbs during the winter, allowing very few other plants to pierce its surface. As for the French

243

'*perce-neige*', I cannot think of it without remembering the sword that Simeon prophesied would pierce Mary's heart.

The snowdrop is thought to be a native of Brittany, and in spite of the naturalized colonies that grow in woodlands and around churches up and down the country it is not counted as indigenous to England. Several of these colonies are on the sites of old monasteries or near their ruins. There are notable examples at Shaftesbury and Wherwell (both Benedictine nunneries) at Walsingham, and at Abbotskerwell in Devon, near the former monastery of Augustinian Canonesses. Three of these snowdrop colonies are at pre-Reformation sites, and it is tempting to imagine that they may have been planted by the nuns as a symbol of purity, and to decorate their chapels at Candlemas.

In the border counties of England and Wales bunches of snowdrops would be brought indoors so that the house would have its own purification at Candlemas. In other areas the practice was frowned on as a superstitious relic of the papist past, and it is undeniable that in the early Protestant era there was a deliberate de-catholicizing of plant names and a suppression of customs that connected them with the Catholic faith. However, farmers continued to set their planting and harvesting programmes by the church calendar, and several of their *aides-mémoire* have survived: 'On Candlemas Day if a thorn be adrop / You can be sure of a good pea crop'; 'A farmer on Candlemas day / should have half his corn and half his hay.' It was also a day when the length of winter could be predicted: 'If Candlemas be fair and bright / Winter will have another flight. / If Candlemas be cloud and rain / Winter will not come again.' In the United States they say that if a wart-hog sees his shadow at Candlemas then the winter is only half done. Other days of the year were singled out for the sowing of different seeds, but Candlemas was supposed to be good for everything.

Church authorities are of the opinion that Candlemas is one of the oldest feasts involving Mary, if not *the* oldest. In Welsh, *Gwyl fair y carhwyllau* means 'Mary's festival of candles'. This is particularly interesting, since 2 February was a cross-quarter day in the old Celtic calendar. In the East, it seems to have been known as 'The fortieth day after Epiphany', but in Constantinople (as early as 543) it is believed to have been kept as the 'The Purification of the Blessed Virgin.' *Saint Andrew's Daily Missal* (pre-Vatican II) claims that the feast was kept in Jerusalem in the fourth century and that it had reached Rome by the seventh, together with its procession of candles. The Greeks called it 'The meeting of Christ with Simeon and Anna', and the old Latin name was

Obviato (meeting). Bede (d. 735) called it *Oblatio Christi ad templum*, which brings us full-circle to the present title of the feast. In the 1960s, the *Saint Andrew's Daily Missal* classifies it as a feast of Our Lord, anticipating the reform of 1969, while retaining the Marian title. There has in fact never been much about Mary's Purification in either the Mass or the Office of the day; Luke, from whom the readings come, is more concerned with the christology of the feast. Whatever the official title, the faithful have probably always kept it as a feast of Our Lord *and* Our Lady. The British will always more easily call it Candlemas, and the French *La Chandeleur*.

Towards Meditation
'We have thought of thy steadfast love, O God, in the mist of thy temple' (Ps 48:9).

There will be snowdrops in my garden, and also in my house chapel if I am in France. In London, I will attend Mass and celebrate with joy this last great feast of light in darkness. Candlemas, as well as having great spiritual significance, is a comforting feast. Outside, the night is usually bitterly cold and often rainy, but we are warm and safe within the church. The candles blessed, the choir sings 'The Lord will come with mighty power and give light to the eyes of all who serve him, Alleluia.' After prayers, the priest lifts his voice in the invitation, 'Let us go in peace to meet the Lord', and then leads the entire congregation round the church. The choir sings the *Nunc dimittis*, and we respond after each verse with, 'A Light to lighten the Gentiles and the glory of thy people Israel'. There is a tremendous collective feeling of family security and fellowship, and a solemn awareness that we are singing about ourselves; we are struck with wonder at the continuity of our faith and at the absolutely real connection we have with the old priest in the Temple holding our Saviour in his arms. Each of us symbolically carries him in the light of the candle we hold. As at the beginning of the Easter Vigil, there is no other light in church. There does not need to be: the church is always packed for Candlemas. The light we make symbolizes many more things than Simeon's prophecy as related to ourselves and our carrying the light of Christ within us. I shall reflect on some of them during the day. Here is last year's list of what the light of Candlemas symbolizes:

the light of example in the submission of Mary and Joseph to the ritual of Purification, even though it was entirely inappropriate to Mary and her Child;

245

the light of our realization that Christ himself willed it so. He submitted to the Law in order to purify it. He willed to become like us in every way. He entered the Temple in demonstration that he had come to rebuild it;

the light of his glorious kingship over Israel and over all the kingdoms of earth;

the light of his sacred priesthood over all priests;

the light of the Spirit that brought Simeon to the Temple to receive the Child that day;

the light that spoke though Simeon of suffering, not only for Mary but for all Israel in the near future and in the far distant future for all of us, and of those who would accept or reject the light;

the light that enabled Simeon to recognize the Child in his arms as the glory of his people, and enabled Anna to acclaim that Child as Messiah and Redeemer;

the light that completed the cycle of prophecy immediately surrounding the birth of the Saviour;

the light of personal fulfilment and peace brought to Simeon and Anna by his presence;

the light of life he is to us;

the light of Christ himself.

Bible Readings

Psalm 49:9–11: We have thought of thy steadfast love, O God, in the midst of thy temple

Malachi 3:1–5: The Lord whom you seek will suddenly come to his temple

Psalm 24:7–10: Let him enter, the King of glory

Hebrews 2:14–18: It was essential that he become like his brothers and sisters

Hebrews 10:5–7: Here I am, come to do thy will

Psalm 45: I address my verses to the king

Exodus 13:1–3a; 11–16: The consecration of the first-born

Isaiah 8:14: The Lord will become a sanctuary, and a stumbling-block

Isaiah 42:13: The Lord advances like a hero

Isaiah 12:5–6: Great in your midst is the Holy One of Israel

Psalm 110: The Lord says to my lord: sit at my right hand

Hebrews 4:15–16: Christ out High Priest

Luke 2:22–40: The Presentation in the Temple

Place of Spiritual Retreat

In the Temple, as in Luke 2

3 FEBRUARY

St Blaise, Bishop and Martyr
(early fourth century)

HOREHOUND *Marrubium vulgare*

Cultivation Notes

This perennial herb has woolly stems and rough greyish
leaves. It grows to a height of up to 18 inches and
produces small white flowers in midsummer.
Horehound favours a dry alkaline soil and enjoys full
sun. Protect from wind and winter rain. Cut back after
flowering for a second crop of leaves. Sow in late
spring and divide established plants as necessary.

History and Lore

The botanical name comes from the
Hebrew *marrob*, meaning bitter juice.
It is mentioned in the *Mishna* and
was possibly one of the bitter herbs
eaten at the Passover. The English name
may come from the Anglo-Saxon *hare*,
meaning hoary-white, and *hune*, the word used
to describe a plant with hairy leaves and stems.
Horehound is native to Britain, central and
western Asia, continental Europe, and the
Canary Isles. In parts of Australia it is regarded as
a weed. The fruit-scented leaves contain vitamin C but have a bitter
flavour. Their use in the treatment of sore throats, coughs, and chest
complaints is thought to go back thousands of years, and it was certainly a
favourite in monastic gardens. Nowadays an expectorant syrup is made
with honey and a strong infusion of the leaves. The juice is supposed to
cure canker worm in trees, and the leaves soaked in milk make an effective
fly killer. Culpeper recommends horehound to soothe the pain of pricking
thorns. I have also found that an application of fresh leaves brings
immediate relief from nettle stings.

Blaise is believed to have been the son of noble Christians. Tradition
has it that as a young man, during the reign of the emperor Licinius, he

247

was consecrated bishop of Sebaste in Armenia. During persecution, he hid in a cave and blessed sick or wounded animals. He is associated with throats because he allegedly saved a boy who was choking to death on a fish bone. Later, when Blaise was in prison, the boy's mother brought food, drink, and candles to him. From this story stems the church ceremony of blessing throats with two candles on his feast-day. Horehound is the obvious plant for him, but not only because of the throat association. The woolly stems and leaves are a reminder that, before being beheaded, Blaise was flayed with iron wool combs. Not surprisingly he is the patron of wool carders. The wool traders of Norwich paid him particular honour. *Parson Woodforde's Diary* gives a detailed description of a long and magnificent procession through the city on 24 March 1783. The man representing St Blaise had pride of place and rode in a phaeton drawn by six horses.

Towards Meditation

It is this woolly aspect of the lore surrounding St Blaise that will preoccupy me today, and indeed the second Office reading is from St Augustine's *Sermon 32*, 'On the Ordination of a Bishop'. It invites us to reflect on Christ's thrice-repeated question to Peter: 'Simon, son of John, do you love me?' Peter is given the chance to cancel out his threefold denial after the arrest of Jesus, the product of fear. Now his threefold affirmation of love banishes his fear, but each time he makes it Christ commands him, 'Feed my sheep' and then goes on to prophesy the martyrdom of Peter. *Feed* the sheep, says Augustine, means *suffer* for them. St Blaise's day is therefore one of concentration on love, service, and sacrifice and of examination as to how we express these in our own lives.

Bible Readings

Psalm 34: Prayer to be set free from fear
James 1:2–4, 12: Standing firm in trials
Romans 8:35–9: Nothing can separate us from Christ's love
Philippians 1:20: Prayer for physical courage
Luke 9:23–6: Losing and gaining life
John 21:15–19: Follow me

Place of Spiritual Retreat

With John, following behind Jesus and Peter, as in John 21

5 FEBRUARY

St Agatha, Virgin and Martyr (dates uncertain)

ALL GOOD *Chenopodium Bonus Henricus*; Good King Henry

Cultivation Notes

This perennial is a member of the goosefoot tribe and, unless you are an expert in plant recognition, picking in the wild is not recommended. Rather, buy seeds or plants from a reputable specialist. The leaves of Good King Henry are broad and arrow-shaped, and the greenish-yellow flowers appear on spikes in early summer. The plant reaches a height of up to twenty inches and likes a deeply dug, well-drained site in full sun. Sow in spring and thin seedlings to fifteen inches apart. Divide established roots in autumn, and allow a year or two before harvesting.

History and Lore

Good Henry is from the German *Guter Heinrich* and distinguishes it from *Mercurialis annua*, or *Böser Heinrich* (Bad Henry). Heinrich features in German folklore somewhat as Robin or Jack and Jill do in English. All Good has been a popular herb since Neolithic times, particularly as food. During the twentieth century, it was overtaken by cultivated spinach, but it is still worth growing. Steam the flower spikes and toss in butter; cook the leaves like spinach, or use in soups and casseroles; peel and boil pen-sized shoots; and eat as a source of vitamins and iron. The leaves can also be used in external compresses to soothe pain. In plant lore All Good represents goodness itself, and it is chosen for St Agatha because her name is Greek for goodness. She is thought to have lived in the third century, probably in Catania or Palermo. Quintanius, a Roman senator, attempted to make her renounce a vow of consecrated virginity by having her put in a brothel. This did not work and he then had her tortured with rods, rack, and fire. Finally her breasts were cut off by soldiers, to whom she allegedly said, 'Are you not ashamed to cut off from a woman that with which your mothers suckled you?' That night an aged man, introducing himself as St Peter, came to her cell and restored her breasts with heavenly ointment. Shortly afterwards Quintanius ordered the renewal of torture, and she was made to roll naked on hot coals, but as she did so, an earthquake shook the town. Back in her cell, Agatha finally died from her injuries. After her death

Quintanius was bitten by one of his horses, and another kicked him into the river. His body was never found. Agatha's veil is later supposed to have saved the town from volcanic destruction. It was waved, according to the legend, before the oncoming lava and halted its advance. Agatha is mentioned in the *Martyrology of Jerome* (*c.* 530) and is invoked against fire and volcanic eruption. Unsurprisingly, she is patroness against diseases of the breast.

Towards Meditation
In today's Office, Methodius of Sicily reflects on Agatha's goodness in name, speech, and action and upon God the true goodness. Virgin martyrs from the eras of early persecution may seem remote from the modern Western Christian woman. (Not quite so remote from Korean and Chinese Christian women, who honour Agatha Kim and Agatha Lin, both martyred in the mid-nineteenth century.) We have not been called to horrific physical martyrdom for being good and loving Christ above all, but all three Agathas teach humility, that virtue from which all the others spring. For I cannot live even one day in the certainty that all my words, thoughts and actions have been good, or show that I love Christ above all.

It is hardly possible to go through St Agatha's day without thinking of the sufferings of those with breast cancer. The scourge is such that most readers will know at least one person who has had it, or who is currently fighting it. Some will be suffering from it themselves. In the past fifteen years, three women close to me have endured the trauma of mastectomy. Readers will make their own grim tallies, and although the publicity is usually about the disease in women, it is far from unknown in men. My intercessory prayer today will be for victims of breast cancer, whatever their gender. One of them, the mother of a beloved student is, as I write, two thirds of the way through chemotherapy, to be followed by radiotherapy, after the removal of a breast and the discovery of pulmonary embolism. Her son comes to me for his lessons most Saturdays. He tells me the latest news of his mother before we grapple with Graham Greene's 'take' on God. I dare not think about what may happen before St Agatha's day comes around next year.

Bible Readings
Psalm 33: Reliance on God
Romans 5:1–5: Sufferings

Matthew 5:10: Blessed are the persecuted

Place of Spiritual Retreat
With the disciples, listening to the Beatitudes as preached by Christ in
Matthew 5

6 FEBRUARY

St Dorothy, Virgin and Martyr, Patron of Gardeners (died *c.* 313)
St Paul Miki and Companions, Martyrs (died 1597)

DOG ROSE *Rosa canina*

This is the most common wild rose in Europe, brought to England by the
Romans some 2,000 years ago. A new hedge can be planted at this time of
year as long as there is no snow or frost on the ground surface. The Apple
Rose, *R. pomifera*, is also appropriate to St Dorothy. It is a medium-sized
shrub with grey-green downy foliage. Its scented flowers are pale pink and
are followed by large apple-shaped hips

APPLE *Malus sylvestris domestica*

Planting can take place this month as long as conditions are favourable.
Otherwise, store newly delivered plants in a frost-free place. Prune
established trees where hard frosts are not normal.

History and Lore
The apple is an ancient symbol of health and plenty. In English lore,
apart from the tag about its keeping the doctor away, there are other
customs attesting to faith in its positive characteristics. It was once
considered almost sacrilegious to burn apple wood indoors as this might
disturb the wellbeing of the house and its inhabitants. The old English
kissing-bough had evergreens and rosy-red apples, and at New Year in
parts of Gloucestershire 'Apple Gifts' were decorated with nuts and
evergreens, both symbolic of immortality and sweetness. In Cornwall
apples were the traditional gift for children on All Hallows Eve, and in
Yorkshire care was taken to thank the tree annually for its gift of fruit. In

South Devon on Epiphany Eve, farmers would bless and toast their best-bearing apple trees in a practice that was more a fertility rite than a Christian blessing. Nevertheless, running through all these customs there is concern for things of lasting value, a respect for creation, and gratitude for its gifts.

Of course the apple also has a negative moral reputation because of its mention in the Genesis account of the Fall. Scholars have argued that biblical apples were in fact oranges, apricots, or even quince, and that the roses were anemones, *cistus narcissus*, tulips, or crocus. They allow a possible exception in the case of 2 Esdras 2, where God says he has prepared roses to grow on 'the seven mighty mountains'. This, they think, could be a reference to the true *Rosa phoenicia*, which has been found growing at heights of up to five thousand feet.

In *The World's First Love*, Fulton Sheen says that the early virgin martyrs wore crowns of roses because death would take them straight to the love of Jesus in heaven and to the joy of being with him eternally. In the mid-nineteenth-century *The Language of Flowers*, a wreath of roses symbolizes beauty and virtue rewarded, while the dog rose signifies pleasure mixed with pain. Dorothy is recorded as having been beheaded in about 313 during the persecution under Diocletian. She was martyred for refusing to marry or to worship idols and is usually represented wearing a crown of roses. Roses and fruit appear next to her. Legend has it that when she was on her way to execution, the judge's secretary, Theophilus, mocked her, saying, 'Send me some fruit and roses, Dorothea, when you get to Paradise.' Immediately after her death an angel brought Theophilus a basket of roses and apples, and before disappearing, said to him, 'From Dorothea in Paradise.' Not surprisingly, the secretary was converted. He too was later martyred under Diocletian. Dorothy's popularity was centred in Italy and Germany, but she was known to Aldhelm (639–709), Abbot of Malmesbury and Bishop of Sherborne. In 1622 her legend inspired a tragedy, *The Virgin Martir*, by John Massinger and Thomas Dekker. She is believed to be buried in the Roman church that bears her name.

Paul Miki was a Japanese aristocrat who became a Jesuit and for a while preached the gospel successfully. In 1597, during the persecution by Hideyoshi, together with twenty-five others, he was seized and tortured near Nagasaki. Each martyr had a part of the left ear cut off and was then bound to a cross. They were set aloft and speared to death one by one. Besides Paul Miki, there were two Jesuit brothers, six Franciscans, and seventeen laymen, one of whom was Korean. Three were young boys. In the early years of the following century several hundred Japanese Christians were also martyred. Paul Miki and his companions were canonized in 1862 and took their place in the Universal calendar in 1970.

Towards Meditation

Even in the minds of informed Christians, tradition is stronger than scholarship, and it is doubtful that the association of the apple with the Fall and of the rose with perfection will ever be shifted. And surely there can be nothing wrong in finding a way into meditation and prayer by reading the biblical passages that mention them. There is also the lovely carol 'Jesus Christ the apple tree', set to music by Elizabeth Poston. I shall reflect upon it today and if possible tour the roses, checking for wind-rock and shoring up defences against the vicious surprises winter may yet inflict. Protective gloves notwithstanding, there will be at least one scratch. The bright blood will show and I will ponder again the nature and difficulty of martyrdom.

We live in an age that strives to eliminate pain altogether. Even a visit to the dentist does not hold the same terrors as it did when I was a child. Our ancestors were more used to pain, but even so we find it difficult to understand how they could willingly submit to the horrific deaths dreamed up by their persecutors. Inevitably we ask ourselves, 'How would I stand up to such a test of faith?' and quail in shame at the likely answer. Western Christians are 'persecuted' today only by an insidious indifference and mockery and by commercial debasement of their major feasts. Most are safe from physical martyrdom. But since Christmas (and not including the Holy Innocents) the Church has commemorated thirty-six martyrs, and we still have Polycarp, Felicity, and Perpetua to come before Lent begins. Why this emphasis? Surely it must be because thinking about the martyrs is bound to involve an exercise in humility, in gratitude for their strengthening of the Faith through the centuries, and in intercessory prayer for those who *are* being tortured and killed for their faith in other parts of the world. And for these reasons, although we may mourn the death of martyrs on earth, we rejoice even more in their glory in heaven.

My confessor has been accused by an atheist friend of belonging to 'a nasty little death cult'. In a recent sermon he made defence: that

Christianity is a cult is arguable, that it is nasty and little is easily challenged, but to say that it is only to do with death is to miss its whole point. Its whole point is that it is to do with *life*, Life in Christ for eternity. As I finish ministering to the roses today, I must ask myself, 'What do I do or say in my little existence to counter the views of those around me? Do I make the most of opportunities to bring Christ to others? Is it possible to make more room in my life for apostleship? Chastened, I go indoors.

Bible Readings
Galatians 2:19–20: The life of Christ lives in me
Matthew 28:16–20: The call to apostleship

Place of Spiritual Retreat
With the disciples, listening to Jesus, as at the end of Matthew's Gospel

8 FEBRUARY

St Jerome Emiliani, Priest (1481–1537)

ELECAMPANE *Inula helenium*; wild sunflower; elfwort; scabwort

Cultivation Notes
This strong and majestic perennial appreciates well-drained soil and sun. Propagate by division, or by seed sown in spring and autumn. Thin to three feet apart. The flowers, which appear in summer, are golden-yellow, shaggy, and aster-like. The leaves are pointed and toothed and up to eighteen inches long. The thick, hairy, and ridged stems can grow up to ten feet, and therefore may require staking. Prune in late summer.

History and Lore
Inula is the Latin name given by Horace, thought to derive from *helenium*, which makes the botanical title tautological. The plant was named after Helen of Troy, who is believed to have been gathering it when she was abducted by Paris. It is native to southern Europe, Western Asia, and southern England, whence it travelled to New England with the settlers. The English name is probably a corruption of the French *Helene* and *campagne*, thus meaning 'country Helen' or 'Helen of the fields'. The thick

brown roots smell of bananas when fresh and of violets when dried. Lift them in the second or third autumn, and slice before drying. Elecampane root contains over 40 per cent insulin, a polysaccharide often recommended to diabetics as a sweetener. In earlier times it was popular for flavouring puddings, fish sauces, sweets, and absinthe. Medicinally, elecampane is expectorant, and it combines well with horehound in the treatment of sore throats and chest complaints. It cleans the system of toxins, is diuretic, and is effective against bacterial and fungal infections. Culpeper went so far as to say that it 'stays the spreading of putrid, pestilential fevers and the plague itself'. Pick the flower heads when fully open and dry for use in winter arrangements, or to add colour to pot-pourri. If they are to be infused for internal use, dry and keep in muslin bags to avoid irritant fibres escaping into the liquid.

Note: Elecampane is not given to pregnant women.

Towards Meditation

Jerome Emiliani was born in Venice in 1481. He became a soldier who commanded a fortress against the League of Cambrai. He was taken prisoner and after escaping gave away his worldly goods and devoted his life to helping the poor. He was ordained in 1518 and later founded hospitals, orphanages, and an order of clerks at Somaschi. He died there at the age of fifty-six and was canonized in 1767. Of all his charitable works the care of orphans was his favourite, and he was named as their patron by Pius XI in 1928.

I have chosen elecampane for him because in 1531 he recovered from the plague, and also because the plant's golden flowers remind me of the extract from one of his letters that is the second reading in today's Office. Jerome is writing to the brothers of his Order. It is clear that he has had to leave them to fend for themselves and that they need encouragement in his absence. God, he tells them, makes his friends holy through trials, deprivation, and fatigue. He tests them like gold in a furnace. He alone knows why he does this, but it is the business of his friends to have him as their only goal and to accept his conditions in a spirit of complete trust. Only then will he work through us. Only then can Jerome's prayer be answered: 'May the Lord be glorified through me among you.' It sounds so simple, but we all know how difficult it is in practice. I suspect Jerome is speaking especially of how we deal with the irritations, setbacks, disappointments, and tensions in our daily routines. These are the tiny martyrdoms to which most of us are called. How often do we fail even in these? So my prayer today will be for more trust, more faith. Perhaps, then, the day before yesterday's questions about apostleship will have a chance of being more satisfactorily answered.

Bible Readings

1 Peter 3:8–9: Love, compassion, and self-effacement

Romans 12:10–11: Brotherly love and respect; untiring effort in God's work

John 13:35: Love for others marks us out as disciples of Christ

Matthew 25:14–30: Being faithful in small things; the parable of the talents

Place of Spiritual Retreat

With the disciples listening to Christ's teaching, as in John 13 or Matthew 25

10 FEBRUARY

St Scholastica, Virgin
(died 543)

DAME'S VIOLET *Hesperis matronalis*; sweet rocket; vesper flower

Cultivation Notes

This delightful biennial (sometimes perennial) needs to be sown in spring or planted in clumps in autumn. It likes sun and some shade and can grow to a height of three feet. The flowers, produced from early to late summer, are usually white, mauve, or purple. A white variety is *H. matronalis* 'Nana', and a purple one, *H. matronalis* 'Purpurea'.

The colour and scent of dame's violet make it a lovely addition to pot-pourri. The leaves were once used to prevent scurvy.

History and Lore

It is chosen for St Scholastica because in England Benedictine nuns are formally addressed as Dame. But there are other reasons. In flower lore the plant represents watchfulness, a quality that Scholastica possessed in more ways than one. The name 'Vesper flower' comes from the fact that it is at its most fragrant after sunset. This too is appropriate for the sister of St Benedict. Also, the plant sometimes sends out new shoots from the old roots. Here I am thinking of the nunneries founded in Australia, Brazil, Peru, and India from our English monasteries of Stanbrook, Tyburn, and St Cecilia's, Isle of Wight. Lastly, Scholastica and Benedict were born in Umbria, and although dame's violet is found throughout Europe and North America, it is native to Italy. As well as being part of the plant's botanical name, *Hesperis* also means 'the Western Land', Italy.

Little is known about Scholastica except that, having been consecrated to God in childhood, she eventually founded the first monastery of Benedictine nuns at Plombariola, near her brother and his monks at Monte Cassino. The only other details are found in the *Dialogues* of St Gregory (*c.* 540–604), a relevant passage of which appears as the second Office reading today. Gregory tells how brother and sister used to meet at a place between their houses to discuss spiritual matters. On one occasion, as the time approached for night silence, Scholastica implored Benedict to stay longer. On his refusal to stay, she prayed. The result was a violent storm, which prevented both of them from returning to their monasteries, and so, just as she had wished, they spent the night in heavenly converse. It was to be their last meeting. Three days later, Benedict, back at Monte Cassino, saw from his window the soul of his sister ascending to heaven in the form of a dove. She was buried in the grave he had prepared for himself.

Towards Meditation

In her *Benedictine Tapestry*, Dame Felicitas Corrigan offers refreshing and wise insights into this story. First of all she corrects the notion that Scholastica is an imagined symbol of the female Benedictine contemplative. She was Benedict's elder sister. Why should it be automatically assumed that she consolidated her childhood dedication by taking the veil at her brother's behest and not as an independent choice? Their age relationship makes it reasonable to ask whether it was not Scholastica's example that lit *his* path, rather than the other way round. Her annual visits to him were natural in a sister, and Dame Felicitas suggests that Scholastica went to share and guide and not merely as a passive receiver of his counsel. The true character of their conversation lies in Gregory's Latin, *vicaria relatione*. Their exchanges were mutual. Scholastica may have known her death was imminent, and perhaps the prayer she offered on Benedict's refusal was her way, with God's help, of teaching the great rule-maker that there are occasions, however rare, when love is the Divine imperative, not legalistic observance.

Next, Dame Felicitas invites us, in the gentlest of terms, to consider the improbability of their not having discussed the *Rule* at all during their annual meetings. Appreciate anew, says our guide, the 'loftiness, sobriety and humanity' of it. Surely, she suggests, it could not have been the product of a masculine mind and personality alone. Does not the sane balance for which it is famous indicate that both male and female were involved in its construction? And is it not more likely that Scholastica was responsible for the kindness and practicality of certain dietary provisions and of the conduct of the infirmary? The implication is that without his sister's restraint, warmth, and compassion even the great Benedict may have been too zealous for his own or anyone else's good. In drawing to a close on the subject of Scholastica, Dame Felicitas admires Gregory's nuances and cautions us not to be taken in by his apparent simplicity. She appreciates his *Plus potuit quae plus amavit* (She prevailed who had the greater love), because of the succinctness of its spiritual lesson. Gregory, she says, is showing us a man obstructing God's wisdom by misguided insistence on rules and a woman, on the other hand, who through total and unfettered trust in God shows forth the love of his Holy Spirit.

Bible Readings
1 Corinthians 1:26–31: God chose what is foolish by human standards
Mark 7:1–13: Warning not to fall short by clinging to human ordinances
Luke 7:37–50: The repentant woman with the jar of nard (Dame Felicitas cites this text in support of her point about love.)

Place of Spiritual Retreat
With the repentant woman, as in Luke 7

11 FEBRUARY

The Apparitions of Our Lady at Lourdes (1858)

ROSES

The three varieties for Our Lady of Lourdes have been chosen because of their characteristics and because, according to Bernadette, a single golden rose rested on each of the Blessed Virgin's feet.

Floribunda, 'Amber queen'
Jack Harkness, 1983; gained worldwide approval; a beautiful golden rose; low growing and sweetly fragrant; flowers in rain or sun.

Hybrid Tea, 'Gloria Dei' ('Peace')
Meilland, 1945; the world's best-loved rose; yellow, edged pink; vigorous and reliable; beautiful from bud to maturity; slightly fragrant; dedicated to peace at the end of World War II; said to have been smuggled out of France in the last diplomatic bag before the fall of the country to the Nazis; still peerless.

Climber, 'Golden showers'
Lammerts, 1957; a worldwide favourite; fragrant; resistant to rain; repeat-flowering; golden yellow, fading to pale yellow in hot sun.

History and Lore
Joseph Fabisch's statue for the grotto is not entirely faithful to Bernadette's description, and he adapted it to satisfy the taste and expectation of his times. The result is that *we* see a grown woman of about five foot nine. *Bernadette* saw a fourteen-year-old girl, about four and a half feet. *Aquero* (see 8 December) actually showed herself as Our Lady of her own Presentation, that is, as she was before the birth of Christ, but looking ahead to it and aware of her own identity and destiny. Hence her famous statement, *I am the Immaculate Conception*, significantly delivered on the feast of the Annunciation. Perhaps her very youth was meant to underline the truth of her saying. Perhaps we are meant to learn how much we miss when we deliberately distort what is revealed to us.

The rest of the detail of the Fabisch statue seems true to Bernadette's description. Our Lady of Lourdes is not rich, jewelled, or queenly, but dressed in white, almost austere simplicity, the only colour being in the blue of the sash and the gold of the foot-roses. Even the rosary is white except for its shining chain. The lack of adornment is refreshing and salutary. Bernadette also conveyed the vivacity of *Aquero*, a quality admittedly difficult to represent in stone, but in my opinion the grotto statue fails to do so at all. Perhaps that was Fabisch's punishment for distorting other details to please fashion – and, by extension, ours for always wanting to see things in our own way and for having closed minds. Bernadette was fit to see the face of Our Lady, and perhaps because we most patently are not, she was never able to describe *Aquero's* features.

Lourdes, by Alan Neame, is an eminently sane study of the place in terms of sociology, economics, church and state politics and history, psychology, and medicine. But today I am not concerned with these aspects of the phenomenon. My business is to re-address its spiritual message, consequences, and relevance. Best to start by reading again the actual words of Our Lady of Lourdes to Bernadette in 1858.

Towards Meditation
18 February: 'That isn't necessary' (in response to the pen and paper Bernadette offered in the hope that *Aquero* would identify herself).
'Will you be kind enough to come here for a fortnight?'
'I don't promise to make you happy in this world, but only in the next.'
23 February: 'I forbid you to repeat this to anyone.' (On this day several educated people were witnesses at the Grotto. It is possible that it was the occasion when Bernadette received the special prayer that she said daily for the rest of her life and also the secrets, which she was never prevailed upon to reveal.)
24 February: 'Penitence! Penitence! Penitence!'
'You must pray to God for sinners.'
'Kiss the ground in penance for the conversion of sinners.'
25 February: 'Drink at the spring and wash in it.'
'Eat some of the weed there.'
2 March: 'Tell the priests that people are to come here in procession and to have a chapel built here.'
3 March: 'Tell the priests to have a chapel built here.'
25 March: 'I am the Immaculate Conception.'
These mostly imperative words, delivered in Bernadette's dialect, seem terse and simple. Perhaps they had to be because heaven was communicating with a poorly educated girl of limited vocabulary. But

their effect is startling and profound. *Aquero* may have appeared as little more than a child, but she does not treat Bernadette as one. Again, by extension, she assumes our adulthood and awareness of individual and social sin. She does not show us her suffering Son. She assumes our acknowledgement that our sins crucified him. She does not warn us of God's fury. She assumes our fear of the Lord. She is neither politically partisan nor exclusively concerned with the welfare and future of France. Her message is universal and for all the time that remains to our race. Our Lady of Lourdes is practical and helpful. She teaches us with absolute clarity what we must do as individuals.

We must have faith and not waste energy seeking proofs; we are invited to intercede through her, not only at her shrines, but wherever we are; worldly happiness should not be our first priority, and we must remember our true goal; we must keep our counsel, control our tongues, and accept with humility that some mysteries should and will remain impenetrable to us; we must particularly heed the threefold call to penitence, not just on our own behalf, but for others who cannot or will not repent; we must pray for conversions; we must drink at the spring of the sacraments, and eat the weed of obedience and humility, however much the world may mock; we must follow Christ in a constant pilgrimage of the heart; our duty to build up his body, the Church, is repeated and therefore particularly important; we must open our eyes and ears, and realize who is reminding us of all this. In sum, it is an exhortation to fulfil Christ's New Law: 'Love God and your neighbour as yourself.' And it is this above all else which convinces me that Bernadette's *Aquero* truly was and is the Blessed Virgin Mary.

Bible Readings
Isaiah 66:10–14: Toward her I send flowing peace, like a river
Luke 1:28: The Annunciation

Place of Spiritual Retreat
With Our Lady on the road to visit Elizabeth

14 FEBRUARY

St Valentine, Martyr (third century)
St Cyril, Monk (826–869)
St Methodius (his brother), Bishop (815–884)

ROSE 'Valentine heart'

This is a medium-sized floribunda. The fragrant blooms are pink with tinges of cream and red towards the base. It is disease resistant, and a major award winner in Britain and elsewhere. In mild areas it can be pruned towards the end of February and new specimens can be planted now if the soil is free from snow and frost.

MOCK ORANGE *Philadelphus*

This well-known deciduous shrub produces white blooms in midsummer. It can be planted in favourable conditions between October and March. The taller varieties grow up to six feet and are ideal as hedge or back-of-border plants (for a hedge plant two feet apart). *P.* 'Virginal' produces pure white double flowers in pendant clusters. *P.* 'Silver showers' grows to three feet. *Philadelphus* likes sun and light shade. Feed with general fertilizer in spring and mulch in April. The flowers dry well for pot-pourri.

History and Lore

There are two traditional Valentines (now accepted as one and the same person). One was a priest who after much preaching and healing was cudgelled and then beheaded on the Flamminian Way in 268 under Claudius Caesar. The other was Bishop of Terni in Umbria. In 273 he was flogged, imprisoned and finally beheaded at the command of Placidus, prefect of the city. Neither of these seems to have any obvious connection with lovers and sweethearts. However, there is an old tradition that the birds mate on 14 February, and in the old Celtic calendar it was a cross quarter day and beneficial for the planting of seed. I have heard of a town somewhere in France that has a shrine to St Valentine to which courting couples make pilgrimage.

In *The Language of Flowers*, *Philadelphus* symbolizes fraternal love, which makes it an obvious choice for the two priest brothers Cyril and Methodius. They were born in Thessalonica. Around 863 they were sent to Moravia and preached the gospel in the vernacular, translated the Scriptures and liturgy into Slavonic, and invented the Glagolithic alphabet, from which the Cyrillic later developed. For this reason they are held to be the founders of Slavonic literature. They went to Rome, taking with them the alleged relics of St Clement, one of the early popes. Cyril died shortly after becoming a monk at the age of forty two. He is buried in San Clemente. Methodius returned to Moravia as Archbishop. He was later imprisoned for two years, and the Pope ordered him to stop the vernacular liturgy. In 880 he was cleared of disobedience, and he eventually died in Czechoslovakia. Pope John Paul II has made Cyril, Methodius, and Benedict joint patrons of Europe.

Towards Meditation

Today's Office reading is from the Slavonic *Life of Constantine* (Cyril's birth name) and gives his dying prayers. They encapsulate the principles on which he led his life. After thanking God for creation, he prays particularly for the flock he is about to leave. Handing them back to God, he prays for their safety from unbelievers; he asks that they may increase in number, that they may be united, and that after his death they will remain steadfast in faith and continue to praise and glorify the Holy Trinity. Finally he blesses God for protection from the malice of invisible enemies, who have thus been unable to capture and destroy him or his flock.

The *Philadelphus* may still be bare today, but in a mild winter buds may already be showing. Whether or no, like any tree or vine, it will eventually produce them if the life within it is properly tended and nurtured. Looking at it, and taught by Christ's metaphor in John 15, I will see in the *Philadelphus* the Church at large and the buds as the new growth Cyril prayed for, springing from the life of Christ within her; will see each Christian community gathered in fraternal love and unity round its own place of worship, the buds being the newly baptized and confirmed in each one; will see each Christian soul abiding in Christ, and he in her, the buds being the beginnings of the fruit of individual prayer and action. Lord, make your Church grow, and make us grow within it. Gather us all together in the unity of your Spirit of truth and love.

Bible Readings

Psalm 89:20–22: God chooses from among his people
Jeremiah 1:4–9: Go where I send you

Jeremiah 3:15: God will give us shepherds
Matthew 28:19–20: Christ is with us always
Mark 16:15–20: The command to proclaim the Gospel
John 15:1–17: Christ the vine, we the branches

Place of Spiritual Retreat

Listening to Christ preaching at the Last Supper, as in John 15, or at the table with the disciples when the risen Lord appeared, as at the end of Mark's Gospel

17 FEBRUARY

The Seven Holy Founders of the Servite Order (thirteenth century)

SEVEN PURPLE CROCUS (indoor and outdoor): *Crocus sativus*; Crocus verna
Suggested varieties: *C. tommasinianus*, flowers in January and February; Dutch hybrid, *C.* 'Remembrance', flowers in February or later.

History and Lore

Crocus is the Greek word for saffron, and saffron is from the Arabic *zaferan*. The plant therefore takes us back to the ancient past. And in eastern Turkey near the Syrian border there still stands the thousand-year-old monastery of *Deir el-Zaferan*, the saffron monastery. The saffron crocus has probably been in England since the Roman era, but its cultivation as a crop is thought to have begun in the early fourteenth century. It is mentioned in a document of 1359, and its cultivation in Essex led to the town of Walden becoming Saffron Walden. Edward VI granted the town's charter in 1549, when the continued importance of the plant was shown by three crocus flowers on the coat of arms. Later in the century it is recorded as growing at Peterhouse College, Cambridge. Aside from its culinary value, and its famous use as a dye, the crocus has also been employed as a disinfectant and as a medicine for improving the sense of humour. The garden crocus, *C. verna*, probably arrived in England about the same time as *C. sativus*.

The Seven Founders of the Servite Order were devout Florentines of the merchant class who belonged to *The Major Society of Our Lady* in their city. Some were married, some vowed to chastity, and some widowed when as a group they left their families and gave away all their possessions for the poor. Their first house was built at Monte Sennario, where for some time they refused to take in aspirants. The new Order was recognized in 1259 and solemnly approved in 1104. Four of the founders became priors, and two founded convents in other countries. The seventh, Alexis Falconieri, outlived all the others, not dying until 1310. It seems from today's second Office reading, which is an extract from the documents on the origin of the Servites, that it was Alexis who described to the writer how the Order began.

Today, there are Servites in all continents of the world. There are 955 friars, of whom seven hundred are priests and eight are bishops. Affiliated to the Friars are twenty-two congregations of Sisters or enclosed nuns, making a total of over five thousand. Added to this are two hundred lay members of Servite Secular Institutes. In 2001 the Servites celebrated their 221st General Chapter and elected their first Mexican Prior General.

The Servites are also known as the Order of Servants of Mary, and this reminds us of their connection with devotion to the Seven Sorrows of Our Lady. The 'Seven Sorrows Rosary' seems to have been in use in the Order at a very early date, since a Bull issued in 1722 by Benedict XIII refers to its recitation as 'a very ancient custom of the Order'. The method of reciting it was not brought in by the General Chapter until 1646. Thirty-one years later all Servite religions were ordered to wear the Seven Sorrows rosary hanging from the right-hand side of their girdles. Since the reform of the Servite Constitutions in 1966, the rosary has not been worn as part of the habit, which now resembles that worn during the first four hundred years of the Order. However, the friars still celebrate and recite it, and so the seven purple crocuses are chosen for the Founders because of this penitential aspect of their spirituality.

Towards Meditation
In 1983, the International Liturgy Commission of the Servites published a *Triduum, In Praise of our Seven First Fathers*. These three services consist of private and vocal prayer, the singing of hymns and psalms, and readings from the Chronicle of the origin of the Order, the Gospels, and the writings of Paul. Each of the three days concentrates on a different aspect of the Founders' charism: the first on their pursuit of the Kingdom as disciples of Christ; the second on their life of fraternal communion; and the third on their spirit of service to God, the Virgin Mary, and God's people.

During this *Triduum*, the Servites seek the help and prayers of their Founders in the renewal of their vocation as servants in their own communities and in a wider world. One does not need to be a Servite to gain spiritual benefit from their *Triduum*. Weather depending, I will pray the Seven Sorrows Rosary at least once during it, either in the garden or by the indoor groups of commemorative crocuses.

Bible Readings from the Servite *Triduum*

Day one

Psalm 84: Longing for God's house

Luke 6:20–2: The Beatitudes

Luke 12:22b–24; 29–30a; 33–4: Watch and have faith

1 Corinthians 1:26–9: God chose what is weak in the world to shame the strong

Philippians 4:4–7: Have no anxiety about anything

Ephesians 6:10; 14–17: Be strong in the Lord

Matthew 11:25–6: No one knows the Father except the Son and anyone to whom the Son chooses to reveal him

Day two

Psalm 133: The joy of fraternal love

John 15:9–10: Abide in my love; keep the commandments

John 17:11; 20–3: Christ prays for the unity of the flock

1 John 4:7–12: Exhortation to love one another

1 Corinthians 13:1–13: The blueprint of love

Day three

Psalm 123: God, the unfailing hope of his people

Matthew 20:25–8: Whoever would be great among you must be your servant

Matthew 23:8–12: You have one Master, the Christ

John 13:13–15: Christ washes the disciples' feet

Romans 12:11–16: Life in the Body of Christ

Galatians 5:13–14: Be servants of each other through love

1 Peter 1:15–16: Be holy in all your conduct

1 Peter 3:8–9: Love the brethren; have a tender heart and a humble mind

1 Peter 4:10–11: Give service through the strength that God supplies

Place of Spiritual Retreat
With Christ and the disciples, as in John 13

18 FEBRUARY

St Bernadette of Lourdes, Virgin (1844–1879)

(Bernadette's date of
commemoration in the
Roman Martyrology is the
anniversary of her death,
16 April, buther feast-day
is celebratedtoday in
France, and this
is followed here.)

SAXIFRAGE
Saxifraga oppositifolium

Cultivation Notes
This creeping perennial appears
early, as soon as the snow melts,
if there has been any. It grows to about an
inch high, and spreads up to two feet. The
pinkish-purple flowers cover the thin stems in March and
April. The plant needs careful treatment, but once established it is long-
lived. It benefits from a sunny site and well-drained soil and appreciates a
mulch of leaf mould or peat. Propagate by extremely careful division, or
by rooting tip cuttings in a cold frame in peat and sand from April to
June.

History and Lore
According to Alan Neame, this was the type of saxifrage eaten by
Bernadette during the ninth apparition, when *Aquero* guided her to the
spring. The word saxifrage comes from the Latin words *saxum* for stone
and *frangere*, to break. Our Lady is a stone-breaker in two senses here. She
used Bernadette to break the stone of the earth so that the spring could be
released, and ever since has used her apparitions at Lourdes to break the

stone of unbelief and futile suffering. The Lourdes saxifrage is called *oppositifolium* because of the growth habit of its leaves, and this reflects the paradoxes in Bernadette's life. She, who was a poor miller's daughter of no great intellectual gift, was chosen to see the Mother of God. She, who later referred to the visions as a private experience of heaven on earth, was to suffer much from curiosity and publicity after they were over. Her life as a nun at Nevers was uneventful, except for the suffering she bore until her early death at 35 from an excruciatingly painful bone disease. She had revealed the curative spring at Lourdes but was not to benefit from it herself. Physically delicate, she was mentally robust and determined, and despite repeated questioning she never disclosed the secrets, or indeed the personal prayer, given to her by Our Lady during the visions. There is no evidence that she was forced to enter the convent. Rather, her life there was hidden as a matter of her own choice. And yet it shines forth now as an example of simplicity, integrity, acceptance, detachment, and balance. The Blessed Virgin kept her word, 'I do not promise to make you happy in this world only in the next.' Surely it must have enabled Bernadette to endure her pain. A commonly seen photograph, taken before she left Lourdes, shows her as a living paradox, as someone who has seen beyond this world, and yet remains in it. Her right eye is in shadow and seems to be the eye of suffering. Her left is serene, full of peaceful acceptance and a yearning love, looking through time towards the heaven she has already glimpsed.

Towards Meditation
Neither Our Lady nor Bernadette ever said that cures would result from exposure to water from the Lourdes spring, and yet miraculous healing has become, at least in the consciousness of the general public, the major point of the place. The faithful know this emphasis is wrong. Lourdes, besides the meanings I drew from it on 11 February, is about the *uncured* in body, mind, and soul, including the millions who never set foot there. It is about how the rest of us relate to and care for them. It is about our attitude to pain and disease and how we deal with them in ourselves and in others. Every Christian must wrestle with these things, and much has been written about them from the standpoint of faith. Vernon Johnson's *Christian Suffering and Bernadette of Lourdes* is an example. It is a series of five sermons preached to the sick at Lourdes during a pilgrimage. The first four are inspired by sayings of Bernadette.

1. My business is to be ill. This was Bernadette's answer on being asked whether she had heard of the cures at Lourdes and her reason for having little interest in them. She did not become a saint because of her encounters with Our Lady, but through silent, patient suffering in the convent at Nevers.

2. Nothing very much. On entering the convent, this was Bernadette's reply to the Reverend Mother, who asked her what she would be able to contribute to the community. Bernadette became a saint because she did nothing very much very well indeed.

3. I ask my sisters to forgive me for the bad example I have set them. Bernadette said this when she was dying and about to receive the Last Rites. The secret of holiness is humility. Bernadette had to compare herself with the perfect humility she had seen in the Mother of God at Lourdes.

4. My God, it is your will. I accept the cup which you have given me. Blessed be your holy name. Imitating Christ in Gethsemane, Bernadette shows utter obedience to God's will.

In the final sermon in *A Farewell to Lourdes,* Fr Johnson shows us that in Christ's obedience and that of all his saints lies the answer to the problem of pain. Through it the sick themselves become ministers to the healthy. The secret is in Christ's words: *Am I not to drink the cup that the Father has given me?* (Jn 18:11).

Even Christians may find it difficult to achieve this imitation of their Master, and it will not do at all for unbelievers, who need the most help. The majority of us will be challenged at some point by the type of question that was asked of me recently. 'Why, if there is a just and merciful God, is your neighbour's daughter dying from leukaemia?' Usually there is sarcasm in the tone of the questioner but in the eyes a desperate hope that we will give a satisfactory answer. We are in the front line and feel totally inadequate. What can we do? What can we say? First, I think we must actively concern ourselves with individual sufferers, and not waste time with well people who just want to catch us out in academic argument. It is useless to try and explain. With the unbelieving sick and their relatives, it is how we act that matters. The plight of my neighbours and their daughter drove me to search for advice. Eventually, I found an article by Sheila Cassidy, a specialist in the palliative care of the terminally ill. Entitled 'Pain and the Paschal Mystery', it crystallized ideas I had already been groping towards, and it was strengthening to see them in the cogent words of someone so experienced. Dr Cassidy says that with the sick one should react intuitively and not with prepared speeches, and that sometimes this leads us to expose our own vulnerability to rejection. She speaks of the 'painful accompaniment' in which we are close to the deep pain of the sufferer and face our own impotence to help. Slowly we find out what view he or she has of God, if any. We find out what the sufferer knows and wants to know. We begin to share a little of the anguish, anger, and despair. We must be open; we must *show* our compassion. We must let people talk and really listen, and when we speak or act it must be with all the caution and sensitivity at our command. Our response is about showing Christ in action, but when speech is necessary the choice of words is crucial. It is worse than useless, says Dr Cassidy, to talk about God as a Father to a woman who was abused by her father as a child. The words of sufferers will often be full of hatred, bitterness, and fear. But we must let them know that they are not going to be judged or abandoned because of this. There is no need to mention God or prayer to create this secure place. And we can call on our own experience of pain and misery, not to tell the present sufferer about them, but to increase our understanding of how he or she *may* be feeling.

Underpinning everything we do in preparing for ministry to the afflicted are our own hidden faith, prayer, suffering, and Scripture reading. These above all else will fit us to answer Christ's call to bind up hearts that are broken. So, as I prepare for Nathalie to make her daily visit from next door, my prayer will be for intuition, sensitivity, caution, openness, and compassion. And in the garden by the saxifrage, I will thank Our Lady and St Bernadette (and Sheila Cassidy) for leading me to ask for these gifts.

Bible Readings
Isaiah 53: The Man of Sorrows
2 Corinthians 1:3–5: He helps us in our troubles, so that we are able to help others
John 18:1–11: Shall I not drink the cup?

Place of Spiritual Retreat
In the Garden of Gethsemane at the arrest of Christ

Note: This entry was written in the depths of winter. The last words Nathalie spoke to me on the subject of her daughter were, 'I do not think she will be with us to see another spring.' As we hugged on New Year's Eve, although nothing else was said, we knew the hollowness of our mutual '*Bonne année*'. Three days later she went south with her dying daughter, husband and younger child to swim with dolphins. We went north for the new school term. Eugenie died in February on the feast of St Bernadette. She was seven years old.

21 FEBRUARY

St Peter Damian, Bishop and Doctor (1007–1072)

COMMON GORSE *Ulex europaeus*
WESTERN GORSE *Ulex gallii*
DWARF GORSE *Ulex minor* (all also known as furze and whin)

Cultivation Notes
Common gorse grows throughout Britain and flowers from January to June. In the south and east, colonies of it are often mixed with dwarf gorse, which flowers from July to November, and in other parts of the country western gorse also flowers from summer to the beginning of winter. Gorse is prolific and fast-growing and its flowers have a delightful coconut vanilla scent.

History and Lore
Gorse has traditionally been used as building material, fuel, stock fodder, and food colouring, and to make chimney brushes. The sight of it growing in abundance brings back childhood memories of walks in Derbyshire with my parents, and of much later forays on Dartmoor where hedges made of stone and gorse brighten that often forbidding terrain with swathes of bright yellow. Linnaeus is supposed to have fallen to his knees with a prayer of thanksgiving when he first saw gorse in England, probably on Putney Heath, although many other places claim to be the site. He would have felt at one, as I do, with the old man in George Meredith's 'Juggling Jerry':

> Yonder came smell of the gorse, so nuttty,
>   Gold-like and warm: it's the prime of May.
> Better than mortar, bricks and putty,
>   Is God's house on a blowing day.

Peter Damian seems to have been a strange mixture of warmth and austerity, and he had a great devotion to the passion of Christ. The thorny thicket-forming gorse, with its vibrant golden flowers, is therefore most suitable for him. He was born at Ravenna and was a child orphan. One of his brothers kept him as a slave until another brother adopted him and provided the best possible education. He became a teacher for a while and then a hermit in the severe Camaldolese branch of the Benedictines at Fonte Avellana in northern Italy. In 1043 he was elected abbot and in 1057, as a result of his assistance to the Holy See through his writings and travelling, was made bishop and cardinal. In spite of this, Peter Damian remained a monk at heart and a promoter of the eremitic life as being superior to community life. After frequent requests to be dispensed from episcopal duties, he was at last allowed to return to Fonte Avellana. His final mission was to Ravenna, where he was sent to restore ecclesiastical stability. He died on the return journey in the monastery at Faenza. St Peter Damian was zealous and intransigent on occasion. His writings reflect the strictness of his preferred life, but he was also loved for his kindness to his monks and penitents.

Towards Meditation
Today the Church turns her attention from the physical suffering of martyrdom to the spiritual trials through which God may choose to sanctify us. The second reading in today's Office is an extract from one of Peter Damian's letters. The title, 'Wait gladly for the joy that follows sadness', bears out what we already know of him. The letter is to someone who is experiencing 'bitterness of soul'. Consolation will come, says the writer. This trial is a necessary part of the education a son must receive before he can take possession of his inheritance. He cites Job as an example of a man being refined by God, beaten like gold under a hammer and fired like a jar in a kiln. We must not chafe under the rod. We must not grumble, lose heart, or be impatient. Trials are a sign that God is refining us in this world to save us in the next. We must read the Scriptures for reassurance and a strengthening of spirit. Then we will be able to wait gladly for the joy that follows sadness. The gorse bush will always help me to remember St Peter Damian and his comforting advice.

Bible Readings
Job 26:1 – 27:6: Job's faith

1 Peter 4:13–14: If you can have some share in the sufferings of Christ, be
   glad
1 Peter 5:10–11: He will confirm, strengthen and support you
2 Corinthians 4:7 – 5:8: The power of Christ is shown in our trials
James 1:2–4: Count it joy when you meet trials
Matthew 28:20: I am with you always

Place of Spiritual Retreat
Resting in Christ's reassurance, as in Matthew 28

22 FEBRUARY

The See of Peter

SCARLET VERBENA *Verbena x hybrida*

Cultivation Notes
From June to autumn this half-hardy annual produces scented primula-
like flowers in clusters at the end of its stems. It will grow to a foot high in
a sunny position in compost-enriched soil. Sow in February and March.
Pinch out later for bushy growth, and for effective ground cover peg down
the shoots with hairpins and deadhead.

History and Lore
Tradition holds 22 February as the day when St Peter was first enthroned
in a bishop's chair at Antioch. The feast celebrating the occasion has been
kept at Rome from the fourth century and is still observed as a symbol of
the unity of the Church founded on the rock of Peter (Mt. 16:18). Since, in
The Language of Flowers, scarlet verbena signifies church unity, it is an
obvious choice, and today is an ideal time to sow some.

Towards Meditation
Preparing the seed trays, I reflect on the triumphalist days of my pre-
Vatican II girlhood. Praying for 'unity' was then seen in terms of the re-
conversion of England to the Roman Catholic faith, and at Benediction
we beseeched Our Lady to 'intercede for our separated brethren, that with
us in the One True Fold they may be united to the Chief Shepherd, the
Vicar of thy Son' (upper case not mine). Benediction itself is far less

common now. Many Catholic churches never have it. The *Prayer for England* is hardly ever heard, even at exclusively Roman Catholic gatherings, and perhaps that is no bad thing. But ancient certainties are shaken. In the 'old days' one could be next to a complete stranger at Mass and know what he believed about the moments of consecration. Now it is anyone's guess. And I can no longer be sure that in celebrating the primacy of the See of Peter I shall be in accord with all Catholics, let alone with all Christians, in honouring his importance. A kind of 'unity' has gone from the Roman Church herself. Whether that unity in a defiant siege mentality was good or bad now seems a matter of individual opinion, as do many other things we learnt in our penny Catechisms. Were pre-conciliar English Catholics really praying for uniformity, not unity? Now our own 'unity' has been dented, are we at liberty to seek a true unity of spirit with Christians of other denominations? It would be unproductive to spend time today pondering the thorny subject of how much has been gained and lost to the Church as a result of Vatican II. Better to go back to the Gospels and to measure my own beliefs and actions against them. Verbena trays finished, the feeling comes to me that Christians produce their best fruit, that their faith is the strongest, when they are persecuted and ridiculed, or when they are not completely comfortable in the societies in which they live, when they are the leaven in the lump. It was so at the beginning of the Church on earth. Maybe it will be so at the end.

Bible Readings

Matthew 16:13–19: You are Peter and upon this rock I will build my Church, and the powers of death shall not prevail against it

John 14:2: In my Father's house there are many mansions

John 10:16: I have other sheep, that are not of this fold; I must bring them also, and they will heed my voice. So there shall be one flock, and one shepherd

John 4:7–26: How is it that you, a Jew, ask a drink of me, a woman of Samaria?

Luke 10:30–7: The Good Samaritan

Acts 11:1–18: The conversion of the Gentiles

Acts 15:7b–9: He made no difference between us and them; he forgave them their sins because they believed

Place of Spiritual Retreat

With Jesus, as in any of the Gospel texts above

23 FEBRUARY

St Polycarp, Bishop and Martyr (*c.* 69–*c.* 155)

FRANKINCENSE *Boswellia sacra*; olibanum; mastic tree
CORIANDER *Coriandrum sativum*

Cultivation Notes

The nearest most Westerners come to owning frankincense is in the form of a purchased fixative for pot-pourri more usually known as *olibanum*. It is a fragrant gum or resin extracted from the bark of certain species of *Boswellia* tree native to Saudi Arabia. This is small with peeling papery bark and produces little white flowers in spring, followed by brown seed capsules. The tree is tender and requires full sun and fairly dry soil in a minimum temperature of 10–15° C (50–9° F) Propagate by semi-ripe cuttings in summer. The hotter and drier the conditions, the finer will be the frankincense produced.

Coriander is a hardy annual that produces dainty, white, bee-tempting flowers in late summer. It grows to a height of two feet and appreciates a sheltered site in full sun. For good seed production, the drier and warmer the better. A cool wet spring followed by a hot dry summer is ideal. Sow direct in late spring and keep moist at seedling stage to prevent later bolting. Collect seeds in August when ripe. They will smell rubbery until then. The ripe seed tastes of oranges, and the scent is reminiscent of baking bread. Always use throughout a whole cooking process, never at the end only. The seed should be crushed to release full flavour and fragrance. Coriander is a useful companion plant, encouraging the growth of anise and repelling aphids and carrot fly. It is an ancient member of the carrot family and the leaves have a vaguely aniseed flavour. Do not grow near fennel.

History and Lore

'Olibanum' is probably from the Greek *libanos*, meaning milk, but there are also the Hebrew *lebonah* and Arabic *luban*. In the classical era frankincense was thought to aid memory and longevity, while in early Middle Eastern cultures, it was one of the most valued trade commodities. Reliefs on the Temple of Queen Hatshepsut at Luxor (*c.* 1512–1483 BC) show frankincense being grown to make youth-preserving face masks. In 1979 James Mandavill reported that in Dhofar, Southern Arabia, the frankincense collection begins in December and reaches a peak between March and May. It is stored in the dry for some months before being traded on the coast. Olibanum is the main ingredient in church incense, but in Arabia it is also used in household fumigation and personal hygiene.

Coriander comes from the Greek *koriannon*, a type of seed thought to have been used as a preserving spice, which smelled of coriander leaves. Even today, dishes *à la grecque* normally contain coriander. It has been cultivated as a culinary and medicinal herb for at least three thousand years. Seeds have been found in tombs of the Pharaohs, and the Israelites, who became familiar with it in Egypt, likened manna to it (Ex. 16:31; Num. 11:7). Coriander grows naturally in the Jordan valley and in many other parts of the Holy Land. It was brought to northern Europe by the Romans who, according to Pliny, combined it with cumin and vinegar to produce a meat-preservative. For a time it was grown commercially in Essex for the gin distillers. Nowadays it is reputedly an ingredient in vermouth and chartreuse. It is also a useful addition to pot-pourri. Today would be a good time to begin a Polycarp pot-pourri, which would include both olibanum and coriander.

Towards Meditation

The second Office reading today is taken from *The Letter of the Church at Smyrna* on the martyrdom of Polycarp, and contains the reasons why I have chosen these plants to commemorate him. It is an eyewitness account, and the writer reports the miracle he saw at Polycarp's burning. When the fire was lit, it formed a wall around the martyr's body, which did not look like burning flesh, but like bread being baked, or like precious metal in a furnace. A fragrance of frankincense and other spices emanated from it. Polycarp, in spite of his importance as a link between the apostles and the early church, is not much celebrated in the West these days. In *The Language of Flowers* coriander symbolizes hidden worth.

Polycarp was a disciple of John the Evangelist. Before he died he confessed to being eighty-six. Having followed Christ all his life, he saw no good reason to deny him at that late stage. This would indicate that Polycarp was baptized as an infant, or at least in early childhood. As Bishop of Smyrna he defended orthodox Christianity against the Gnostics. By his late thirties he had become friendly with Ignatius of Antioch, who was martyred around 107 and who asked Polycarp to take care of his own church at Antioch. Towards the end of his life Polycarp conferred with Pope Anicetus on the dating of Easter, eventually agreeing with him to differ in brotherly love over their two systems. Anicetus is reputed to have asked Polycarp to celebrate Mass in the papal chapel during this visit.

Today is an occasion for thanksgiving because the letter in the Office gives a most impressive and moving sense of connection with the early Fathers and with John the Evangelist himself. Moreover, the account is the first authentic one of its kind, and shows that the Christians of Smyrna venerated their aged bishop as a saint even before his martyrdom. From it we know that he exerted authority, even over his executioners, who attempted to nail him to the pyre. He brushed them aside with the promise that the Lord, who would give him strength to bear the fire, would also give him the courage to remain in it. And so he was not nailed, only bound. His final prayer was one of praise and thanksgiving that God had found him worthy to share the suffering of Christ.

Bible Readings
Psalm 31: Be thou a rock of refuge for me
Revelation 2:8–10: To the angel of the church in Smyrna ... I know your
    tribulation ... Be faithful unto death and I will give you the crown of
    life
John 12:24–6: If a grain of wheat dies, it yields a rich harvest

Place of Spiritual Retreat
With Philip and Andrew when they went to Jesus with the message from
Greeks who wished to see him, as in John 12

27 FEBRUARY (28 IN LEAP YEARS)

St Gabriel of Our Lady of Sorrows, Religious (1838–1862)

SANICLE *Sanicula europaea*
BUGLE *Ajuga reptans*; sicklewort; middle comfrey; herb carpenter

Cultivation Notes
Sanicle is perennial and grows to a height of two feet. Its pale pink or greeny-white flowers appear on umbels in early summer. The leaves have

five pointed sections and the seed
cases are burr-like and cling to clothing.
It likes thickets and shady moist places.

Bugle is also perennial, but evergreen, with
a squarish stalk and rather hairy leaves. It
bears blue flowers in small spikes from late
spring to midsummer, and grows to about
six inches. Its creeping habit makes it a
good ground cover plant. The leaves are
oval and dark green, tinged with purple.
Like sanicle, it favours shade and damp,
and does well under shrubs or hedges.
Sow in autumn or spring and thin
to a foot apart to allow for spreading.
Propagate by the runners, also in
autumn or spring.

History and Lore
Sanicle was once believed to be a panacea,
and there is a theory that the name is a
corruption of 'St Nicholas', who is traditionally
thought to have been a great healer. However,
it is just as likely that the name comes from the Latin *sanus*, meaning clean
or healthy. In his *Niewe Herball or Historie of Plantes* (1578), Henry Lyte
says, 'The iuyce of Sanicle dronken, doth make whole and sound all
inward, and outward woundes and hurtes.' And according to Culpeper it
'heals green wounds or any ulcers speedily'. Modern herbalism uses it in
the treatment of sore throats, septic wounds, leucorrhoea, and diarrhoea,
and also claims that it stops internal haemorrhage.

Culpeper had an even greater respect for bugle. 'If the virtues of it make
you fall in love with it (as they will if you be wise), keep a syrup of it to take
inwardly and an ointment and plaister of it to use outwardly always by
you.' He also recommends it to counter the effects of alcohol abuse. 'Those
that give themselves much to drinking are troubled with strange fancies,
strange sights in the night or voices. These I have known cured by taking
only two spoonfuls of the syrup of this herb two hours after supper on going
to bed.' Bugle is now known to be mildly analgesic, astringent, and laxative.
It is used in modern herbalism to arrest internal haemorrhage.

Towards Meditation

Born into a middle-class family, Francis Possenti was schooled by the Jesuits in his home town of Spoleto, and as a youth considered joining them. However, at the age of 18, after serious illness and the death of his sister, he entered the Passionist novitiate at Morrovale. He took the name Gabriel of Our Lady of Sorrows and received the habit on her feast-day in 1856. He belonged to the Confraternity of the Seven Dolours and kept a perpetual light burning before a *Pietà* in his room. Gabriel trained for the priesthood, but his ordination was deferred because of the difficulties and dangers of travel at the time. Writing to his father, he said with characteristic cheerfulness and resignation that he was left with only minor orders. 'But God has so willed. And as He wills, so do I.' In the early summer of 1857 Gabriel caught a severe cold and bronchitis. His condition improved temporarily in the dry mountain air of Isola, but tuberculosis was eventually diagnosed. To him, it was what the Italian proverb calls 'the disease of the blessed'. The slowness with which it consumes its victims appealed to him because it would give him time to prepare for death. In mid-February 1862 he suffered a violent haemorrhage and received the Last Rites. He died aged twenty-four on 27 February 1862. A biography, *St Gabriel, Passionist*, by Fr Camillus, CP, conveys its subject's heroic effort to attain holiness in a small and hidden way. This, together with his undaunted cheerfulness and outstanding devotion to the Mother of Sorrows, marked him out from his brothers. He was canonized in 1920.

I first encountered St Gabriel forty years ago when I was given the Seven Sorrows rosary previously mentioned, and I have been devoted to it and to him ever since. I am unlikely to forget him, or indeed the Mother of Sorrows, because the early weekday Masses at my London parish church are offered in a side chapel dedicated to her. In France on St Gabriel's day I will contemplate the carpet of bugle leaves and wonder whether an infusion of them might have eased his suffering. And I will take away two phrases for meditation: 'small things' and 'cheerfulness in adversity'.

In the absence of bugle or sanicle, the latter virtue is symbolized by white chrysanthemums in *The Language of Flowers*.

Bible Readings

Psalm 31:19–24: In the shelter of your presence you hide them
Psalm 116:16–17: O Lord, I am your servant

Ecclesiasticus (Sirach) 11:12–13: The eyes of the Lord look upon him for his good

1 John 2:14–17: He that does the will of God abides for ever

Revelation 3:20: Behold I stand at the gate and knock

Mark 10:13–21: Receive the kingdom of God as a child; sell what you have, give to the poor

Place of Spiritual Retreat

With Jesus and the rich young man, as in Mark 10

MARCH

1 MARCH

St David, Monk and Bishop (*c*. 520–588), Patron of Wales

LEEK *Allium porrum* (see Part I, Thursday Week 2 in Advent)
DAFFODIL *Narcissus*. This is the common trumpet type of *Narcissus*. 'February gold' and 'Golden harvest' are recommended.

History and Lore

The daffodil was officially adopted as the national flower of Wales at the investiture of Edward Prince of Wales in 1911, but the leek's credentials as an emblem are far more historically valid. Tradition has it that when the Saxons invaded the country in the sixth century, King Cadwallader's men were ordered to wear leeks in their caps to distinguish them from the enemy. Shakespeare indicates through Fluellen that the Welsh wore leeks much later when fighting with Henry V in France, and that they 'did good service in a garden where leeks did grow, wearing leeks in their Monmouth caps, which your majesty know, to this hour is an honourable badge of the service; and I do believe your majesty takes no scorn to wear the leek upon St Tavy's Day' (Henry V, Act 4, scene 8). There is too, a verse in an ancient manuscript in the British Museum:

> I like the leeke above all herbes and floures;
> When first we wore the same, the field was ours,
> The leeke is white and green, whereby is meant
> That Britaines are both stout and eminente.
> Next to the lion and the unicorn
> The leeke the fairest emblym that is worn.

Towards Meditation

David is the most ancient saint of the British Isles to be celebrated in this book and as such connects us with our native Christian forbears. Reliable facts about him are few, but he is traditionally thought to have trained under Illtyd (d. early sixth century), who was reputedly the most learned British philosopher and biblical scholar of his time. It is claimed that Illtyd was in his turn a disciple of Germanus of Auxerre (d. 446). Germanus had been called twice by the British bishops to help them combat Pelagianism, which was then rife. (This heresy was named after the British monk Pelagius, who promoted the view that Adam's sin affected no one but himself. Human infants are not born with a predisposition to sin. He also denied that human salvation was an act of Divine Grace and taught that human beings can save themselves.) While he was in Britain, Germanus visited the shrine of St Alban and exchanged relics of the apostles for earth from the tomb of the first British martyr. If Illtyd was a pupil of Germanus we can be certain of the orthodoxy of David's later preaching. Moreover, the connection between these men is a reminder that Christianity was well established in parts of Britain long before Augustine's arrival in Kent in 597, by which time Alban had been dead for at least 290 years, Germanus for 140, Illtyd since the beginning of the sixth century, and David himself for nine years.

David was a monk and had founded several monasteries before being consecrated bishop and Primate of Wales. He established his see at Mynyw (St David's) in Monmouthshire, where he was also Abbot. He was noted for his preaching and works of mercy. Personal austerity earned him the nickname *Aquaticus*, either because he drank only water or because he was given to total immersion in cold water as a means of self-discipline. He is usually pictured wearing bishop's vestments, and a dove commemorates his attendance at the Synod of Brevi. Today's reflection on his life and time, and on the influences on him, inspires thanksgiving for the beginnings and the continuity of faith in our islands.

Bible Readings
Psalm 40: I have told the glad news of deliverance in the great congregation
Philippians 3:8–14: I press on towards the goal
Matthew 5:13–16: You are the salt of the earth . . . the light of the world

Place of Spiritual Retreat
Listening to Jesus' description of true discipleship, as in Matthew 5

4 MARCH

St Casimir, Confessor (1458–1484)

LUNGWORT* *Pulmonaria officinalis*; Jerusalem cowslip; soldiers and sailors

Cultivation Notes

This hardy herbaceous perennial grows to a height of twelve inches and produces clusters of flowers in mid to late spring. These are pink at first but later turn a purplish-blue. The leaves are hairy, white-spotted, and ovate. Lungwort thrives in the shade of trees or shrubs. Seed can be sown outdoors in the spring, but germination may be slow, and it is better to set out plants in late autumn. Water in dry weather and cut back established plants in autumn. Harvest flowering plants in early summer and dry for later use.

History and Lore

The botanical name comes from Latin *pulmo* for lung, probably because of the *Doctrine of Signatures*. This theory, described in *The Art of Simples* (William Coles, 1656), held that a plant's appearance was a divine indication as to how it should be used medicinally. In the case of lungwort, the mottled leaves were reminiscent of diseased lungs, and so it was used to treat a variety of chest ailments. It does in fact have soothing, astringent, and expectorant qualities and is still employed in modern herbalism to relieve coughs, bronchitis, and catarrh.

Towards Meditation

Casimir was born at Cracow, son of Casimir IV, king of Poland. At the age of thirteen he was sent by his father to claim the throne of Hungary but withdrew his army in a refusal to wage war on another Christian country. His father punished him with three months' imprisonment. Casimir also refused to marry, preferring a life of celibacy, prayer, and austerity. His hallmarks were firm faith in the Eucharist, love of the poor, and deep devotion to the Blessed Virgin Mary. He frequently said the twelfth-century hymn ascribed to Bernard of Cluny, *Omni die dic Mariae*, and a copy of it was buried with him. (This is the original of our hymn, 'Daily, daily, sing to Mary.') Casimir died from a lung-wasting disease at

---

* Lungwort is legally restricted in some countries and can irritate sensitive skins.

the age of twenty-six, and his tomb at Vilna was claimed as the site of many miracles. He was canonized in 1521 and is patron of Poland and Lithuania. Whether I can see any lungwort today or not, I will meditate on that hymn and beseech Our Lady to pray for an increase in our love and respect for the Eucharist, for her Son's poor, for a decrease in our concern for material possessions, and for all sufferers from lung disease.

Bible Readings
Ecclesiasticus (Sirach) 29:8–13: Lay up your treasure according to the commandments
1 Timothy 6:6–11: The love of money is the root of all evils
Matthew 6:19–24: Lay up for yourselves treasures in heaven; you cannot serve God and mammon

Place of Spiritual Retreat
With the disciples listening to Christ, as in Matthew 6

7 MARCH

SS Perpetua and Felicity, Martyrs (died 203)

RAMBLER ROSE 'Félicité perpétue'

Cultivation Notes
This rose was introduced in 1827 and is still vigorous and reliable. Do not prune, but cut out the dead wood. It has glossy dark green leaves and slightly fragrant flowers that appear in midsummer. These are borne in clusters and begin as red-tipped buds. In full bloom, they are creamy-white, small, rosette-shaped, and double, all of which characteristics suit them to today's martyrs.

History and Lore
Perpetua and Felicity were killed at Carthage in the persecution by Septimus Severus. He had forbidden any new Christian conversions, so catechumens knew they were risking the death penalty. Perpetua, a young married woman, was twenty-two when she was arrested, and had recently given birth to a son. She took him to prison with her and was accompanied by several others, including Felicity, a pregnant slave.

There were four men in the group, but the records seem to concentrate on the witness of the women. While in prison, Felicity gave birth to a daughter. The men were eventually thrown to leopards, and the women to a mad heifer. The survivors were later finished off by the sword.

Towards Meditation

The account of the deaths of these Christian mothers in today's second Office reading was partly written or dictated by the martyrs themselves and completed by a contemporary, probably an eyewitness (possibly Tertullian, c. 150–c. 212). This makes the testimony particularly moving and precious. It is so vivid that one can smell the animals and the blood of their victims. One can hear the brutal sarcasm in the baying of the crowd. When one of the men, fatally bitten by a leopard, was drenched in the blood of his 'second baptism', the roar went up, 'Well washed! Well washed!' Or perhaps the shout came from the Christians in the crowd who thus acknowledged that the martyr had indeed been saved. The gladiator assigned to cut the throat of Perpetua was a novice and trembled at his task. She herself had to guide his hand. There is a sad omission from the Office account. We are not told what happened to the babies of Perpetua and Felicity, and can only hope that they were taken to safety by other Christians.

Bible Readings

Romans 8:34–5, 37: Jesus is at God's right hand and pleads for us. Who shall separate us from his love? We triumph through his power

Revelation 7:13–17: They have washed their robes and made them white in the blood of the Lamb

Matthew 5:10–12: Blessed are those who are persecuted

Matthew 10:34–9: He who loses his life for my sake will find it

Place of Spiritual Retreat

Listening to the teaching of Jesus, as in the Matthew texts above

8 MARCH

St John of God, Religious (1495–1550)

LUPIN *Lupinus polyphillus*

Cultivation Notes

This familiar herbaceous garden perennial grows to a height of four feet and produces flowers of various colours in late spring and early summer. These are followed by long pods containing the flat, round, white seeds. Lupins grow well in sandy soil in sun or light shade. Sow in spring or plant in groups from October to March. Mulch established plants annually, and top-dress with compost or old manure. Water in dry weather. Deadhead to encourage a second crop of flowers, and to discourage seedlings. Cut dead stems to the ground in autumn. Watch out for slugs!

History and Lore

The white lupin was common in Culpeper's day, and he recommends its seeds for external treatment 'against deformities of the skin, scabby ulcers, scald heads and other cutaneous distempers'. They are still used in modern herbalism, soaked in water and applied to ulcers. Cosmetically, they can be bruised for a cleansing facial steam. It is thought that the lupin may absorb radiation, and it has been planted around the nuclear disaster area at Chernobyl.

Note: The raw seed is toxic if eaten.

Towards Meditation

John of God was Portuguese and spent many dangerous years as a mercenary in the Spanish army. After this, he became a shepherd in Andalusia and in early middle age was converted to a life dedicated to the poor. He first planned, despite the risk of martyrdom, to work with Christian slaves in North Africa. He eventually found himself in Gibraltar, peddling holy books and pictures. His trade was so successful that in 1538 he opened a repository in Granada. There he suffered a period of mental breakdown, wandering the streets, tearing his hair, and giving away the stock of his shop. Perhaps this was caused by the brutality, poverty, and suffering he had seen all his life and by frustration that he was still not serving God practically in alleviating them. John of Avila, a well-known preacher, took him in charge, and when he came out of hospital John of God rented a house and took in sick and poor people. He was efficient, devoted to his patients, and led a life marked by prayer, austerity, and a boundless energy. He received a religious habit from the bishop and continued work for the sick poor for the next decade. In a letter in today's Office he lists some of their illnesses and conditions. His house was open to the maimed, dumb, insane, paralytic, and senile; to lepers and cancer victims; and to children, travellers, and pilgrims. No charge was made and John was often so heavily in debt that he dared not go out for fear of arrest. But through it all he trusted in God and only regretted that he could not help more people. His final illness was brought on by his rescue of a drowning man. John of God died at the altar of his chapel at the age of fifty-five. His followers took vows and became the Brother Hospitallers, claiming St John of God as their founder. He is also patron of hospitals and booksellers.

In *The Language of Flowers* the lupin symbolizes both veracity and dejection. It seems suitable for St John because of his pursuit of his true calling, and the time in his life when failure to find it caused mental breakdown. His experience reminds us of the need to ask frequently in prayer whether the work we do has been chosen for us by God. Remembering St John's association with hospitals, I will make a supply of lupin lotion and a herbal disinfectant, much easier on the hands and better for the environment than the chemical wonder-products so much vaunted these days.

Note: Other plants that share the lupin's disinfectant qualities are bergamot, juniper, lavender, eucalyptus, and Norway spruce.

Bible Readings
Isaiah 58:7–8: Share your bed with the hungry and bring the homeless poor into your house
Matthew 26:31–46: The separation of the sheep from goats: as you did it to one of the least of these my brethren, you did it to me

Place of Spiritual Retreat
Listening to Jesus with the disciples, as in Matthew 26

9 MARCH

St Frances of Rome, Religious (1384–1440)

NARCISSUS 'Angel'

'Angel' belongs to the small-cupped group of narcissi. Its flowers are all white and are produced singly on stems that grow to a height of eighteen inches.

History and Lore

Frances of Rome was born into a wealthy but devout family. However, they refused to allow her to become a nun, and at the age of thirteen she was married to Lorenzo Ponziano. Authorities are divided as to how many children she had. Some suggest as many as six. We do know, however, that the first was born when she was only sixteen. From the beginning of her marriage, she devoted herself to the relief of Rome's poor and sick. In 1408 the city was captured by the Neapolitans, and as the Ponziano family were known to be papal supporters, they were subjected to attack. Their estates were confiscated, the house ruined, and Lorenzo banished. Frances continued her works of mercy and suffered personally as a result. In 1425, after the deaths of two of her children, she founded a religious community, on Benedictine lines, to help carry out her mission. Later they became known as the Oblates of Torre de'Specchi. After Lorenzo's death in 1436 Frances entered the community herself. She remained there for the rest of her life and became its superior. She is buried in the church named after her, Santa Francesca Romana. Her community still exists. Even during her lifetime St Frances gained a reputation for miracles and bilocation. This is perhaps why she was later made patron saint of motorists. But probably best known is her extended series of visions of her guardian angel, hence my choice of today's flower.

St Frances of Rome died on 9 March 1440 at the age of fifty-six. She was canonized in 1608.

Towards Meditation

St Frances' holiness, even before she entered her community, was of an order few Christian wives ever reach. Apparently, during forty years of marriage, she succeeded in never annoying her husband. Most of us have no hope of emulating her in *that* achievement! Today's Office reading from her biography shows her heroic love and patience. But there is something homely, gentle, and normal about her. She is not off-puttingly pious as an example of Christian married womanhood. In any case she is as dear to me as are my other married favourites, Jane Frances de Chantal, and Louise de Marillac (1591–1660). Narcissus 'Angel' can be late to bloom in a cold spring. I will go anxiously down the garden to look for it. Surely at least the leaves will be showing. Contemplating them will be to acknowledge that these three saints achieved what I constantly struggle and fail to do: namely, to accept my lot and feed the sheep Christ has given me to care for. Nevertheless, Frances, Jane, and Louise give me courage and renewed determination, and I thank God for them.

Bible Readings

Ruth 3:10–11: My fellow townsmen know that you are a woman of worth
Mark 14:3–9: Let her alone ... she has done a beautiful thing
Luke 10:38–41: One thing is needful. Mary has chosen the better portion

Place of Spiritual Retreat

With Jesus in Bethany, as in Luke 10, or in the house of Simon the Leper, as in Mark 14

APPENDIX 1

AN EXAMPLE OF HOW THIS BOOK CAN BE USED TO PLAN RETREATS OR QUIET DAYS

Saint Benedict's Winter Harvest in England and France

During January and at the beginning of March the Benedictines commemorate a group of ten saints who followed the Rule of Saint Benedict and whose lives bore great fruit for monasticism and for Christian life and education in general in England and France. They are not celebrated in the Universal Calendar, but I include them as a reminder of the huge contribution the Benedictines and Cistercians have made to the Church as a whole and because, between them, they exemplify so many of the charisms and preoccupations that have, over the centuries, come to be regarded as characteristic of their Orders.

15 January: SS Maurus and Placidus (sixth century), Benedictines

Hollyhock Althaea (Alcea) rosea
This popular cottage garden flower arrived in Europe from the East in the sixteenth century. Its English name is thought to mean 'holy mallow', *hoc* being Old English for mallow. Normally biennial or a short-lived perennial, it can reach a height of eight feet. Watch for rust and slug damage. The hollyhock traditionally symbolizes fruitfulness and is chosen particularly for Maurus in acknowledgement of the fruit borne of his labours in south west France.

Maurus was of noble birth and became a disciple of Benedict at Monte Cassino. He is traditionally noted for his obedience. According to the *Dialogues* of Gregory the Great, Maurus, on Benedict's command, unconsciously walked on the water in order to save the boy Placidus from drowning. There are dubious stories of Placidus' later martyrdom in Sicily. These led to a feast for him on 5 October, and he was for a long time held as patron of novices in Benedictine houses. In 1915, however, the Benedictines themselves recommended that his feast should be suppressed, and so he comes to share commemoration with his traditional rescuer.

Maurus died in 565, reputedly having established Benedictine monasticism in the southern Charente and Dordogne in France. In the twelfth century Maurus' monastic descendants were excavating the rock cliff behind their convent at Aubeterre-sur-Dronne when they broke through into a vast subterranean church with a nave over twenty metres high. In the centre, hewn out of the rock floor, is a baptistery for total immersion, dating from the ninth century if not several centuries earlier. (Local tradition holds that it was built by near-contemporaries of Maurus.) In the apse there is a hexagonal monument, probably a mausoleum, resembling the one that covers the tomb of Joseph of Arimathea under the church of the Holy Sepulchre in Jerusalem. The nave of the Aubeterre church is bordered on three sides by galleries that are reached by steps carved into the rock. In 1958, a burial chamber was discovered at the south end of the nave, containing a hundred sarcophagi, and about thirty years ago further excavation revealed another chamber underneath the church itself.

Those twelfth-century monks are supposed to have made their discovery by accident, but I like to entertain the possibility that, suspecting the church was there from stories handed down by previous generations of their Order, they were actually *looking* for it. The foot of a rocky cliff perched precariously over a valley was not typical terrain for a Benedictine foundation, and I wonder whether they had been sent as prospectors from one of several nearby monasteries. At any rate, in the cavernous depths of the Aubeterre monolithic Church of Saint Jean, one experiences a profound connectedness with *Saint Maur* and with those whose remains rest in its burial chamber. The place provokes a sense of Christian continuity that is far more stirring to faith than the Placidus legend. Since the late 1990s, as a result of priest shortage, the parish of Aubeterre has encompassed eight outlying parishes, most of which have medieval churches. The ageing *abbé* who looked after all of them retired in 2001, worn out and ill from his labours. As there is no diocesan priest available to replace him, his flock, which includes many expatriate Britons, has been bereft of a shepherd since his departure. Efforts are now being made – in England and France – to find a son, or sons, of St Benedict who will follow in the steps of St Maurus by coming 'home' to Aubeterre and ministering to its community.

2 March: SS Cedd (died 664) and Chad (died 672), Benedictines

Candytuft *Iberis*

This annual produces white, red, lilac, or pink flowers from May to September. It normally grows to about nine inches and can be sown in its flowering position between March and May. In *The Language of Flowers* it represents architecture, so it is given to Cedd and Chad for the monasteries they built and symbolically to Chad as the founding architect of the see of Lichfield.

Cedd and his brother Chad were educated at Lindisfarne by Aidan (died 651) and Finan (abbot of Lindisfarne 651–61). After successfully evangelizing Essex, Cedd was consecrated bishop of the East Saxons by Finan. He founded monasteries at Tilbury and Bradwell-on-Sea and at Lastingham in North Yorkshire, where he became Abbot. He acted as interpreter at the Synod of Whitby in 663–4 and shortly afterwards died of the plague at Lastingham. He had accepted the decisions of the Synod for his own diocese, and his building at Bradwell is Roman in style, resembling early Christian churches in Kent.

Aidan sent Chad to Ireland for part of his training, and Bede (673–735) records him as humble, devout, and apostolically zealous. He eventually succeeded his brother as Abbot of Lastingham and was consecrated Bishop of the Mercians in 669 by Theodore, Archbishop of Canterbury (died 690). Chad's episcopate laid the foundations for the later see of Lichfield, where he established a monastery. He was venerated as a saint immediately after his death, and cures of both people and cattle were claimed at his tomb in Lichfield. At the Dissolution of the Monasteries his shrine was spared for a while but was finally destroyed. Recusants are believed to have rescued and preserved some of his relics, and several of his bones are venerated at the Roman Catholic Metropolitan Cathedral of Saint Chad in Birmingham.

12 January: St Benedict Biscop (628–689), Benedictine

Bear's breeches *Acanthus spinosus*

This hardy herbaceous plant is majestic and handsome. Depending on variety, it reaches a height of two to five feet. It has dark green indented leaves and produces white, pink, or purple flowers from July to September. Plant in March or April where it will later enjoy full sun.

In *The Language of Flowers* it represents the Arts, and so it is appropriate for a saint who brought so much music and painting from the Continent to enhance the liturgy in his native Britain.

Born into a noble Northumbrian family, this Benedict is known to have made no less than six journeys to Rome, the first with Wilfrid (633–709) to visit the tombs of the Apostles. On his second return journey he became a monk at Lérins. In 669 he returned from his third visit with Theodore, the new Archbishop of Canterbury, and became Abbot there for a while. In 674 he founded the abbey at Wearmouth and became its first abbot. The rule was based on the Benedictine practice he had seen on his travels. He imported stonemasons and glaziers, who passed on their skills to the locals. From his fourth and fifth journeys he brought back liturgical books, religious pictures, calendars, and relics. In 682 he founded the monastery at Jarrow and from a final visit to Rome brought back yet more books and sacred pictures. Bede, who was entrusted to him at an early age, could not have achieved his own scholarship without the library assembled by Benedict Biscop. A glimpse of his other priorities is to be found in his final conference to his monks, in which he exhorted them to elect a new abbot for his manner of life and not out of considerations of nobility or class.

19 January: St Wulstan (1008–1095), Benedictine

Water lily *Nymphaea*
A wide range of water lilies is available, and it is essential to consider the size of your water feature before planting one. Novice aquatic gardeners should take advice. Suffice it to say here that water lilies need still water. You cannot have a water lily and a fountain in the same pond! The water lily signifies eloquence and is given to Wulstan for his articulacy in his native Old English.

Wulstan was an Anglo-Saxon, born at Itchington in Warwickshire. He became a monk at Worcester and eventually prior there. Later as bishop he combined the two callings to great effect. He is believed to have been the first English bishop to make systematic visitations in his diocese, preaching, baptizing, and counselling. He has maintained a reputation for eloquence in English, and, regardless of the legend that he was not well educated, under his care Worcester became a centre for Old English literature and culture. He enjoyed good health and died at the age of eighty-seven. The cathedral crypt, rebuilt by him with an insistence on stone, is still extant in part. Perhaps his most admirable achievement was the abolition of the trade in slaves from Bristol to Viking Ireland.

26 January: SS Alberic (died 1109), Robert of Molesme (died 1110), and Stephen Harding (died 1134), Cistercians

Holy or *blessed thistle* Cnicus benedictus; Cardus benedictus
This annual plant was first grown in monastery herb gardens as a cure-all; in the sixteenth century it was used against the plague. It does have antiseptic and antibiotic properties and is still grown today for use in the pharmaceutical industry. It produces single yellow flowers and grows to a height of about two feet. Traditionally, the holy thistle symbolizes austerity and independence, which makes it appropriate for men who displayed both qualities in their foundation and observance of a strict form of Benedictine Rule.

Alberic's early life is unrecorded, but he is known to have been a hermit near Châtillon-sur-Seine. He invited Robert, then Abbot of Tonnerre, and some companions to join him in making a settlement at Molesme, with Robert as abbot and himself as prior. Disputes arose and finally, together with Robert, Stephen, and all their followers, he moved to Cîteaux, near Dijon, with the intention of living the Rule of St Benedict in strict observance. Robert's departure caused Molesme to deteriorate even further, and he eventually returned there as abbot, a post he kept until he died at the age of eighty-three. Stephen Harding became third abbot of Cîteaux on the death of Alberic. The three men traditionally share the honour of founding the Cistercians, but it is believed to have been Stephen who wrote down the Constitutions. Born in the south west of England, he is thought to have been a monk of Sherborne who returned for a while to lay life before joining the community at Molesme on a return journey from Rome. At Cîteaux, it was Stephen who received Bernard and his followers. Their arrival gave a wonderful impetus to the progress of the reformed ideal. Clairvaux, with Bernard as abbot, was founded during Stephen's abbacy at Cîteaux, and he lived to see the foundation of Tintern, Fountains, and Rievaulx in his native land. The *Cîteaux Bible* is thought to be his work.

11 January: St Aelred (1110–1167), Cistercian

Greater monk's rhubarb *Rumex Alpinus*; monk's rhubarb; patience dock
This plant, a member of the dock family, is now infrequently found
outside the mountainous regions of Europe. Culpeper includes it in his
Herbal, so perhaps it was more common in the England of his time. He
claims that 'the root expels stone, provokes urine, and helps the dimness of
sight'. We know that Aelred suffered from gallstones and can only hope
that monk's rhubarb grew near Rievaulx in the twelfth century and was
used to ease the pain suffered by this great monk.

Aelred was born near Durham, was educated there, and joined the recently
founded abbey of Rievaulx in 1134. He became abbot at Revesby in
Lincolnshire in 1143 but was recalled to be abbot of Rievaulx four years
later. The abbey flourished under his rule and became the largest Cistercian
house in England, with over a hundred choir monks and five hundred lay
brothers. He is reputed to have been sensitive, discreet, possessed of a gentle
holiness, and a softening influence on the austerity of the Rule. He preached
at Westminster Abbey for the translation of Edward the Confessor in 1163.
His written legacy includes Lives of Edward, Ninian, and the saints of
Hexham; sermons on Isaiah; a treatise on friendship; and an unfinished
work on the soul. He suffered agonies from the stone but frequently visited
new Cistercian foundations in Scotland until illness eventually made
travelling impossible. He died at Rievaulx and was buried in the Chapter
House, his remains later being moved to the church.

* * *

The commemoration of these saints leads to an examination of the Rule
that inspired and governed them. As we shall see, there has always been –
and still is – a great deal in the Rule of St Benedict that is relevant to lay
Christians. Indeed, in its salutary penultimate sentence Benedict says,
'Whoever you are, if you wish to follow the path to God, make use of this
little Rule for beginners.' So let us follow his advice.

PLANNING A RETREAT OR QUIET DAY

Purpose
Using plants as visual springboards, to awaken or renew our appreciation

of the Rule's relevance as inspiration, guide, and discipline in contemporary lay Christian life.

Preparation

During the previous summer:

1. Grow or buy, and then dry, Acanthus, Candytuft, and Canterbury Bell. It is illegal to pick wild flowers, so if you do not have Bee Orchis or Wood Anemone in the garden, find a picture of them to add to a collage.
2. Collect pictures of plants in the foregoing list and make Benedictine collages. Ask your church community to collect pictures and assemble a 'bank' of them for retreatants to make collages or other art-work on the day(s).
3. Aim to have as many 'live' samples of the plants as possible. Advertise the need at church and among your friends and colleagues at work.

During the preceding months/weeks:

1. To ensure the smooth running of a group retreat at church, ask for specialist 'officers' for the day(s), e.g. chaplain, kitchener, gardener, musical director, artist, embroiderer, mistress or master of ceremonies, readers, cantors, etc.
2. Establish beforehand who will be doing what during the manual and creative labour sessions during the day(s). If you are planning a quiet day at home decide your activities for these times in advance.
3. Explore the possibility of inviting outside speakers to give conferences on the Benedictine vows and traditional works, and on the history and practice of plainchant.

The day beforehand:

Make arrangements from assembled plants and decorate the church, retreat rooms, or home with them. Group the plants according to their relevance, either to the Benedictine Rule or to traditional works (see Retreat Content below). Display collage.

Retreat Content

Any Benedictine day must include time for Mass and the Divine Office, reading and study, and manual/creative labour. Around this backbone, plan time for private prayer, social interchange, silent meals (with reader), choir practice (or a talk with practical demonstration on the chant), and two conferences, one on Benedictine vows, and the other on traditional Benedictine works. Each should be followed by a period for private reflection on the questions they raise. This is certainly a lot to fit into a Saturday parish retreat, and a solution could be to have the choir practice and second conference on Sunday morning before the main Mass of the day and to conclude the retreat with a social lunch where talking is allowed. (At home, one would spend the conference time in reading, meditation, and praying the chant through listening to recordings of it.)

NOTES FOR THE CONFERENCES

The Benedictine Vows

Stability
Introduced by WESTERN RED CEDAR *Thuya plicata*
Western red cedar was introduced to Britain in 1853 from the west coast of the United States, where it grows from Alaska to California. It is not really a cedar and was given its name by early European settlers, who thought it was related to the cedar of Lebanon. The wood has many uses in carpentry and building, and it is planted near young deciduous trees to protect them. It can reach a height of over 80 feet but can be controlled to make a good hedge. In plant lore it signifies stability, and I used it to enclose my herb garden for this reason. On a physical level, the vow of Stability binds Benedictine monks or nuns to a specific house; but its metaphorical meaning clearly applies to lay people as well.

Questions:
How loyal am I to the house of faith? How much am I truly fixed on Christ? How justified am I in praying Psalm 38:7: 'My heart is steadfast O Lord, my heart is steadfast'? (I favour the Common Bible translation because of 'stead' meaning 'a home or dwelling', so that in the psalm the word means being loyal and fixed to our true home with God.)

Conversion of manners
By this vow, Benedictines promise to be chaste and to embrace poverty.

(a) Chastity
Introduced by CHASTE TREE, *Vitex agnus-castus* (see also under 'Vocation' in Part One: Ordinary Time) and WATER LILY, *Nymphaea* (see under St Wulstan, above)

The chaste tree, or monk's pepper, is a deciduous ornamental shrub or small tree, growing to a height of up to fifteen feet. In summer it bears small lilac flowers, scented and carried on spikes. The plant has long been an emblem of virtue, but here it symbolizes physical chastity as opposed to purity of heart, which is traditionally represented by the water lily.

As Esther de Waal points out in *Seeking God: The Way of St Benedict*, he does not isolate 'sex' as an overriding problem. For him it is only one aspect of our lives that needs to be regulated. He mentions chastity separately only once in Chapter 4, where the injunction 'Love chastity' is number 63 in a list of 72 'Instruments of Good Works' or, as he calls them at the end of the chapter, 'the tools of our spiritual craft'. Perhaps it comes so low down on the list because if we have managed to observe the preceding 62 injunctions, chastity will no longer be an effort, but something we actively love and pursue. In any case chastity is not merely a synonym for virginity or celibacy. It is also about being pure in spirit and about exercising control and moderation of all our bodily desires; it is about rejecting the pursuit of the physical gratifications the world has to offer as a driving priority. It is about a total conversion of attitude and about really desiring Christ above all else. In these terms it is possible for lay people to be chaste, even though they may not be virginal or celibate.

(b) Poverty

Introduced by WOOD ANEMONE, *Anemone nemorosa*

This graceful and delicate plant flowers from March to May in deciduous woodland. It is recognizable by a ring of three leaves about two thirds of the way up the stem, which can reach a height of twelve inches. Its white flowers open and face upward to the sun but close and droop in cloudy weather and at the end of the day. It is a member of the windflower family and so is able, despite its fragile appearance, to withstand quite rough weather. Perhaps that is why it is traditionally associated with Christian poverty.

For Benedictines poverty as part of their second vow means the renunciation of all possessions. It is a literal interpretation of, and obedience to, Christ's command that we should leave everything and follow him. In Chapter 33 of the Rule Benedict reminds us of the practice among early Christians: 'Neither did anyone say or think that anything whatever was his own' (Acts 4:32). It is however, not merely a question of giving up material possessions, but of truly being able to dismiss them as valueless in comparison with the riches and gifts of the Spirit.

Here again the vow is about attitude. *Conversion of Manners* could therefore be translated as a total *volte face* in one's approach to living. It is to listen to and to give oneself to the words of Benedict, and of St Paul before him: 'Let your minds be remade, your nature transformed' (Rom. 12:1–21).

Question:
How far, with regard to chastity and poverty, in attitude and action, have I truly renounced the world's mind for the mind of Christ?

Obedience
Introduced by BROOM, *Cytisus scoparius*
Wild broom produces its golden pea-like flowers in May and June. It is similar to gorse, but it is not thorny and can grow to a height of seven feet. Traditionally, it symbolizes obedience, possibly because of its pliant branches.

It has often been said that obedience is the hardest vow to keep. This is no surprise since it strikes at the very roots of our headstrong wilfulness, at our self-determination and self-orientation. In his Chapter 5, on obedience, Benedict says that inspiration will be found in Christ's saying: 'I come not to do my own will, but the will of him who sent me' (Jn 6:38). To be obedient to superiors is to be obedient to God, who said, 'He who hears you, hears me' (Lk. 10:16). Obedience should be immediate and cheerful: 'God loves a cheerful giver' (2 Cor. 9:7). It should be unquestioning, even if the task seems impossible. In Chapter 68 Benedict gives room for appeal only if the task has been tried to the best of a monk's ability. And even then, if the abbot persists, the monk must go back and continue to do his best, 'trusting in God's help'. The vow is about seeking and doing God's will, not an enslavement to the will of human authority.

Questions:

How does the vow of obedience relate to my professional, private and parish life?

Am I difficult to manage? Do I carp destructively behind the back of the boss, my friends, or the clergy and church officers? How easy am I for others to work, socialize, and worship with?

How genuinely do I seek to know and do God's will? How easily do I give up?

Benedictine Works

The 'Opus Dei'

Introduced by the PRAYER PLANT, *Maranta leuconeura kerchoveana*

Perhaps the easiest of the *Maranta* group to grow, this house plant likes a moist compost and tepid watering, which is reduced in winter. It grows best in partial shade. The plant folds and raises its leaves at night, and this probably accounts for its English name. It is a characteristic that reminds me of the time when Matins, the first Office of the day, was universally said or sung during the small hours. Also, the prayer plant reminds me of the Rosary, because it has ten symmetrical splodges on each of its leaves.

The *Opus Dei* is the Divine Office, consisting of the Office of Readings or Vigils (formerly the night Office of Matins); Morning Prayer (formerly Lauds); Prayer During the Morning and Afternoon (formerly Terce, Sext and None); Evening Prayer (formerly Vespers); and Night Prayer (formerly Compline).

All Benedictines should daily, in community, recite or preferably sing the full Divine Office. It is the work of God, the universal prayer of the Church. In 1974, desiring that more lay people would make it part of their daily spiritual practice, the Church made it available in the vernacular. Most of us should be able to find the time to pray either Morning, Evening or Night Prayer, and these are published together in a relatively inexpensive volume. The present retreat should offer a taster of the full Daily Office, with those who are used to it helping those who are not to find their way about it. If the Mass is the mortice, then the Office is the tenon that the Church has, over centuries, crafted to fit it. This retreat is an opportunity to demonstrate just how perfectly it does so.

Questions:
If I do not already say the Office or part of it each day, am I prepared to find the time to experiment with it for a while, and to search for its riches? Can I begin to obey Benedict and regularly 'sing his [God's] praises with a psalm' (Ps. 47:7)?

'Lectio divina'
Introduced by BULRUSH, *Cyperus papyrus (Scirpus lacustris)*
If it is not to run rampant, bulrush needs careful management in a domestic pond. It can be bought already dried or found in streams in the wild. The 'paper reeds by the brooks' of Isaiah 19:7 were almost certainly bulrushes, and the scroll eaten by Ezekiel was equally likely to have been made from them: '"Eat this scroll that I give you and fill your stomach with it." Then I ate it; and it was in my mouth as sweet as honey' (Ezek. 3:3). The prophet's literal and spiritual consumption of the scroll prefigures the ways in which we too partake of the word. The bulrush is symbolic of the written word in general but, in a specifically Christian sense, of the written word of God. It is also an appropriate emblem for *lectio divina*, a phrase coined by St Benedict for any reading in pursuit of spiritual understanding. All Benedictines spend time each day thus occupied.

Questions:
How much time do I spend reading in search of spiritual understanding? Could I not make time for more? Do I pray for Christ's enlightening presence before I read? 'And beginning with Moses and all the prophets, he interpreted to them in all the scriptures the things concerning himself' (Lk. 24:27).

Manual labour
Introduced by BEE ORCHIS, *Orphrys apifera*; FLAX, *Linum usitatissimum*
The bee orchis is the traditional symbol for industry. Its flower is so marked as to make it appear that a female bumble-bee is resting on it. In a Benedictine context, bees of any kind never fail to remind me of the late Brother Adam of Buckfast Abbey in Devon, who became an internationally recognized expert in the keeping and breeding of honey-bees.

Flax signifies domestic industry. There are two types, the taller of which is used to make fibre. The shorter and more flowery variety yields linseed oil.

The Benedictine day balances spiritual and intellectual pursuits with physical work. 'Idleness is the enemy of the soul', says Benedict in Chapter 48 of the Rule. Most lay people cannot *avoid* manual labour. Our problem is to find enough time for prayer, and for creative leisure. However, all members of families could do well to read Chapter 35, on 'Weekly Kitchen Service'. Benedict is adamant that no one should be excused it unless he is ill or at work on a project judged by the abbot to be of greater importance. In larger monasteries, the cellarer (housekeeper/bursar) may also be excused. The monk entering on his week's service must publicly ask for God's assistance in carrying out his duty, and at the end of his week he must thank God for the help God has given. In Benedictine terms 'kitchen service' means more than cooking and serving meals. It also involves cleaning, laundering, and the washing of the brothers' feet at the end of the week. There is a wise touch in this chapter where Benedict instructs that the meal servers should be allowed a portion over their daily allowance so that they may serve their brothers uncomplainingly and without fatigue.

Questions:
Are things fairly organized in my home, or is one person bearing the brunt of the chores? Am I pulling my weight? Do I treat my spouse or other family members as unpaid servants? How often do I fail to do my share in a cheerful manner? Am I imbued with a spirit of loving service of others? How often do I fail to ask God's help in my work, and to thank him when he sustains me in it?

Hospitality
Introduced by OAK, *Quercus robur*, and HOLLY, *Ilex aquifolium* (see Tuesday Week One in Advent and 19 December respectively)
When they are found together, oak and holly are traditionally representative of hospitality.

The constant coming and going of guests was the norm in monasteries when Benedict wrote his Rule. His Chapter 53, on how they should be received and treated, is one of the longest and most detailed in the Rule. Benedict points out that in welcoming guests, the brothers are really welcoming Christ, particularly if they are poor or pilgrims. He cites Christ in Matthew 25:35: 'I was a stranger and you welcomed me.' He is, however, obviously very much aware of the dangers inherent in contact with the outside world. For this reason he is particular about the rituals for the reception and departure of guests, and stresses that their quarters should be staffed by tried and tested brothers. The rest of the community, although they will honour all guests in charity, must not enter into conversation with them without permission. On a practical note, he states that there should always be plenty of beds available. (I wonder if this is a contribution that Dame Felicitas Corrigan would suspect St Scholastica of having made!)

Questions:
What is my reaction to being 'dropped in on' when I am busy doing something else? What are my criteria and motives for inviting people into my home?
How open am I to other people? How well and how often do I truly listen to them?
Do I make strangers and visitors welcome in church? How often do I turn my back on people I find distasteful, irritating, or boring? Do I pray for discernment as to how and with whom I should spend time?

Education
Introduced by the WILD CHERRY TREE, *Prunus avium*
The wild cherry can grow to a height of 40 feet and produces white blossom in spring. It is still used as rootstock on which to grow some of its more prolifically fruiting descendants. Its wood is of good quality. Perhaps it is for these reasons that in *The Language of Flowers* it signifies a good education.

The ten saints whose lives are briefly summarized above were part of the foundation of English and French Benedictine/Cistercian thirst to acquire and disseminate knowledge in the service of God. Henrician Dissolution and Reformation notwithstanding, their monastic descendants continue with that work in our own day all over the world.

Questions:
What do I want to know, and why do I want to know it?
What do I want to convey to others of my knowledge, and why?
What contribution do I make in my own community to learning and teaching and to spreading the Gospel? Is there more God wants me to do? When did I last say to God, 'Here I am Lord, send me.'

Arts

Introduced by BEAR'S BREECHES, *Acanthus* spinosus (Arts; see 12 January, Benedict Biscop, p. 288); CANDYTUFT, *Iberis* (Architecture; see 2 March, Cedd and Chad, p. 288)

As with education, a proper study of the Benedictine/Cistercian contribution to music, art, literature, and architecture would yield enough material for several retreats of more than a day's duration. But here we are concerned with what Benedict says about the artistically gifted. In Chapter 57, he is clearly aware that the most likely sin of the artist or artisan is pride in his achievement, and in the financial benefit it brings to the monastery. If a brother displays such pride, he is to be taken from his specialist craft and made to do ordinary work until he comes to his senses. Benedict does not say so in as many words, but the message is plain. Talent is God-given, and to him alone must the praise and glory be given.

Questions:

Whatever my talents, how often do I forget that I did not create them or give them to myself?

When my work is successful, how often do I praise and congratulate myself instead of God?

Loving

Introduced by any self-coloured PINK, *Dianthus* (Love; see 29 December, St Thomas Becket, p. 202)

Brothers must love each other, despite faults in body and soul. This is the burden of the penultimate chapter of St Benedict's Rule. It is the keystone, and perhaps the most difficult to lay as the foundation of one's conduct and attitude, whether in the monastery, church community, or secular workplace. As Christ is present in our guests, he is present too in the person we do not get on with; in the person who trips us up and makes us look and feel foolish; and in the person who refutes our arguments. Worse, for our souls, he is in the person we presume to look down on.

Question:

How do I express love?

Place of Spiritual Retreat

On the road to Emmaus, as in Luke 24

Further Reading

Ashton, Michael. *Monasteries*. London: Batsford, 1993.

Bellinger, Aidan, OSB (ed.). *Downside: A Pictorial History*. Stratton-on-the-Fosse, Bath: Downside Abbey Publications, 2000.

Benedictines of Stanbrook Abbey. *In a Great Tradition. Tribute to Dame Laurentia McLachlan, Abbess of Stanbrook. By the Benedictines of Stanbrook*. London: John Murray, 1956.

Brabbs, Derry. *Abbeys and Monasteries of Britian*. London: Weidenfeld, 1999.

Clutterbuck, Robin. *A History of Buckfast Abbey*. Buckfast Abbey, 1994.

Coldicott, Diana K. *Hampshire Nunneries*. Phillimore (English Local History, Gale Prize), 1989.

Corrigan, Felicitas, OSB. *Benedictine Tapestry*. London: Darton, Longman & Todd, 1991.

Corrigan, Felicitas, OSB. *The Nun, the Infidel and the Superman: The Remarkable Friendships of Dame Laurentia McLachlan with Sydney Cockerell, Bernard Shaw, and Others*. Chicago: University of Chicago Press, 1985.

Godden, Rumer. *In This House of Brede*. London: Pan/Macmillan, 1991.

Suggestions for Plainchant Choir Practice

Introduction of the eight tones (see Introduction in the *Liber Usualis*)

Missa de Angelis (see *Kyriale* in the *Graduale Romanum*)

Alma Redemptoris; *Ubi Caritas*; *Adoro te devote* (see *Liber Usualis*)

Suggested Anglican Chant for the Psalms

Garrett; Smart; Atkins; Bairstow; Knight; Wilton; Turle; Goodenough; Wesley (Samuel); Mann; Cooke; Nares; Stanford. All on *Psalms of David from King's*. Willcock, EMI Classics

Music for Listening

Gregorian Chant: The Complete Remastered 1930 Recordings. Monks of Solesmes Abbey Choir. Pearl Mono

Ubi Caritas (motet): Duruflé, Fauré, Poulenc. All on *Requiem motets*. Choir of St John's, Cambridge. George Guest, Decca

Anton Bruckner. *Locus Iste* (motet)

Henry Purcell. 'Love divine all loves excelling.' Joseph Haydn. *Missa Brevis in C* (Mass for the Visitation with plainchant in English). Both on St Mary's, Bourne Street choir recording. Whitetower Records (apply to St Mary's, Bourne Street, London, SW1)

Monks of Glenstal Abbey. 'The Beatitudes' (write to the abbey)

APPENDIX 2

USEFUL ADDRESSES

SUPPLIERS

Bulbs
Orchard Nurseries,
Orchard Place, Flint House Road, Three Holes, Wisbech, Cambs PE14
9JN
Tel. & Fax 01354 638613; e-mail info@orchard-nurseries.co.uk;
www.orchard-nurseries.co.uk

Carncairn Daffodils (the only supplier of *Narcissus* 'Angel' listed in RHS
Plantfinder)
c/o Houston's Mill, 10 Buchna Road, Broughshane, Ballymena, Co.
Antrim, N. Ireland BT42 4NJ
Tel. 028 256 2805; Fax 028 2586 2700;
e-mail carnccairndaffodils@broughshanecommunity.com;
www.broughshanecommunity.com

Dried Flower Arranging
Caroline Alexander,
The Hop Shop, Castle Farm, Shoreham, Sevenoaks, Kent TN14 7UB
Tel. 01959 523219; Fax 01959 524220; www.hopshop.co.uk

Joanna Sheen Ltd,
P.O. Box 52, Newton Abbot, South Devon
Tel. 01626 872405; Fax 01626 872265

Hedges, Fruit, Trees and Shrubs
Buckingham Nurseries and Garden Centre,
Tingewick Road, Buckingham MK18 4AE
Tel. 0845 3456269; Fax 01280 815491; e-mail enquiries@hedging.co.uk;
www.hedging.co.uk

Reads,
Hales Hall, Loddon, Norfolk NR14 6QW
Tel. 01508 548395; Fax 01508 548040; e-mail plants@readsnursery.co.uk;
www.readsnursery.co.uk

Herbs
Dave & Mon Holtom,
Barwinnock Herbs, Barrhill, Ayrshire KA26 0RB
Tel. 01465 821338; Fax: 0870 7059196; e-mail herbs@barwinnock.com

Organic Gardening (vegetable and flower seeds, plants and green manures)
Send for catalogue to
The Organic Gardening Catalogue,
Riverdene Business Park, Molesey Road, Hersham, Surrey KT12 4RG
Tel. 01932 253666; Fax 01932 252707; e-mail chaseorg@aol.com;
www.OrganicCatalogue.com

HDRA – The Organic Organisation,
Ryton Organic Gardens, Coventry CV8 3LG
Tel. *(for membership)* 024 7630 8210; e-mail membership @hdra.org.uk;
www.hdra.org.uk

Pinks
Mark and Elaine Trenear,
Southview Nurseries, Chequers Lane, Eversley Cross, Hook, Hampshire
RG27 0NT
Tel: 01189 732206

Pot Pourri Materials
G. Baldwin & Co.,
171/173 Walworth Road, London SE17 1RW
Tel. 020 7703 5550; www.baldwins.co.uk

Neal's Yard Remedies
Tel. 0161 831 7875

Napiers Direct
Tel. 0131 553 3500; www.napiers.net

Essential Oils
Tel. 01608 659544; www.essentiallyoils.com

Rare and Unusual Plants Specialists
Larch Cottage Nurseries,
Melkinthorpe, Penrith, Cumbria CA10 2DR
Tel. 01931 712404; Fax: 01931 712727;
e-mail larchcottage.freeserve.co.uk; www.larchcottagenurseries.co.uk

Roses
(Three addresses given to ensure availability of all roses mentioned in this book)

Apuldram Roses,
Apuldram Lane, Dell Quay, Chichester, West Sussex PO20 7EG
Tel. 01243 785769; Fax 01243 536973

Peter Beales Roses,
London Road, Attelborough, Norfolk NR17 1AY
Tel. 01953 454707; Fax 01953 456845; e-mail sales@classicroses.co.uk;
www.classicroses.co.uk

Fryer's Roses,
Knutsford, Cheshire WA16 0SX
Tel. 01565 755455; Fax 01565 653755;
e-mail rosesales@fryers.roses.co.uk; www.fryers.co.uk

Wildflowers
Scott's Wildflowers,
Swallow Hill Barn, 1 Common Side, Distington, Workington, Cumbria
CA14 4PU
Tel. 01946 830486; e-mail Wildflowers@btinternet.com;
www.scottswildflowers.co.uk

SOME BENEDICTINE HOUSES OFFERING RETREAT ACCOMMODATION

Monks (Roman Catholic)
Ealing Abbey,
Charlbury Grove, London W5 2DY
Tel. 020 8862 2100; http://members.aol.com/ealingmonk

Buckfast Abbey,
(Men in Monastic Guest House; men and women in Southgate Retreat House)
Buckfastleigh, Devon TQ11 0EE
Tel. 01364 645500/550/590; Fax 01364 643891;
e-mail enquiries@buckfast.org.uk; http://www.buckfast.org.uk

Glenstal Abbey,
Murroe, Co. Limerick, Ireland
e-mail guestmaster@glenstal.org; www.glenstal.org

Washington Abbey (St. Anselm's),
4501 South Dakota Avenue, N.E., Washington D.C. 20017, U.S.A.
e-mail dcabbey@erols.com; http://saintanselms.org

Monks (Anglican)
Elmore Abbey,
Church Lane, Speen, Newbury, Berkshire RG14 1SA
Tel. 01635 33080

St Gregory's Abbey,
56500 Abbey Road, Three Rivers, Michigan 49093-9595, U.S.A.
www.geocities.com/stgregorysabbey

Nuns (Roman Catholic)
Stanbrook Abbey,
Callow End, Worcester WR2 4TD
Tel. 01905 830209/307; e-mail secretary@stanbrook.org.uk;
www.stanbrookabbey.org.uk

Priory of St Mildred, *(open to married couples)*
Minster Abbey, Ramsgate, Kent CT12 4HF
Tel. 01843 821254

Nuns (Anglican)

Edgware Abbey,
St Mary at the Cross, Priory Field Drive, Edgware, Middlesex HA8 9PZ
Tel. 0208 958 7868; e-mail nuns.osb.edgware@btclick.com

Holy Cross Convent,
Rempstone Hall, Rempstone, Loughborough LE12 6RG
Tel. 01509 880336; http://orders.anglican.org/arcyb/chc.html

St. Hilda's Priory,
Sneaton Castle, Whitby, North Yorkshire YO21 3QN
Tel. 01947 602079

(The Order of the Holy Paraclete also has convents at Rievaulx, York, Leicester, and Dundee. Visitors are welcome at them all.)
e-mail ohppriorywhitby@btinternet.com; http://www.ohpwhitby.org

Some Cistercian Retreat Houses

Monks (Roman Catholic)

Mount Melleray Abbey,
Cappoquin, Co. Waterford, Ireland
e-mail mountmellerayabbey@eircom.net

Sancta Maria Abbey (Nunraw),
Garvald, Haddington, East Lothian EH41 4LW
Tel. 01620 830223/228; e-mail domdonald@yahoo.co.uk;
www.nunraw.org.uk

Nuns (Roman Catholic)

Cistercians of Esquermes,
Monastery of Our Lady of Hyning, Carnforth, Lancashire LA5 9SE
Tel. 01524 73284

La Trappe (l'Abbaye Notre Dame de Bonne-Esperance),
Echourgnac, 24410 Dordogne, France

Miscellaneous
Xaverian Brothers,
32 Strawberry Hill Road, Twickenham, Middlesex TW1 4PU

Daughters of Saint Francis de Sales
All enquiries to:
Revd. Gerald Flood,
1 Haig Road, Biggin Hill, Kent TN16 3LJ

Servite Friars,
St Mary's Priory, 264 Fulham Road, London SW10 9EL

Monastery of the Visitation,
Waldron, Heathfield, East Sussex TN21 ORX

Tyburn Convent,
8 Hyde Park Gate, London W2 2LJ
Tel. 0207 723 7262
Web. http://tyburnconvent.org.uk

The Quiet Garden Trust, Revd. Philip D. Roderick, Director,
Stoke Park Farm, Park Road, Stoke Poges, Buckinghamshire SL2 4PG
Tel. 01753 643050; e-mail quiet.gardens@ukonline.co.uk

Rufiji Leprosy Trust,
(Reg Charity No. 286242): Field Address:
The Project Officer, Kindwitwi Leprosy Care Centre, Box Two, Utete,
Rufiji, Tanzania
Secretary:
Mrs Valerie S. Mead, 17 Harbutts, Bathampton, Bath BA2 6TA

William Whitehead, Director of Music,
Church of St Mary the Virgin, Bourne Street, London SW1W 8JJ
Tel. 0207 730 7455; www.stmarythevirgin.org.uk

SELECT BIBLIOGRAPHY

Adams, Peter. *Successful Bonsai Growing*. London: Ward Lock, 1985.

Addis, W. E. and T. Arnold (rev. T. B. Scannell). *A Catholic Dictionary*. London: Virtue & Co., 1928.

Alexander, D. and P. *The Lion Concise Bible Handbook*. Oxford: Lion Publishing, 1980.

Allison Peers, E. (ed. and trans.). *The Complete Works of Saint John of the Cross*. London: Burns & Oates, 1954.

Ampleforth Abbey. *Benedictine Year Book*. Ampleforth: English Benedictine Congregation Trust, 2002.

Anson, Peter F. *The Religious Orders and Congregations of Great Britain and Ireland*. Callow End: Stanbrook Abbey Press, 1949.

Armstrong, Christophe (sel.). *Evelyn Underhill*. Masters of Prayer Series. London: Church House Publishing, 1986.

Baker, Margaret. *Folklore and Customs of Rural England*. Newton Abbot: David & Charles, 1974.

Bartram, Douglas. *Climbing Plants*. London: John Gifford, 1968.

Benedictine Monks of Solesmes Abbey. *The Liber Usualis with Introduction and Rubrics in English*. Tournai: Desclée, 1957.

— *Graduale Romanum*. Tournai: Desclée, 1974.

Benson, R. H. *Lourdes*. London: Manresa Press, 1914.

Beresford, John (ed.). *Woodforde – Passages from the Five Volumes of the 'Diary of a Country Parson' 1758–1802*. Oxford: OUP, 1935.

Bettley, Kate (ed.). *Classical Good CD Guide*. Teddington: Gramophone Publications/B&W, 2002.

Boardman, Brigid, and Philip Jebb, OSB. *In a Quiet Garden*. Stratton-on-the-Fosse: Downside Abbey, 2000.

Bowman, Leonard J. *A Retreat with Saint Bonaventure: The Tree of Life*. Shaftesbury: Element, 1993.

Bown, Deni. *Encyclopedia of Herbs and their Uses*. London: Dorling Kindersley, 1995.

Bremner, Lesley. *The Complete Book of Herbs*. London: Guild Publishing/ Dorling Kindersley, 1988.

Brownell Jameson, Anna. *Legends of the Madonna*. London: Hutchinson & Co., n.d.

Buchman, Dian Dincin. *Herbal Medicine*. London: Herb Society/Random Century, 1987.

Bunyan, John. *The Pilgrim's Progress*. London: Blackie, n.d.

Burrows, Ruth. *Guidelines for Mystical Prayer (from a twentieth-century Carmelite)*. London: Catholic Book Club, 1976.

Bute, John, Marquess of. *The Roman Breviary in English*. 4 vols. Edinburgh and London: William Blackwood & Sons, 1908.

Caird, G. B. *Saint Luke*. Pelican Gospel Commentaries. Harmondsworth: Penguin Books, 1963.

Camillus, Fr, OP. *Saint Gabriel, Passionist*. New York: P.J. Kennedy & Sons, 1923.

Campbell-Culver, Maggie. *The Origin of Plants*. London: Headline, 2001.

Cecil Kerr, Lady. *The Miraculous Medal as Revealed to Catherine Labouré*. London: Catholic Truth Society, n.d.

Chaumeton, H. *Les plantes aromatiques*. Solarama, 1981.

Clarke, Nora. *Christmas Traditions*. London: Grisewood & Dempsey (Kingfisher Books), 1992.

Compson, Wendy and Margaret Lockley. *A Flower Arranger's Garden*. Calverton: Floraprint, 1981.

Cornwell, John. *Powers of Darkness, Powers of Light*. London: Viking, 1991.

Corrigan, Dame Felicitas, OSB. *Benedictine Tapestry*. London: Darton, Longman & Todd, 1991.

Cullum, Elizabeth. *A Cottage Herbal*. Newton Abbot: David & Charles, 1975.

Culpeper, Nicholas. *Complete Herbal*. London: Foulsham, n.d.

Davis, Brian. *Flowering Trees and Shrubs*. London: Pelham Books, 1988.

Day, Brian. *A Chronicle of Folklore and Customs*. London: Hamlyn, 1998.

de Sales, St Francis. *Introduction to the Devout Life*. Trans. John K. Ryan. New York: Doubleday Image Books, 1972.

de Waal, Esther. *Seeking God – The Way of Saint Benedict*. London: Collins Fount/Faith Press, 1984.

— *A Seven-Day Journey with Thomas Merton*. Ann Arbor, MI: Servant Publications, 1992.

Dearmer, Percy (words ed.), Ralph Vaughan Williams, and Martin Shaw (music eds). *Songs of Praise* (full music edn) Oxford: OUP, 1947.

Divine Office. Vol. 1: Advent, Christmastide and Weeks 1–9 of the Year. London: Wm Collins Sons & Co. Ltd, 1974.

Division of Christian Education of the National Council of the Churches of Christ in the United States of America. *Revised Standard Version Common Bible with Apocrypha & Deuterocanonical Books*. Glasgow: William Collins, 1995.

Durka, Gloria. *Praying with Hildegard of Bingen*. Minnesota: Saint Mary's Press Christian Brothers Publications, 1991.

Ealing Abbey. *Ordo for the Liturgy of the Hours and the Eucharist in the Churches of the English Benedictine Congregation*. London: Ealing Abbey, 2002.

Ellwood Post, W. *Saints, Signs and Symbols*. London: SPCK, 1964.

Épinal Glossary. Ed. J. D. Pheifer. Oxford: Clarendon Press, 1974.

Farmer, D. H. *The Oxford Dictionary of Saints*. 5th edn. Oxford: OUP, 2002.

Field Guide to Trees and Shrubs of Britain. London: Reader's Digest Association, 2001.

Fitzgerald, G., CSP, *Handbook of the Mass*. Mahwah, NJ: Paulist Press, 1982.

Fleming, David A., SM (comp.). *The Fire and the Cloud: An Anthology of Catholic Spirituality (from Ignatius of Antioch to Thomas Merton)*. London: Geoffrey Chapman, 1978.

Formby, H., OP. *The Book of the Holy Rosary – a Popular Exposition of its Fifteen Mysteries*. London: Burns & Oates, 1872.

Gordon, Lesley. *Green Magic*. London: Webb & Bower, 1977.

Gordon, Vroni. *Shrubs and Trees*. Bristol: Paragon, 1999.

Goudge, Elizabeth (comp.). *A Book of Comfort – An Anthology*. London: Collins Fount, 1979.

Hay, Roy (consultant ed.). *The Gardening Year*. London: Reader's Digest Association, 1968.

— *Illustrated Guide to Gardening*. London: Reader's Digest Association, 1975.

Hepper, F. Nigel. *Illustrated Encyclopaedia of Bible Plants*. London: Inter-Varsity Press, 1992.

Herbert, Maryse, and Francis Moulla. *L'église souterraine Saint-Jean-Baptiste d'Aubeterre-sur-Dronne: De la source antique au Saint-Sepulcre*. Angoulême: Les Presses de QWERTY Impressions, 1992.

Hessayon, D. G. *The Flowering Shrub Expert*. London: Transworld/Reader's Digest Association, 2000.

— *The Gold Plated House Plant Expert*. London: Century, 1987.

— *The Fruit Expert*. Waltham Cross: PBI Publications, 1990.

— *The Rose Expert*. London: Transworld, 1999.

Hierarchies of Australia, England and Wales, and Ireland. *The Divine Office, Vol. One*. Glasgow: William Collins, 1974.

Hindley, Geoffrey (ed.). *Larousse Encyclopedia of Music*. London: Hamlyn, 1979.

Hollings, Michael, and Etta Gullick. *The One Who Listens – A Book of Prayer*. Great Wakering: Mayhew-McCrimmon, 1971.

Illustrated Bible Dictionary. 3 vols. Leicester: Inter-Varsity Press, 1988.

International Committee on English in the Liturgy, Inc. *The People's Daily Missal*. Dublin and Alcester: Goodliffe Neale, 1974.

Jackson, Kenneth Hurlstone (ed.). *A Celtic Miscellany. Translations from the Celtic Traditions*. Penguin Classics. Harmondsworth: Penguin, 1971.

Johns, C. A. *Flowers of the Field*. London: Routledge, 1913.

Johnson, Lady Bird, and Carlton B. Lee. *Wildflowers across America*. New York: Abbeville Press, 1993.

Johnson, Vernon. *Christian Suffering and Bernadette of Lourdes*. London: Catholic Truth Society, 1984.

Keller, Phillip. *A Shepherd Looks at Psalm 23*. London: Pickering & Inglis, 1981.

— *A Shepherd Looks at the Fruits of the Spirit*. London: Marshall Pickering/HarperCollins, 1991.

Kelly, J. N. D. *The Oxford Dictionary of Popes*. Oxford: Oxford University Press, 1986.

Kenneth, Bro., C. G. A. *John Mason Neale*. Masters of Prayer Series. London: Church House Publishing, 1986.

Lambert Ortez, E. *Encyclopedia of Herbs, Spices and Flavourings*. London: Dorling Kindersley, 1992.

Lane, Tony. *The Lion Concise Handbook of Christian Thought*. Oxford: Lion Publishing, 1984.

Larousse. *Encyclopédie des plantes médicinales*. Paris: Larousse Bordas, 1997.

Lefebvre, Gaspar, OSB and the monks of St Andrew's Abbey (eds.). *Saint Andrew Daily Missal*. Tournai: Biblica, 1962.

Lemoine, Cécile. *La flore du sud-ouest*. Editions Sud-ouest, 1990.

Lenox-Conyngham, A. 'In the Catholic Tradition – Saint Ambrose', *Priests and People*, vol. 6, no. 12 (1992).

Lord, T., J. Cubey, M. Grant, and A. Whiteley (eds.). *Royal Horticultural Society Plant Finder*. London: Dorling Kindersley, annual publication.

Lynd, Robert (ed.). *An Anthology of Modern Verse*. London: Methuen & Co., 1933.

Mabey, R. *Flora Britannica*. London: Chatto & Windus, 1998.

Macmillan, Hugh. *Bible Teaching in Nature*. London: Macmillan & Co., 1878.

Marnham, Patrick. *Lourdes: A Modern Pilgrimage*. London: Heinemann, 1980.

Martin, Brian. *John Henry Newman*. Masters of Prayer Series. London: Church House Publishing, 1986.

Martin, W. Keble. *The New Concise British Flora*. London: Ebury Press/ Michael Joseph, 1982.

Matthews, Edward. *Saint Stephen Handbook for Altar Servers*. London: Collins Liturgical Publications, 1988.

Mattock, J., S. McCann, F. Witchell, and P. Wood. *The Complete Book of Roses*. London: Ward Lock, 1994.

Mayhew, Kevin, T. Barr, and R. Kelly (eds.). *Hymns Old and New*. Leigh-on-Sea: Kevin Mayhew, 1983.

Meisel, A. C., and M. L. del Mastro (trans.). *The Rule of Saint Benedict*. New York: Doubleday Image Books, 1975.

Michael, Pamela. *A Country Harvest*. London: Peerage Books, 1986.

Neame, Alan. *The Happening at Lourdes*. London: Catholic Book Club, 1968.

Oldmeadow, K. L. *The Folklore of Herbs*. Birmingham: Cornish Bros., 1946.

Parker, Helen (ed.). *Perennials: Royal Horticultural Society Plant Guide*. London: Dorling Kindersley, 1996.

Petti, Antony, and Geoffrey Laycock. *New Catholic Hymnal* (full edition). London: Faber Music, 1971.

Pittaway, Andy and Bernard Scofield. *Country Bazaar: A Handbook to Country Pleasures*. London, Fontana/Collins, 1976.

Potterton, D. (ed.). *Culpeper's Colour Herbal (with modern medicinal applications)*. London: W. Foulsham & Co. Ltd., 1997.

Purveux, Susan. *Plant That Name*. London: Michael Joseph, 1996.

Reader's Digest. *Field Guide to the Wild Flowers of Britain*. London: Reader's Digest Association, 2000.

Reader's Digest. *Hints and Tips from Times Past*. London: Reader's Digest Association, 2000.

Reader's Digest. *Field Guide to the Trees aand Shrubs of Britain*. London: Reader's Digest Association, 2001.

Reid, Shirley. *Herbs for the Home and Garden*. London: Bookmark, 1992.

Roberts, Margaret. *Pot-Pourri Making*. Auckland, NZ: David Bateman, 1988.

Rodheiser, Ronald, OMI. *The Spiritual Life according to St John of the Cross; The Spiritual Life as a Transformation of Love, according to St John of the Cross* (two cassettes: recordings of talks given by Fr Rodheiser at All Hallows College, Dublin). Dublin: Veritas Video Productions, 1983.

Ryan, John K. (trans.). *Introduction to the Devout Life*. New York: Doubleday Image Books, 1972.

Sandon, Nick (ed.). *The Octave of the Nativity: Essays and Notes on Ten*

Liturgical Reconstructions for Christmas. London: British Broadcasting Corporation, 1984.

Segall, Barbara. *The Herb Garden Month by Month*. Newton Abbot: David & Charles, 1994.

Sheen, Bishop Fulton J. *The World's First Love*. London: Burns & Oates, 1953.

Sheen, Joanna, and Caroline Alexander. *Dried Flower Gardening*. London: Ward Lock, 1996.

Sherley-Price, Leo. *Bede – Ecclesiastical History of the English People*. Trans. and Rev. R. E. Latham. London: Penguin Books, 1990.

Shewell-Cooper, W. E. *Plants, Flowers and Herbs of the Bible*. Berkhampstead: Arthur James, 1988.

Songs of Praise (full music edition). Oxford: OUP, 1947.

Step, E. *Wayside and Woodland Blossoms*. Revised A. B. Jackson. London: Frederick Warne, 1941.

Stevenson, Violet. *Flower Arranging & House Plants*. London: Sphere, 1973.

Sutton & Sons. *The Culture of Flowers and Vegetables*. London: Simpkin, Marshall, Hamilton, Kent, 1904.

Sutton, David. *Larousse Pocket Guide – Wild Flowers*. London: Kingfisher, 1995.

Sutton, David. *Larousse Pocket Guide: Trees of Britain*. London: Kingfisher, 1995.

Teilhard de Chardin, Pierre, SJ. *The Heart of Matter*. London: Collins, 1978.

Timms, George, and others (eds.). *The New Catholic Hymnal*. Norwich: Canterbury Press, 1986.

Tyack, G. S. *Lore and Legend of the English Church*. London: William Andrews, 1899.

Vedel, H. and J. Lange. *Trees and Bushes*. Trans. C. H. R. Hillman. Adapted by H. L. Edlin. London: Methuen, 1960.

Walpole, J. *Roses in a Suffolk Garden*. Woodpit: Images Publications, 1990.

Ward, Maisie. *Splendour of the Rosary*. London: Sheed & Ward, 1946.

Werfl, Franz. *The Song of Bernadette: A Novel*. London: Hamish Hamilton, 1942.

Woodbridge, J. D. (ed.). *Great Leaders of the Christian Church*. Chicago, IL: Moody Press, 1986.